T0211250

Lecture Notes in Computer Science 9899

Commenced Publication in 1973
Founding and Former Series Editors:
Gerhard Goos, Juris Hartmanis, and Jan van Leeuwen

More information about this series at http://www.springer.com/series/7407

Kim Guldstrand Larsen · Igor Potapov
Jiří Srba (Eds.)

Reachability Problems

10th International Workshop, RP 2016
Aalborg, Denmark, September 19–21, 2016
Proceedings

 Springer

Editors
Kim Guldstrand Larsen
Aalborg University
Aalborg
Denmark

Jiří Srba
Aalborg University
Aalborg
Denmark

Igor Potapov
University of Liverpool
Liverpool
UK

ISSN 0302-9743 ISSN 1611-3349 (electronic)
Lecture Notes in Computer Science
ISBN 978-3-319-45993-6 ISBN 978-3-319-45994-3 (eBook)
DOI 10.1007/978-3-319-45994-3

Library of Congress Control Number: 2016949624

LNCS Sublibrary: SL1 – Theoretical Computer Science and General Issues

Printed on acid-free paper

This Springer imprint is published by Springer Nature
The registered company is Springer International Publishing AG Switzerland

Preface

This volume contains the papers presented at the 10th International Workshop on Reachability Problems (RP), held on September 19–21, 2016, at Aalborg University, Denmark. Previous workshops in the series were located at: the University of Warsaw (2015), the University of Oxford (2014), Uppsala University (2013), the University of Bordeaux (2012), the University of Genoa (2011), Masaryk University Brno (2010), École Polytechnique (2009), the University of Liverpool (2008), and Turku University (2007).

The aim of the conference is to bring together scholars from diverse fields with a shared interest in reachability problems, and to promote the exploration of new approaches for the modelling and analysis of computational processes by combining mathematical, algorithmic, and computational techniques. Topics of interest include (but are not limited to): reachability for infinite state systems; rewriting systems; reachability analysis in counter/timed/cellular/communicating automata; Petri nets; computational aspects of semigroups, groups, and rings; reachability in dynamical and hybrid systems; frontiers between decidable and undecidable reachability problems; complexity and decidability aspects; predictability in iterative maps, and new computational paradigms. The invited speakers at the 2016 workshop were:

- Alain Finkel, ENS de Cachan, France
- Axel Legay, INRIA, Rennes Cedex, France
- Jaco van de Pol, University of Twente, Netherlands.

The workshop received 18 submissions. Each submission was reviewed by three Program Committee (PC) members. The members of the PC and the list of external reviewers can be found on the next two pages. The PC is grateful for the high quality work produced by these external reviewers. Based on these reviews, the PC decided to accept 11 papers, in addition to the three invited talks. Overall this volume contains 11 contributed papers and 2 papers by invited speakers. The workshop also provided the opportunity to researchers to give informal presentations, prepared shortly before the event, informing the participants about current research and work in progress.

We gratefully acknowledge the help of Rikke W. Uhrenholt in organizing the event, as well as CISS (Center for Embedded Software Systems) for the financial support. It is also a pleasure to thank the team behind the EasyChair system and the Lecture Notes in Computer Science team at Springer, who together made the production of this volume possible in time for the workshop. Finally, we thank all the authors for their high-quality contributions, and the participants for making RP 2016 a success.

September 2016

Kim Guldstrand Larsen
Igor Potapov
Jiří Srba

Organization

Program Committee

Filippo Bonchi	University of Pisa, Italy
Tomas Brazdil	Masaryk University, Czech Republic
Thomas Brihaye	Université de Mons, France
Krishnendu Chatterjee	Institute of Science and Technology (IST), Austria
Javier Esparza	Technical University of Munich, Germany
Kousha Etessami	University of Edinburgh, UK
Gilles Geeraerts	Université libre de Bruxelles, Belgium
Kim Guldstrand Larsen	Aalborg University, Denmark
Stefan Göller	LSV, CNRS & ENS Cachan, France
Tero Harju	University of Turku, Finland
Petr Jancar	Technical University of Ostrava, Czech Republic
Sławomir Lasota	Warsaw University, Poland
Oded Maler	CNRS-VERIMAG, France
Nicolas Markey	LSV, CNRS & ENS Cachan, France
Richard Mayr	University of Edinburgh, UK
Pierre McKenzie	Université de Montréal, Canada
Igor Potapov	The University of Liverpool, UK
Alexander Rabinovich	Tel Aviv University, Israel
Jiří Srba	Aalborg University, Denmark
Igor Walukiewicz	CNRS, LaBRI, France
James Worrell	Oxford University, UK
Lijun Zhang	Institute of Software, Chinese Academy of Sciences, China

Additional Reviewers

Della Monica, Dario	Kurganskyy, Oleksiy	Sproston, Jeremy
Ferrère, Thomas	Lin, Anthony Widjaja	Totzke, Patrick
Habermehl, Peter	Manuel, Amaldev	Trivedi, Ashutosh
Hahn, Ernst Moritz	Mazowiecki, Filip	Turrini, Andrea
Kopczynski, Eryk	Mélot, Hadrien	
Kuperberg, Denis	Semukhin, Pavel	

Abstracts of Invited Talks

The Ideal Theory for WSTS

Alain Finkel

LSV, ENS Cachan and CNRS, Université Paris-Saclay, Cachan, France
finkel@lsv.ens-cachan.fr

Abstract. We begin with a survey on well structured transition systems and, in particular, we present the ideal framework which was recently used to obtain new deep results on Petri nets and extensions. We argue that the theory of ideals prompts a renewal of the theory of WSTS by providing a way to define a new class of monotonic systems, the so-called Well Behaved Transition Systems, which properly contains WSTS, and for which coverability is still decidable by a forward algorithm. We then recall the completion of WSTS which leads to defining a conceptual Karp-Miller procedure that terminates in more cases than the generalized Karp-Miller procedure on extensions of Petri nets.

Rare Events for Statistical Model Checking: An Overview

Axel Legay, Sean Sedwards, and Louis-Marie Traonouez

Inria Rennes – Bretagne Atlantique, Rennes, France

Abstract. This invited paper surveys several simulation-based approaches to compute the probability of rare bugs in complex systems. The paper also describes how those techniques can be implemented in the professional toolset Plasma.

High Performance Reachability
Algorithms – Extensions – Interface

Jaco van de Pol

University of Twente, Enschede, The Netherlands

Abstract. Reachability analysis is heavily used in the verification of complex systems with discrete dynamics. Due to the combinatorial nature of data and processes, the graphs corresponding to their state space become very large. Algorithmic improvements can lead to exponential gains, as witnessed by BDD technology (binary decision diagrams) and POR (partial order reduction). Implementing these algorithms on massively parallel hardware can yield several extra orders of speedup. However, parallelising graph analysis applications is notoriously hard.

This invited lecture will address the many challenges in designing parallel graph algorithms and discuss the intricacies of symbolic verification algorithms for reachability and liveness. We will also address the required effort to develop prototypes that demonstrate actual speedup on distributed and multi-core computers. We will share the experience we gained with the LTSmin toolset[1].

LTSmin offers distributed and parallel algorithms for explicit-state model checking (with POR) and symbolic reachability analysis (with BDDs). It offers LTL model checking (linear-time liveness properties) and mu-calculus model checking (a powerful branching time logic). At the same time, it provides this functionality to a wide variety of specification formalisms, including process algebras, timed automata, Petri nets, and languages in the Promela and B-families.

The key to this generality is an interface that abstracts from language details on the one hand, but exposes sufficient model structure on the other hand. Our PINS interface is based on state vectors and disjunctive transition groups, and equipped with static information on transitions, like their read/write dependencies on variables, and their mutual independence.

We will also shortly discuss the limitations and future perspectives of integrating more analysis algorithms, or more specification formalisms, or verify software directly, and of exploiting heterogeneous hardware, for instance GPU clusters.

---

[1] http://fmt.cs.utwente.nl/tools/ltsmin

Contents

The Ideal Theory for WSTS

Alain Finkel[✉]

LSV, ENS Cachan and CNRS, Université Paris-Saclay, Cachan, France
finkel@lsv.ens-cachan.fr

Abstract. We begin with a survey on well structured transition systems and, in particular, we present the ideal framework [FG09a, BFM14] which was recently used to obtain new deep results on Petri nets and extensions. We argue that the theory of ideals prompts a renewal of the theory of WSTS by providing a way to define a new class of monotonic systems, the so-called Well Behaved Transition Systems, which properly contains WSTS, and for which coverability is still decidable by a forward algorithm. We then recall the completion of WSTS which leads to defining a conceptual Karp-Miller procedure that terminates in more cases than the generalized Karp-Miller procedure on extensions of Petri nets.

1 Introduction

Context. "The concept of a *well-structured transition system* (WSTS) arose thirty years ago, in 1987 precisely [Fin87, Fin90], where such systems were initially called *structured transition systems* and shown to have decidable termination and boundedness problems. WSTS were developed for the purpose of capturing properties common to a wide range of formal models (generating infinite-state systems) used in model-checking, system verification and concurrent programming. The coverability for such systems — given states s, t, decide whether $s \rightarrow^* t_1 \geq t$ for some t_1 – was shown decidable in 1996 [AČJYK96, AČJT00], thus generalizing the decidability of coverability for lossy channel systems [AJ93] but also generalizing a much older result by Arnold and Latteux [AL78, Theorem 5, p. 391], published in French and thus less accessible, stating that coverability for vector addition systems with resets is decidable. It is interesting to note that the algorithm used by Arnold and Latteux in 1979 is an instance of the backward algorithm presented in [AČJYK96] and applied to $\mathbb{N}^n$."[1]

Ideals Everywhere? We believe that we have only now begun to understand that all (?) existing forward coverability algorithms were based on the use of ideals, i.e., directed downward closed sets, and on the fact that the *cover*, $\downarrow Post^*(s)$,

This paper contains results and parts of texts of the following published papers [FG09a, FG09b, FG12, BFM14, BFM16b] and also some results from a paper "Well Behaved Transition Systems" [BFM16a], in preparation with Michael Blondin and Pierre McKenzie.

[1] This citation is drawn from our paper [BFM16a].

© Springer International Publishing Switzerland 2016
K.G. Larsen et al. (Eds.): RP 2016, LNCS 9899, pp. 1–22, 2016.
DOI: 10.1007/978-3-319-45994-3_1

i.e., the downward closure of the reachability set from s, is equal to a finite union of ideals. Indeed, we may say now that the algorithm of Karp and Miller [KM69], for coverability in Petri nets, computes a finite set of ideals whose union is equal to the *cover*. Finkel introduced the framework of WSTS [Fin87,Fin90] and generalized the Karp-Miller procedure to a class of complete WSTS by building a non-effective completion of the set of states (the completion is done by quotienting equivalent increasing sequences of states; this construction is equivalent to the ideals completion), and replacing ω-accelerations of strictly increasing sequences of states (in Petri nets) by least upper bounds.

Emerson and Namjoshi [EN98] take into account the labeling of WSTS and consequently adapt the generalized Karp-Miller algorithm to model-checking. They assume the existence of a compatible dcpo (a dcpo is a directed complete partial ordering), and generalize the Karp-Miller procedure to the case of broadcast protocols. However, termination is then not guaranteed [EFM99], and in fact neither is the existence of a finite representation of the cover. This problem was solved latter in [FG09a].

Abdulla, Collomb-Annichini, Bouajjani and Jonsson proposed a forward procedure for lossy channel systems [ACABJ04a] using downward-closed regular languages as symbolic representations. We realize now that these symbolic representations were the ideals! In [GRvB06b,GRvB06a], Ganty, Geeraerts, Raskin and Van Begin proposed the first forward procedure for solving the coverability problem for general WSTS equipped with an effective adequate domain of limits, or equipped with a finite set D used as a parameter to tune the precision of an abstract domain. Both solutions ensure that every downward-closed set has a finite representation and still ideals were implicit but they were not seen as the crucial mathematical object. Abdulla, Deneux, Mahata and Nylén also proposed a symbolic framework for dealing with downward-closed sets for Timed Petri nets [ADMN04] and this was still a story of ideals.

The starting point of the series of papers entitled *Forward analysis for WSTS, part I: Completions* [FG09a], and *Forward analysis for WSTS, part II: Complete WSTS* [FG09b,FG12], both written with Jean Goubault-Larrecq, came from our desire to derive similar general algorithms working *forwards*, namely algorithms computing the *cover* of any WSTS (and not for a particular class of WSTS). Our initial completion (of the set of states) was originally based on topology (the completion by sobrification), orderings (the completion by ideals) and the strong connection between both; after some years, we may now only work with the ideals completion [BFM16b] which is quite simple. While computing the cover allows one to decide coverability, by testing whether $t \in \downarrow Post^*(s)$, it also allows to decide whether the reachability sct, $Post^*(s)$, is finite (the boundedness problem). No backward algorithm can decide this. In fact, boundedness is undecidable in general, e.g., on reset Petri nets [DFS98]. So computing the cover is not possible for general WSTS. Despite this, the known forward algorithms are felt to be more efficient than backward procedures in general: e.g., for lossy channel systems, although the backward procedure always terminates, only a (necessarily non-terminating) forward procedure is implemented in the TREX tool [ABJ98]. Another argument in favor of forward procedures is the following: for depth-bounded processes, a fragment of the π-calculus, the backward algorithm of [AČJT00] is not applicable when the maximal depth of configurations is not known in advance because, in this case, the predecessor configurations are not effectively computable [WZH10]. But the *forward* Expand, Enlarge and Check algorithm of [GRvB07], which operates on complete WSTS, solves coverability even though the depth of the process is not known a priori [WZH10].

Our Contribution. Most of the material in Sects. 2, 5 and 6 of this paper is not original and appeared in previous papers [FG09a, FG09b, FG12, BFM14, BFM16b]. Section 3 is a survey on WSTS. Section 4 presents the ideals framework and some recent and deep results using ideals. Section 4 also recalls the Erdös and Tarsky Theorem that says that a quasi-ordered set X is without infinite antichain if and only if every downward closed subset of X is equal to a finite union of ideals. This Theorem paves the way to the new definition of *Well Behaved Transition System (WBTS)*, more general than WSTS, with its decidability of coverability [BFM16a] by a forward coverability algorithm.

In Sect. 5, we introduce the completion of a WSTS and building on our own theory of completions [FG09a, BFM16b], we recall that ω^2-*WSTS* are the right class of WSTS to consider: the completion $\widehat{S}$ of a WSTS S is a WSTS if and only if S is an ω^2-WSTS. All naturally occurring WSTS are in fact ω^2-WSTS. Despite the fact that $\mathbf{Clover}_{\mathfrak{S}}$ cannot terminate on all inputs, that $\mathfrak{S}$ is an ω^2 WSTS will ensure *progress*, i.e., will ensure that every opportunity of accelerating a loop will eventually be taken by $\mathbf{Clover}_{\mathfrak{S}}$.

In Sect. 6, we recall *complete WSTS* which are functional WSTS $\mathfrak{S} = (S, \xrightarrow{F}, \leq)$ where $(S, \leq)$ is a wqo and a continuous dcpo and every function in F is partial ω-continuous. This allows us to design a conceptual procedure $\mathbf{Clover}_{\mathfrak{S}}$ that looks for a finite representation (we say now, a finite set of ideals) of the cover. Our procedure also terminates in more cases than the well-known (generalized) Karp-Miller procedure [EN98, Fin90].

2 Preliminaries

2.1 Orderings

We borrow from theories of order, as used in model-checking [EN98, FS01], and also from domain theory [AJ94, GHK+03].

Let X be a set and let $\leq \subseteq X \times X$. The relation $\leq$ is a *quasi-ordering* if it is reflexive and transitive. If $\leq$ is additionally antisymmetric, then $\leq$ is a *partial order*. We write $\geq$ for the converse quasi-ordering, $<$ for the associated strict ordering $(\leq \setminus \geq)$. There is also an associated equivalence relation $\equiv$, defined as $\leq \cap \geq$. A set X with a partial ordering $\leq$ is a *poset* $(X, \leq)$, or just X when $\leq$ is clear. If X is merely quasi-ordered by $\leq$, then the quotient $X/\equiv$ is ordered by the relation induced by $\leq$ on equivalence classes. So there is not much difference in dealing with quasi-orderings or partial orderings, and we shall essentially be concerned with the latter.

The set X is *well-founded (under $\leq$)* if there is no infinite strictly decreasing sequence $x_0 > x_1 > \ldots$ of elements of X. An *antichain (under $\leq$)* is a subset $A \subseteq X$ of pairwise incomparable elements, i.e. for every $a, b \in A$, $a \not\leq b$ and $b \not\leq a$. We say that a quasi-ordering $\leq$ is a *well-quasi-ordering* for X if X is well-founded and contains no infinite antichain under $\leq$.

Let $A \subseteq X$, we define the *downward closure* and *upward closure* of A respectively as $\uparrow A \stackrel{\text{def}}{=} \{x \in X : x \geq a \text{ for some } a \in A\}$ and $\downarrow A \stackrel{\text{def}}{=} \{x \in X : x \leq a \text{ for some } a \in A\}$. A subset $A \subseteq X$ is said to be *downward closed* if $A = \downarrow A$ and *upward closed* if $A = \uparrow A$. An *ideal* is a downward closed subset $I \subseteq X$ that is also *directed*, i.e. it is nonempty and for every $a, b \in I$, there exists $c \in I$ such that $a \leq c$ and $b \leq c$. Chains, i.e., totally ordered subsets, and one-element sets are examples of directed subsets. The set of ideals of X is denoted $\mathsf{Ideals}(X) \stackrel{\text{def}}{=} \{I \subseteq X : I = \downarrow I \text{ and } I \text{ is directed}\}$.

An *upper bound* $x \in X$ of $E \subseteq X$ is such that $y \leq x$ for every $y \in E$. The *least upper bound (lub)* of a set E, if it exists, is written $\mathrm{lub}(E)$. An element x of E is *maximal* (resp. minimal) iff $\uparrow x \cap E = \{x\}$ (resp. $\downarrow x \cap E = \{x\}$). Write $\mathrm{Max}\, E$ (resp. $\mathrm{Min}\, E$) for the set of maximal (resp. minimal) elements of E.

A *dcpo* is a poset in which every directed subset has a least upper bound. For any subset E of a dcpo X, let $\mathrm{Lub}(E) = \{\mathrm{lub}(D) \mid D \text{ directed subset of } E\}$. Clearly, $E \subseteq \mathrm{Lub}(E)$; $\mathrm{Lub}(E)$ can be thought of E plus all limits from elements of E. When $\leq$ is a well partial ordering that also turns X into a dcpo, we say that X is a *directed complete well order*, or *dcwo*.

3   A Survey on Well-Structured Transition Systems

The theory of WSTS has now been used for 30 years as a foundation for verification in various models, such as (monotonic extensions of) Petri nets, broadcast protocols, fragments of the pi-calculus, rewriting systems, lossy systems, timed Petri nets, etc. Two journal papers synthesise the known results and show the possible applications [AČJT00, FS01].

3.1   Monotonic Transition Systems

A *transition system* is a pair $\mathfrak{S} = (S, \rightarrow)$ of a set S, whose elements are called *states*, and a *transition relation* $\rightarrow \subseteq S \times S$. We write $s \rightarrow s'$ for $(s, s') \in \rightarrow$. Let $\stackrel{*}{\rightarrow}$ be the transitive and reflexive closure of the relation $\rightarrow$. We write $Post_{\mathfrak{S}}(s) = \{s' \in S \mid s \rightarrow s'\}$ for the set of immediate successors of the state s. The *reachability set* of a transition system $\mathfrak{S} = (S, \rightarrow)$ from an initial state s_0 is $Post^*_{\mathfrak{S}}(s_0) = \{s \in S \mid s_0 \stackrel{*}{\rightarrow} s\}$. The *reachability tree* $RT(S, \rightarrow, s_0)$ of a transition system $(S, \rightarrow)$ with an initial state s_0 is defined as follows: the root is labeled by s_0 and there is an arc between two nodes n, n' labeled by the states s, s' iff $s \rightarrow s'$.

We shall be interested in effective transition systems. Intuitively, a transition system $(S, \rightarrow)$ is *effective* iff one can compute the set of successors $Post_{\mathfrak{S}}(s)$ of any state s. We shall take this to imply that $Post_{\mathfrak{S}}(s)$ is finite (for simplicity, transition systems are supposed to be finitely banching), and each of its elements is computable. Formally, one would need to find a representation of the states $s \in S$. For reasons of readability, we shall make an abuse of language, and say that the pair $(S, \rightarrow)$ is itself an effective transition system in this case, leaving the representation of states and the *post* function implicit (see [FG12] for more precise definitions).

We say that an ordered transition system $\mathfrak{S} = (S, \rightarrow, \leq)$, where $\leq$ is a quasi ordering, is *monotonic* (resp. *strictly monotonic*) iff for all $s, s', s_1 \in S$ such that $s \rightarrow s'$ and $s_1 \geq s$ (resp. $s_1 > s$), there exists an $s_1' \in S$ such that $s_1 \xrightarrow{*} s_1'$ and $s_1' \geq s'$ (resp. $s_1' > s'$). $\mathfrak{S}$ is *transitive monotonic* iff for all $s, s', s_1 \in S$ such that $s \rightarrow s'$ and $s_1 \geq s$, there exists an $s_1' \in S$ such that $s_1 \xrightarrow{+} s_1'$ and $s_1' \geq s'$. $\mathfrak{S}$ is *strongly monotonic* iff for all $s, s', s_1 \in S$ such that $s \rightarrow s'$ and $s_1 \geq s$, there exists an $s_1' \in S$ such that $s_1 \rightarrow s_1'$ and $s_1' \geq s'$. These variations on monotonicity were studied in [Fin87,FS01]. Originally, three different definitions of monotonicity (hence six definitions with the strict variant) were given in [Fin87] and four with the stuttering variant (resp. eight) were studied in [FS01].

3.2 The Properties

Finite representations of $Post_{\mathfrak{S}}^*(s)$, e.g., as Presburger formulae or finite automata, usually don't exist even for monotonic transition systems (not even speaking of being computable). However, the *cover* set $Cover_{\mathfrak{S}}(s) = \downarrow Post_{\mathfrak{S}}^*(\downarrow s)$ ($= \downarrow Post_{\mathfrak{S}}^*(s)$ when $\mathfrak{S}$ is monotonic) will be much better behaved. Note that being able to compute the cover allows one to decide *coverability* ($t \in Cover_{\mathfrak{S}}(s)$?), and *boundedness* (is $Post_{\mathfrak{S}}^*(s)$ finite?). Let us recall that the *control-state reachability problem* (when the set S of states is $S = Q \times X$ with Q a finite set of control states) can be reduced to coverability. However, the *repeated control state reachability problem* (does there exist an infinite computation that visits infinitely often a control state q?) cannot be reduced to coverability.

The *eventuality* property for a given upward closed set I, is the following property: $\mathrm{EG}\,I$ is true in a state s_0 iff there is a computation from s_0 in which all states are in I. Given two labeled transition systems $\mathfrak{S}_1 = (S_1, \rightarrow_1)$ and $\mathfrak{S}_2 = (S_2, \rightarrow_2)$, on the same alphabet Σ, the relation $R \subseteq S_1 \times S_2$ is a *simulation* of $\mathfrak{S}_1$ by $\mathfrak{S}_2$ if for each $(s_1, s_2) \in R$, $s_1' \in S_1$ and $a \in \Sigma$, if $s_1 \xrightarrow{a} s_1'$ then there exists $s_2' \in S_2$ such that $s_2 \xrightarrow{a} s_2'$ and $(s_1', s_2') \in R$. We say that $s_1 \in S_1$ is *simulated* by $s_2 \in S_2$ if there is a simulation R of $\mathfrak{S}_1$ by $\mathfrak{S}_2$ such that $(s_1, s_2) \in R$.

3.3 Well-Structured Transition Systems

WSTS were originally thought of as generalizations of Petri nets (and classes of FIFO nets) in which the set of states (called markings) of a Petri net with n places, $\mathbb{N}^n$, is abstracted into a set X equipped with a wqo $\leq$; the Petri net transitions (which are particular affine translations from $\mathbb{N}^n$ into $\mathbb{N}^n$) are abstracted to general recursive monotonic relations in X. WSTS were defined and studied in the author's PhD thesis in 1986, the results were presented at ICALP'87 [Fin87] and published in the journal "information and computation" [Fin90].

Definition 1 [Fin87,Fin90]. *A* Well Structured Transition System *(WSTS)* $\mathfrak{S} = (S, \rightarrow, \leq)$ *is a monotonic transition system such that* $(S, \leq)$ *is wqo.*

We will need *effective WSTS* $\mathfrak{S} = (S, \rightarrow, \leq)$, i.e., $(S, \rightarrow)$ is effective and $\leq$ is decidable. Generally WSTS are finitely banching. Some of the decidability results [BFM14] do not require this but, for simplicity, we will make this assumption. A WSTS (or more generally, an ordered transition system) $\mathfrak{S} = (S, \rightarrow, \leq)$ has the *effective PredBasis* property if there exists an algorithm which computes $\uparrow Pre(\uparrow s)$ for each $s \in S$; $\mathfrak{S}$ is *intersection effective* if there is an algorithm which computes a finite basis of $\uparrow s \cap \uparrow s'$, for all states $s, s' \in S$.

We now summarize the main decidability results on WSTS till the year 2000.

Theorem 1. *The following are* decidable:

- *Termination, for effective transitive monotonic WSTS [Fin87, FS01].*
- *Boundedness, for effective strictly monotonic transitive WSTS [Fin87, FS01].*
- *Coverability (hence control-state reachability), for effective WSTS with effective PredBasis ([AČJYK96], extended in [FS01]).*
- *Eventuality, for effective strongly monotonic finitely branching WSTS (see [KS96, AČJT00], extended in [FS01]).*
- *Simulation of a labeled WSTS by a finite automaton, for intersection effective and effective strongly monotonic WSTS with effective PredBasis [AČJYK96].*
- *Simulation of a finite automaton by a labeled WSTS, for effective strongly monotonic WSTS [AČJYK96].*

The following are undecidable:

- *Reachability, for effective strongly strictly monotonic WSTS (Transfer Petri nets, [DFS98]).*
- *Repeated control-state reachability (hence LTL), for effective strongly strictly monotonic WSTS (Transfer Petri nets, [DFS98]).*   □

To prove these decidability results we alternatively use forward and backward algorithms. Termination, boundedness, eventuality and one part of simulation can be proved by using a forward algorithm that builds the so-called Finite Reachability Tree (FRT) [Fin87]: we develop the reachability tree until a state larger than or equal to one of its ancestors is encountered, in which case the current branch is definitely closed. The place-boundedness problem (to decide whether a place can contain an unbounded number of tokens) is undecidable for transfer Petri nets [DFS98], although they are strongly and strictly monotonic WSTS. It is decidable for Petri nets. This requires a richer structure than the FRT, the Karp-Miller tree. The set of labels of the Karp-Miller tree is a finite representation of the cover.

Almost all the assumptions used above are necessary:

Theorem 2. *The following are* undecidable:

- *Termination, for transitive monotonic WSTS.*
- *Boundedness, for effective strongly monotonic WSTS.*
- *Coverability, for effective strongly strictly monotonic WSTS.* □

For termination, Turing machines are transitive WSTS for which the termination ordering $\leq_{termination}$ is undecidable [FS01]. For the second claim, Reset Petri nets have an undecidable bounded problem, and are effective strongly monotonic WSTS; but they are not strictly monotonic [DFS98]. For the last claim, there are WSTS composed two recursive strictly monotonic functions from $\mathbb{N}^2$ into $\mathbb{N}^2$ that are not recursive on $\mathbb{N}^2_\omega$, hence there are no algorithm computing a PredBasis [FMP04].

The status of eventuality and simulation is open: for each of these properties, we know of no natural class of WSTS for which this property would be undecidable.

3.4 WSTS Everywhere[2]

Here are *some* (this is not an exhaustive list) of the papers that introduced new points of view, in our opinion:

Forward Coverability Algorithm and Forward Analysis for WSTS
    Ganty, Geeraerts, Raskin and Van Begin proposed a new forward procedure for deciding the coverability problem [GRB04, GRvB06a, GRvB06b]. This was the first forward procedure for this problem in the general framework of WSTS (to which they explicitly added, to the set of states, an Adequate Domain of Limits). Their procedure computes a sufficient part (to decide coverability) of a finite representation of the cover.
    Goubault-Larrecq and I began in 2009 a series entitled *"Forward analysis for WSTS, Part I: Completions"* [FG09a] and *"Forward Analysis for WSTS, Part II: Complete WSTS"* [FG09b] in which we provide the missing theoretical fundations of finite representations of downward closed sets. Most of used ordering in WSTS are ω^2-ordering and in fact also better quasi ordering. This allows to extend the wqo to the completion of a WSTS and the completed system is still a WSTS. An ω^2-ordering that is extended on downward closed sets is also a wqo [FG09a, FG09b, AN00]. This work, based on both order and topology, allowed us to design a conceptual coverability set procedure for *all* WSTS. Bounded WSTS [CFS11] are a particular recursive class of WSTS for which our coverability set procedure terminates.
Expressive Power of WSTS
    In [ADB07, GRB07], Abdulla, Delzanno, Geeraerts, Raskin and Van Begin studied the expressive power of WSTS by means of the set of coverability languages which are well-adapted to WSTS. Bonnet, Finkel,

---

[2] "WSTS Everywhere" was the title of our survey with Philippe Schnoebelen [FS01].

Haddad and Rosa-Velardo proposed in [BFHR11] to use a new tool, the order type of posets, to prove, for example, that the class of all WSTS with set of states of type $\mathbb{N}^n$ are less expressive than WSTS with set of states of type $\mathbb{N}^{n+1}$. This strategy unifies the previous proofs and allows to compare models of different natures, such as lossy channel systems and timed Petrinets.

Petri Net Extensions and Complexity of WSTS

Affine Petri nets extensions were studied a long time ago by Valk [Val78] under the name *self modified nets*; more recently, many Petri nets extensions were studied like recursive Petri nets [HP07], PRS [May00], Reset/Transfer Petri nets [DFS98, DJS99] and affine well-structured nets [FMP04]. More recently, since the first paper on Petri nets with data (which extend affine nets) by Lazić, Newcomb, Ouaknine, Roscoe and Worrell [LNO+07], many authors like Rosa-Velardo, Frutos-Escrig [RdF07, RMdF11], Lazić, Haddad, Schmitz and Schnoebelen have began to study the complexity for many classes of Petri net extensions where tokens carry data: data nets, Petri data nets, ν-Petri nets, ordered and unordered data Petri nets. D. Figueira, S. Figueira, Schmitz and Schnoebelen began the study of the ordinal-recusive complexity of general WSTS. They characterized the ordinal length of bad sequences of vectors of integers [FFSS11] (using the Dickson lemma) and of words [SS11] (using the Higman lemma). Haddad, Schmitz and Schnoebelen showed *"how to reliably compute fast-growing functions with timed-arc Petri nets and data nets. They provided ordinal-recursive lower bounds on the complexity of the main decidable properties (safety, termination, regular simulation, etc.) of these models. Since these new lower bounds match the upper bounds that one can derive from wqo theory, they precisely characterise the computational power of these so-called" enriched "nets"* in [HSS12].

In [BHM15], Badouel, Hélouët and Morvan addressed a WSTS extension of Petri Nets whose transitions manipulate structured data via patterns and queries. Very recently, Hofman, Lasota, Lazić, Leroux, Schmitz and Totzke extended the construction of coverability trees to Petri Nets with Unordered Data [HLL+16] and Lazić and Schmitz proved that coverability for ν-Petri nets is complete for "double Ackermann" time [LS16a].

Pushdown VASS and Well-Structured Pushdown Systems

Mixing pushdown and counters is possible even if one reaches undecidability or high complexity. Cai, Ogawa, Lazić, Leroux, Sutre, Totzke studied reachability and coverability for VASS with a stack and subclasses of Pushdown WSTS. Coverability is decidable for one dimensional Pushdown VASS but it is Tower-hard (while Boundedness is in exponential time) and its decidability is an open problem for general Pushdown VASS [Laz13, LST15b, LST15a, BLP15].

We could also quote other applications and use of the WSTS theory to: *Well-Structured Graph Transformation Systems* [BDK+12, KS14, BG14]; to decide properties in the *pi-Calculus* [Mey08, ZWH12, HMM14, BG14]; and we could also mention the recent paper from Lasota [Las16] who proposes an interesting *"WQO Dichotomy Conjecture: under a mild assumption, either a data domain exhibits a well quasi-order (in which case one can apply the general setting of well-structured transition systems to solve problems like coverability or boundedness), or essentially all the decision problems are undecidable for Petri nets over that data domain."*.

4 The Ideal Framework of Ideals

Recall that an *ideal* is a downward closed subset $I \subseteq X$ that is also *directed*, i.e. it is nonempty and for every $a, b \in I$, there exists $c \in I$ such that $a \leq c$ and $b \leq c$. The set of ideals of X is denoted $\mathsf{Ideals}(X) \stackrel{\text{def}}{=} \{I \subseteq X : I = \downarrow I$ and I is directed$\}$.

The two following examples come from [BFM16b].

Example 1. Let us consider the ideals of $\mathbb{N}^d$. It can be shown that

$$\mathsf{Ideals}(\mathbb{N}^d) = \underbrace{\mathsf{Ideals}(\mathbb{N}) \times \mathsf{Ideals}(\mathbb{N}) \times \cdots \times \mathsf{Ideals}(\mathbb{N})}_{d \text{ times}}$$

and that $I \in \mathsf{Ideals}(\mathbb{N})$ is either $\mathbb{N}$ or of the form $\downarrow x$ for some $x \in \mathbb{N}$. Therefore, any ideal $I \in \mathsf{Ideals}(\mathbb{N}^d)$ may be represented by some $x \in \mathbb{N}_\omega^d$ where $x_i = \omega$ represents $\mathbb{N}$ and $x_i = y$ represents $\downarrow y$. Consider the following downward closed set

$$X = \{(x_1, x_2) \in \mathbb{N}^2 : (x_1 \leq 4) \vee (x_1 \leq 8 \wedge x_2 \leq 10) \vee (x_2 \leq 5)\}.$$

As illustrated in Fig. 1, it is possible to write X as the following finite union of ideals:

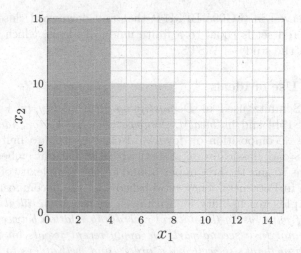

Fig. 1. Decomposition of $X = \{(x_1, x_2) \in \mathbb{N}^2 : (x_1 \leq 4) \vee (x_1 \leq 8 \wedge x_2 \leq 10) \vee (x_2 \leq 5)\}$ into finitely many ideals. The three ideals $\downarrow 4 \times \mathbb{N}, \downarrow 8 \times \downarrow 10$ and $\mathbb{N} \times \downarrow 5$ appear respectively in blue, orange and green. (Color figure online)

$$\downarrow 4 \times \mathbb{N} \cup \ \downarrow 8 \times \downarrow 10 \ \cup \ \mathbb{N} \times \downarrow 5$$

which can be represented by $\{(4, \omega), (8, 10), (\omega, 5)\}$.

Example 2. It has been recently shown that downward closed languages (under the subword ordering) coincide with the class of *strictly piecewise-testable languages* [RHB+10]. Previously, downward closed languages were studied and used in [ACABJ04a] for representing infinite reachability subsets of lossy channel systems; it is proved that every downward closed language on Σ^*, where Σ is a finite alphabet, is a finite union of *products* $P_1 P_2 \cdots P_m$ where each P_i is either $\{\varepsilon, \sigma\}$ for some $\sigma \in \Sigma$, or A^* for some $A \subseteq \Sigma$. It has been remarked in [FG09a] that every ideal $I \in \mathsf{Ideals}(\Sigma^*)$, is exactly a product $I = P_1 P_2 \cdots P_m$ like in [ACABJ04a]. Following [FG09a], the previous result on downward closed languages is then a particular instance of a more general result: every downward closed set (here a downward closed language on Σ^*), in a wqo, is a finite union of ideals.

For example, consider the language of words over $\Sigma = \{a, b, c\}$ where the first letter does not reappear, *i.e.*, let

$$L = \{w \in \Sigma^+ : w_i \neq w_1 \text{ for } 1 < i \leq |w|\}$$

$$= a\{b, c\}^* \cup b\{a, c\}^* \cup c\{a, b\}^*.$$

It can be shown that

$$\downarrow L = L \cup \{w \in \Sigma^* : |w|_\sigma = 0 \text{ for some } \sigma \in \Sigma\}$$

$$= L \cup \{a, b\}^* \cup \{a, c\}^* \cup \{b, c\}^*$$

$$= \{a, \varepsilon\}\{b, c\}^* \cup \{b, \varepsilon\}\{a, c\}^* \cup \{c, \varepsilon\}\{a, b\}^*.$$

Hence, $\downarrow L$ decomposes into finitely many ideals.

It was observed in [FG09a, BFM14] that any downward closed subset of a well-quasi-ordered set is equal to a finite union of ideals, which led to further applications in the study of WSTS.

4.1   Recent Use of Ideals

– Leroux et Schmitz used in *Demystifying Reachability in Vector Addition Systems* [LS15b] and in *Ideal Decompositions for Vector Addition Systems* [LS16b] the decomposition of downward closed sets into finite many ideals on runs (instead classically on states) with the natural embedding relation between runs to give the first upper bound for the complexity of the reachability problem in Petri nets. They established that the decomposition produced by the complex reachability algorithm is, in fact, *"the ideal decomposition of the set of runs, using the natural embedding relation between runs as well quasi ordering. In a second part, we apply recent results on the complexity of termination thanks to well quasi orders and well orders to obtain a cubic Ackermann upper bound for the decomposition algorithms, thus providing the first known upper bounds for general VAS reachability."*

- Lazić and Schmitz studied in *The Ideal View on Rackoff's Coverability Technique* [LS15a, BLP15] the well-known Rackoff coverability algorithm and they renewed the study by using the ideals framework: *We take a dual view on the backward coverability algorithm, by considering successively the sets of configurations that do not cover y in 0, 1, 2, . . . or fewer steps. Such sets are downwards-closed, and enjoy a (usually effective) canonical representation as finite unions of ideals. We show that, in the case of VAS, this dual view exhibits an additional structural property of ω -monotonicity, which allows to derive the desired doubly-exponential bound.*
- Lazić and Schmitz proved in *The Complexity of Coverability in ν-Petri Nets* [LS16a] that coverability for ν-Petri nets is complete for "double Ackermann" time by using the ideals framework with the multiset ordering. They proved that the ν-Petri nets are ideally effective and they studied the length of controlled descending chains of downwards-closed sets which are finite unions of ideals. The proof deeply relies on ideals.
- Hofman, Lasota, Lazić, Leroux, Schmitz and Totzke studied in *Coverability Trees for Petri Nets with Unordered Data* [HLL+16] *"an extension of classical Petri nets where tokens carry values from a countable data domain, that can be tested for equality upon firing transitions. These Unordered Data Petri Nets (UDPN) are well-structured and therefore allow generic decision procedures for several verification problems including coverability and boundedness. We show how to construct a finite representation of the coverability set in terms of its ideal decomposition."*.
- Blondin, Finkel and McKenzie studied in *Handling Infinitely Branching Well-structured Transition Systems* [BFM14, BFM16b] coverability, termination and boundedness for infinitely branching WSTS. *"Here we develop tools to handle infinitely branching WSTS by exploiting the crucial property that in the (ideal) completion of a well-quasi-ordered set, downward-closed sets are finite unions of ideals. Then, using these tools, we derive decidability results and we delineate the undecidability frontier in the case of the termination, the maintainability and the coverability problems. Coverability and boundedness under new effectiveness conditions are shown decidable."*

Other applications of ideals arrive: Goubault-Larrecq and Schmitz showed using effective representations for tree ideals that it entails the decidability of piecewise testable separability when the input languages are regular [GLS16].

4.2   Decomposition of Downward Closed Sets into Ideals

Even if it was observed that any downward closed subset of a well-quasi-ordered set is equal to a finite union of ideals, here, we stress the fact that such finite decompositions also exist in quasi-ordered sets with *no infinite antichain*. The existence of such a decomposition has been proved numerous times (for partial orderings instead of quasi-orderings) in the order theory community under different terminologies, and is a particular case of a more general result of Erdös & Tarski [ET43]. But, to the best of our knowledge, this has never been remarked neither used in the verification community.

Theorem 3 [ET43, Bon75, Fra86, BFM16a]. *A countable quasi-ordered set X contains no infinite antichain if, and only if, every downward closed subset of X is equal to a finite union of ideals.*

We give a self-contained proof of this result in [BFM16a].

Theorem 3 allows us, as in [BFM14], to define a canonical finite decomposition of a downward closed subset $D \subseteq X$, that is, the (finite) set IdealDecomp(D) of maximal ideals contained in D under inclusion.

4.3   Well Behaved Transition Systems

Since downward closed sets decompose in finitely ideals, we may use the forward coverability algorithm and then we are motivated to define a new class of monotonic transition systems.

Definition 2 [BFM16a]. *A Well Behaved Transition System (WBTS) is a monotonic transition system $\mathfrak{S} = (S, \rightarrow, \leq)$ such that $(S, \leq)$ contains no infinite antichain.*

Every WSTS is trivially a WBTS but, for example, a one counter automaton on $\mathbb{Z}$ is a WBTS but it is not a WSTS, for the usual ordering.

We describe effectiveness hypotheses that allow manipulating downward closed sets in WBTS.

Definition 3 [BFM16a]. *A class C of WBTS $\mathfrak{S}$ is ideally effective if*

- *the function mapping the encoding of a state s of an ordered transition system to the encoding of the ideal $\downarrow s$ is computable;*
- *inclusion of ideals is decidable;*
- *the downward closure $\downarrow post(I)$ expressed as a finite union of ideals is computable from the ideal I.*

Let us emphasize that an ideally effective WBTS is effective and post-effective: S embeds into Ideals(S) hence S is also decidable; the inequation $s \leq t$ is equivalent to $\downarrow s \subseteq \downarrow t$ hence it is decidable; and computing $post(s)$ boils down to computing $post(\downarrow s)$.

Remark 1. Enforcing WBTS to be ideally effective is not an issue for virtually all useful models. Indeed, a large scope of WBTS are ideally effective [FG09a]: ideally effective WSTS, Petri nets, VASS and their extensions (with resets, transfers, affine functions), lossy channel systems and extensions with data.

We recently proved in [BFM16a] that coverability is decidable for ideally effective Well Behaved Transition Systems.

Theorem 4 [BFM16a]. *Coverability is decidable for ideally effective Well Behaved Transition Systems.*

5 Completion of WSTS and Accelerations[3]

5.1 Completion of a WSTS

The ideal completion of a WSTS is useful to define lub-accelerations (that are defined in the completed set of states, i.e., in the set S completed with lubs) ; then one may design coverability set procedures like abstracted Karp Miller procedures working on states and lubs, i.e., "limits of states". Let us recall that S is canonically included in $\mathsf{Ideals}(S)$, that $\mathsf{Ideals}(S)$ is a continuous dcpo, and in the case of continuous dcpos, the set S with its set of lubs, is isomorphic to $\mathsf{Ideals}(S)$. The following definition extends [FG09b] to non-functional WSTS and uses the ideal completion instead of the more complex sober topological completion.

Definition 4 [BFM14, FG09b]. *The completion $\widehat{\mathfrak{S}}$ of a WSTS $\mathfrak{S} = (S, \rightarrow, \leq)$ is the ordered transition system $\widehat{\mathfrak{S}} = (\widehat{S}, \rightsquigarrow, \subseteq)$ where $\widehat{S} = \mathsf{Ideals}(S)$ and $I \rightsquigarrow J$ if $J \in idealdecomp(\downarrow Post_{\widehat{\mathfrak{S}}}(I))$.*

It would seem clear that the construction of the completion $\widehat{\mathfrak{S}} = (\widehat{S}, \rightsquigarrow, \subseteq)$ of a WSTS $\mathfrak{S} = (S, \rightarrow, \leq)$ be, again, a WSTS. We shall recall that this is not the case. The only missing ingredient to show that $\widehat{\mathfrak{S}}$ is a WSTS is to check that $\widehat{S}$ is well-ordered by inclusion. And this is not the case, the Rado wqo is a well known example.

When is $\widehat{X}$ well-ordered by inclusion? We shall see that there is a definite answer: when X is ω^2-wqo. Hence, when the original wqo $\leq$ is also a ω^2-wqo, the ordered set ($\mathsf{Ideals}(S), \subseteq$) is also a wqo and then the completion of a such WSTS would be still a WSTS.

In fact, the completion can be extended to *WBTS* since the completion only needs a quasi ordering without infinite antichains.

Definition 5 [BFM16a]. *The completion $\widehat{\mathfrak{S}}$ of a WBTS $\mathfrak{S} = (S, \rightarrow, \leq)$ is the ordered transition system $\widehat{\mathfrak{S}} = (\widehat{S}, \rightsquigarrow, \subseteq)$ where $\widehat{S} = \mathsf{Ideals}(S)$ and $I \rightsquigarrow J$ if $J \in \mathsf{IdealDecomp}(\downarrow Post_{\widehat{\mathfrak{S}}}(I))$.*

Let us remark that the completion of a WBTS is not necessarily a WBTS. Take X to be Rado's structure X_{Rado} [Rad54], i.e., $\{(m, n) \in \mathbb{N}^2 \mid m < n\}$, ordered by $\leq_{\mathrm{Rado}}$: $(m, n) \leq_{\mathrm{Rado}} (m', n')$ iff $m = m'$ and $n \leq n'$, or $n < m'$. It is well-known that $\leq_{\mathrm{Rado}}$ is a well quasi-ordering, hence without infinite antichains. Since the completion of the Rado ordering contains the infinite set of the ω_i [Sect. 5.3, Lemma 1], which is an infinite antichain, we conclude that the completion of a WBTS is not necessarily a WBTS.

---

[3] The text of Sects. 5.2, 5.3, 5.4 and 5.5 is drawn from the paper [FG12].

5.2   Lub-Accelerations

A subset U of a dcpo X is (Scott-)*open* iff U is upward-closed, and for any directed subset D of X such that $\mathrm{lub}(D) \in U$, some element of D is already in U. A *partial ω-continuous* map $f : X \to X$, where $(X, \leq)$ is a dcpo, is a partial map whose domain $\mathrm{dom}\, f$ is upward-closed, and such that for every directed subset D *in* $\mathrm{dom}\, f$, $\mathrm{lub}(f(D)) = f(\mathrm{lub}(D))$. The composition of two partial ω-continuous maps again yields a partial ω-continuous map. This is all we require when we define accelerations. The *closed* sets are the complements of open sets. Every closed set is downward-closed. On a dcpo, the closed subsets are the subsets B that are both downward-closed and *inductive*, i.e., such that $\mathrm{Lub}(B) = B$. An inductive subset of X is none other than a sub-dcpo of X. The *closure* $cl(A)$ of $A \subseteq X$ is the smallest closed set containing A. This should not be confused with the *inductive closure* $\mathrm{Ind}(A)$ of A, which is obtained as the smallest inductive subset B containing A. In general, $\downarrow A \subseteq \mathrm{Lub}(\downarrow A) \subseteq \mathrm{Ind}(\downarrow A) \subseteq cl(A)$, and all inclusions can be strict. All this nitpicking is irrelevant when X is a *continuous* dcpo, and A is downward-closed in X. In this case indeed, $\mathrm{Lub}(A) = \mathrm{Ind}(A) = cl(A)$. This is well-known, see e.g., [FG09a, Proposition 3.5], and will play an important role in our constructions. As a matter in fact, the fact that $\mathrm{Lub}(A) = cl(A)$, in the particular case of continuous dcpos, is required for lub-accelerations to ever reach the closure of the set of states that are reachable in a transition system.

In [FG12], we illustrate that ω^2-wqo are crucial to establish a *progress* property that consists to make infinitely often lub-accelerations.

The reasons why the original Karp-Miller procedure terminates on (ordinary) Petri nets are two-fold. First, when $\widehat{X} = \mathbb{N}_\omega^k$, one cannot lub-accelerate more than k times, because each lub-acceleration introduces a new ω component to the label of the produced state, which will not disappear in later node extensions. This is specific to Petri nets, and already fails for reset Petri nets, where ω components do disappear. The second reason is of more general applicability: $\widehat{X} = \mathbb{N}_\omega^k$ is wpo, and this implies that along every infinite branch of the tree thus constructed, case (*) will eventually happen, and in fact will happen infinitely many times. Call this *progress*: along any infinite path, one will lub-accelerate infinitely often. In the original Karp-Miller procedure for Petri nets, this will entail termination.

As we have already announced, for WSTS other than Petri nets, termination cannot be ensured. But at least we would like to ensure progress. The argument above shows that progress is obtained provided $\widehat{X}$ is wqo. *This* is our main motivation in characterizing those wqos X such that $\widehat{X}$ is wqo again.

5.3   The Rado Structure

We now return to the purpose of this section: showing that $\widehat{X}$ is well-ordered iff X is ω^2-wqo. We start by showing that, in some cases, $\widehat{X}$ is indeed *not* well-ordered.

Recall that X is Rado's structure X_{Rado} [Rad54], i.e., $\{(m,n) \in \mathbb{N}^2 \mid m < n\}$, ordered by $\leq_{\mathrm{Rado}}$: $(m,n) \leq_{\mathrm{Rado}} (m',n')$ iff $m = m'$ and $n \leq n'$, or $n < m'$. It is well-known that $\leq_{\mathrm{Rado}}$ is a well quasi-ordering, and that $\mathbb{P}(X_{\mathrm{Rado}})$ is not well-quasi-ordered by $\leq^{\sharp}_{\mathrm{Rado}}$, defined as $A \leq^{\sharp}_{\mathrm{Rado}} B$ iff for every $y \in B$, there is a $x \in A$ such that $x \leq_{\mathrm{Rado}} y$ [Jan99]. (Equivalently, $A \leq^{\sharp}_{\mathrm{Rado}} B$ iff $\uparrow B \subseteq \uparrow A$.)

Consider indeed $\omega_i = \{(i,n) \mid n \geq i+1\} \cup \{(m,n) \in X_{\mathrm{Rado}} \mid n \leq i-1\}$, for each $i \in \mathbb{N}$. This is pictured as the dark blue (or dark grey) region in Fig. 2, and arises naturally in Lemma 1 below. Note that ω_i is downward-closed in $\leq_{\mathrm{Rado}}$. Consider the complement $\overline{\omega}_i$ of ω_i, and note that $\overline{\omega}_i \leq^{\sharp}_{\mathrm{Rado}} \overline{\omega}_j$ iff $\uparrow \overline{\omega}_j \subseteq \uparrow \overline{\omega}_i$, iff $\overline{\omega}_j \subseteq \overline{\omega}_i$ (since $\overline{\omega}_i$ is upward-closed), iff $\omega_i \subseteq \omega_j$. However, when $i < j$, (i,j) is in ω_i but not in ω_j, so $\overline{\omega}_i \not\leq^{\sharp}_{\mathrm{Rado}} \overline{\omega}_j$. So $(\overline{\omega}_i)_{i \in \mathbb{N}}$ is an infinite sequence of $\mathbb{P}(X_{\mathrm{Rado}})$ from which one cannot extract any infinite ascending chain. Hence $\mathbb{P}(X_{\mathrm{Rado}})$ is indeed not wqo. Since $\widehat{X_{\mathrm{Rado}}} = \mathsf{Ideals}(X_{\mathrm{Rado}})$, let us examine the structure of directed subsets of X_{Rado}.

Lemma 1 [FG12]. *The downward-closed directed subsets of X_{Rado}, apart from those of the form $\downarrow(m,n)$, are of the form $\omega_i = \{(i,n) \mid n \geq i+1\} \cup \{(m,n) \in X_{Rado} \mid n \leq i-1\}$, or $\omega = X_{Rado}$.*

See Fig. 2 for a pictorial representation of ω_i.

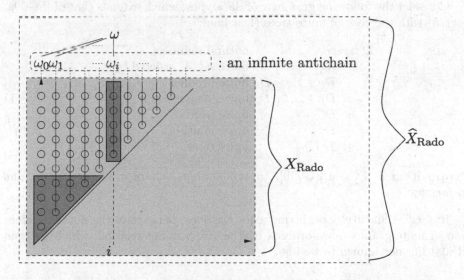

Fig. 2. Ideals in Rado's structure

5.4 ω^2-WSTS

Recall here the working definition in [Jan99]: a well-quasi-order X is ω^2-*wqo* if and only if it does not contain an (isomorphic copy of) X_{Rado}; here we use Jančar's definition, as it is more tractable than the complex definition of [Mar94]. Jančar proved that X is ω^2-*wqo* iff $(\mathbb{P}(X), \leq^{\sharp})$ is wqo (where $A \leq^{\sharp} B$ iff for every

$b \in B$, there is an $a \in A$ such that $a \leq b$ or equivalently iff $\uparrow B \subseteq \uparrow A$ iff $B \subseteq \uparrow A$).
We have shown that the above is the only case that can go bad:

Proposition 1 [FG09b]. *Let S be a well-quasi-order. Then $\widehat{S}$ is well-quasi-ordered by inclusion iff S is ω^2-wqo.*

Let an ω^2-*WSTS* be any WSTS whose underlying poset is ω^2-wqo. It follows:

Theorem 5 [FG09b]. *Let $\mathfrak{S} = (S, \rightarrow, \leq)$ be a WSTS. Then $\widehat{\mathfrak{S}}$ is a WSTS iff $\mathfrak{S}$ is an ω^2-WSTS.* □

Note that $\widehat{S} = \mathsf{Ideals}(S)$ is an algebraic dcpo [AJ94], whence $\widehat{S}$ is a continuous dcwo as soon as S is ω^2-wqo.

5.5 Are ω^2-wqos Ubiquitous?

X_{Rado} is an example of a wqo that is not ω^2-wqo. It is natural to ask whether this is the norm or an exception. We claim that all wqos used in the verification literature are in fact ω^2-wpo.

Consider the following grammar of datatypes, which extends that of [FG09a, Sect. 5] with the case of finite trees (last line):

$$
\begin{array}{lll}
D ::= & \mathbb{N} & \text{natural numbers} \\
| & A_{\leq} & \text{finite set } A, \text{ ordered by } \leq \\
| & D_1 \times \ldots \times D_k & \text{finite product} \\
| & D_1 + \ldots + D_k & \text{finite, disjoint sum} \\
| & D^* & \text{finite words} \\
| & D^{\circledast} & \text{finite multisets} \\
| & \mathcal{T}(D) & \text{finite trees}
\end{array} \tag{1}
$$

Proposition 2 [FG09a, FG09b]. *Every datatype defined in (1) is ω^2-wqo, and in fact bqo.*

In fact, all naturally occurring wqos are bqos, perhaps to the notable exception of finite graphs quasi-ordered by the graph minor relation, which are wqo [RS04] but not known to be bqo.

6   A Conceptual Karp-Miller Procedure[4]

An argument in favor of computing clovers is Emerson and Namjoshi's [EN98] approach to model-checking *liveness* properties of WSTS, which uses a finite (coverability) graph based on the clover. Since WSTS enjoy the finite path property ([EN98], Definition 7), model-checking liveness properties is decidable for WSTS for which the clover is computable. This motivate us to *try* to compute the clover for classes of WSTS, even though it is not computable in general. The

---

[4] The content of Sect. 6 is mainly drawn from the paper [FG12].

key to designing some form of a Karp-Miller procedure, such as the **Clover**$_{\mathfrak{S}}$ procedure below is being able to *compute* lub-accelerations. To define and to compute lub-accelerations, one will use functional WSTS and one will accelerate compositions of functions. Complete WSTS is the framework to define and compute lub-accelerations.

Definition 6 (Complete WSTS [FG12]). *A complete transition system is a functional transition system* $\mathfrak{S} = (S, \xrightarrow{F}, \leq)$ *where* $(S, \leq)$ *is a continuous dcwo and every function in F is partial ω-continuous. A complete WSTS is a functional WSTS that is complete as a functional transition system.*

Let us remark that complete WSTS are strongly monotonic and that $\widehat{S} = \mathsf{Ideals}(S)$ is always a continuous dcpo [AJ94, Proposition 2.2.22], hence the completion of a WSTS (resp. a WBTS) is a complete WSTS (resp. a WBTS).

The point in complete WSTS is that one can *accelerate* loops:

Definition 7 (Lub-Acceleration [FG12]). *Let* $(X, \leq)$ *be a dcpo, $f : X \to X$ be partial ω-continuous. The* lub-acceleration $f^\infty : X \to X$ *is defined by:* dom f^∞ = dom f, *and for any $x \in$ dom f, if $x < f(x)$ then $f^\infty(x) = \mathrm{lub}\{f^n(x) \mid n \in \mathbb{N}\}$, else $f^\infty(x) = f(x)$.*

Note that if $x \leq f(x)$, then $f(x) \in$ dom f, and $f(x) \leq f^2(x)$. By induction, we can show that $\{f^n(x) \mid n \in \mathbb{N}\}$ is an increasing sequence, so that the definition makes sense.

Remark 2. In [FG09b], we define, only for complete WSTS, the *clover* as the finite set (not necessarily computable) of maximal elements of the least upper bounds of the cover: more precisely, the *clover* $Clover_{\mathfrak{S}}(s_0)$ of the state $s_0 \in S$ is $\mathrm{Max\,Lub}(Cover_{\mathfrak{S}}(s_0))$. Now we may extend the previous definition of $Clover$ to any WBTS as follows: $Clover_{\mathfrak{S}}(s_0) \overset{\mathrm{def}}{=} \mathsf{IdealDecomp}(Cover_{\mathfrak{S}}(s_0))$ where

$\mathsf{IdealDecomp}(Cover_{\mathfrak{S}}(s_0))$ is the canonical ideal decomposition of $Cover_{\mathfrak{S}}(s_0)$. Then each maximal element in $\mathrm{Lub}(Cover_{\mathfrak{S}}(s_0))$ can be identified with a maximal ideal in $\mathsf{IdealDecomp}(Cover_{\mathfrak{S}}(s_0))$. Lub-accelerations in WBTS could be defined for functional *complete* WBTS.

Definition 8 (∞-Effective [FG12]). *An effective complete functional WSTS* $\mathfrak{S} = (S, \xrightarrow{F}, \leq)$ *is ∞-effective iff every function g^∞ is computable, for every $g \in F^*$, where F^* is the set of all compositions of maps in F.*

E.g., the completion of a Petri net is ∞-effective: not only is $\mathbb{N}_\omega^k$ a wpo, but every composition of transitions $g \in F^*$ is of the form $g(\boldsymbol{x}) = \boldsymbol{x} + \delta$, where $\delta \in \mathbb{Z}^k$. If $\boldsymbol{x} < g(\boldsymbol{x})$ then $\delta \in \mathbb{N}^k \setminus \{0\}$. Write $\boldsymbol{x}_i$ the ith component of $\boldsymbol{x}$, it follows that $g^\infty(\boldsymbol{x})$ is the tuple whose ith component is $\boldsymbol{x}_i$ if $\delta_i = 0$, ω otherwise.

Let $\mathfrak{S}$ be an ∞-effective WSTS, and write $A \leq^\flat B$ iff $\downarrow A \subseteq \downarrow B$, i.e., iff every element of A is below some element of B. The following is a simple procedure which computes the clover of its input $s_0 \in S$ (when it terminates):

Procedure Clover$_\mathfrak{S}(s_0)$:

1. $A \leftarrow \{s_0\}$;
2. **while** $Post_\mathfrak{S}(A) \not\leq^b A$ **do**
   (a) Choose fairly (see below) $(g, a) \in F^* \times A$ such that $a \in \text{dom}\, g$;
   (b) $A \leftarrow A \cup \{g^\infty(a)\}$;
3. **return** Max A;

The reader will find in [FG12] arguments showing that **Clover$_\mathfrak{S}$** is well-defined and all its lines are computable by assumption, provided we make clear what we mean by fair choice in line (a).

We use a *fixpoint test* (line 2) that is not in the Karp-Miller algorithm; and this improvement allows **Clover$_\mathfrak{S}$** to terminate in *more cases* than the Karp-Miller procedure when it is used for extended Petri nets (for reset Petri nets for instance, which are a special case of the affine maps above). To decide whether the current set A, which is always an under-approximation of $Clover_\mathfrak{S}(s_0)$, is the clover, it is enough to decide whether $Post_\mathfrak{S}(A) \leq^b A$.

7   Conclusion and Perspectives

We have made a (partial) survey on WSTS among the tens of papers related to WSTS. Then we have presented the new (for the verification community) framework of ideals and we have shown how it has been used in recent papers concerning decidability and complexity of different Petri nets extensions. We have also presented the new definition of Well Behaved Transition Systems, which extends WSTS, and where coverability is still decidable [BFM16a]. We have recalled the framework in [FG12] of *complete WSTS*, and of *completions* of WSTS, on which forward reachability analyses can be conducted, using the *clover*, i.e., the set of maximal elements of the cover. For complete WSTS, the clover is finite, describes the cover exactly and it is computed by a simple procedure, **Clover$_\mathfrak{S}$**, for ∞-effective complete WSTS $\mathfrak{S}$.

From [BFM16a], one could extend the Clover's definition and the procedure **Clover$_\mathfrak{S}$** to WBTS. In the future, it would be interesting to investigate all of the previous questions for *WBTS* instead of WSTS.

Acknowledgement. I would like to thank Michael Blondin, Jean Goubault-Larrecq and Pierre McKenzie for fruitful discussions and for having allowed me to use some parts of common papers.

References

[ABJ98] Abdulla, P., Bouajjani, A., Jonsson, B.: On-the-fly analysis of systems with unbounded, lossy Fifo channels. In: Hu, A.J., Vardi, M.Y. (eds.) CAV 1898. LNCS, vol. 1427, pp. 305–318. Springer, Heidelberg (1998)

[ACABJ04a] Abdulla, P.A., Collomb-Annichini, A., Bouajjani, A., Jonsson, B.: Using forward reachability analysis for verification of lossy channel systems. Formal Methods Syst. Des. **25**(1), 39–65 (2004)

[AČJT00] Abdulla, P.A., Čerāns, K., Jonsson, B., Tsay, Y.-K.: Algorithmic analysis of programs with well quasi-ordered domains. Inf. Comput. **160**(1–2), 109–127 (2000)

[AČJYK96] Abdulla, P.A., Čerāns, K., Jonsson, B., Yih-Kuen, T.: General decidability theorems for infinite-state systems. In: 11th LICS, pp. 313–321 (1996)

[ADB07] Abdulla, P.A., Delzanno, G., Van Begin, L.: Comparing the expressive power of well-structured transition systems. In: Duparc, J., Henzinger, T.A. (eds.) CSL 2007. LNCS, vol. 4646, pp. 99–114. Springer, Heidelberg (2007)

[ADMN04] Abdulla, P.A., Deneux, J., Mahata, P., Nylén, A.: Forward reachability analysis of timed Petri nets. In: Lakhnech, Y., Yovine, S. (eds.) FOR-MATS/FTRTFT 2004. LNCS, vol. 3253, pp. 343–362. Springer, Heidelberg (2004)

[AJ93] Abdulla, P., Jonsson, B.: Verifying programs with unreliable channels. In: Proceedings of the 8th LICS, pp. 160–170 (1993)

[AJ94] Abramsky, S., Jung, A.: Domain theory. In: Abramsky, S., Gabbay, D.M., Maibaum, T.S.E. (eds.) Handbook of Logic in Computer Science, vol. 3, pp. 1–168. Oxford University Press (1994)

[AL78] Arnold, A., Latteux, M.: Recursivite et cones rationnels fermes par inter-section. Calcolo **15**(4), 381–394 (1978)

[AN00] Abdulla, P.A., Nylén, A.: Better is better than well: on efficient verification of infinite-state systems. In: Proceedings of 14th IEEE Symposium, LICS 2000, pp. 132–140 (2000)

[BDK+12] Bertrand, N., Delzanno, G., König, B., Sangnier, A., Stückrath, J.: On the decidability status of reachability and coverability in graph trans-formation systems. In: Tiwari, A. (ed.) 23rd RTA 2012, Nagoya, Japan, 28 May–2 June 2012. LIPIcs, vol. 15, pp. 101–116. Schloss Dagstuhl - Leibniz-Zentrum fuer Informatik (2012)

[BFHR11] Bonnet, R., Finkel, A., Haddad, S., Rosa-Velardo, F.: Ordinal theory for expressiveness of well structured transition systems. In: Hofmann, M. (ed.) FOSSACS 2011. LNCS, vol. 6604, pp. 153–167. Springer, Heidelberg (2011)

[BFM14] Blondin, M., Finkel, A., McKenzie, P.: Handling infinitely branching WSTS. In: Esparza, J., Fraigniaud, P., Husfeldt, T., Koutsoupias, E. (eds.) ICALP 2014, Part II. LNCS, vol. 8573, pp. 13–25. Springer, Hei-delberg (2014)

[BFM16a] Blondin, M., Finkel, A., McKenzie, P.: Well Behaved Transition Systems (2016, in preparation)

[BFM16b] Blondin, M., Finkel, A., McKenzie, P.: Handling infinitely branching well-structured transition systems. Inf. Comput. (2016, submitted)

[BG14] Baldan, P., Gorla, D. (eds.): CONCUR 2014. LNCS, vol. 8704. Springer, Heidelberg (2014)

[BHM15] Badouel, E., Hélouët, L., Morvan, C.: Petri nets with structured data. In: Devillers, R., Valmari, A. (eds.) PETRI NETS 2015. LNCS, vol. 9115, pp. 212–233. Springer, Heidelberg (2015)

[BLP15] Bojanczyk, M., Lasota, S., Potapov, I. (eds.): RP 2015. LNCS, vol. 9328. Springer, Heidelberg (2015). doi:10.1007/978-3-319-24537-9_7

[Bon75] Bonnet, R.: On the cardinality of the set of initial intervals of a partially ordered set. In: Infinite, Finite Sets: To Paul Erdös on His 60th Birthday, pp. 189–198 (1975)

[CFS11] Chambart, P., Finkel, A., Schmitz, S.: Forward analysis and model checking for trace bounded WSTS. In: Kristensen, L.M., Petrucci, L. (eds.) PETRI NETS 2011. LNCS, vol. 6709, pp. 49–68. Springer, Heidelberg (2011)

[DFS98] Dufourd, C., Finkel, A., Schnoebelen, P.: Reset nets between decidability and undecidability. In: Larsen, K.G., Skyum, S., Winskel, G. (eds.) ICALP 1998. LNCS, vol. 1443, pp. 103–115. Springer, Heidelberg (1998)

[DJS99] Dufourd, C., Jančar, P., Schnoebelen, P.: Boundedness of reset P/T nets. In: Wiedermann, J., Van Emde Boas, P., Nielsen, M. (eds.) ICALP 1999. LNCS, vol. 1644, pp. 301–310. Springer, Heidelberg (1999)

[EFM99] Esparza, J., Finkel, A., Mayr, R.: On the verification of broadcast protocols. In: 14th LICS, pp. 352–359 (1999)

[EN98] Allen Emerson, E., Namjoshi, K.S.: On model-checking for non-deterministic infinite-state systems. In: 13th LICS, pp. 70–80 (1998)

[ET43] Erdös, P., Tarski, A.: On families of mutually exclusive sets. Ann. Math. 2(44), 315–329 (1943)

[FFSS11] Figueira, D., Figueira, S., Schmitz, S., Schnoebelen, P.: Ackermannian and primitive-recursive bounds with Dickson's lemma. In: 26th Annual IEEE LICS, Toronto, Ontario, Canada, 21–24 June 2011, pp. 269–278. IEEE Computer Society (2011)

[FG09a] Finkel, A., Goubault-Larrecq, J.: Forward analysis for WSTS, part I: completions. In: Albers, S., Marion, J.-Y. (eds.) 26th Annual STACS 2009. Leibniz International Proceedings in Informatics, vol. 3, pp. 433–444. Leibniz-Zentrum für Informatik, Freiburg (2009)

[FG09b] Finkel, A., Goubault-Larrecq, J.: Forward analysis for WSTS, part II: complete WSTS. In: Albers, S., Marchetti-Spaccamela, A., Matias, Y., Nikoletseas, S., Thomas, W. (eds.) ICALP 2009, Part II. LNCS, vol. 5556, pp. 188–199. Springer, Heidelberg (2009)

[FG12] Finkel, A., Goubault-Larrecq, J.: Forward analysis for WSTS, part II: complete WSTS. Logical Methods Comput. Sci. 8(3:28), 1–35 (2012)

[Fin87] Finkel, A.: A generalization of the procedure of Karp and Miller to well structured transition systems. In: Ottmann, T. (ed.) ICALP 1987. LNCS, vol. 267, pp. 499–508. Springer, Heidelberg (1987)

[Fin90] Finkel, A.: Reduction and covering of infinite reachability trees. Inf. Comput. 89(2), 144–179 (1990)

[FMP04] Finkel, A., McKenzie, P., Picaronny, C.: A well-structured framework for analysing Petri net extensions. Inf. Comput. 195(1–2), 1–29 (2004)

[Fra86] Fraïssé, R.: Theory of relations. Stud. Logic Found. Math. 118, 1–456 (1986)

[FS01] Finkel, A., Schnoebelen, P.: Well-structured transition systems everywhere!. Theoret. Comput. Sci. 256(1–2), 63–92 (2001)

[GHK+03] Gierz, G., Hofmann, K.H., Keimel, K., Lawson, J.D., Mislove, M., Scott, D.S.: Continuous lattices and domains. In: Encyclopedia of Mathematics and its Applications, vol. 93. Cambridge University Press (2003)

[GLS16] Goubault-Larrecq, J., Schmitz, S.: Deciding piecewise testable separability for regular tree languages. In: Calamoneri, T., Gorla, D., Rabani, Y., Sangiorgi, D., Mitzenmacher, M. (eds.) 43rd ICALP 2016, Proceedings Leibniz International Proceedings in Informatics, Rome, Italy, 12–15 July 2016, pp. 97:1–97:14. Leibniz-Zentrum für Informatik (2016)

[GRB04]   Geeraerts, G., Raskin, J.-F., Van Begin, L.: Expand, enlarge, and check: new algorithms for the coverability problem of WSTS. In: Lodaya, K., Mahajan, M. (eds.) FSTTCS 2004. LNCS, vol. 3328, pp. 287–298. Springer, Heidelberg (2004)

[GRB07]   Geeraerts, G., Raskin, J.-F., Van Begin, L.: Well-structured languages. Acta Inf. **44**(3–4), 249–288 (2007)

[GRvB06a] Ganty, P., Raskin, J.-F., Van Begin, L.: A complete abstract interpretation framework for coverability properties of WSTS. In: Emerson, E.A., Namjoshi, K.S. (eds.) VMCAI 2006. LNCS, vol. 3855, pp. 49–64. Springer, Heidelberg (2006)

[GRvB06b] Geeraerts, G., Raskin, J.-F., Van Begin, L.: Expand, enlarge and check: new algorithms for the coverability problem of WSTS. J. Comput. Syst. Sci. **72**(1), 180–203 (2006)

[GRvB07] Geeraerts, G., Raskin, J.-F., Van Begin, L.: On the efficient computation of the minimal coverability set for Petri nets. In: Namjoshi, K.S., Yoneda, T., Higashino, T., Okamura, Y. (eds.) ATVA 2007. LNCS, vol. 4762, pp. 98–113. Springer, Heidelberg (2007)

[HLL+16] Hofman, P., Lasota, S., Lazic, R., Leroux, J., Schmitz, S., Totzke, P.: Coverability trees for Petri nets with unordered data. In: Jacobs, B., Löding, C. (eds.) FOSSACS 2016. LNCS, vol. 9634, pp. 445–461. Springer, Heidelberg (2016). doi:10.1007/978-3-662-49630-5_26

[HMM14]   Hüchting, R., Majumdar, R., Meyer, R.: Bounds on mobility. In: Baldan and Gorla [BG14], pp. 357–371

[HP07]   Haddad, S., Poitrenaud, D.: Recursive Petri nets. Acta Inf. **44**(7–8), 463–508 (2007)

[HSS12]   Haddad, S., Schmitz, S., Schnoebelen, P.: The ordinal-recursive complexity of timed-arc petri nets, data nets, and other enriched nets. In: 27th Annual IEEE LICS, Dubrovnik, Croatia, 25–28 June 2012, pp. 355–364. IEEE Computer Society (2012)

[Jan99]   Jančar, P.: A note on well quasi-orderings for powersets. Inf. Process. Lett. **72**(5–6), 155–160 (1999)

[KM69]   Karp, R.M., Miller, R.E.: Parallel program schemata. J. Comput. Syst. Sci. **3**(2), 147–195 (1969)

[KS96]   Kouchnarenko, O., Schnoebelen, P.: A model for recursive-parallel programs. Electron. Notes Theor. Comput. Sci. **5**, 30 (1996)

[KS14]   König, B., Stückrath, J.: A general framework for well-structured graph transformation systems. In: Baldan and Gorla [BG14], pp. 467–481

[Las16]   Lasota, S.: Decidability border for Petri nets with data: WQO dichotomy conjecture. In: Kordon, F., Moldt, D. (eds.) PETRI NETS 2016. LNCS, vol. 9698, pp. 20–36. Springer, Heidelberg (2016). doi:10.1007/978-3-319-39086-4_3

[Laz13]   Lazić, R.: The reachability problem for vector addition systems with a stack is not elementary. CoRR, abs/1310.1767 (2013)

[LNO+07] Lazić, R.S., Newcomb, T., Ouaknine, J., Roscoe, A.W., Worrell, J.B.: Nets with tokens which carry data. In: Kleijn, J., Yakovlev, A. (eds.) ICATPN 2007. LNCS, vol. 4546, pp. 301–320. Springer, Heidelberg (2007)

[LS15a]   Lazić, R., Schmitz, S.: The ideal view on rackoff's coverability technique. In: Bojanczyk et al. [BLP15], pp. 76–88

[LS15b]   Leroux, J., Schmitz, S.: Demystifying reachability in vector addition systems. In: 30th Annual ACM/IEEE LICS, Kyoto, Japan, 6–10 July 2015, pp. 56–67. IEEE Computer Society (2015)

[LS16a] Lazić, R., Schmitz, S.: The complexity of coverability in -Petri nets. In: LICS 2016. ACM Press, New York (2016)

[LS16b] Leroux, J., Schmitz, S.: Ideal decompositions for vector addition systems (invited talk). In: Ollinger, N., Vollmer, H. (eds.) 33rd STACS 2016, Orléans, France, 17–20 February 2016. LIPIcs, vol. 47, pp. 1:1–1:13 (2016)

[LST15a] Leroux, J., Sutre, G., Totzke, P.: On boundedness problems for pushdown vector addition systems. In: Bojanczyk et al. [BLP15], pp. 101–113

[LST15b] Leroux, J., Sutre, G., Totzke, P.: On the coverability problem for pushdown vector addition systems in one dimension. In: Halldórsson, M.M., Iwama, K., Kobayashi, N., Speckmann, B. (eds.) ICALP 2015. LNCS, vol. 9135, pp. 324–336. Springer, Heidelberg (2015)

[Mar94] Marcone, A.: Foundations of BQO theory. Trans. Am. Math. Soc. **345**(2), 641–660 (1994)

[May00] Mayr, R.: Process rewrite systems. Inf. Comput. **156**(1–2), 264–286 (2000)

[Mey08] Meyer, R.: On boundedness in depth in the pi-calculus. In: Ausiello, G., Karhumäki, J., Mauri, G., Luke Ong, C.-H. (eds.) TCS 2008. IFIP, vol. 273, pp. 477–489. Springer, Heidelberg (2008)

[Rad54] Rado, R.: Partial well-ordering of sets of vectors. Mathematika **1**, 89–95 (1954)

[RdF07] Rosa-Velardo, F., de Frutos-Escrig, D.: Name creation vs. replication in Petri net systems. In: Kleijn, J., Yakovlev, A. (eds.) ICATPN 2007. LNCS, vol. 4546, pp. 402–422. Springer, Heidelberg (2007)

[RHB+10] Rogers, J., Heinz, J., Bailey, G., Edlefsen, M., Visscher, M., Wellcome, D., Wibel, S.: On languages piecewise testable in the strict sense. In: Ebert, C., Jäger, G., Michaelis, J. (eds.) MOL 10/11. LNCS, vol. 6149, pp. 255–265. Springer, Heidelberg (2010)

[RMdF11] Rosa-Velardo, F., Martos-Salgado, M., de Frutos-Escrig, D.: Accelerations for the coverability set of Petri nets with names. Fundam. Inform. **113**(3–4), 313–341 (2011)

[RS04] Robertson, N., Seymour, P.D.: Graph minors. XX. Wagner's conjecture. J. Comb. Theory Ser. B **92**(2), 325–357 (2004)

[SS11] Schmitz, S., Schnoebelen, P.: Multiply-recursive upper bounds with Higman's Lemma. In: Aceto, L., Henzinger, M., Sgall, J. (eds.) ICALP 2011, Part II. LNCS, vol. 6756, pp. 441–452. Springer, Heidelberg (2011)

[Val78] Valk, R.: Self-modidying nets, a natural extension of Petri nets. In: Ausiello, G., Böhm, C. (eds.) ICALP 1978. LNCS, vol. 62, pp. 464–476. Springer, Heidelberg (1978)

[WZH10] Wies, T., Zufferey, D., Henzinger, T.A.: Forward analysis of depth-bounded processes. In: Ong, L. (ed.) FOSSACS 2010. LNCS, vol. 6014, pp. 94–108. Springer, Heidelberg (2010)

[ZWH12] Zufferey, D., Wies, T., Henzinger, T.A.: Ideal abstractions for well-structured transition systems. In: Kuncak, V., Rybalchenko, A. (eds.) VMCAI 2012. LNCS, vol. 7148, pp. 445–460. Springer, Heidelberg (2012)

Rare Events for Statistical Model Checking
an Overview

Axel Legay, Sean Sedwards, and Louis-Marie Traonouez[✉]

Inria Rennes – Bretagne Atlantique, Rennes, France
louis-marie.traonouez@inria.fr

Abstract. This invited paper surveys several simulation-based approaches to compute the probability of rare bugs in complex systems. The paper also describes how those techniques can be implemented in the professional toolset Plasma.

1 Introduction

Model checking offers the possibility to automatically verify the correctness of complex systems or detect bugs [7]. In many practical applications it is also useful to quantify the probability of a property (e.g., system failure), so the concept of model checking has been extended to probabilistic systems [2]. This form is frequently referred to as *numerical* model checking.

To give results with certainty, numerical model checking algorithms effectively perform an exhaustive traversal of the states of the system. In most real applications, however, the state space is intractable, scaling exponentially with the number of independent state variables (the 'state explosion problem' [6]). Abstraction and symmetry reduction may make certain classes of systems tractable, but these techniques are not generally applicable. This limitation has prompted the development of *statistical* model checking (SMC), which employs an executable model of the system to estimate the probability of a property from simulations.

SMC is a Monte Carlo method which takes advantage of robust statistical techniques to bound the error of the estimated result (e.g., [22,26]). To quantify a property it is necessary to observe the property, while increasing the number of observations generally increases the confidence of the estimate. Rare properties are often highly relevant to system performance (e.g., bugs and system failure are required to be rare) but pose a problem for statistical model checking because they are difficult to observe. Fortunately, rare event techniques such as *importance sampling* [17,19] and *importance splitting* [18,19,24] may be successfully applied to statistical model checking.

Importance sampling and importance splitting have been widely applied to specific simulation problems in science and engineering. Importance sampling works by estimating a result using weighted simulations and then compensating for the weights. Importance splitting works by reformulating the rare probability as a product of less rare probabilities conditioned on levels that must be achieved.

© Springer International Publishing Switzerland 2016
K.G. Larsen et al. (Eds.): RP 2016, LNCS 9899, pp. 23–35, 2016.
DOI: 10.1007/978-3-319-45994-3_2

In this invited paper, we summarize our contributions on importance sampling and splitting. Then, we discuss their implementation within the Plasma toolset.

2   Command Based Importance Sampling

Importance sampling works by simulating a probabilistic system under a weighted (*importance sampling*) measure that makes a rare property more likely to be seen [16]. It then compensates the results by the weights, to estimate the probability under the original measure. When simulating Markov Chains, this compensation is typically performed on the fly with almost no additional overhead.

Given a set of finite traces $\omega \in \Omega$ and a function $z : \Omega \to \{0, 1\}$ that returns 1 iff a trace satisfies some property, the importance sampling estimator is given by

$$\sum_{i=1}^{N} z(\omega_i) \frac{\mathrm{d}f(\omega_i)}{\mathrm{d}f'(\omega_i)}.$$

N is the number of simulation traces ω_i generated under the importance sampling measure f', while f is the original measure. $\frac{\mathrm{d}f}{\mathrm{d}f'}$ is the *likelihood ratio*.

For importance sampling to be effective it is necessary to define a "good" importance sampling distribution: (i) the property of interest must be seen frequently in simulations and (ii) the distribution of the simulation traces that satisfy the property in the importance sampling distribution must be as close as possible to the normalised distribution of the same traces in the original distribution. Failure to consider both (i) and (ii) can result in underestimated probability with overestimated confidence.

Since the main motivation of importance sampling is to reduce the computational burden, the process of finding a good importance sampling distribution must maintain the scaling advantage of SMC and, in particular, should not iterate over all the states or transitions of the system. We therefore consider parametrised importance sampling distributions, where our parametrisation is over the syntax of stochastic *guarded commands*, a common low level modelling language of probabilistic systems[1].

Each command has the form (*guard, rate, action*). The *guard* enables the command and is a predicate over the state variables of the model. The *rate* is a function from the state variables to $\mathbb{R}_{>0}$, defining the rate of an exponential distribution. The *action* is an update function that modifies the state variables. In general, each command defines a set of semantically linked transitions in the resulting Markov chain.

The semantics of a stochastic guarded command is a Markov jump process. The semantics of a parallel composition of commands is a system of concurrent Markov jump processes. Sample execution traces can be generated by discrete-event simulation. In any state, zero or more commands may be enabled. If no commands are enabled the system is in a halting state. In all other cases the enabled

---

[1] http://www.prismmodelchecker.org/manual/ThePRISMLanguage/.

commands "compete" to execute their actions: sample times are drawn from the exponential distributions defined by their rates and the shortest time "wins".

2.1   The Cross-Entropy Method

The "cross-entropy method" [25] is an optimisation technique based on minimising the Kullback-Leibler divergence between a parametrised importance sampling distribution and the theoretically optimum distribution, without having an explicit description of the latter.

Given a system whose distribution is described by parametrised measure $f : \Omega \times \Lambda \to \mathbb{R}$, where Λ is the set of possible vectors of parameters, using the cross-entropy method it is possible to construct the following iterative process that converges to an estimate of λ^*, the optimal vector of parameters:

$$\lambda^{(j+1)} = \arg\max_{\lambda} \sum_{i=1}^{N} z(\omega_i^{(j)}) L^{(j)}(\omega_i^{(j)}) \log \mathrm{d}f(\omega_i^{(j)}, \lambda) \tag{1}$$

N is the number of simulation runs generated on each of the j iterations, $\lambda^{(j)}$ is the jth set of estimated parameters, $L^{(j)}(\omega) = \mathrm{d}f(\omega, \mu)/\mathrm{d}f(\omega, \lambda^{(j)})$ is the jth likelihood ratio (μ is the original vector of parameters), $\omega_i^{(j)}$ is the ith path generated using $f(\cdot, \lambda^{(i)})$ and $\mathrm{d}f(\omega_i^{(j)}, \lambda)$ is the probability of path $\omega_i^{(j)}$ under the distribution $f(\cdot, \lambda^{(j)})$.

2.2   Cross-Entropy Minimisation Algorithm

We consider a system of n stochastic guarded commands with vector of rate functions $\eta = (\eta_1, \ldots, \eta_n)$ and corresponding vector of parameters $\lambda = (\lambda_1, \ldots, \lambda_n)$. In any given state x_s, reached after s transitions, the probability that command $k \in \{1 \ldots n\}$ is chosen is given by

$$\frac{\lambda_k \eta_k(x_s)}{\langle \eta(x_s), \lambda \rangle},$$

where η is explicitly parametrised by x_s to emphasise its state dependence and the notation $\langle \cdot, \cdot \rangle$ denotes a scalar product. Let $U_k(\omega)$ be the number of transitions of type k occurring in ω. We therefore have

$$\mathrm{d}f(\omega, \lambda) = \prod_{k}^{n} \left((\lambda_k)^{U_k(\omega)} \prod_{s \in J_k(\omega)} \frac{\eta_k(x_s)}{\langle \eta(x_s), \lambda \rangle} \right).$$

We define $\eta_k^{(i)}(x_s)$ and $\eta^{(i)}(x_s)$ as the respective values of η_k and η functions in state x_s of the ith trace. We substitute the previous expressions in the cross-entropy estimator (1) and for compactness substitute $z_i = z(\omega_i)$, $u_i(k) = U_k(\omega_i)$ and $l_i = L^{(j)}(\omega_i)$ to get

$$\arg\max_{\lambda} \sum_{i=1}^{N} l_i z_i \log \prod_{k}^{n} \left(\lambda_k^{u_i(k)} \prod_{s \in J_k^{(i)}} \frac{\eta_k^{(i)}(x_s)}{\langle \eta^{(i)}(x_s), \lambda \rangle} \right)$$

$$= \arg\max_{\lambda} \sum_{i=1}^{N} \sum_{k}^{n} l_i z_i$$

$$\left(u_i(k) \log(\lambda_k) + \sum_{s \in J_k^{(i)}} \log(\eta_k^{(i)}(x_s)) - \sum_{s \in J_k^{(i)}} \log(\langle \eta^{(i)}(x_s), \lambda \rangle) \right) \qquad (2)$$

We denote the argument of the arg max in (2) as $F(\lambda)$ and derive the following partial differential equation:

$$\frac{\partial F}{\partial \lambda_k}(\lambda) = 0 \Leftrightarrow \sum_{i=1}^{N} l_i z_i \left(\frac{u_i(k)}{\lambda_k} - \sum_{s=1}^{|\omega_i|} \frac{\eta_k^{(i)}(x_s)}{\langle \eta^{(i)}(x_s), \lambda \rangle} \right) = 0 \qquad (3)$$

The quantity $|\omega_i|$ is the length of path ω_i.

Theorem 1 ([12]). *A solution of (3) is almost surely a unique maximum, up to a normalising scalar.*

The fact that there is a unique optimum makes it possible to use (3) to construct an iterative process that converges to λ^*:

$$\lambda_k^{(j+1)} = \frac{\sum_{i=1}^{N} l_i z_i u_i(k)}{\sum_{i=1}^{N} l_i z_i \sum_{s=1}^{|\omega_i|} \frac{\eta_k^{(i)}(x_s)}{\langle \eta^{(i)}(x_s), \lambda^{(j)} \rangle}}. \qquad (4)$$

A rare property does not imply that good parameters are rare, hence (4) may be initialised by selecting vectors of parameters at random until one is found that allows some traces that satisfy the property to be observed. An alternative initialisation strategy is to simply choose the outgoing transition from every state uniformly at random from those that are enabled.

3   Importance Sampling for Timed Systems

The foregoing approach considers continuous time in the context of continuous time Markov chains (CTMC), where time delays in each state are sampled from exponential distributions. To reason on the stochastic performance of complex timed systems, the model of Stochastic Timed Automata (STA) [8] extends Timed Automata (TA) [1] with both exponential and continuous distributions. Work on closely related models [21] suggests that tractable analytical solutions exist only for special cases. Monte Carlo approaches provide an approximative alternative to analysis, but they incur the problem of rare events.

The added complexity of the STA model prevents a direct application of our approach for Markov chains, however in recent work we are applying importance sampling to STA by taking advantage of the symbolic data structures used to analyse TA. Our approach is to construct a simulation kernel based on a "zone graph" representation of an STA that excludes zones where the property fails. The probability corresponding to these "dead ends" is redistributed to the adjacent zones in proportion to the original probability of reaching them. The calculation is performed on the fly during simulation, by numerically solving an integral whose polynomial form is known a priori. All simulated traces reach goal states, while the change of measure is guaranteed by construction to reduce the variance of estimates with respect to the standard Monte Carlo estimator. Our early experimental results demonstrate substantial reductions of variance.

4   Importance Splitting

The earliest application of importance splitting is perhaps that of [17,18], where it is used to calculate the probability that neutrons pass through certain shielding materials. This physical example provides a convenient analogy for the more general case. The system comprises a source of neutrons aimed at one side of a shield of thickness T. The distance traveled by a neutron in the shield defines a monotonic sequence of levels $l_0 = 0 < l_1 < l_2 < \ldots < l_n = T$, such that reaching a given level implies having reached all the lower levels. While the overall probability of passing through the shield is small, the probability of passing from one level to another can be made arbitrarily close to 1 by reducing the distance between levels. Denoting the abstract level of a neutron as l, the probability of a neutron reaching level l_i can be expressed as $P(l \geq l_i) = P(l \geq l_i \mid l \geq l_{i-1})P(l \geq l_{i-1})$. Defining $\gamma = P(l \geq l_m)$ and $P(l \geq l_0) = 1$, we get

$$\gamma = \prod_{i=1}^{m} P(l \geq l_i \mid l \geq l_{i-1}). \tag{5}$$

Each term of (5) is necessarily greater than or equal to γ, making their estimation easier.

The general procedure is as follows. At each level a number of simulations are generated, starting from a distribution of initial states that corresponds to reaching the current level. It starts by estimating $P(l \geq l_1 | l \geq l_0)$, where the distribution of initial states for l_0 is usually given (often a single state). Simulations are stopped as soon as they reach the next level; the final states becoming the empirical distribution of initial states for the next level. Simulations that do not reach the next level (or reach some other stopping criterion) are discarded. In general, $P(l \geq l_i | l \geq l_{i-1})$ is estimated by the number of simulation traces that reach l_i, divided by the total number of traces started from l_{i-1}. Simulations that reached the next level are continued from where they stopped. To avoid a progressive reduction of the number of simulations, the generated distribution of initial states is sampled to provide additional initial states for new simulations, thus replacing those that were discarded.

4.1   Score Function

The concept of levels can be generalised to arbitrary systems and properties in the context of SMC, treating l and l_i in (5) as values of a score function over the model-property product automaton. Intuitively, a score function discriminates good paths from bad, assigning higher scores to paths that more nearly satisfy the overall property. Since the choice of levels is crucial to the effectiveness of importance splitting, various ways to construct score functions from a temporal logic property are proposed in [13].

Formally, given a set of finite trace prefixes $\omega \in \Omega$, an ideal score function $S : \Omega \to \mathbb{R}$ has the characteristics $S(\omega) > S(\omega') \iff \mathrm{P}(\models \varphi \mid \omega) > \mathrm{P}(\models \varphi \mid \omega')$, where $\mathrm{P}(\models \varphi \mid \omega)$ is the probability of eventually satisfying φ given prefix ω. Intuitively, ω has a higher score than ω' iff there is more chance of satisfying φ by continuing ω than by continuing ω'. The minimum requirement of a score function is $S(\omega) \geq s_\varphi \iff \omega \models \varphi$, where s_φ is an arbitrary value denoting that φ is satisfied. Any trace that satisfies φ must have a score of at least s_φ and any trace that does not satisfy φ must have a score less than s_φ. In what follows we assume that (5) refers to scores.

4.2   Fixed Levels Algorithm

The fixed level algorithm follows from the general procedure previously presented. Its advantages are that it is simple, it has low computational overhead and the resulting estimate is unbiased. Its disadvantage is that the levels must often be guessed by trial and error – adding to the overall computational cost.

In Algorithm 1, $\tilde{\gamma}$ is an unbiased estimate (see, e.g., [9]). Furthermore, from Proposition 3 in [4], we can deduce the following $(1 - \alpha)$ confidence interval:

$$CI = \left[\hat{\gamma} / \left(1 + \frac{z_\alpha \sigma}{\sqrt{n}} \right), \hat{\gamma} / \left(1 - \frac{z_\alpha \sigma}{\sqrt{n}} \right) \right] \quad \text{with} \quad \sigma^2 \geq \sum_{i=1}^{m} \frac{1 - \gamma_i}{\gamma_i}. \tag{6}$$

Confidence is specified via z_α, the $1 - \alpha/2$ quantile of the standard normal distribution, while n is the per-level simulation budget. We infer from (6) that for a given γ the confidence is maximised by making both the number of levels m and the simulation budget n large, with all γ_i equal.

4.3   Adaptive Levels Algorithms

In general, however, score functions will not equally divide the conditional probabilities of the levels, as required by (6) to minimise variance. In the worst case, one or more of the conditional probabilities will be too low for the algorithm to pass between levels. Finding good or even reasonable levels by trial and error may be computationally expensive and has prompted the development of adaptive algorithms that discover optimal levels on the fly [5,13,14]. Instead of pre-defining levels, the user specifies the proportion of simulations to retain

---

Algorithm 1. Fixed levels

Let $(\tau_k)_{1 \leq k \leq m}$ be the sequence of thresholds with $\tau_m = \tau_\varphi$
Let *stop* be a termination condition
$\forall j \in \{1, \ldots, n\}$, set prefix $\tilde{\omega}_j^1 = \epsilon$ (empty path)
for $1 \leq k \leq m$ **do**

> $\forall j \in \{1, \ldots, n\}$, using prefix $\tilde{\omega}_j^k$, generate path ω_j^k until $(S(\omega_j^k) \geq \tau_k) \vee stop$
> $I_k = \{\forall j \in \{1, \ldots, n\} : S(\omega_j^k) \geq \tau_k\}$
> $\tilde{\gamma}_k = \frac{|I_k|}{n}$
> $\forall j \in I_k, \tilde{\omega}_j^{k+1} = \omega_j^k$
> $\forall j \notin I_k$, let $\tilde{\omega}_j^{k+1}$ be a copy of ω_i^k with $i \in I_k$ chosen uniformly randomly

$\tilde{\gamma} = \prod_{k=1}^m \tilde{\gamma}_k$

---

after each iteration. This proportion generally defines all but the final conditional probability in (5).

Adaptive importance splitting algorithms first perform a number of simulations until the overall property is decided, storing the resulting traces of the model-property automaton. Each trace induces a sequence of scores and a corresponding maximum score. The algorithm finds a level that is less than or equal to the maximum score of the desired proportion of simulations to retain. The simulations whose maximum score is below this current level are discarded. New simulations to replace the discarded ones are initialised with states corresponding to the current level, chosen at random from the retained simulations. The new simulations are continued until the overall property is decided and the procedure is repeated until a sufficient proportion of simulations satisfy the overall property.

Algorithm 2 is an optimized adaptive algorithm that rejects a minimum number of simulations at each level (ideally 1, the one with a minimum score). This maximises the confidence for a given score function.

5 Plasma Lab Implementation

Plasma Lab [3] is a modular platform for statistical model-checking. The tool offers a series of SMC algorithms, included advanced techniques for rare events simulation, distributed SMC, non-determinism, and optimization. They are used with several modeling formalisms and simulators. The main difference between Plasma Lab and other SMC tools is that Plasma Lab proposes an API abstraction of the concepts of stochastic model simulator, property checker (monitoring) and SMC algorithm. In other words, the tool has been designed to be capable of using external simulators, input languages, or SMC algorithms. This not only reduces the effort of integrating new algorithms, but also allows us to create direct plug-in interfaces with industry used specification tools. The latter being done without using extra compilers.

Plasma Lab architecture is illustrated by the graph in Fig. 1. The core of Plasma Lab is a light-weight controller that manages the experiments and the

---

Algorithm 2. Optimized adaptive levels

Let $\tau_\varphi = \min\{S(\omega) \mid \omega \models \varphi\}$ be the minimum score of paths that satisfy φ

$k = 1$

$\forall j \in \{1,\dots,n\}$, generate path ω_j^k

repeat

    Let $T = \{S(\omega_j^k), \forall j \in \{1,\dots,n\}\}$

    $\tau_k = \min T$

    $\tau_k = \min(\tau_k, \tau_\varphi)$

    $I_k = \{j \in \{1,\dots,n\} : S(\omega_j^k) > \tau_k\}$

    $\tilde\gamma_k = \frac{|I_k|}{n}$

    $\forall j \in I_k,\ \omega_j^{k+1} = \omega_j^k$

    for $j \notin I_k$ **do**

        choose uniformly randomly $l \in I_k$

        $\tilde\omega_j^{k+1} = \max\limits_{|\omega|}\{\omega \in pref(\omega_l^k) : S(\omega) < \tau_k\}$

        generate path ω_j^{k+1} with prefix $\tilde\omega_j^{k+1}$

    $m = k$

    $k = k + 1$

until $\tau_k > \tau_\varphi$;

$\tilde\gamma = \prod_{k=1}^m \tilde\gamma_k$

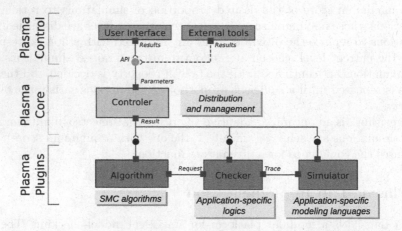

Fig. 1. Plasma Lab architecture.

distribution mechanism. It implements an API that allows to control the experiments either through user interfaces or through external tools. It loads three types of plugins: 1. algorithms, 2. checkers, and 3. simulators. These plugins communicate with each other and with the controller through the API. The tool currently supports the following plugins for modeling language:

- Reactive Module Language (RML), the input language of the tool Prism for Markov chains models.
- Biological language for writing chemical reactions.

- Simulink diagrams, using an interface to control the simulator of Matlab/ Simulink
- SystemC models, using an external tool to instrument SystemC models and generate a C++ executable used by the plugin.

5.1 Importance Sampling Implementation

We have implemented importance sampling for the RML, allowing the user to specify sampling parameters that modify transition rates. These rates are automatically used by Plasma Lab SMC algorithms to compute probabilities or rewards using the new sampling measure.

We have also implemented the cross-entropy minimization technique to iteratively find an optimal parameters distribution. The initial parameters distribution can be determined by selecting transitions uniformly at random.

5.2 Importance Splitting Implementation

Importance splitting algorithms require the user to specify a score function over the model-property product automaton. This automaton is usually hidden in the implementation of the checker plugin. Therefore Plasma Lab includes a specific checker plugin for importance splitting that facilitates the construction of score functions. The plugin allows to write small observers automata to check properties over traces and compute the score function. These observers are written with a syntax similar to the RML, using the notion of 'guarded commands' [10] with sequential semantics. This does not restrict the type of model being analyzed that can be different than RML.

These observers implement a subset of the BLTL logic presented in [15]. This subset ensures that the size of the property automaton does not depend on the bounds of temporal operators. As importance splitting algorithms require to restart simulations from random states (including the state of the property automaton), limiting the memory needed by this automaton facilitates the distribution of the simulations over network computer grids. Finally the tool allows to translate BLTL properties from this subset into observers. The user needs only to edit the produced observers to compute an adequate score function for the property.

5.3 Distributed SMC Algorithms

Simple Monte Carlo SMC may be efficiently distributed because once initialised, simulations are executed independently and the result is communicated at the end with just a single bit of information (i.e., whether the property was satisfied or not). Importance sampling and the cross entropy algorithms can be distributed as easily.

By contrast, the simulations of importance splitting are dependent because scores generated during the course of each simulation must be processed centrally. The amount of central processing can be minimised by reducing the number of levels, but this generally reduces the variance reduction performance.

In [15] we propose a distributed fixed level importance splitting algorithm. It benefits from our welterweight observers to share states between the clients responsible for the simulations and the server responsible for dispatching the simulations. We also show that a distributed adaptive algorithms would be inefficient because the number of levels is too high and consequently the number of simulations between each level is too low to benefit from the distribution.

Alternatively, entire instances of the importance splitting algorithms may be distributed and their estimates averaged, with each instance using a proportionally reduced simulation budget. This is the approach used in Plasma Lab to distribute importance splitting algorithms, but note that if the budget is reduced too far, the algorithm will fail to pass from one level to the next (because no trace achieves a high enough score) and no valid estimate will be produced.

5.4   Importance Sampling Results

Repair Model. We first apply our cross-entropy minimisation algorithm to a repair model from [23], using $N = 10000$ simulations per iteration. The system comprises six types of subsystems containing $(5, 4, 6, 3, 7, 5)$ components that may fail independently. The system's evolution begins with no failures and with various probabilistic rates the components fail and are repaired. The respective failure and repair rates are $(2.5\epsilon, \epsilon, 5\epsilon, 3\epsilon, \epsilon, 5\epsilon)$, $\epsilon = 0.001$, and $(1.0, 1.5, 1.0, 2.0, 1.0, 1.5)$. Each subsystem type is modelled by two guarded commands: one for failure and one for repair. The property under investigation is the probability of a complete failure of a subsystem (i.e., the failure of all components of one type), given an initial condition of no failures. This can be expressed in temporal logic as $\Pr[\mathbf{X}(\neg init \, \mathbf{U} \, failure)]$.

Figure 2 plots the estimated probability and sample variance during the course of the algorithm, superimposed on a grey line denoting the true probability calculated by PRISM. The long term average agrees well with the true value (an error of -1.7 %, based on an average excluding the first two estimates). Without importance sampling we expect the variance of probability estimates of rare events to be approximately equal to the probability, hence Fig. 2 suggests that our importance sampling parameters provide a variance reduction of more than 10^5.

Chemical System. We next consider a chemically reacting system of five molecular species (A, B, C, D, E) modelled by three guarded commands with correspondingly named variables:

$$(A > 0 \wedge B > 0, A \times B, A \leftarrow A - 1; B \leftarrow B - 1; C \leftarrow C + 1)$$
$$(C > 0, C, C \leftarrow C - 1; D \leftarrow D + 1)$$
$$(D > 0, D, D \leftarrow D - 1; E \leftarrow E + 1)$$

When simulated, A and B tend to combine rapidly to form C, which peaks before decaying slowly to D. The production of D also peaks, while E rises monotonically.

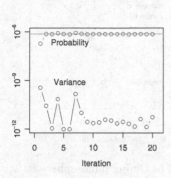

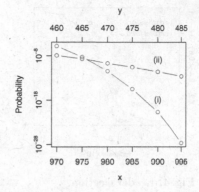

Fig. 2. Repair model.   **Fig. 3.** Chemical system.

With an initial vector of values $(1000, 1000, 0, 0, 0)$, we use $N = 1000$ simulations per iteration to estimate the probabilities of the following rare properties: (i) $\mathbf{F}^{3000} C \geq x, x \in \{970, 975, 980, 985, 990, 995\}$ and (ii) $\mathbf{F}^{3000} D \geq y, y \in \{460, 465, 470, 475, 480, 485\}$. We see from the results plotted in Fig. 3 that it is possible to estimate extremely low probabilities with very few simulations. Note that although the model is intractable to numerical analysis, we have verified the estimates via independent simulation experiments.

5.5 Importance Splitting Results

We provide experimental results of two case-studies analysed with Plasma Lab importance splitting algorithms. For each model we performed a number of experiments to compare the performance of the fixed and adaptive importance splitting algorithms with and without distribution, using different simulation budgets and levels. Our results are illustrated in the form of empirical cumulative probability distributions of 100 estimates, noting that a perfect (zero variance) estimator distribution would be represented by a single step. The probabilities we estimate are all close to 10^{-6} and are marked on the figures with a vertical line. Since we are not able to use numerical techniques to calculate the true probabilities, we use the average of 200 low variance estimates as our best overall estimate.

As a reference, we applied the adaptive algorithm to each model using a single computational thread. We chose parameters to maximise the number of levels and thus minimise the variance for a given score function and budget. The resulting distributions, sampled at every tenth percentile, are plotted with circular markers in the figures. Over these points we superimpose the results of applying a single instance of the fixed level algorithm with just a few levels. We also superimpose the average estimates of five parallel threads running the fixed level algorithm, using the same levels (Figs. 4 and 5).

Leader Election. Our leader election case study is based on the PRISM model of the synchronous leader election protocol of [11]. With $N = 20$ processes and

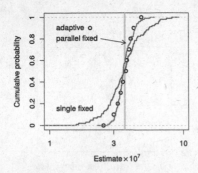
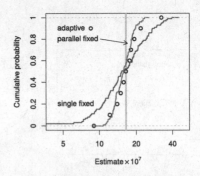

Fig. 4. Leader election.   **Fig. 5.** Dining philosophers.

$K = 6$ probabilistic choices the model has approximately 1.2×10^{18} states. We consider the probability of the property $\mathbf{G}^{420} \neg elected$, where *elected* denotes the state where a leader has been elected. Our chosen score function uses the time bound of the $\mathbf{G}$ operator to give nominal scores between 0 and 420. The model constrains these to only 20 actual levels (some scores are equivalent with respect to the model and property), but with evenly distributed probability. For the fixed level algorithm we use scores of 70, 140, 210, 280, 350 and 420.

Dining Philosophers. Our dining philosophers case study extends the PRISM model of the fair probabilistic protocol of [20]. With 150 philosophers our model contains approximately 2.3×10^{144} states. We consider the probability of the property $\mathbf{F}^{30} Phil\ eats$, where *Phil* is the name of an arbitrary philosopher. The adaptive algorithm uses the heuristic score function described in [14], which includes the five logical levels used by the fixed level algorithm. Between these levels the heuristic favours short paths, based on the assumption that as time runs out the property is less likely to be satisfied.

References

1. Alur, R., Dill, D.L.: A theory of timed automata. Theor. Comput. Sci. **126**(2), 183–235 (1994)
2. Baier, C., Katoen, J.-P.: Principles of Model Checking. Representation and Mind Series. The MIT Press, Cambridge (2008)
3. Boyer, B., Corre, K., Legay, A., Sedwards, S.: PLASMA-lab: a flexible, distributable statistical model checking library. In: Joshi, K., Siegle, M., Stoelinga, M., D'Argenio, P.R. (eds.) QEST 2013. LNCS, vol. 8054, pp. 160–164. Springer, Heidelberg (2013)
4. Cérou, F., Del Moral, P., Furon, T., Guyader, A.: Sequential Monte Carlo for rare event estimation. Stat. Comput. **22**, 795–808 (2012)
5. Cérou, F., Guyader, A.: Adaptive multilevel splitting for rare event analysis. Stoch. Anal. Appl. **25**, 417–443 (2007)
6. Clarke, E., Emerson, E.A., Sifakis, J.: Model checking: algorithmic verification and debugging. Commun. ACM **52**(11), 74–84 (2009)

7. Clarke Jr., E.M., Grumberg, O., Peled, D.A.: Model Checking. MIT Press, Cambridge (1999)
8. David, A., Larsen, K.G., Legay, A., Mikučionis, M., Poulsen, D.B., van Vliet, J., Wang, Z.: Statistical model checking for networks of priced timed automata. In: Fahrenberg, U., Tripakis, S. (eds.) FORMATS 2011. LNCS, vol. 6919, pp. 80–96. Springer, Heidelberg (2011)
9. Del Moral, P.: Feynman-Kac Formulae: Genealogical and Interacting Particle Systems with Applications. Probability and Its Applications. Springer, New York (2004)
10. Dijkstra, E.W.: Guarded commands, nondeterminacy and formal derivation of programs. Commun. ACM **18**(8), 453–457 (1975)
11. Itai, A., Rodeh, M.: Symmetry breaking in distributed networks. Inf. Comput. **88**(1), 60–87 (1990)
12. Jegourel, C., Legay, A., Sedwards, S.: Cross-entropy optimisation of importance sampling parameters for statistical model checking. In: Madhusudan, P., Seshia, S.A. (eds.) CAV 2012. LNCS, vol. 7358, pp. 327–342. Springer, Heidelberg (2012)
13. Jegourel, C., Legay, A., Sedwards, S.: Importance splitting for statistical model checking rare properties. In: Sharygina, N., Veith, H. (eds.) CAV 2013. LNCS, vol. 8044, pp. 576–591. Springer, Heidelberg (2013)
14. Jegourel, C., Legay, A., Sedwards, S.: An Effective Heuristic for Adaptive Importance Splitting in Statistical Model Checking. In: Margaria, T., Steffen, B. (eds.) ISoLA 2014, Part II. LNCS, vol. 8803, pp. 143–159. Springer, Heidelberg (2014)
15. Jegourel, C., Legay, A., Sedwards, S., Traonouez, L.-M.: Distributed verification of rare properties using importance splitting observers. In: ECEASST, vol. 72 (2015)
16. Kahn, H.: Stochastic (Monte Carlo) attenuation analysis. Technical report P-88, Rand Corporation, July 1949
17. Kahn, H.: Random sampling (Monte Carlo) techniques in neutron attenuation problems. Nucleonics **6**(5), 27 (1950)
18. Kahn, H., Harris, T.E.: Estimation of particle transmission by random sampling. In: Applied Mathematics. Series 12, vol. 5. National Bureau of Standards (1951)
19. Kahn, H., Marshall, A.W.: Methods of reducing sample size in Monte Carlo computations. Oper. Res. **1**(5), 263–278 (1953)
20. Lehmann, D., Rabin, M.O.: On the advantage of free choice: a symmetric and fully distributed solution to the dining philosophers problem. In: Proceedings of the 8th Annual Symposium on Principles of Programming Languages, pp. 133–138 (1981)
21. Maler, O., Larsen, K.G., Krogh, B.H.: On zone-based analysis of duration probabilistic automata. In: 12th International Workshop on Verification of Infinite-State Systems (INFINITY), pp. 33–46 (2010)
22. Okamoto, M.: Some inequalities relating to the partial sum of binomial probabilities. Ann. Inst. Stat. Math. **10**, 29–35 (1959)
23. Ridder, A.: Importance sampling simulations of markovian reliability systems using cross-entropy. Ann. Oper. Res. **134**, 119–136 (2005)
24. Rosenbluth, M.N., Rosenbluth, A.W.: Monte Carlo calculation of the average extension of molecular chains. J. Chem. Phys. **23**(2) (1955)
25. Rubinstein, R.: The cross-entropy method for combinatorial and continuous optimization. In: Methodology and Computing in Applied Probability, vol. 1, pp. 127–190. Kluwer Academic (1999)
26. Wald, A.: Sequential tests of statistical hypotheses. Ann. Math. Stat. **16**(2), 117–186 (1945)

On the Complexity of Resource-Bounded Logics

Natasha Alechina[1], Nils Bulling[2(✉)], Stephane Demri[3], and Brian Logan[1]

[1] University of Nottingham, Nottingham, UK
[2] TU Delft, Delft, Netherlands
n.bulling@tudelft.nl
[3] LSV, CNRS, ENS Cachan, Cachan, France

Abstract. We revisit decidability results for resource-bounded logics and use decision problems for vector addition systems with states (VASS) to characterise the complexity of (decidable) model-checking problems. We show that the model-checking problem for the logic RB±ATL is 2EXPTIME-complete by using recent results on alternating VASS. In addition, we establish that the model-checking problem for RBTL is decidable and has the same complexity as for RBTL* (the extension of RBTL with arbitrary path formulae), namely EXPSPACE-complete, proving a new decidability result as a by-product of the approach. Finally, we establish that the model-checking problem for RB±ATL* is decidable by a reduction to parity games, and show how to synthesise values for resource parameters.

1 Introduction

Resource-bounded logics [2,3,10–12,29] extend alternating-time temporal logic (ATL) [5] by adding transitions that produce and consume resources to the models. As shown in [2], the introduction of implicit counters in the models (i.e. variables interpreted by natural numbers) and the ability to quantify over strategies for a given set of agents can lead to undecidability, or decidability with a very high worst-case upper bound on the complexity of the model checking problem.

The nature of the strategy modalities means that reasoning about resources has similarities to the analysis of runs of vector addition systems with states (a.k.a. VASS) [27], and more specifically to games on VASS, see e.g. [9]. In this paper, we exploit results on VASS in order to analyse the model-checking problem for resource-bounded logics. Model-checking problems on VASS based on temporal logics and games are not always decidable, or at least quite difficult to solve, but sharp results exist. Temporal logics on VASS often lead to undecidable model-checking problems, see e.g. [17,18], and this is more common with branching-time temporal logics such as CTL [18], or when the atomic formulae can state properties about the counter values [22]. However, there are exceptions. For example, CTL model-checking on one-counter VASS is PSPACE-complete [19,32] (see also [34]). Similarly, the control-state repeated reachability problem for VASS is shown to be decidable in [23], and this is generalised to full

© Springer International Publishing Switzerland 2016
K.G. Larsen et al. (Eds.): RP 2016, LNCS 9899, pp. 36–50, 2016.
DOI: 10.1007/978-3-319-45994-3_3

LTL (for which the atomic formulae are exactly control states) in [21], where the model-checking problem for LTL on VASS is shown to be EXPSPACE-complete. Also in [23], a strict fragment of LTL restricted to the "infinitely often" temporal operator GF and atomic formulae stating properties on counter values is shown decidable by a reduction into the reachability problem for VASS.

As far as games for VASS are concerned, the situation is even less encouraging. Two-player games on VASS in which each player can freely update the counter values are undecidable, even with simple winning conditions such as the reachability of a given control state [9]. However, asymmetric VASS games in which at most one player can freely update the counter values and where the winning conditions are simple, are decidable [31]. In addition, the game on asymmetric VASS with reachability of a control state (a slight variant of single-sided VASS in [1] or alternating VASS in [13]) has been shown to be 2EXPTIME-complete [13], and decidable with parity conditions [1,24]. The non-termination problem for symmetric games is 2EXPTIME-complete (the upper bound is from [26] and the lower bound is from [13]).

In this paper, we establish formal relationships between model-checking problems for resource-bounded logics and decision problems for alternating VASS (also known as single-sided VASS). We then use these relationships to show new results for the decidability and complexity of model-checking resource-bounded logics. Ours is not the first work in this direction. There are clear similarities between resource values and counter values, and the semantics of resource-bounded logics are inherently game-based. Previous work has explored the connections with counter machines, either to obtain undecidability, or to obtain lower bounds on complexity, e.g., [2,11].

We give optimal complexity upper bounds and new decidability results, including for resource-bounded logics with enriched path formulae as those in CTL* [16]. First, we show that the model-checking problem for RB±ATL is 2EXPTIME-complete (Theorems 1 and 2), and that RB±ATL restricted to a bounded number of resources is in EXPTIME. The 2EXPTIME lower bound is obtained by a reduction from the state reachability problem for alternating VASS (AVASS) [13], whereas the upper bound is established by a reduction to the state reachability and the termination problems for AVASS (both problems are needed). These results are obtained by using formal relationships between strategies in concurrent game structures and proofs in AVASS, and the key observation is that only asymmetric VASS are needed. The formal relationships also allow us to show that the model-checking problem for RB±ATL* (a new logic naturally extending RB±ATL) is decidable by a reduction to the parity game problem for AVASS [1] (Theorem 4). To the best of our knowledge, the complexity of the parity game problem for AVASS is still open. We also show that resource parameters can be effectively computed in the parameterised version of RB±ATL* (Theorem 5), due to the fact that the Pareto frontier for any parity game on single-sided VASS is computable [1, Theorem 4]. As far as we know, this is the first time that resource values are synthesised in resource-bounded logics (see also [25]). Lastly, we show that the model-checking problems for RBTL [10] and its extension RBTL* are EXPSPACE-complete, and that RBTL restricted to a bounded number of resources is in PSPACE.

2   Alternating VASS Preliminaries

We write $\mathbb{N}$ (resp. $\mathbb{Z}$) for the set of natural numbers (resp. integers) and $[m, m']$ with $m, m' \in \mathbb{Z}$ to denote the set $\{j \in \mathbb{Z} : m \leq j \leq m'\}$. Given a dimension $r \geq 1$ and $a \in \mathbb{Z}$, we write $\boldsymbol{a} \in \mathbb{Z}^r$ to denote the vector of dimension r with all components equal to a. For each $\boldsymbol{x} \in \mathbb{Z}^r$, we write $\boldsymbol{x}(1), \ldots, \boldsymbol{x}(r)$ for the entries of $\boldsymbol{x}$. For each $\boldsymbol{x}, \boldsymbol{y} \in \mathbb{Z}^r$, $\boldsymbol{x} \preceq \boldsymbol{y} \overset{\text{def}}{\Leftrightarrow}$ for every $i \in [1, r]$, we have $\boldsymbol{x}(i) \leq \boldsymbol{y}(i)$. We also write $\boldsymbol{x} \prec \boldsymbol{y}$ when $\boldsymbol{x} \preceq \boldsymbol{y}$ and $\boldsymbol{x} \neq \boldsymbol{y}$.

A binary tree $\mathfrak{T}$, which may contain nodes with one child, is a non-empty subset of $\{1, 2\}^*$ such that, for all $\mathfrak{n} \in \{1, 2\}^*$ and $i \in \{1, 2\}$, $\mathfrak{n} \cdot i \in \mathfrak{T}$ implies $\mathfrak{n} \in \mathfrak{T}$ and, $\mathfrak{n} \cdot 2 \in \mathfrak{T}$ implies $\mathfrak{n} \cdot 1 \in \mathfrak{T}$. The nodes of $\mathfrak{T}$ are its *elements*. The root of $\mathfrak{T}$ is ε, the empty word. All notions such as parent, first child, second child, subtree and leaf, have their standard meanings. The height of $\mathfrak{T}$ is the length, i.e. the number of nodes, of the longest simple path from the root to a leaf.

An *alternating VASS* (AVASS) [13] is a tuple $\mathcal{A} = (Q, r, R_1, R_2)$ such that (1) Q is a finite set of *locations* (a.k.a. *control states*) and $r \geq 0$ is the number of resource values, (2) R_1 is a finite subset of $Q \times \mathbb{Z}^r \times Q$ (*unary rules*) and (3) R_2 is a finite subset of Q^3 (*fork rules*). A *derivation skeleton* of $\mathcal{A}$ is a labelling $\mathcal{D} : \mathfrak{T} \to (R_1 \cup R_2 \cup \{\bot\})$ such that: (1) $\mathfrak{T}$ is a (possibly infinite) binary tree (subset of $\{1, 2\}^*$ with standard conditions), (2) if $\mathfrak{n}$ has one child in $\mathfrak{T}$, then $\mathcal{D}(\mathfrak{n}) \in R_1$, (3) if $\mathfrak{n}$ has two children in $\mathfrak{T}$, then $\mathcal{D}(\mathfrak{n}) \in R_2$ and (4) if $\mathfrak{n}$ is a leaf in $\mathfrak{T}$, then $\mathcal{D}(\mathfrak{n}) = \bot$. A *derivation* of $\mathcal{A}$ based on $\mathcal{D}$ is a labelling $\hat{\mathcal{D}} : \mathfrak{T} \to Q \times \mathbb{Z}^r$ such that: (1) if $\mathfrak{n}$ has one child $\mathfrak{n}'$ in $\mathfrak{T}$, $\mathcal{D}(\mathfrak{n}) = (q, \boldsymbol{u}, q')$ and $\hat{\mathcal{D}}(\mathfrak{n}) = (q, \boldsymbol{v})$, then $\hat{\mathcal{D}}(\mathfrak{n}') = (q', \boldsymbol{v} + \boldsymbol{u})$ and (2) if $\mathfrak{n}$ has two children $\mathfrak{n}'$ and $\mathfrak{n}''$ in $\mathfrak{T}$, $\mathcal{D}(\mathfrak{n}) = (q, q_1, q_2)$ and $\hat{\mathcal{D}}(\mathfrak{n}) = (q, \boldsymbol{v})$, then $\hat{\mathcal{D}}(\mathfrak{n}') = (q_1, \boldsymbol{v})$ and $\hat{\mathcal{D}}(\mathfrak{n}'') = (q_2, \boldsymbol{v})$. So, fork rules do not update the resources and whence, there is an asymmetry between unary rules and fork rules (this makes a difference with branching VASS, see e.g. [15, 33]). This is a useful feature when dealing with the proponent restriction condition in RB±ATL. A derivation $\hat{\mathcal{D}}$ is *admissible* whenever $\hat{\mathcal{D}} : \mathfrak{T} \to Q \times \mathbb{N}^r$, i.e. only natural numbers occur in it. An admissible derivation is also called a *proof*.

The *state reachability problem* for AVASS is as follows: given an AVASS $\mathcal{A}$ and control states q_0 and q_f, is there a finite proof of AVASS whose root is equal to $(q_0, \boldsymbol{0})$ and each leaf belongs to $\{q_f\} \times \mathbb{N}^r$? When $\mathcal{A}$ has no fork rules, $\mathcal{A}$ is essentially a VASS [27] and the above problem is an instance of the coverability problem, which is known to be EXPSPACE-complete [28, 30] (see also [7, 14]). The *non-termination problem* for AVASS is as follows: given an AVASS $\mathcal{A}$ and a control state q_0, is there a proof whose root is equal to $(q_0, \boldsymbol{0})$ and all the maximal branches are infinite?

Proposition 1. [13, 26] *The state reachability and non-termination problems for AVASS are* 2EXPTIME-*complete.*

Decidability of these problems were first established in [31] by using monotonicity of the games. The 2EXPTIME upper bound is preserved if we assume that the root is labelled by $(q_0, \boldsymbol{b})$ with $\boldsymbol{b} \in \mathbb{N}^r$ encoded with a binary representation (see Lemma 1).

In the sequel, we shall also admit fork rules of any arity $\alpha \geq 1$, and therefore, in such slightly extended AVASS the set of fork rules R_2 is a finite subset of $\bigcup_{\beta \geq 2} Q^\beta$.

Lemma 1. *The following extension of the state reachability and non-termination problems for AVASS remains in* 2EXPTIME:

- *Fork rules can be α-ary for any $\alpha \geq 1$ (but there are only a finite amount of them).*
- *Reachability is related to a subset $Q_f \subseteq Q$ (instead of a singleton set).*
- *The initial configuration is $(q_0, \boldsymbol{b})$ with $\boldsymbol{b} \in \mathbb{N}^r$ instead of the fixed tuple $\mathbf{0}$.*
- *The value ω is allowed in $\boldsymbol{b}$ in the initial configuration $(q_0, \boldsymbol{b})$, where for all $n \in \mathbb{Z}$, we have $\omega = n + \omega = \omega + n$.*

The rather standard proof consists in using Proposition 1 by simulating a non-binary fork by a linear-size gadget made of unary and binary fork rules and by adding binary fork rules from states in Q_f to a new single final state (alternatively, one could add unary rules with effect $\mathbf{0}$). The third item in Lemma 1 can be handled by adding a new unary rule with effect $\boldsymbol{b}$ whereas the fourth one amounts to ignore the components with the root value ω.

The notions of derivation skeleton, derivation and proof are also extended to general trees $\mathfrak{T} \subseteq (\mathbb{N} \setminus \{0\})^*$. The set of finite words $\mathfrak{T} \subseteq (\mathbb{N} \setminus \{0\})^*$ is a (not necessarily binary) *tree* iff for all $\mathfrak{n} \in (\mathbb{N} \setminus \{0\})^*$ and $i \in (\mathbb{N} \setminus \{0\})$, $\mathfrak{n} \cdot i \in \mathfrak{T}$ implies $\mathfrak{n} \in \mathfrak{T}$ and, $\mathfrak{n} \cdot i \in \mathfrak{T}$ and $i > 1$ imply $\mathfrak{n} \cdot (i-1) \in \mathfrak{T}$. Such AVASS correspond to a *single-sided VASS* [1,6].

In what follows, by a VASS we mean an alternating VASS without any fork rule and write it as $\mathcal{V} = (Q, r, R)$ where R is a finite set of unary rules. Given a VASS $\mathcal{V}$, its transition system $\mathfrak{TS}(\mathcal{V}) \overset{\text{def}}{=} (\mathfrak{W}, \to, L)$ is such that: (1) $\mathfrak{W} \overset{\text{def}}{=} Q \times \mathbb{N}^r$, (2) L is a truth assigment with elements of Q also understood as propositional variables and $L(q) \overset{\text{def}}{=} \{q\} \times \mathbb{N}^r$ and (3) $\to$ is a binary relation on $\mathfrak{W}$ such that $(q, \boldsymbol{v}) \to (q', \boldsymbol{v}')$ iff there is a unary rule $(q, \boldsymbol{u}, q')$ in R such that $\boldsymbol{v}' = \boldsymbol{v} + \boldsymbol{u}$ where '+' is the component-wise addition on $\mathbb{N}^r$. As usual, we also write $\overset{*}{\to}$ to denote the reflexive and transitive closure of $\to$. Since $\mathfrak{TS}(\mathcal{V})$ is a Kripke-style structure, it can be used to interpret modal or temporal formulae (e.g., LTL or CTL formulae) where atomic formulae refer to control states. Since alternating-time temporal logics such as ATL or ATL* are strict extensions of CTL or CTL* respectively, complexity hardness results for temporal logics can be lifted to such logics. A known result which will be useful in the sequel is that the model-checking problem for LTL on VASS is EXPSPACE-complete (the atomic formulae/propositions are control states) and it is PSPACE-complete for a fixed number of resources [21].

Below, we consider AVASS with a finite set of fork rules included in $\bigcup_{\beta>2} Q^\beta$, and where the proofs are trees with nodes labelled by elements in $Q \times (\mathbb{N} \cup \{\omega\})^r$. Given an AVASS $\mathcal{A} = (Q, r, R_1, R_2)$, a *colouring* col is a map $Q \to [0, p]$ for some $p \geq 0$. The *parity game problem* for AVASS is as follows: given an AVASS $\mathcal{A}$, a control state q_0, $\boldsymbol{b} \in (\mathbb{N} \cup \{\omega\})^r$ and col : $Q \to [0, p]$, is there a proof the root of which is equal to $(q_0, \boldsymbol{b})$, all the maximal branches are infinite and the maximal colour that appears infinitely often along each branch is even (the colour of each node is induced by col)?

Proposition 2. [1, Corollary 2] *The parity game problem for AVASS is decidable.*

To be precise, [1, Corollary 2] states the result for single-sided VASS that can be viewed as AVASS such that the set Q of control states is partitioned into $Q = Q_1 \uplus Q_2$, unary rules start by states in Q_1, fork rules start by states in Q_2 and there is at most one fork rule starting in the same control state (necessarily, belonging to Q_2). The problem for AVASS can be reduced to that for single-sided VASS. It is not difficult to show that the state reachability and non-termination problems for AVASS can be understood as subproblems of the parity game problem and therefore their decidability also follows from [1]. However, the situation is different in the case of complexity. While the exact complexity of the parity game problem is unknown, the state reachability and non-termination problems for AVASS are shown to be 2EXPTIME-hard in [13], the state reachability problem is shown to be in 2EXPTIME in [13] and the non-termination problem is proved to be in 2EXPTIME in [26]. It has been shown recently that the parity game problem is in TOWER [24].

This decidability result has been strenghtened in [1] in the following way. Given $\mathcal{A}$, q_0 and col : $Q \to [0, p]$, the set of tuples $\boldsymbol{b} \in (\mathbb{N} \cup \{\omega\})^r$ for which there is a positive solution to the parity game problem is upward closed and computable. This means that it can be represented effectively by a Boolean combination of atomic constraints of the form either $\mathbf{x}_i \geq k$ where $i \in [1, r]$ and $k \in \mathbb{N}$ or $\mathbf{x}_i = \omega$. Indeed, since the set is upward closed, by Dickson's Lemma, it has a finite set of minimal elements (with respect to the well-quasi-ordering $\preceq$ slightly extended to accomodate the addition of the value ω) that allows one to define easily the symbolic representation in terms of atomic constraints of the form $\mathbf{x} \geq k$. The *Pareto frontier* of $\mathcal{A}$, q_0 and col : $Q \to [0, p]$ is defined as the set of minimal elements in $(\mathbb{N} \cup \{\omega\})^r$ for which there is a positive solution to the parity game problem.

Proposition 3. [1, Theorem 4] *The Pareto frontier for any parity game on single-sided VASS is computable.*

3   The Logic RB±ATL and Variants

We consider the logics RB±ATL and RB±ATL*. The logic RB±ATL was introduced in [3,4], and extends ATL [5] with resources. RB±ATL* extends RB±ATL to allow path formulae to be any LTL-like formula.

Let PROP be a countably infinite set of atomic propositions. The models for the logics RB±ATL and RB±ATL* are the structures introduced in Definition 1 below. These are concurrent game structures from [5], but enriched with a cost function that specifies how resources are produced or consumed. At some abstract level, a structure is equipped with r counters and the transitions can perform increments and decrements.

Definition 1. *A resource-bounded concurrent game structure* $\mathfrak{M}$ *is a tuple of the form* $(Agt, S, Act, r, \mathsf{act}, \mathsf{cost}, \delta, L)$ *such that:*

- *Agt is a non-empty finite set of agents (by default* $Agt = [1, k]$ *for some* $k \geq 1$*).*
- *S is a set of states and $r \geq 1$ is the number of resources.*
- *Act is a non-empty set of actions with a distinguished action* idle.
- $\mathsf{act} : Agt \times S \rightarrow \mathcal{P}(Act)$ *is the* action manager function *such that for all a and s we have* $\mathtt{idle} \in \mathsf{act}(a, s)$.
- $\mathsf{cost} : S \times Agt \times Act \rightarrow \mathbb{Z}^r$ *is the (partial) cost function so that* $\mathsf{cost}(s, a, \mathtt{a})$ *is defined exactly when* $\mathtt{a} \in \mathsf{act}(a, s)$. *Moreover,* $\mathsf{cost}(s, a, \mathtt{idle}) = \mathbf{0}$.
- $\delta : S \times (Agt \rightarrow Act) \rightarrow S$ *is the (partial) transition function such that δ is defined on $(s, \mathfrak{f})$ whenever for all agents $a \in Agt$, we have $\mathfrak{f}(a) \in \mathsf{act}(a, s)$.*
- $L : \mathrm{PROP} \rightarrow \mathcal{P}(S)$ *is a truth assignment (the definition can be adapted when finite subsets of PROP are involved).*

The map δ is also viewed as a deterministic relation with transitions of the form $s \xrightarrow{(\mathtt{a}_1, \ldots, \mathtt{a}_k)} s'$ where $\delta(s, \mathfrak{f}) = s'$ and for all $i \in [1, k] = Agt$, we have $\mathfrak{f}(i) = \mathtt{a}_i$. We say that $\mathfrak{M}$ is finite whenever S and Act are finite sets and L is restricted to a finite subset of PROP. For instance, the idle action is considered in [3,4], where motivations for considering such a distinguished action are given. Given a *coalition* $A \subseteq Agt$ and a state s, a *joint action* by A in s is a map $\mathfrak{f} : A \rightarrow Act$ such that, for all agents $a \in A$, we have $\mathfrak{f}(a) \in \mathsf{act}(a, s)$. The set of joint actions by A in s is denoted $D_A(s)$. Given a state s, the set of joint actions by Agt in s is denoted $D(s)$ (instead of $D_{Agt}(s)$) and the map δ is defined only for such joint actions. We write $\mathfrak{f} \sqsubseteq \mathfrak{g}$ whenever $\mathfrak{g}$ is a conservative extension of $\mathfrak{f}$, i.e. $\mathrm{dom}(\mathfrak{f}) \subseteq \mathrm{dom}(\mathfrak{g})$ and, $\mathfrak{f}$ and $\mathfrak{g}$ agree on $\mathrm{dom}(\mathfrak{f})$.

Given a joint action $\mathfrak{f} \in D_A(s)$, we write $\mathsf{out}(s, \mathfrak{f})$ to denote $\{s' \in S \mid$ there is $\mathfrak{g} \in D(s)$ such that $\mathfrak{f} \sqsubseteq \mathfrak{g}$ and $s' = \delta(s, \mathfrak{g})\}$. For instance, $\mathsf{out}(s, \mathfrak{f})$ is a singleton set when $\mathfrak{f} \in D(s)$ since δ is a map and not a relation. Given a joint action $\mathfrak{f} \in D_A(s)$ and a state s, the *cost* of any transition fired from s following $\mathfrak{f}$ (restricted to A by definition) is as follows: $\mathsf{cost}_A(s, \mathfrak{f}) \overset{\mathrm{def}}{=} \sum_{a \in A} \mathsf{cost}(s, a, \mathfrak{f}(a))$. In a sense, the value $\mathsf{cost}_A(s, \mathfrak{f})$ does not depend on the costs related to the agents in $(Agt \setminus A)$, or equivalently, the cost related to the agents in $(Agt \setminus A)$ is reduced to zero.

A *computation* λ is a finite sequence or an ω-sequence of the form $s_0 \xrightarrow{\mathfrak{f}_0} s_1 \xrightarrow{\mathfrak{f}_1} s_2 \ldots$ such that for all $i < |\lambda| - 1$, we have $s_{i+1} \in \delta(s_i, \mathfrak{f}_i)$. Here, $|\lambda|$ denotes the length of λ, each s_i is a state and each $\mathfrak{f}_i$ belongs to $D(s_i)$. For instance $|s_0 \xrightarrow{\mathfrak{f}_0} s_1 \cdots \xrightarrow{\mathfrak{f}_{n-1}} s_n| = n+1$ and $|s_0 \xrightarrow{\mathfrak{f}_0} s_1 \cdots \xrightarrow{\mathfrak{f}_{n-1}} \cdots| = \omega$ for any infinite computation.

So, in full generality, in a computation, a transition between two successive states is labelled by a joint action: this is not strictly needed for the forthcoming developments but it provides a more general notion that might be used in other contexts (for instance, if the winning condition of forthcoming strategies depends on the actions of all the agents and not only on those for the agents in A or on the visited states). A *strategy* F_A for the coalition A is a map from the set of finite computations to the set of joint actions by A such that $F_A(s_0 \xrightarrow{f_0} s_1 \cdots \xrightarrow{f_{n-1}} s_n) \in D_A(s_n)$. A computation $\lambda = s_0 \xrightarrow{f_0} s_1 \xrightarrow{f_1} s_2 \cdots$ *respects* the strategy F_A iff for all $i < |\lambda|$, we have, $s_{i+1} \in \text{out}(s_i, F_A(s_0 \xrightarrow{f_0} s_1 \ldots \xrightarrow{f_{i-1}} s_i))$. A computation λ that respects F_A is *maximal* whenever it cannot be extended further while respecting the strategy. Note that maximal computations respecting F_A are infinite. The set of all maximal computations that respect the strategy F_A and that start at the state s is denoted by $\text{out}(s, F_A)$. So far, no resource value has been involved in computations. Below, we shall quantify over maximal computations that respect a strategy and therefore for defining a strategy we can restrict ourselves to finite computations that respect it so far.

Given a bound $\boldsymbol{b} \in (\mathbb{N} \cup \{\omega\})^r$, a computation $\lambda = s_0 \xrightarrow{f_0} s_1 \xrightarrow{f_1} s_2 \ldots$ in $\text{out}(s, F_A)$ is $\boldsymbol{b}$-*consistent* iff for all $i < |\lambda|$, we have $\boldsymbol{0} \preceq (\sum_{j=0}^{i-1} \text{cost}_A(s_j, F_A(s_0 \xrightarrow{f_0} s_1 \ldots \xrightarrow{f_{j-1}} s_j)) + \boldsymbol{b})$. Whenever $\boldsymbol{b}(i) = \omega$, this can be viewed as a means to disregard what happens on the ith resource (assuming that $n + \omega = \omega$ for any $n \in \mathbb{Z}$). Indeed, $\boldsymbol{b}(i) = \omega$ amounts to guarantee from the beginning of the computation that there is an infinite supply of resources on the ith component. Note also that the above condition is slightly different from the one in [4] but strictly equivalent. We have decided to adopt that notation in order to show more easily the relationships with VASS decision problems. So, for a computation $\lambda = s_0 \xrightarrow{f_0} s_1 \xrightarrow{f_1} s_2 \ldots$ and a coalition A, there is an underlying sequence $\boldsymbol{v}_0, \boldsymbol{v}_1, \ldots$ of resource values so that $\boldsymbol{v}_0 \overset{\text{def}}{=} \boldsymbol{b}$ and for all $i < |\lambda| - 1$, we have $\boldsymbol{v}_{i+1} \overset{\text{def}}{=} \boldsymbol{v}_i + \text{cost}_A(s_i, F_A(s_0 \xrightarrow{f_0} s_1 \ldots \xrightarrow{f_{i-1}} s_i))$. The values of the sequence only depend on the agents in A, which is often called the *proponent restriction condition*.

The set of all the $\boldsymbol{b}$-consistent (infinite) computations is denoted by $\text{out}(s, F_A, \boldsymbol{b})$. A $\boldsymbol{b}$-*strategy* F_A *with respect to* s is a strategy such that $\text{out}(s, F_A) = \text{out}(s, F_A, \boldsymbol{b})$. This definition also slightly differs from the one in [4] that is not relative to a given state and therefore in [4] the equality should hold for all the states.

So far, we have provided the main definitions about resource-bounded concurrent game structures and strategies. Let us present now the logic RB±ATL. Given a set of agents $Agt = \{a_1, \ldots, a_k\}$ and $r \geq 1$, we write RB±ATL (Agt, r) to denote the resource-bounded logic with k agents and r resources whose models are resource-bounded concurrent game structures with the same parameters. Formulae of RB±ATL (Agt, r) are defined according to the grammar:

$$\phi ::= p \mid \neg\phi \mid \phi \wedge \phi \mid \langle\!\langle A^{\boldsymbol{b}} \rangle\!\rangle \bigcirc \phi \mid \langle\!\langle A^{\boldsymbol{b}} \rangle\!\rangle \square \phi \mid \langle\!\langle A^{\boldsymbol{b}} \rangle\!\rangle \phi \mathcal{U} \phi,$$

where $p \in PROP$, $A \subseteq Agt$ and $\boldsymbol{b} \in (\mathbb{N} \cup \{\omega\})^r$. The size of a formula is computed from a DAG representation and the integers are encoded in binary. Note that forthcoming hardness results do not use the conciseness of the DAG representation (with respect to the tree representation).

The satisfaction relation $\models$ is defined inductively as follows assuming that $\mathfrak{M}$ is an RB$\pm$ATL (Agt, r) model (we omit the obvious cases for the Boolean connectives): $\mathfrak{M}, s \models p \overset{\text{def}}{\Leftrightarrow} s \in L(p)$ and,

$\mathfrak{M}, s \models \langle\langle A^{\boldsymbol{b}} \rangle\rangle \bigcirc \phi \overset{\text{def}}{\Leftrightarrow}$ there is a $\boldsymbol{b}$-strategy F_A w.r.t. s such that for all $s_0 \overset{\text{fo}}{\longrightarrow}$ $s_1 \ldots \in \text{out}(s, F_A)$, we have $\mathfrak{M}, s_1 \models \phi$

$\mathfrak{M}, s \models \langle\langle A^{\boldsymbol{b}} \rangle\rangle \Box \phi \overset{\text{def}}{\Leftrightarrow}$ there is a $\boldsymbol{b}$-strategy F_A w.r.t. s such that for all $\lambda = s_0 \overset{\text{fo}}{\longrightarrow}$ $s_1 \ldots \in \text{out}(s, F_A)$, for all $i < |\lambda|$, we have $\mathfrak{M}, s_i \models \phi$

$\mathfrak{M}, s \models \langle\langle A^{\boldsymbol{b}} \rangle\rangle \phi_1 \mathcal{U} \phi_2 \overset{\text{def}}{\Leftrightarrow}$ there is a $\boldsymbol{b}$-strategy F_A w.r.t. s such that for all $\lambda = s_0 \overset{\text{fo}}{\longrightarrow} s_1 \ldots \in \text{out}(s, F_A)$, there is some $i < |\lambda|$ such that $\mathfrak{M}, s_i \models \phi_2$ and for all $j \in [0, i-1]$, we have $\mathfrak{M}, s_j \models \phi_1$.

Since all the maximal computations are infinite, the index i involved for clauses above related to $\langle\langle A^{\boldsymbol{b}} \rangle\rangle \Box$ or $\langle\langle A^{\boldsymbol{b}} \rangle\rangle \mathcal{U}$ can take any value in $\mathbb{N}$. The presence of the idle action allows the extension of a strategy as soon as a given condition is satisfied along the computations. For instance, $\mathfrak{M}, s \models \langle\langle A^{\boldsymbol{b}} \rangle\rangle \bigcirc \phi$ is equivalent to the existence of $\mathfrak{f} \in D_A(s)$ such that for all $\mathfrak{g} \sqsupseteq \mathfrak{f}$, we have $\mathfrak{M}, s' \models \phi$ with $\delta(s, \mathfrak{g}) = s'$ and $\boldsymbol{0} \preceq \boldsymbol{b} + \text{cost}_A(s, \mathfrak{f})$. A strategy modality $\langle\langle A^{\boldsymbol{b}} \rangle\rangle$ reduces the impact of the function cost in two ways. If the ith component of $\boldsymbol{b}$ is equal to ω, then there are no constraints on the ith resource along the computation. The restriction of cost to opponent agents in $(Agt \setminus A)$ is also reduced to $\boldsymbol{0}$ (so without any impact on consistency).

Obviously, RB$\pm$ATL (Agt, r) is a quantitative variant of ATL [5] in which resource values are computed along the computations.

The *model-checking problem for* RB$\pm$ATL is as follows: given $k, r \geq 1$ (in unary), a formula ϕ in RB$\pm$ATL $([1, k], r)$, a finite RB$\pm$ATL $([1, k], r)$ model $\mathfrak{M}$ and a state s, is $\mathfrak{M}, s \models \phi$? The encoding of k and r in unary is unessential since the size of $\mathfrak{M}$ with an explicit representation of all the transitions is over $k + r$.

Proposition 4. *[3, Theorem 1] The model-checking problem for RB$\pm$ATL is decidable.*

We also consider RB$\pm$ATL*, an extension of RB$\pm$ATL in which the path formulae can be any LTL-like formula, in particular a temporal operator may no longer be preceded by a cooperation modality. This is a new logic although its definition follows a classical schema for branching-time temporal logics. Given a set of agents $Agt = [1, k]$ and $r \geq 1$, we write RB$\pm$ATL* (Agt, r) to denote the resource-bounded logic with k agents and r resources whose models are resource-bounded concurrent game structures with the same parameters. The *parameterised version* of RB$\pm$ATL* denoted by ParRB$\pm$ATL* admits formulae as RB$\pm$ATL* except that the values $\boldsymbol{b} \in (\mathbb{N} \cup \{\omega\})^r$ are replaced by tuples of variables within $\mathtt{VAR} = \{\mathtt{x_1}, \mathtt{x_2}, \ldots\}$. Here is a typical formula in ParRB$\pm$ATL*:

$$\langle\langle \{1\}^{(\mathtt{x_1}, \mathtt{x_2})} \rangle\rangle \top \mathcal{U} q_f \wedge \langle\langle \{2\}^{(\mathtt{x_2}, \mathtt{x_3})} \rangle\rangle \top \mathcal{U} q'_f.$$

Given a parameterised (state or path) formula ϕ with variables $\mathtt{x_1}, \ldots, \mathtt{x_n}$ and a map $\mathfrak{v} : \{\mathtt{x_1}, \ldots, \mathtt{x_n}\} \to (\mathbb{N} \cup \{\omega\})$, we write $\mathfrak{v}(\phi)$ to denote the formula in RB$\pm$ATL* obtained from ϕ by replacing each occurrence of a variable $\mathtt{x}$ by $\mathfrak{v}(\mathtt{x})$. The *parameterised model-checking problem for* ParRB$\pm$ATL* is as follows: given $k, r \geq 1$ (in unary), a state formula ϕ in ParRB$\pm$ATL* $([1, k], r)$, a finite RB$\pm$ATL* $([1, k], r)$ model $\mathfrak{M}$ and a state s, compute the set of maps $\mathfrak{v}$ such that $\mathfrak{M}, s \models_s \mathfrak{v}(\phi)$. Here, computing means to be able to characterise the set of maps $\mathfrak{v}$ with $\mathfrak{M}, s \models_s \mathfrak{v}(\phi)$, by using a symbolic representation with nice computational properties. We can show that we only need Boolean combinations of atomic formulae of the form either $\mathtt{x} \geq k$ where $k \in \mathbb{N}$ or $\mathtt{x} = \omega$.

4   The Complexity of RB$\pm$ATL

The results in this section are obtained by elaborating on correspondences between AVASS decision problems, and the existence of strategies in RB$\pm$ATL. We show a 2EXPTIME-hardness result by a reduction from the state reachability problem for AVASS. This improves the EXPSPACE-hardness result in [4]. It is also worth noting that in the proof of Theorem 1, the presence of the idle action requires a bit of work.

Theorem 1. *The model-checking problem for RB$\pm$ATL is* 2EXPTIME-*hard.*

The upper bound is proved by designing a labelling algorithm as done in [4] but the main difference with [4] rests on the fact that we explicitly call subroutines that solve decision problems on AVASS. Let $\mathfrak{M}$ be a finite resource-bounded concurrent game structure, $A \subseteq Agt$ be a coalition, F_A be a strategy and s be a state. We construct an AVASS $\mathcal{A}_{\mathfrak{M}, A, s}$ such that the set of computations respecting F_A and starting from s corresponds to a derivation skeleton whose root is labelled by a unary rule with first state s. Moreover, if F_A is $\boldsymbol{b}$-strategy w.r.t. s, then the derivation skeleton can be turned into a proof whose root is labelled by $(s, \boldsymbol{b})$.

Given $\mathfrak{M} = (Agt, S, Act, r, \mathsf{act}, \mathsf{cost}, \delta, L)$, the AVASS $\mathcal{A}_{\mathfrak{M}, A, s} \stackrel{\text{def}}{=} (Q, r, R_1, R_2)$ is built as follows:

$$Q \stackrel{\text{def}}{=} \{s\} \cup \{(s', \mathfrak{f}) \mid s' \in S, \mathfrak{f} \in D_A(s')\} \cup \{(\mathfrak{g}, s') \mid s', s'' \in S, \mathfrak{g} \in D(s''), \delta(s'', \mathfrak{g}) = s'\}.$$

- The set R_1 contains the following rules: (1) for all $\mathfrak{f} \in D_A(s)$, $(s, \mathsf{cost}_A(s, \mathfrak{f}), (s, \mathfrak{f}))$ and (2) for all $(\mathfrak{g}, s') \in Q$, for all $\mathfrak{f} \in D_A(s')$, $((\mathfrak{g}, s'), \mathsf{cost}_A(s', \mathfrak{f}), (s', \mathfrak{f}))$.

– The set R_2 contains the following rules. For all $(s', f) \in Q$, let
$\{(g_1, s_1), \ldots, (g_\alpha, s_\alpha)\} = \{(g, s'') \in Q \mid s'' \in \delta(s', g), g \in D(s'), f \sqsubseteq g\}$.
The set is non-empty thanks to constraints on the idle action. We add the
fork rule $((s', f), (g_1, s_1), \ldots, (g_\alpha, s_\alpha))$. In order to define unambiguously that
rule, we assume an arbitrary ordering on Q.

It is worth noting that s has a special status in Q simply because any proof
whose root configuration contains s has no predecessor configuration. Any deriva-
tion skeleton from $\mathcal{A}_{\mathfrak{M}, A, s}$ has to alternate the rules in R_1 and the rules in R_2, by
construction. For every (s', f) in Q, there is a unique fork rule starting by (s', f)
and the construction applies also in the degenerate cases, i.e. when $A = Agt$ or
when $A = \emptyset$ (assuming that $\mathsf{cost}(s', f) = \mathbf{0}$ for the unique $f \in D_\emptyset(s')$). The main
property of $\mathcal{A}_{\mathfrak{M}, A, s}$ is stated below.

Lemma 2. *There is a b-strategy w.r.t. s in $\mathfrak{M}$ iff there is a proof in $\mathcal{A}_{\mathfrak{M}, A, s}$
whose root is labelled by (s, b) and every maximal branch is infinite.*

Theorem 2. *The model-checking problem for $RB\pm ATL$ is in 2EXPTIME.*

An AVASS of the form $\mathcal{A}_{\mathfrak{M}, A, s}^{S'}$ is defined as the restriction of $\mathcal{A}_{\mathfrak{M}, A, s}$ in which
the opponent coalition has no way to go out of S'. The algorithm is given below
with the essential property: $GMC(\mathfrak{M}, \psi) = \{s \mid \mathfrak{M}, s \models \psi\}$.

Corollary 1. *For any fixed $r \geq 1$, the model-checking problem for $RB\pm ATL$
restricted to at most r resources is in EXPTIME. For $r \geq 4$, the problem is
EXPTIME-hard.*

We invoke [26, Theorem 3.4] and [13, Theorem 3.1] since for a bound r, the
state reachability and the non-termination problems can be solved in EXPTIME.
EXPTIME-hardness ($r \geq 4$) is due to [13, Proposition 4.2] and to the proof of
Theorem 1.

5   More Path Formulae While Preserving Decidability

In this section, we study the model-checking problem for resource-bounded logics
where the path formulae can be any LTL-like formula. In doing so, we also
illustrate the versatility of our formalisation, by showing how it can be used
to establish complexity results for the model-checking problem for the logics
RBTL* and RB$\pm$ATL*.

5.1   The Logic RBTL* and its Complexity

The models of the logic RBTL* are structures of the form (Q, r, R, L) where
(Q, r, R) is a VASS and L is a truth assignment built on elements of Q understood
as propositional variables, so that $L(q) = \{q\}$ (see e.g [10, Sect. 3]). In order to
fit the usual terminology, below, an infinite proof in (Q, r, R) is called a *path* or
run and it can be represented by $\lambda = (q_0, \mathbf{v}_0) \to (q_1, \mathbf{v}_1) \ldots$. We write $\lambda[i, +\infty)$
to denote the run starting from $(q_i, \mathbf{v}_i)$ taken from λ as a suffix and $\lambda(i)$ to
denote the configuration $(q_i, \mathbf{v}_i)$.

Algorithm 1. An algorithm for RB±ATL model checking.

1: **procedure** GMC($\mathfrak{M}, \phi$)
2:   **case** ϕ **of**
3:     p: **return** $\{s \in S \mid p \in L(s)\}$
4:     $\neg\psi$: **return** $S \setminus GMC(\mathfrak{M}, \psi)$
5:     $\psi_1 \wedge \psi_2$: **return** $GMC(\mathfrak{M}, \psi_1) \cap GMC(\mathfrak{M}, \psi_2)$
6:     $\langle\langle A^b \rangle\rangle \bigcirc \psi$: **return** $\{s \mid \exists\, \mathfrak{f} \in D_A(s), 0 \preceq b + \mathrm{cost}_A(s, \mathfrak{f}),$ for all $\mathfrak{f} \sqsubseteq \mathfrak{g} \in$
          $D(s),\ \delta(s, \mathfrak{g}) \in GMC(\mathfrak{M}, \psi)\}$
7:     $\langle\langle A^b \rangle\rangle \square \psi$: $S_1 := GMC(\mathfrak{M}, \psi)$
8:         **if** $s \in S_1$ **then return** $\{s \mid \mathcal{A}^{S_1}_{\mathfrak{M}, A, s}, (s, b)$ is non-terminating$\}$ **end if**
9:         **if** $s \notin S_1$ **then return** $\emptyset$ **end if**
10:    $\langle\langle A^b \rangle\rangle \psi_1 \mathcal{U} \psi_2$: **return** $\{s \mid \mathcal{A}^{S_1 \cup S_2}_{\mathfrak{M}, A, s}, (s, b), S_2'$ is a positive instance of state reachability$\}$
          with $S_1 = GMC(\mathfrak{M}, \psi_1),\ S_2 = GMC(\mathfrak{M}, \psi_2),\ S_2' = \{(\mathfrak{g}, s') \in Q \mid s' \in$
          $S_2\} \cup \{s' \in Q \mid s' = s,\ s \in S_2\}$
11:   **end case**
12: **end procedure**

The *state formulae* ϕ and the *path formulae* Φ of RBTL* are defined by mutual recursion with the grammar (relatively to Q and r)

$$\phi ::= q \mid \neg\phi \mid (\phi \wedge \phi) \mid \langle b \rangle\, \Phi$$
$$\Phi ::= \phi \mid \neg\Phi \mid (\Phi \wedge \Phi) \mid \bigcirc \Phi \mid (\Phi \mathcal{U} \Phi) \mid \square\Phi$$

where $q \in Q$ and $b \in (\mathbb{N} \cup \{\omega\})^r$. Syntactically, every state formula is also a path formula according to this grammar, and this reflects the fact that a path uniquely identifies a control state in which a formula is interpreted: its starting control state. We present the semantics for RBTL* by distinguishing the state formulae from the path formulae. The two satisfaction relations $\models_s$ and $\models_p$ are defined as follows (clauses for the Boolean connectives are omitted).

$\mathfrak{M}, q \models_s q'$ iff $q' = q$
$\mathfrak{M}, q \models_s \langle b \rangle\Phi$ iff there is an infinite run λ starting at (q, b) such that $\mathfrak{M}, \lambda \models_p \Phi$
$\mathfrak{M}, \lambda \models_p \phi$ iff $\mathfrak{M}, q_0 \models_s \phi$ for state formulae ϕ with $\lambda(0) = (q_0, v_0)$
$\mathfrak{M}, \lambda \models_p \bigcirc\Phi$ iff $\mathfrak{M}, \lambda[1, +\infty) \models_p \Phi$
$\mathfrak{M}, \lambda \models_p \Phi \mathcal{U} \Psi$ iff there is $i \geq 0$ such that $\mathfrak{M}, \lambda[i, +\infty) \models_p \Psi$ and
          for every $j \in [0, i-1]$, we have $\mathfrak{M}, \lambda[j, +\infty) \models_p \Phi$
$\mathfrak{M}, \lambda \models_p \square\Phi$ iff for all $i \geq 0$, $\mathfrak{M}, \lambda[i, +\infty) \models_p \Phi$.

The model-checking problem for RBTL* is as follows: given a model $\mathfrak{M}, q$ and a state formula ϕ, is it $\mathfrak{M}, q \models_s \phi$? The logic RBTL is the fragment of RBTL* in which any subformula whose outermost connective is in $\{\mathcal{U}, \bigcirc, \square\}$, is preceded by some $\langle b \rangle$. The problem for RBTL is already EXPSPACE-hard since the state reachability problem for VASS can be reduced easily to it. The EXPSPACE lower bound for the model-checking problem for RBTL can be matched with the upper bound for RBTL*.

Theorem 3. *The model-checking problems for RBTL and RBTL* are* EXPSPACE-*complete.*

We can obtain a improved complexity result if the number of resources is considered fixed.

Corollary 2. *For any fixed $r \geq 1$, the model-checking problem for RBTL* restricted to at most r resources is in* PSPACE.

The PSPACE upper bound is then a consequence of [21, Theorem 4.1]. Again, if r is fixed but greater than two, then the model-checking problem for RBTL* restricted to at most r resources is PSPACE-hard since the state reachability problem for VASS of dimension two is PSPACE-complete [8]. When $r = 1$, the model-checking problem for RBTL* restricted to at most one resource is NP-hard since the state reachability for VASS of dimension one is NP-complete [20].

5.2 Decidability of RB±ATL*

In order to illustrate the reduction from the model-checking problem for RB±ATL* into the parity game problem, we briefly present a notion of synchronisation. Let $\mathfrak{M} = (Agt, S, Act, r, \mathsf{act}, \mathsf{cost}, \delta, L)$ be a resource-bounded concurrent game structure. Given $p_1, \ldots, p_n$, we write Σ_n to denote $\mathcal{P}(\{p_1, \ldots, p_n\})$ and $L_n(s') \stackrel{\text{def}}{=} \{p_i \mid i \in [1, n], \ s' \in L(p_i)\}$ for all $s' \in S$. So, $L_n(s') \in \Sigma_n$.

Let $\mathcal{A}_{\mathfrak{M},A,s} = (Q, r, R_1, R_2)$ be the AVASS defined from $\mathfrak{M}$, A and s, and let $\mathbb{A} = (Q', q'_0, \delta' : Q' \times \Sigma_n \to Q', \mathsf{col} : Q' \to [0, p])$ be a deterministic parity automaton over Σ_n. The principle of the *synchronised product* $\mathcal{A}_{\mathfrak{M},A,s} \otimes \mathbb{A}$ defined below is the following. Any (infinite) branch of a proof of $\mathcal{A}_{\mathfrak{M},A,s}$ contains control states of the form s, $(s', \mathfrak{f})$ or $(\mathfrak{g}, s')$ where s is a distinguished state of $\mathfrak{M}$, s' is any state, $\mathfrak{f} \in D_A(s')$ and $\mathfrak{g}$ is a joint action in $D(s'')$ with $\delta(s'', \mathfrak{g}) = s'$. By construction, $(s', \mathfrak{f})$ is preceded by a state of the form either $(\mathfrak{g}, s')$ or s' (if $s' - s$). So an infinite branch of the form $(s_0, u_0) \ ((s_0, \mathfrak{f}_0), u_1) \ ((\mathfrak{g}_1, s_1), u_1) \ ((s_1, \mathfrak{f}_1), u_2) \ ((\mathfrak{g}_2, s_2), u_2) \cdots$ leads to the ω-word $L_n(s_0) \ L_n(s_1) \ L_n(s_2) \cdots$ that admits a unique run in $\mathbb{A}$ (thanks to determinism). Above, we slightly abuse notation since we identify a branch with its label. Given an infinite branch $s_0 \xrightarrow{u_0} (s_0, \mathfrak{f}_0) \to (\mathfrak{g}^1_{k_1}, s^1_{k_1}) \xrightarrow{u_1} (s^1_{k_1}, \mathfrak{f}_1) \to (\mathfrak{g}^2_{k_2}, s^2_{k_2}) \xrightarrow{u_2} (s^2_{k_2}, \mathfrak{f}_2) \to (\mathfrak{g}^3_{k_3}, s^3_{k_3}) \cdots$ in a proof of $\mathcal{A}_{\mathfrak{M},A,s}$, its L_n-*projection* is simply defined as the ω-word $L_n(s_0) \ L_n(s^1_{k_1}) \ L_n(s^2_{k_2}) \ L_n(s^3_{k_3}) \cdots$ in Σ_n^ω.

The control states of $\mathcal{A}_{\mathfrak{M},A,s} \otimes \mathbb{A}$ are pairs in $Q \times Q'$ and the second components are therefore control states in Q' as they appear for the unique run on $L_n(s_0) \ L_n(s_1) \ L_n(s_2) \cdots$.

Let us define the AVASS $\mathcal{A}_{\mathfrak{M},A,s} \otimes \mathbb{A} \stackrel{\text{def}}{=} (Q'', r, R'_1, R'_2)$ such that $Q'' \stackrel{\text{def}}{=} Q \times Q'$ and:

- For each $s \xrightarrow{u} (s, \mathfrak{f}) \in R_1$, R'_1 contains the unary rule $(s, q'_0) \xrightarrow{u} ((s, \mathfrak{f}), q'_0)$.
- For each $(\mathfrak{g}, s') \xrightarrow{u} (s', \mathfrak{f}) \in R_1$, and for each $q \in Q'$, R'_1 contains the rule $((\mathfrak{g}, s'), q) \xrightarrow{u} ((s', \mathfrak{f}), q)$. So, firing a unary rule from $\mathcal{A}_{\mathfrak{M},A,s}$ does not change the second component.

– For each $((s', \mathfrak{f}), (\mathfrak{g}_1, s_1), \ldots, (\mathfrak{g}_\alpha, s_\alpha)) \in R_2$ and for each $q \in Q'$, we add in R_2' $(((s', \mathfrak{f}), q), ((\mathfrak{g}_1, s_1), \delta(q, L_n(s'))), \ldots, ((\mathfrak{g}_\alpha, s_\alpha), \delta(q, L_n(s'))))$. Firing a fork rule from $\mathcal{A}_{\mathfrak{M}, A, s}$ changes the second component in a unique way depending on q and $L_n(s')$.

Again, there is a unique fork rule starting by the control state $((s', \mathfrak{f}), q)$.

Let us define the colouring $\mathrm{col}' : Q'' \to [0, p]$ such that for all $(q, q') \in Q''$, we have $\mathrm{col}'((q, q')) \stackrel{\mathrm{def}}{=} \mathrm{col}(q')$. The synchronised product satisfies the essential property for the automata-based approach (as for temporal logics). This is the most natural way to inherit colours from $\mathbb{A}$ to $\mathcal{A}_{\mathfrak{M}, A, s} \otimes \mathbb{A}$.

Lemma 3. *Let $(s, \boldsymbol{b}) \in Q \times (\mathbb{N} \cup \{\omega\})^r$. The statements below are equivalent:*

(I) *$\mathcal{A}_{\mathfrak{M}, A, s}$ has a proof the root of which is equal to $(s, \boldsymbol{b})$, all the maximal branches are infinite and the L_n-projection of each infinite branch belongs to the language accepted by $\mathbb{A}$ (i.e. to $\mathrm{L}(\mathbb{A})$).*

(II) *$\mathcal{A}_{\mathfrak{M}, A, s} \otimes \mathbb{A}$ has a proof the root of which is equal to $((s, q_0'), \boldsymbol{b})$, all the maximal branches are infinite and the maximal colour that appears infinitely often is even.*

Theorem 4. *The model-checking problem for RB±ATL* is decidable.*

Lemma 3 is essential to establish Theorem 4 since its proof uses the product between an alternating VASS and a deterministic parity automaton recognizing ω-words. This is reminiscent of the proof of [5, Theorem 5.6] about the 2EXPTIME upper bound for the ATL* model-checking problem. Rabin tree automata of the proof of [5, Theorem 5.6] are replaced by deterministic parity automata for encoding the LTL formulae and by alternating VASS (with counters) as outcome of the synchronisation.

Theorem 5. *The parameterised model-checking problem for ParRB±ATL* is decidable.*

The proof of Theorem 5 is based on a global model-checking algorithm that is essentially based on Lemma 3 and on [1, Theorem 4]. Synthesising resource values has been also considered in [25].

6   Concluding Remarks

We have related model-checking problems for resource-bounded logics and decision problems for AVASS. Though such relationships should not come as a complete surprise, we obtained new complexity and decidability results. We prove that the model-checking problem for RB±ATL introduced in [3,4] is 2EXPTIME-complete. No complexity upper bound was known so far. We have introduced the logic RB±ATL* that extends RB±ATL, and we have shown that the model-checking problem is decidable. The same hold for the parameterised version ParRB±ATL*, i.e. it is decidable to compute the set of resource bounds for which the given parameterised formula is satisfied. We have also shown that the model-checking problem for RBTL* introduced in [10] is EXPSPACE-complete. No complexity upper bound for RBTL was known so far as well as the decidability status for RBTL*. We believe that the simple framework we have proposed could be used to obtain further results for new resource-bounded logics.

Acknowledgements. We would like to thank the anonymous reviewers for their numerous suggestions that helped us improve the quality of the paper.

References

1. Abdulla, P.A., Mayr, R., Sangnier, A., Sproston, J.: Solving parity games on integer vectors. In: D'Argenio, P.R., Melgratti, H. (eds.) CONCUR 2013 – Concurrency Theory. LNCS, vol. 8052, pp. 106–120. Springer, Heidelberg (2013)
2. Alechina, N., Bulling, N., Logan, B., Nguyen, H.: On the boundary of (un)decidability: decidable model-checking for a fragment of resource agent logic. In: IJCAI 2015, pp. 1494–1501. AAAI Press (2015)
3. Alechina, N., Logan, B., Nguyen, H., Raimondi, F.: Decidable model-checking for a resource logic with production of resources. In: ECAI 2014, pp. 9–14 (2014)
4. Alechina, N., Logan, B., Nguyen, H., Raimondi, F.: Technical report: model-checking for resource-bounded ATL with production and consumption of resources. CoRR abs/1504.06766 (2015)
5. Alur, R., Henzinger, T., Kupferman, O.: Alternating-time temporal logic. JACM 49(5), 672–713 (2002)
6. Bérard, B., Haddad, S., Sassolas, M., Sznajder, N.: Concurrent games on VASS with inhibition. In: Koutny, M., Ulidowski, I. (eds.) CONCUR 2012. LNCS, vol. 7454, pp. 39–52. Springer, Heidelberg (2012)
7. Blockelet, M., Schmitz, S.: Model checking coverability graphs of vector addition systems. In: Murlak, F., Sankowski, P. (eds.) MFCS 2011. LNCS, vol. 6907, pp. 108–119. Springer, Heidelberg (2011)
8. Blondin, M., Finkel, A., Göller, S., Haase, C., McKenzie, P.: Reachability in two-dimensional vector addition systems with states is PSPACE-complete. In: LICS 2015, pp. 32–43. ACM Press (2015)
9. Brázdil, T., Jančar, P., Kučera, A.: Reachability games on extended vector addition systems with states. In: Abramsky, S., Gavoille, C., Kirchner, C., Meyer auf der Heide, F., Spirakis, P.G. (eds.) ICALP 2010. LNCS, vol. 6199, pp. 478–489. Springer, Heidelberg (2010)
10. Bulling, N., Farwer, B.: Expressing properties of resource-bounded systems: the logics RTL* and RTL. In: Dix, J., Fisher, M., Novák, P. (eds.) CLIMA X. LNCS, vol. 6214, pp. 22–45. Springer, Heidelberg (2010)
11. Bulling, N., Farwer, B.: On the (un-)decidability of model-checking resource-bounded agents. In: ECAI 2010, pp. 567–572 (2010)
12. Bulling, N., Nguyen, H.: Model checking resource bounded systems with shared resources via alternating Büchi pushdown systems. In: Chen, O., Torroni, P., Villata, S., Hsu, J., Omicini, A. (eds.) PRIMA 2015. LNCS, vol. 9387, pp. 640–649. Springer, Heidelberg (2015)
13. Courtois, J.-B., Schmitz, S.: Alternating vector addition systems with states. In: Csuhaj-Varjú, E., Dietzfelbinger, M., Ésik, Z. (eds.) MFCS 2014, Part I. LNCS, vol. 8634, pp. 220–231. Springer, Heidelberg (2014)

14. Demri, S.: On selective unboundedness of VASS. JCSS **79**(5), 689–713 (2013)
15. Demri, S., Jurdziński, M., Lachish, O., Lazić, R.: The covering and boundedness problems for branching vector addition systems. JCSS **79**(1), 23–38 (2013)
16. Emerson, A.: Temporal and modal logic. In: Handbook of Theoretical Computer Science, pp. 996–1072. Elsevier (1990)
17. Esparza, J.: On the decidability of model checking for several μ-calculi and Petri nets. In: Tison, J. (ed.) ICALP 1994. LNCS, vol. 787, pp. 115–129. Springer, Heidelberg (1994)
18. Esparza, J.: Decidability and complexity of Petri net problems - an introduction. In: Reisig, W., Rozenberg, G. (eds.) Advances in Petri Nets 1998. LNCS, vol. 1491, pp. 374–428. Springer, Heidelberg (1998)
19. Göller, S., Lohrey, M.: Branching-time model checking of one-counter processes and timed automata. SIAM J. Comput. **42**(3), 884–923 (2013)
20. Haase, C.: On the complexity of model checking counter automata. Ph.D. thesis, University of Oxford (2012)
21. Habermehl, P.: On the complexity of the linear-time mu-calculus for Petri nets. In: Azéma, P., Balbo, G. (eds.) Application and Theory of Petri Nets 1997. LNCS, vol. 1248, pp. 102–116. Springer, Heidelberg (1997)
22. Howell, R., Rosier, L.: Problems concerning fairness and temporal logic for conflict-free Petri nets. TCS **64**, 305–329 (1989)
23. Jančar, P.: Decidability of a temporal logic problem for Petri nets. TCS **74**(1), 71–93 (1990)
24. Jančar, P.: On reachability-related games on vector addition systems with states. In: Bojańczyk, M., Lasota, S., Potapov, I. (eds.) RP 2015. LNCS, vol. 9328, pp. 50–62. Springer, Heidelberg (2015)
25. Juhl, L., Larsen, K., Raskin, J.-F.: Optimal bounds for multiweighted and parametrised energy games. In: Liu, Z., Woodcock, J., Zhu, H. (eds.) Theories of Programming and Formal Methods. LNCS, vol. 8051, pp. 244–255. Springer, Heidelberg (2013)
26. Jurdziński, M., Lazić, R., Schmitz, S.: Fixed-dimensional energy games are in pseudo-polynomial time. In: Halldórsson, M.M., Iwama, K., Kobayashi, N., Speckmann, B. (eds.) ICALP 2015. LNCS, vol. 9135, pp. 260–272. Springer, Heidelberg (2015)
27. Karp, R., Miller, R.: Parallel program schemata. JCSS **3**(2), 147–195 (1969)
28. Lipton, R.: The reachability problem requires exponential space. Technical Report 62, Department of Computer Science, Yale University (1976)
29. Monica, D.D., Napoli, M., Parente, M.: On a logic for coalitional games with priced-resource agents. ENTCS **278**, 215–228 (2011)
30. Rackoff, C.: The covering and boundedness problems for vector addition systems. TCS **6**(2), 223–231 (1978)
31. Raskin, J.-F., Samuelides, M., Begin, L.V.: Games for counting abstractions. ENTCS **128**(6), 69–85 (2005)
32. Serre, O.: Parity games played on transition graphs of one-counter processes. In: Aceto, L., Ingólfsdóttir, A. (eds.) FOSSACS 2006. LNCS, vol. 3921, pp. 337–351. Springer, Heidelberg (2006)
33. Verma, K., Goubault-Larrecq, J.: Karp-miller trees for a branching extension of VASS. Discrete Math. Theor. Comput. Sci. **7**, 217–230 (2005)
34. Vester, S.: On the complexity of model-checking branching and alternating-time temporallogics in one-counter systems. In: Finkbeiner, B., Pu, G., Zhang, L. (eds.) ATVA 2015. LNCS, vol. 9364, pp. 361–377. Springer, Heidelberg (2015)

Plain, Bounded, Reversible, Persistent, and k-marked Petri Nets Have Marked Graph Reachability Graphs

Eike Best and Harro Wimmel[(⊠)]

Department of Computing Science, Carl von Ossietzky Universität Oldenburg,
26111 Oldenburg, Germany
{eike.best,harro.wimmel}@informatik.uni-oldenburg.de

Abstract. In workflow specifications, it is desirable that k customers can use a system interference-freely, so that no customer is disturbed by other activities on the same workflow. In a Petri net representation of a workflow, this corresponds to allowing initial k-markings, in which the number of tokens on each place is a multiple of k, and to require that every global activity is separable, that is, can be viewed as k individual activities, each acting as if the initial marking had one k'th of its values. In this paper, it is shown that, if $k \geq 2$, if such a Petri net is plain, and if its reachability graph is finite, reversible, and persistent, then the latter is isomorphic to the reachability graph of a marked graph.

The problem has been mentioned as open in a paper by Best and Darondeau from 2011, and its resolution rests on a more recent (2014) characterisation of the reachability graphs of marked graph Petri nets. This characterisation involves the notion of backward persistence, i.e., persistence in the reverse reachability graph, as well as some other properties which are true in the given context. The technical contribution of this paper is to prove that backward persistence is implied by the properties of plainness, boundedness, reversibility and persistence, provided the greatest common divisor of the token counts in the initial state is greater than 1. The existence of a suitable marked graph then follows.

1 Introduction

Persistence of a Petri net means that once a transition is enabled, it cannot be disabled, except possibly by its own occurrence [8]. This property describes a very general notion of conflict-freeness, in the sense that all conflicts are, at most, due to different ways of scheduling concurrent activities. Separability of a Petri net N with an initial marking $k \cdot M_0$ means that the system $(N, k \cdot M_0)$ behaves in the same way as k disjoint parallel instances of the system (N, M_0), that is, the same net N with an initial marking M_0 [6]. In [2], it has been proved that

---

E. Best and H. Wimmel—Supported by DFG (German Research Foundation) through grant Be 1267/15-1 ARS (Algorithms for Reengineering and Synthesis).

K.G. Larsen et al. (Eds.): RP 2016, LNCS 9899, pp. 51–62, 2016.
DOI: 10.1007/978-3-319-45994-3_4

plain, bounded, reversible, and persistent Petri nets enjoy this property.[1] More precisely, in a plain, bounded, reversible, and persistent net N with marking $k \cdot M_0$, every execution sequence belongs to the shuffle product [10] of k firing sequences running in k parallel instances of N with marking M_0.

Separability is of practical significance in the context of workflow systems, and it is closely related to a property known as workflow serialisability [6]. Usually, serialisability allows several customers to be able to execute the same workflow without interfering with each other. In [6], separability has been motivated as follows:

> If we associate to each firing the consumption of some resource, like money or energy, then separability implies that the consumption of a batch of cases equals the sum of the individual consumptions.

There are other practical benefits of separability. For instance, separability implies that a large group of similar nets with small markings can be simulated and represented by a single small net with a large marking.

In the present paper, we focus on the case that $k \geq 2$, i.e., the case that two or more "customers" execute a given Petri net. We shall prove that plain, bounded, reversible and persistent Petri nets with an initial marking of the form $k \cdot M_0$, with $k \geq 2$ (or, equivalently, such that the gcd of the initial token distribution is greater than one) actually have a reachability graph which is isomorphic to the reachability graph of a marked graph [4]. This contrasts, perhaps surprisingly, with the case that $k = 1$, for which examples without marked graph equivalent can be found.

The remaining sections of the paper are organised as follows. Section 2 presents the technical background (labelled transition systems and Petri nets). In Sect. 3, we introduce the key behavioural notions necessary to understand the rest of the paper, along with examples and citations of known results. Section 4 contains the proof of a special case of our main theorem. This special case already embodies the main difficulty of the proof. In Sect. 5, we proceed to proving the main result announced in the title of this paper. Section 6 concludes and presents some ideas for further research.

2   Formal Definitions

This section contains basic definitions relating to labelled transition systems (lts) and to Petri nets. Some properties of lts (such as determinism and backward determinism) are defined explicitly, since they will be referred to in proofs, even though they are automatically satisfied for Petri nets.

A finite labelled transition system with initial state is a tuple $TS = (S, \rightarrow, T, s_0)$ with nodes S, edge labels T, edges $\rightarrow \subseteq (S \times T \times S)$, and an initial state

---

[1] Plainness means that there are no arc weights > 1. Boundedness means that the state space is finite. Reversibility means that the initial marking can be reached from every reachable marking.

$s_0 \in S$. A label t is enabled at $s \in S$, written as $s[t\rangle$, if $\exists s' \in S: (s, t, s') \in \to$, and backward enabled at s, written as $[t\rangle s$, if $\exists s' \in S: (s', t, s) \in \to$. We also write $s[t\rangle s'$ if $(s, t, s') \in \to$. This can be extended, as usual, to $s[\sigma\rangle s'$ (or $s \xrightarrow{\sigma} s'$) for sequences $\sigma \in T^*$. The set of states reachable from s is denoted by $[s\rangle$. A function Φ is called a T-vector if $\Phi: T \to \mathbb{N}$, and a unit T-vector if $\Phi: T \to \{0, 1\}$. The support of a T-vector Φ is $supp(\Phi) = \{t \in T \mid \Phi(t) > 0\}$. Two T-vectors Φ_1, Φ_2 are label-disjoint if $\forall t \in T: \Phi_1(t) = 0 \vee \Phi_2(t) = 0$. For a finite sequence $\sigma \in T^*$, the Parikh vector $\Psi(\sigma)$ of σ is a T-vector defined by $\Psi(\sigma)(t) =$ the number of occurrences of t in σ. An lts $TS = (S, \to, T, s_0)$ is called finite if S and T (and hence also $\to$) are finite sets; totally reachable if $[s_0\rangle = S$ (i.e., every state is reachable from s_0); (forward) deterministic if for any states $s, s', s'' \in [s_0\rangle$ and label $t \in T$, $(s[t\rangle s' \wedge s[t\rangle s'') \Rightarrow s' = s''$; (i.e., the state reached from s after firing t is unique); backward deterministic if for any states $s, s', s'' \in [s_0\rangle$ and label $t \in T$, $(s'[t\rangle s \wedge s''[t\rangle s) \Rightarrow s' = s''$; live if $\forall t \in T \; \forall s \in [s_0\rangle \; \exists s^t \in [s\rangle: s'[t\rangle$ (i.e., transitions remain eventually firable); reversible if $\forall s \in [s_0\rangle: s_0 \in [s\rangle$ (i.e., s_0 always remains reachable); (forward) persistent [8] if for all reachable states s, s', s'', and labels t, t', if $s[t\rangle s'$ and $s[t'\rangle s''$ with $t \neq t'$, then there is some (reachable) state $r \in S$ such that both $s'[t'\rangle r$ and $s''[t\rangle r$ (i.e., once two different labels are both enabled, neither can disable the other, and executing both, in any order, leads to the same state); and backward persistent if for all reachable states s, s', s'', and labels t, t', if $s'[t\rangle s$ and $s''[t'\rangle s$ and $t \neq t'$, then there is some reachable state $r \in S$ such that both $r[t'\rangle s'$ and $r[t\rangle s''$ (i.e., persistence in backward direction). Two lts $TS_1 = (S_1, \to_1, T, s_{01})$ and $TS_2 = (S_2, \to_2, T, s_{02})$ are isomorphic, denoted by $TS_1 \cong TS_2$, if there is a bijection $\zeta: S_1 \to S_2$ with $\zeta(s_{01}) = s_{02}$ and $(s, t, s') \in \to_1 \Leftrightarrow (\zeta(s), t, \zeta(s')) \in \to_2$, for all $s, s' \in S_1$.

A Petri net is denoted by $N = (P, T, F)$ where P is a finite set of places, T is a finite set of transitions, and F is the flow function $F: ((P \times T) \cup (T \times P)) \to \mathbb{N}$ specifying the arc weights. A marking is a P-vector $M: P \to \mathbb{N}$, indicating the number of tokens in each place. An initially marked net (or a net system, or system, for short) is a net together with an initial marking M_0. A system is denoted by $\Sigma = (P, T, F, M_0)$ or, equivalently, by $\Sigma = (N, M_0)$ with $N = (P, T, F)$. If $\Sigma = (P, T, F, M_0)$ and $\Sigma' = (P', T', F', M_0')$ with $(P \cup T) \cap (P' \cup T') = \emptyset$, then the disjoint sum $\Sigma \oplus \Sigma'$ is defined as $(P \cup P', T \cup T', F \cup F', M_0 \cup M_0')$. If $k \in \mathbb{N}$ and M is a marking, then the k-multiple marking $k \cdot M$ is defined by $(k \cdot M)(p) = k \cdot (M(p))$ for every place p. We denote by $\gcd(M_0)$ the number $\gcd\{M_0(p) \mid p \in P\}$. A marking M is called a k-marking if k divides $\gcd(M)$ (note that every marking is a 1-marking). For an element $x \in (P \cup T)$, we write $^\bullet x = \{t \in T \mid F(t, x) > 0\}$ and $x^\bullet = \{t \in T \mid F(x, t) > 0\}$. For a sequence $\tau \in T^*$, we write $^\bullet\tau = \{p \in P \mid \exists t \in T: \Psi(\tau)(t) > 0 \wedge p \in {}^\bullet t\}$ and $\tau^\bullet = \{p \in P \mid \exists t \in T: \Psi(\tau)(t) > 0 \wedge p \in t^\bullet\}$. A net N is called plain if no arc weight exceeds 1; connected if it is weakly connected as a graph; pure or side-place free if $\forall p \in P: (p^\bullet \cap {}^\bullet p) = \emptyset$; and a marked graph [4] if it is plain and $\forall p \in P: |{}^\bullet p| = 1 = |p^\bullet|$. A transition $t \in T$ is enabled at a marking M, denoted by $M[t\rangle$, if $\forall p \in P: M(p) \geq F(p, t)$. The firing of t leads from M to M', denoted by $M[t\rangle M'$, if $M[t\rangle$ and $M'(p) = M(p) - F(p, t) + F(t, p)$. The set of markings reachable from

M by repeated firings is denoted by $[M\rangle$. The reachability graph $RG(\Sigma)$ of an initially marked net $\Sigma = (P, T, F, M_0)$ is the labelled transition system with the set of vertices $[M_0\rangle$, initial state M_0, label set T, and set of edges $\{(M, t, M') \mid M, M' \in [M_0\rangle \wedge M[t\rangle M'\}$. Σ is bounded if and only if its reachability graph is finite. All other notions defined for labelled transition systems apply *verbatim* to Petri nets through their reachability graphs. An initially marked net is always totally reachable (by the definition of its reachability graph) and both forward and backward deterministic (by the fact that if $M[t\rangle M'$, then there is a unique linear-algebraic relationship between M, t, and M'). A system Σ is called *pbrp* if it is plain, bounded, reversible, and persistent.

3   Persistence, Small Cycles, Separability, Marked Graphs

Any marked graph system $\Sigma = (P, T, F, M_0)$ is persistent, because if $a \neq b$ for $a, b \in T$, then there is no common pre-place p of a and b, i.e., for all $p \in P$, either $F(p, a) = 0$ or $F(p, b) = 0$, or both. The converse is not true; for instance, $TS_2 = RG(\Sigma_2)$ in Fig. 2 is persistent but not a marked graph.[2] Persistent transition systems enjoy a property of small cycles, as follows.

Definition 1. DISJOINT SMALL CYCLE PROPERTY
Let $TS = (S, \rightarrow, T, s_0)$ be a transition system. A nontrivial (i.e.: non-empty) cycle $s[\sigma\rangle s$ around a state $s \in [s_0\rangle$ is small if there is no nontrivial cycle $s'[\sigma'\rangle s'$ with $s' \in [s_0\rangle$ and $\Psi(\sigma') \lneqq \Psi(\sigma)$, where $\lneqq = (\leq \cap \neq)$.[3]

TS will be said to have the disjoint small cycle property if there exist a number n and a set of mutually label-disjoint T-vectors $\Upsilon_1, \ldots, \Upsilon_n \colon T \to \mathbb{N}$ such that

$$\{\Upsilon_1, \ldots, \Upsilon_n\} = \{\Psi(\beta) \mid \text{there is a reachable state } s \text{ and a small cycle } s[\beta\rangle s\}$$

If this property is satisfied, we shall abbreviate it to $\mathbf{P}\{\mathbf{\Upsilon_1}, \ldots, \mathbf{\Upsilon_n}\}$ (for **P**arikh vectors of small cycles). The special case that $n = 1$ and $\Upsilon_1 = 1$ (i.e., Υ_1 is the unit vector with no zero entries) will be abbreviated by **P1**.   □1

For example, both TS_1 and TS_2, shown respectively in Figs. 1 and 2, satisfy **P1**, the first with Parikh vector $\Upsilon_1 = (1\,1)$ and the second with Parikh vector $\Upsilon_1 = (1\,1\,1\,1)$.

Theorem 1. SMALL CYCLE AND PBRP NET DECOMPOSITION [1]
Let $\Sigma = (P, T, F, M_0)$ be a pbrp net system with reachability graph $RG = (S, \rightarrow, T, M_0)$.

---

[2] There does not even exist *any* marked graph system generating TS_2 shown in Fig. 2, by Theorem 3 below and the fact that TS_2 is not backward persistent.

[3] Small cycles do not have proper subcycles, but this condition is not sufficient: no proper subset of a small cycle may form a cycle anywhere in TS, not even in a permuted way.

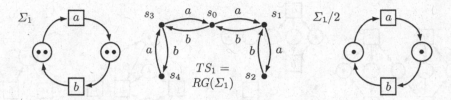

Fig. 1. A 2-marked pbrp Petri net Σ_1 (l.h.s.) and its reachability graph (middle). The system $\Sigma_1/2$ (defined structurally as Σ_1, but with half the initial marking) is shown on the right-hand side.

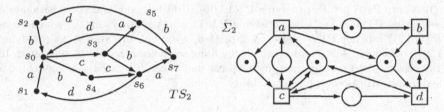

Fig. 2. A transition system TS_2 with initial state s_0 (l.h.s.). TS_2 is not backward persistent at s_0. A non-2-marked pbrp Petri net Σ_2 generating TS_2 (r.h.s.).

(1) *There is a number $n \leq |T|$ and Parikh vectors $\Upsilon_1, \ldots, \Upsilon_n$ such that*
    $\mathbf{P}\{\Upsilon_1, \ldots, \Upsilon_n\}$ *holds in RG.*

(2) *There are n pbrp nets $\Sigma_1, \ldots, \Sigma_n$, where for every $1 \leq i \leq n$, Σ_i has transition set $T_i = supp(\Upsilon_i)$ and satisfies $\mathbf{P1}\{\Upsilon_i'\}$, where Υ_i' is Υ_i restricted to T_i, and moreover, $RG(\Sigma) \cong RG(\Sigma_1 \oplus \ldots \oplus \Sigma_n)$.* □ 1

In (2), every Σ_i can be defined by a fresh copy of the same places and the same marking as Σ, except that transitions t satisfying $\Upsilon_i(t) = 0$ and their surrounding arcs are omitted. For example, in Fig. 3, the pbrp system Σ_3 generates two label-disjoint cycles with unit Parikh vectors in its reachability graph. A decomposition into two transition- (and place-) disjoint systems Σ_{31} and Σ_{32}, as guaranteed by Theorem 1(2), is also shown in the figure. The system Σ_4 shown in Fig. 3 generates a single cycle with a non-unit Parikh vector. By a result in [4], this implies that no marked graph can have an isomorphic reachability graph. The system Σ_5 has arc weights > 1 and thus falls outside the class of Petri nets we consider here (but satisfies some of the properties defined above).

All k-marked pbrp systems enjoy a further property of separability, defined as follows.

Definition 2. SEPARABILITY
Let $k \geq 1$ and let $\Sigma = (N, k \cdot M)$ be any net with a k-marking $k \cdot M$. A firing sequence $(k \cdot M)[\sigma\rangle$ is called k-separable from $k \cdot M$ if there exist k sequences $\sigma_1, \ldots, \sigma_k$ such that

$$(\forall j, 1 \leq j \leq k\colon M[\sigma_j\rangle \text{ in } (N, M)) \quad \text{and} \quad \sigma \in \bigsqcup_{j=1}^{k} \sigma_j$$

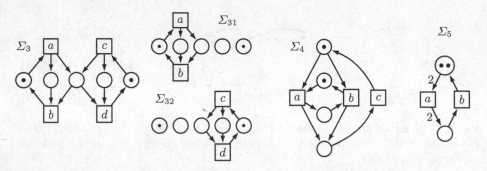

Fig. 3. A pbrp Petri net Σ_3 satisfying $\mathbf{P}\{(1\,1\,0\,0),(0\,0\,1\,1)\}$, and its decomposition into Σ_{31} satisfying $\mathbf{P1}$ and Σ_{32}, also satisfying $\mathbf{P1}$ (l.h.s.). A pbrp system Σ_4 which satisfies $\mathbf{P}\{(1\,1\,2)\}$ but not $\mathbf{P1}$ (middle). A 2-marked, non-plain brp system Σ_5 satisfying $\mathbf{P}\{(1\,2)\}$ (right-hand side), and in which the firing sequence a cannot be separated. In Σ_3, the central place is redundant, in the sense that it can be erased, leaving behind a marked graph with isomorphic reachability graph.

where ⊔⊔ denotes the shuffle product ("arbitrary interleaving") operator. A k-net is separable if every sequence firable in its initial marking is separable from this k-marking.   □2

As an example, consider $k = 2$ and the system Σ_1 shown on the left-hand side of Fig. 1. Σ_1 has a firing sequence $\sigma = abbbaaaabbbba$ which can be separated by σ_1 and σ_2 as follows:

$$
\begin{aligned}
\sigma \; &: (2 \cdot M_0)\ [abbbaaaabbbba\rangle && \text{in } \Sigma_1 \\
\sigma_1 &: M_0\ [baabba\rangle\ M_1 && \text{in } \Sigma_1/2 \\
\sigma_2 &: M_0\ [abbaab\rangle\ M_1\ [b\rangle\ M_2 && \text{in } \Sigma_1/2
\end{aligned}
\tag{1}
$$

It can be seen that σ is indeed a shuffle of the two sequences σ_1 and σ_2 shown in (1), and that indeed, both σ_1 and σ_2 are firable from M_0 in the system $\Sigma_1/2$ shown on the right-hand side of Fig. 1.

Theorem 2. SEPARABILITY, AND UNIT T-VECTOR DECOMPOSABILITY [2]
Let $\Sigma = (N, k \cdot M_0)$ be a pbrp system. Then every firing sequence $k \cdot M_0[\sigma\rangle$ can be separated. Assume, in addition, that $k \geq 2$. Then Σ satisfies $\mathbf{P}\{\Upsilon_1, \ldots, \Upsilon_n\}$ with mutually label-disjoint unit T-vectors $\Upsilon_1, \ldots, \Upsilon_n$.   □2

Intuitively, separability means that a system $\Sigma = (P, T, F, k \cdot M_0)$ with a k-marking $k \cdot M_0$ can be viewed as equivalent (in terms of firing sequences) with k disjoint copies of the system (P, T, F, M_0). The main ingredient of the proof of the first part of Theorem 2 is the fact that the letters in a firing sequence σ of $\Sigma = (P, T, F, k \cdot M_0)$ can be moved leftward according to their frequencies, as exemplified in (1). The 2-marked system Σ_5 displayed in Fig. 3 shows the importance of plainness for separability.

It is known from classic theory [4,9] that every live and bounded (plain) marked graph is a pbrp system. However, there exist pbrp nets which are not marked graphs; see, for instance Σ_2 (Fig. 2) and Σ_4 (Fig. 3). If $k \geq 2$ in the initial marking $k \cdot M_0$, the second part of Theorem 2 ensures that every small cycle is generated by a *unit* Parikh vector. The property that all small cycles are unit cycles is another well-known characteristic of live and bounded marked graphs. This raises the following question: Does there exist a k-marked pbrp system, with $k \geq 2$, which does not have a marked graph reachability graph? In answering it, we will make use of the following, more recent, result.

Theorem 3. MARKED GRAPH SYNTHESIS [3]
Assume that a finite transition system TS is totally reachable, deterministic, persistent, backward persistent, reversible, and satisfies **P1**. *Then there is a connected, live and bounded marked graph Σ' with $RG(\Sigma') \cong TS$.*   □ 3

4 Proving Backward Persistence

This is the core section of our paper. In it, we show the backward persistence of k-marked pbrp systems with $k \geq 2$ under the assumption that **P1** holds. We can then easily see the existence of a marked graph with an isomorphic reachability graph. In Sect. 5, we shall complete the theory by deriving a marked graph representation of arbitrary k-marked prbp systems (without **P1**).

Our proof is built upon a series of small facts about persistent systems. We shall mention the most significant ones before starting the main proof. Keller's theorem [7], in the following form, often serves as a useful tool for proving such small facts. For sequences $\sigma, \tau \in T^*$, let $\tau \overset{\bullet}{-} \sigma$ denote the sequence left after erasing successively in τ the leftmost occurrences of all symbols from σ, read from left to right. Keller's theorem states that in a deterministic and persistent transition system, if $s[\tau\rangle$ and $s[\sigma\rangle$ for some $s \in [s_0\rangle$, then $\Psi(\tau(\sigma \overset{\bullet}{-} \tau)) = \Psi(\sigma(\tau \overset{\bullet}{-} \sigma))$ and $s[\tau(\sigma \overset{\bullet}{-} \tau)\rangle\widehat{s}$ and $s[\sigma(\tau \overset{\bullet}{-} \sigma)\rangle\widehat{s}$ for some state $\widehat{s} \in [s_0\rangle$.

Throughout this section, sequences in T^* will be denoted by small Greek letters, and q, s, s_1 etc. denote reachable states.

Proposition 1. PUSHING CYCLES, AND BACKWARD CYCLIC EXTENSIONS
Let $TS = (S, \rightarrow, T, s_0)$ be a deterministic, persistent transition system.

(1) *If $s \in [s_0\rangle$ and $s[\kappa\rangle s[\gamma\rangle s'$, then there is some sequence $\kappa' \in T^*$ with $\Psi(\kappa') = \Psi(\kappa)$ and $s'[\kappa'\rangle s'$.*
(2) *Suppose that TS is also reversible. If $s, s' \in [s_0\rangle$ and $s[\kappa\rangle s$, then there is some sequence $\kappa' \in T^*$ with $\Psi(\kappa') = \Psi(\kappa)$ and $s'[\kappa'\rangle s'$.*
(3) *Suppose that TS is also reversible and satisfies* **P1**. *If $q \in [s_0\rangle$ and $q[\tau\rangle q'$ with $\Psi(\tau) \leq 1$, then there is some sequence $\tau' \in T^*$ with $q'[\tau'\tau\rangle q'$ and $\Psi(\tau'\tau) = 1$.*

Proof.

(1): Keller's theorem, applied to $s[\kappa\gamma\rangle s'$ and $s[\gamma\rangle s'$, yields

$$s[\kappa\gamma\rangle s'[\gamma \overset{\bullet}{-} (\kappa\gamma))\rangle\widehat{s} \quad \text{and} \quad s[\gamma\rangle s'[(\kappa\gamma) \overset{\bullet}{-} \gamma\rangle\widehat{s}$$

The first conjunct yields $s' = \hat{s}$, and the second conjunct yields $s'[\kappa'\rangle s'$ with $\kappa' = (\kappa\gamma)\overset{\bullet}{-}\gamma$.

(2): Consequence of (1) and reversibility.

(3): Using (2), let κ be such that $q[\kappa\rangle q$ is a small cycle with Parikh vector 1. By Keller's theorem, $q[\tau\rangle q'[\kappa\overset{\bullet}{-}\tau\rangle q''$. By $\Psi(\tau) \leq 1 = \Psi(\kappa)$ (the equality being due to **P1**), $\Psi(\kappa) = \Psi(\tau(\kappa\overset{\bullet}{-}\tau))$. By determinism and the cyclicity of κ, $q'' = q$. With $\tau' = (\kappa\overset{\bullet}{-}\tau)$, we get $q[\tau\rangle q'[\tau'\rangle q[\tau\rangle q'$. By $\Psi(\tau) \leq \Psi(\kappa)$, $\Psi(\tau'\tau)=\Psi(\kappa)=1$.   □1

The following theorem is our central result. Its proof makes reference to Table 1, which depicts the pattern arising from the separation of a sequence σ according to the first part of Theorem 2.

Table 1. A tableau explaining the separation of a firing sequence σ firable from $k \cdot M_0$ in a pbrp system $(N, k \cdot M_0)$. This generalises equation (1) above. The lines denote sequences which can be fired from M_0 with $\Psi(\sigma) = \sum_{i=1}^{k} \Psi(\sigma_i)$. Starting with $k \cdot M_0$, any line can arbitrarily be interleaved with other lines, but the ordering within a line cannot, in general, be changed.

$$k \begin{cases} \sigma_1: & M_0 \longrightarrow M_1 \\ & + \qquad + \\ \sigma_2: & M_0 \longrightarrow M_1 \longrightarrow M_2 \\ & + \qquad + \qquad + \\ \vdots \quad \vdots \quad \vdots \quad \vdots \quad \cdots \quad \longrightarrow M_{k-1} \\ & + \qquad + \qquad + \qquad\qquad + \\ \sigma_k: & M_0 \longrightarrow M_1 \longrightarrow M_2 \cdots \longrightarrow M_{k-1} \longrightarrow M_k \end{cases}$$

letters occur: k times $k-1$ times   2 times   1 times

Theorem 4. k-MARKED PRPB NETS SATISFYING **P1** ARE BACKWARD PERSISTENT

Suppose that $\Sigma = (N, k \cdot M_0)$ is a pbrp system satisfying **P1**, *and that $k \geq 2$. Then Σ is backward persistent.*

Proof. Let $N = (P, T, F)$. Assume that there are two transitions $a, b \in T$ and states $s, s_1, s_2 \in [k \cdot M_0\rangle$ such that $s_1[a\rangle s$ and $s_2[b\rangle s$ in Σ. We want to show that there is a state $s' \in [k \cdot M_0\rangle$ such that $s'[a\rangle s_2$ and $s'[b\rangle s_1$.

By Proposition 1(3) (letting $q = s_1$, $\tau = a$, and $q' = s$), we find a cycle $s[\alpha\rangle s_1[a\rangle s$ with $\Psi(\alpha a) = 1$. A similar cyclic extension can be done at state s_2 for b yielding $s[\beta b\rangle s$. By total reachability, s can be reached from the initial state by some firing sequence γ resulting in $k \cdot M_0[\gamma\rangle s[\alpha a\rangle s$ and $k \cdot M_0[\gamma\rangle s[\beta b\rangle s$.

By separability (Definition 2), we find α_i and β_i ($1 \leq i \leq k$) such that $\gamma\alpha a \in \bigsqcup_{i=1}^{k}\alpha_i$ and $\gamma\beta b \in \bigsqcup_{i=1}^{k}\beta_i$. If we name markings according to Table 1 we get $M_0[\alpha_i\rangle M_i$ and $M_0[\beta_i\rangle M_i$ for $1 \leq i \leq k$, and each α_i/β_i forms one line in the table. To see that we reach the same marking M_i in both cases, note that $\Psi(\gamma\alpha a) = \Psi(\gamma\beta b)$ and thus the number of occurrences of each transition is the same in both sequences, i.e. $\Psi(\alpha_i) = \Psi(\beta_i)$ for $1 \leq i \leq k$.

Since $\gamma\alpha a$ is some interleaving of the α_i's and ends with an a, so must one of the α_i, i.e. we find j_1 with $1 \leq j_1 \leq k$ and α' such that $\alpha_{j_1} = \alpha'a$. Analogously, there are j_2 and β' with $\beta_{j_2} = \beta'b$. We distinguish two cases:

Case 1: $j_1 \neq j_2$ (which implies $k \geq 2$).

So, the lines in Table 1 where a and b occur as the last transition are different ones. Essentially, we can find an interleaving of these two lines where a and b occur as the last two transitions. Let $\gamma' \in T^*$ be the sequence obtained by concatenation of all α_i except α_{j_1} and α_{j_2}. Then we can fire $k \cdot M_0[\gamma'\alpha_{j_1}\beta_{j_2}\rangle s$ as each α_i can be fired from M_0 and $\Psi(\alpha_{j_2}) = \Psi(\beta_{j_2})$. Thus, we can also fire $k \cdot M_0[\gamma'\alpha'\beta'\rangle s'[ab\rangle s$ and $k \cdot M_0[\gamma'\alpha'\beta'\rangle s'[ba\rangle s$. By backward determinism at s, we conclude $s'[b\rangle s_1[a\rangle s$ and $s'[a\rangle s_2[b\rangle s$.

Case 2: $j_1 = j_2$.

When separating $k \cdot M_0[\gamma\alpha a\rangle s$ and $k \cdot M_0[\gamma\beta b\rangle s$ we can fire either $M_0[\alpha_{j_1}\rangle M_{j_1}$ with last letter a or $M_0[\beta_{j_1}\rangle M_{j_1}$ with last letter b in the j_1th line of Table 1, but we do not know where the letter a or b will show up in the other sequence. Especially, we cannot directly guarantee that a and b will be the last two letters. To see that this is possible, we need to visit the state $k \cdot M_{j_1}$. We can reach $k \cdot M_{j_1}$ from $k \cdot M_0$ by firing α_{j_1} k times simultaneously, or alternatively by firing the Parikh-equivalent interleavings $k \cdot M_0[(\alpha_{j_1})^{k-2}\alpha'\beta'ab\rangle k \cdot M_{j_1}$ and $k \cdot M_0[(\alpha_{j_1})^{k-2}\alpha'\beta'ba\rangle k \cdot M_{j_1}$ (since $k \geq 2$). By Proposition 1(3) (with $q' = k \cdot M_{j_1}$ and $\tau = ab$ or $\tau = ba$), we find small cycles $k \cdot M_{j_1}[\tau'ab\rangle k \cdot M_{j_1}$ and $k \cdot M_{j_1}[\tau'ba\rangle k \cdot M_{j_1}$. Since $\Psi(\tau'ab) = 1 = \Psi(\tau'ba)$, separability implies $M_{j_1}[\tau'ab\rangle M_{j_1}$ and $M_{j_1}[\tau'ba\rangle M_{j_1}$. (By Theorem 2, for $k \cdot M_{j_1}[\tau'ab\rangle$ separation is possible and will result – with a new instantiation of Table 1 – in some sequences $\sigma_1, \ldots, \sigma_k$. Since $\sigma_1, \ldots, \sigma_{k-1}$ may only contain letters which occur more than once in $\tau'ab$, $\sigma_1 = \ldots = \sigma_{k-1} = \varepsilon$, and consequently, $\sigma_k = \tau'ab$ and $M_{j_1}[\tau'ab\rangle$. Since $\tau'ab$ does not change the token distribution in the net, even $M_{j_1}[\tau'ab\rangle M_{j_1}$ holds. The same argument can be used for $\tau'ba$.) Now we need to remember that s was the goal marking in $k \cdot M_0[\gamma\alpha a\rangle s$, which the separation previously decomposed such that $s = \sum_{i=1}^{k} M_i$ (the sum of the rightmost markings of each line in Table 1). As M_{j_1} occurs in this sum, $M_{j_1} \leq s$, and by monotonicity of the firing rule, $s[\tau'\rangle s'[ab\rangle s$ as well as $s[\tau'\rangle s'[ba\rangle s$ with some intermediate state s'. By backward determinism at s, we obtain once again $s'[b\rangle s_1[a\rangle s$ and $s'[a\rangle s_2[b\rangle s$.   □ 4

In order to illustrate this proof, let us assume that there is a pbrp system $\Sigma = (N, k \cdot M_0)$ satisfying **P1** with TS_2 from Fig. 2 as its reachability graph and $k \geq 2$. Since $s_1[a\rangle s_0$ and $s_2[b\rangle s_0$, we can find the cyclic extensions $\alpha a = cbda$ and $\beta b = cadb$ firable at $s = s_0$. Separating these sequences leads to $\alpha_i = \varepsilon = \beta_i$ for $i < k$, $\alpha_k = cbda$, and $\beta_k = cabd$ (since every transition occurs exactly once), so we enter Case 2 with $j_1 = j_2 = k$. Since $k \geq 2$, we should find $k \cdot M_0[(cbda)^{k-2}(cbd)(cad)ab\rangle k \cdot M_k$ and $k \cdot M_0[(cbda)^{k-2}(cbd)(cad)ba\rangle k \cdot M_k$.

By Proposition 1(3), we should find small cycles $k \cdot M_k[\tau'ab\rangle k \cdot M_k[\tau'ba\rangle k \cdot M_k$. Unfortunately, since $s_0 \xrightarrow{\alpha_k} s_0$ and $k \cdot M_0[(\alpha_k)^k\rangle k \cdot M_k$, the marking $k \cdot M_k$ is represented by s_0 in TS_2. Due to the missing backward persistence for a and b at s_0, there are no paths $\tau'ab$ or $\tau'ba$ ending in $k \cdot M_k$, no matter how we choose τ'. The assumed net system Σ cannot exist.

Corollary 1. *Suppose that* $\Sigma = (N, k \cdot M_0)$, *with* $N = (P, T, F)$ *and* $k \geq 2$, *is a pbrp system satisfying* **P1**. *Then there exists a connected, live and bounded marked graph* Σ' *with* $RG(\Sigma) \cong RG(\Sigma')$.

Proof. Σ is totally reachable and deterministic by virtue of being a Petri net reachability graph. Σ is persistent and reversible because it is a pbrp system, and it satisfies **P1** by assumption. Moreover, Σ is backward persistent by Theorem 4. Hence Theorem 3 applies, and we can find a suitable marked graph by this theorem.   □1

5   Main Result

Theorem 5. EXISTENCE OF SIMULATING MARKED GRAPHS
Suppose that $\Sigma = (N, k \cdot M_0)$ *is a pbrp system, with* $N = (P, T, F)$ *and* $k \geq 2$. *Then there is a live and bounded marked graph* Σ' *such that* $RG(\Sigma)$ *and* $RG(\Sigma')$ *are isomorphic.*

Proof. We reduce the problem by decomposing Σ. Let $\Sigma_1, \ldots, \Sigma_n$ be the systems defined just after Theorem 1(2). Then, according to Theorem 1(2), $RG(\Sigma) \cong RG(\Sigma_1 \oplus \ldots \oplus \Sigma_n)$. Let T_i be the set of transitions of Σ_i. The sets T_i are mutually disjoint, since the small cycles they stem from are also mutually disjoint. Σ_i is k-marked by definition, and by $RG(\Sigma) \cong RG(\Sigma_1 \oplus \ldots \oplus \Sigma_n)$, its firing sequences are precisely the firing sequences of Σ restricted to T_i^*.

By $k \geq 2$, and by the second part of Theorem 2, Σ_i satisfies **P1**, for every $1 \leq i \leq n$. We can apply Corollary 1, proving that there exists a connected, live and bounded marked graph Σ_i' with $RG(\Sigma_i') \cong RG(\Sigma_i)$. Define $\Sigma' = \Sigma_1' \oplus \ldots \oplus \Sigma_n'$. Now we get

$$RG(\Sigma) \cong RG(\Sigma_1 \oplus \ldots \oplus \Sigma_n) \text{ (by Theorem 1(2))}$$
$$\cong RG(\Sigma_1' \oplus \ldots \oplus \Sigma_n') \text{ (by the definition of the } \Sigma_i, \text{ and by Corollary 1)}$$
$$\cong RG(\Sigma') \qquad\qquad \text{ (by the definition of } \Sigma')$$

Hence $RG(\Sigma) \cong RG(\Sigma')$ by the transitivity of isomorphism. Moreover, Σ' is a live and bounded (not necessarily connected) marked graph since a disjoint sum of live and bounded marked graphs is again a live and bounded marked graph.   □5

For an example, see Fig. 4. The reachability graph of the system shown on the left-hand side is backward persistent. Theorem 5 applies, allowing us to find a live and bounded marked graph with an isomorphic reachability graph. Such a marked graph is shown on the right-hand side of Fig. 4. In fact, according to the results of [3], it is the only place-minimal such graph (up to isomorphism of Petri nets).

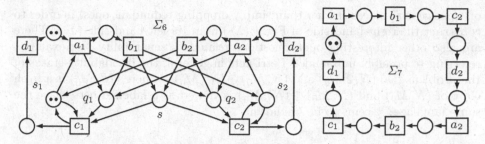

Fig. 4. A pbrp and backward persistent 2-net Σ_6 which is not a marked graph (l.h.s.) and a marked graph Σ_7 with $RG(\Sigma_6) \cong RG(\Sigma_7)$, obtained according to Theorem 5 (r.h.s.). Note that none of the places of Σ_6 is redundant, and that dropping the non-marked-graph places s_1, q_1, s, s_2, q_2 from Σ_6 does not create a reachability-isomorphic marked graph.

6 Concluding Remarks

The notion of a k-marked Petri net has been inspired by workflow applications. Already some time ago, the second part of Theorem 2 suggested that in this context, initial k-markings can have strong consequences, provided $k \geq 2$. The main Theorem 5 proved in this paper serves to reinforce this intuition. It strengthens Theorem 2, in the sense that plain, bounded, reversible, and persistent Petri nets with an initial marking satisfying $\gcd(M_0) \geq 2$ not only exhibit some of the characteristics of live and bounded marked graphs, but can completely be simulated by them. The exact characterisation of marked graph reachability graphs contained in [3] has been instrumental in getting this result, the essential property proved in the present paper being backward persistence.

A rather wide spectrum of different notions of conflict-freeness exists in Petri net theory, and not all simulation relationships have been fully investigated. Within this spectrum, marked graphs are on the restrictive end, while persistent nets are on the permissive end. Intermediate notions can be defined, such as the notion of structural conflict-freeness [5]. Our results suggest that this spectrum collapses for prbp systems with initial k-markings satifying $k \geq 2$.

The repercussions for workflow modelling by Petri nets are not completely clear. On the one hand, one might feel that our results limit the modelling power of persistent Petri nets in the workflow context. On the other hand, the results might also suggest that conflicts should be introduced carefully in workflow nets, so that violations of serialisability are localisable to well-delineated, non-marked graph, substructures of a system.

There are various ways in which one might proceed. For example, it makes a difference whether a k-marked net or its k'th fraction is postulated as persistent, and it is not known whether our results can be strengthened if only the latter but not the former is assumed. Also, it is not clear what happens if reversibility is weakened to liveness (or what happens under other straightforward modifications, for that matter). One might ask whether there exists a sophisticated way of "massaging" places (rather than simply dropping redundant ones) in order to construct the right-hand side of Fig. 4 (Σ_7) from its left-hand side (Σ_6). There are also other interesting open questions related to separability. For example, referring to possibly unbounded Petri nets in general, the decidability status of the problem "Do $(N, 2 \cdot M_0)$ and $(N, M_0) \oplus (N', M_0')$ – where (N', M_0') is a fresh copy of (N, M_0) and $(N, M_0) \oplus (N', M_0')$ is viewed as a labelled net – have the same language?" seems to be unknown.

References

1. Best, E., Darondeau, P.: A decomposition theorem for finite persistent transition systems. Acta Informatica **46**(3), 237–254 (2009)
2. Best, E., Darondeau, P.: Separability in persistent Petri nets. Fundam. Inform. **113**(3–4), 179–203 (2011)
3. Best, E., Devillers, R.: Characterisation of the state spaces of marked graph Petri nets. To be published in Information and Computation (2016). http://www.sciencedirect.com/science/article/pii/S0890540116300207
4. Commoner, F., Holt, A.W., Even, S., Pnueli, A.: Marked directed graphs. J. Comput. Syst. Sci. **5**(5), 511–523 (1971)
5. van Glabbeek, R.J., Goltz, U., Schicke, J.-W.: On causal semantics of Petri nets. In: Katoen, J.-P., König, B. (eds.) CONCUR 2011. LNCS, vol. 6901, pp. 43–59. Springer, Heidelberg (2011)
6. van Hee, K.M., Sidorova, N., Voorhoeve, M.: Soundness and separability of workflow nets in the stepwise refinement approach. In: van der Aalst, W.M.P., Best, E. (eds.) ICATPN 2003. LNCS, vol. 2679, pp. 337–356. Springer, Heidelberg (2003)
7. Keller, R.M.: A fundamental theorem of asynchronous parallel computation. In: Feng, T.Y. (ed.) Parallel Processing. LNCS, vol. 24, pp. 102–112. Springer, Heidelberg (1975)
8. Landweber, L.H., Robertson, E.L.: Properties of conflict-free and persistent Petri nets. JACM **25**(3), 352–364 (1978)
9. Murata, T.: Petri nets: properties, analysis and applications. Proc. IEEE **77**(4), 541–580 (1989)
10. https://en.wikipedia.org/wiki/Shuffle_algebra

Reachability Predicates for Graph Assertions

Giorgio Delzanno[✉]

DIBRIS, University of Genova, Via Dodecaneso, 35, 16146 Genova, Italy
giorgio.delzanno@unige.it

Abstract. We introduce a logic-based formalism to specify updates on
arbitrary graphs. For the resulting language called GLog, we introduce an
assertional language for reasoning about infinite sets of graph configurations in which we use reachability predicates to specify paths of arbitrary
length. For the considered assertional language and a restricted class of
update rules, we define a symbolic procedure to compute predecessor
configurations.

1 Introduction

Verification of distributed algorithm is a challenging task. This kind of algorithms are often defined for an arbitrary number of nodes connected in arbitrary
ways. Furthermore, the behavior of individual nodes is often constrained by values (time-stamps, sequence numbers, identifiers, etc.) that are exchanged during
a protocol run. As shown, e.g., in [5], update rules working on graph patterns
with a completely specified shape (e.g. edge relabeling etc.) combined with symbolic representation of values associated to individual nodes are often sufficient
to specify complex protocols. However, reasoning on this kind of specifications
requires assertional languages that can express properties on graph patterns that
represent minimal constraints on a possible infinite set of configurations. More
specifically, for protocols like AODV [4], whose aim is to dynamically create and
maintain routing tables, correctness is formulated in terms of properties like loop
freedom, i.e., absence of loops in the graph induced by the information stored in
routing tables.

In this paper we define a logic-based specification language, called GLog,
for expressing updates on graph transition systems. GLog is based on binary
predicates that can be used to specify the existence of nodes and edges with
given labels and to update both shape and labels of subgraph. Furthermore, we
consider conditions defined in first order logic over our binary predicates. We
then define an assertional language with two types of atomic formulas, namely
$link(p, X, Y)$ and $path(p, X, Y)$ to specify the existence resp. of links and paths
connecting two generic nodes X and Y resp. with an edge with label p or with a
path consisting of edges with label p only. The denotation of assertions consists of
infinite set of configurations that satisfy the minimal constraints enforced by link-
and path-formulas. Concerning the expressiveness of the assertional languages,
we only admit equality constraints (implicitly defined by multiple occurrences
of the same variable as in the assertion $link(p, X, X)$ denoting a loop on the

© Springer International Publishing Switzerland 2016
K.G. Larsen et al. (Eds.): RP 2016, LNCS 9899, pp. 63–76, 2016.
DOI: 10.1007/978-3-319-45994-3_5

node associated to X). Furthermore, we do not impose extra conditions like disjointness of paths and link generated after instantiating constraints contained in the same assertion. For instance, the assertion $link(p, X, Y), path(p, Z, T)$ can be instantiated with graphs in which the path connecting the nodes associated to Z and T contains the link connecting nodes associated to X and Y that satisfies $link(p, X, Y)$. For the resulting constraints, we define symbolic operators for the containment test and for computing predecessors working directly on assertions. We consider here a restricted form of updates rules, called relabeling rules, to simplify the presentation of the computation of pre-conditions. We discuss possible extensions involving relations over data associated to nodes and edges. Furthermore, we show how the proposed operations can be applied in order to define a symbolic fixpoint computation engine working on assertions.

This work is a preliminary study towards the definition of automated procedures for computing preconditions (and fixpoint computations based on the resulting operators) over graph assertions with reachability predicates. Differently from other approaches based on richer assertional languages, see e.g., the framework defined in [3], in this paper we sacrifice expressiveness of assertions to gain effectiveness in the construction of symbolic operations. Furthermore, we limit the study of possible extensions to features (sequence numbers, timestamps, identifiers) that could be useful to verification of interesting classes of protocols (e.g. loop freedom in AODV).

1.1   Related Work

The paper by German and Sistla [9] is one of the seminal works on parameterized verification. In this work concurrent and distributed systems are represented by means of automata communicating via rendez-vous in the style of Petri nets. Model checking has been extended to infinite-state systems with broadcast communication by Emerson and Namjoshi in [7]. For verification of infinite-state systems with rendez-vous and broadcast communication, it is possible to apply counter abstraction, i.e., an abstraction that keeps track of the number of components in each possible state [1,15,19–21]. MAP [8] is a tool based on transformations of constraint logic programs that can be applied to infinite-state systems with linear configurations and relations over data variables. MCMT [16] is a symbolic backward reachability engine based on SMT solvers that can handle parameterized systems with linear configurations. The MCMT tool is based on the EPR fragment of first order logic with arrays and applies different types of heuristics including invariant generation to reduce the state space. PFS [17] and UNDIP [18] are tool specifically devised to handle parameterized systems. AUGUR 2 [11] is a tool devised for the analysis of Graph Transformation Systems using approximated unfoldings based on Petri nets. PETRUCHIO [12] is a tool that extracts a Petri net representation from specifications of dynamic networks based π-calculus. UNCOVER [14,22] is a tool that performs a symbolic backward reachability analysis for GTS with universally quantified conditions. The tool exploits a generalization of monotonic abstraction to quantifications over graph patterns as a heuristic to manipulate infinite sets of configurations using minimal constraints (given in form of graphs) only. UNCONVER can be viewed as the counterpart of UNDIP and PFS for systems in which configurations have a graph structure. Differently from [13,14,22], our assertional language can be applied to define (violations of) invariants that involve reachability predicates. This kind of specification language is inspired to the path expressions used to express application conditions in Groove [10]. In this setting the applications conditions are applied to finite graph configurations. Differently from [10], the semantics of our language associates infinite set of configurations to assertions. Symbolic operations are defined in order to take into consideration our extended semantics.

2   GLog

In this section we will define a logic-based presentation of evolving graphs called GLog, GLog generalizes the BLog language in [5]. GLog formulas are based on a simple relational calculus that can be used to express updates of configurations defined by sets of ground atoms. Ground atoms define relations, i.e., labelled links, between "nodes". More formally, let P be a finite set of names of binary relations, $\mathcal{N}$ a denumerable set of node identifiers, and V be a denumerable set of variables. Our logic has no function symbols but can be instantiated with elements from $\mathcal{N}$. An atomic formula is a formula $p(x, y)$, where $p \subset P$, $x, y \in V$. A ground atom is a formula $p(n, m)$, where $n, m \in \mathcal{N}$. A literal is either an atomic formula or the negation $\neg A$ of an atomic formula A. A formula is a first order formula built on literals, namely, any literal is a formula, conjunctions, disjunctions, universally and existentially quantified formulas are still formulas. The set of free variables of a formula F, namely $FV(F)$, is the minimal set satisfying $FV(p(x, y)) = \{x, y\}$, $FV(A \vee B) = FV(A) \cup FV(B)$, $FV(A \wedge B) = FV(A) \cap FV(B)$, $FV(\neg A) = FV(A)$, $FV(\forall v.A) = FV(A) \setminus \{v\}$, and $FV(\exists v.A) = FV(A) \setminus \{v\}$. Given $S = \{F_1, \ldots, F_n\}$, we define $FV(S) = FV(F_1) \cup \ldots \cup FV(F_n)$. Quantified formulas we will be used as application conditions of rules. Configurations can be viewed as models in which to evaluate a formula. For this reason, we will consider free variables in guards to restrict the range of identifiers occurring in a configuration. To define instantiations of free variables, we consider injective mappings. We use injective mappings in order to give a unique interpretation of a formula like $p(X, E) \wedge p(Y, F)$, i.e., X, Y, E, F refer to distinct nodes. We allow multiple occurrences of the same variable to implicitly model equality constraints. An interpretation is an injective mapping σ from V to $\mathcal{N}$. For a formula F we use $F\sigma$ as an abbreviation for $\hat{\sigma}(F)$, where $\hat{\sigma}$ is the natural extension of σ to terms. For a set $S = \{A_1, \ldots, A_n\}$, we use $S\sigma$ to denote the set $\{A_1\sigma, \ldots, A_n\sigma\}$.

2.1   Update Rules

Update rules consists of conditions defined by quantified formulas with no function symbols, a deletion and an addition set. The deletion (resp. addition) set defines the set of ground atoms that have to be cancelled from (resp. added to) the current configuration. A rule has the following form $\langle C, D, A \rangle$, where C is a quantified formula, D and A are two sets of atomic formulas with variables in V, and such that $FV(A) \cup FV(D) \subseteq FV(C)$.

To fix an operational semantics for our language we need a support for the interpretation of relations and variables. We will consider a sort of Herbrand semantics for relations. Namely, we first consider two denumerable sets $\mathcal{N}$ and $\mathcal{E}$ of nodes and edges identifiers, respectively. A configuration is a set Δ of ground atomic formulas. A configuration implicitly defines a graph in which directed edges are represented by atomic formulas whose predicate nameacts as edge label.

We use $\Delta \models A$ to define the satisfiability relation of a quantified formula A s.t. $FV(A) = \emptyset$. Let $A[n/X]$ denote the formula obtained by replacing each free occurrence of X with n. The relation is defined by induction as follows.

- $\Delta \models A$, if $A \in \Delta$;
- $\Delta \models A \wedge B$, if $\Delta \models A$ and $\Delta \models B$;
- $\Delta \models \neg A$, if $\Delta \not\models A$;
- $\Delta \models \forall X.A$, if $\Delta \models A[n/X]$ for each $n \in \mathcal{N}$;
- $\Delta \models \exists X.A$, if $\Delta \models A[n/X]$ for some $n \in \mathcal{N}$.

Given a configuration Δ, we say that the quantified formula A is satisfied in Δ, if there exists an interpretation σ s.t. $A\sigma$ is satisfiable.

In order to apply a rule $\langle C, D, A \rangle$ to Δ, there must be an interpretation σ that satisfies the quantified formula C. The same interpretation σ is then applied to the atomic formulas in D and A. The resulting sets of atoms, say D' and A' respectively, are deleted from and added to Δ, respectively.

2.2 Transition System

A protocol $\mathcal{P}$ is a set of rules. The operational semantics of $\mathcal{P}$ is given by a transition system $T_{\mathcal{P}} = \langle \mathcal{C}, \rightarrow \rangle$, where $\mathcal{C}$ is the set of possible configurations, i.e., finite subsets of ground atoms, and $\rightarrow \subseteq \mathcal{C} \times \mathcal{C}$ is a relation defined as follows. For $\Delta, \Delta' \in \mathcal{C}$ and a rule $\langle C, D, A \rangle \in \mathcal{P}$, $\Delta \rightarrow \Delta'$ if there exists σ s.t. $\Delta \models C\sigma$ and $\Delta' = (\Delta \setminus D\sigma) \cup A\sigma$. A computation is a sequence of configurations $\Delta_0 \Delta_1 \ldots$ s.t. $\Delta_i \rightarrow \Delta_{i+1}$ for $i \geq 0$.

We use $\rightarrow^*$ to denote the reflexive and transitive closure of $\rightarrow$. In a single step of the operational semantics a rule is evaluated in the current configuration by taking a sort of closed-word assumption, i.e., ground atoms that do not occur in a configuration are evaluated to false. Furthermore, atomic formulas that are not deleted are transferred from the current to the successor configuration. The latter property can be viewed then as a sort of frame axiom. It is important to notice that, in general, a configuration Δ has several possible successors. Indeed, depending of the chosen interpretation of free variables the same rule can be applied to different subsets of ground atoms contained in the same configuration.

For a set S of configurations, we define the *Post* and *Pre* operators as follows $Post(S) = \{\Delta' \mid \exists \Delta \in S, \ \Delta \rightarrow \Delta'\}$ and $Pre(S) = \{\Delta' \mid \exists \Delta \in S, \ \Delta' \rightarrow \Delta\}$.

We use $Post^*(S)$ (resp. $Pre^*(S)$) to denote the reflexive-transitive closure of $Post$ (resp. Pre).

Decision Problem. We consider decision problems that generalize the standard notion of reachability between configurations. The key point is to reason about an infinite set of initial configurations in order to prove properties for protocol instances with an arbitrary number of nodes and edges. For this purpose, we introduce the $\exists$-reachability problem defined as follows.

Definition 1. *Given a protocol $\mathcal{P}$, a set of target configurations T and a possibly infinite set of initial configurations I, $\exists$-reachability is satisfied for $\mathcal{P}$, I and T, written $\exists Reach(\mathcal{P}, I, T)$, if there exists $\Delta \in T$ and a configuration Δ_1 s.t. $\Delta_1 \in Post^*(I)$ and $\Delta \subseteq \Delta_1$.*

In other words $\exists Reach(\mathcal{P}, I, T)$ holds if there exists a configuration $\Delta_0 \in I$ s.t. $\Delta_0 \rightarrow^* \Delta_1$ and $\Delta \subseteq \Delta_1$ for some $\Delta \in T$. $\exists$-Reachability is an undecidable problem [5].

3   Assertional Language

In this section we introduce an assertional language that can be used to define properties on configurations. The assertional language is designed to express minimal constraints on sets of configurations. We consider here two types of constraints: links and paths. For instance, we use assertions like

$$\exists X, Y.link(p, X, Z), path(q, X, Y)$$

to denote all configurations with at least a link with label p connecting two nodes n and m and a path in which links have label q connecting the same nodes.

Definition 2. *An atomic assertion has one of the following forms: $link(p, x, y)$, $path(p, x, y)$, where $p \in P$, $x, y \in V$.*
   An assertion is a formula $\exists X_1, \dots, X_k.A_1, \dots, A_n$ where

- *$A_1, \dots, A_n$ is an abbreviation for the conjunction $A_1 \wedge \dots \wedge A_n$,*
- *A_i is an atomic assertion for $i : 1, \dots, n$,*
- *and, finally, $FV(A_1 \wedge \dots \dots \wedge A_n) = \{X_1, \dots, X_k\}$.*

The semantics of atomic formulas is defined as follows:

- $\Delta \models link(p, n, m)$, if $p(n, m) \in \Delta$;
- $\Delta \models path(p, n, m)$, if there exist $v_1, \dots, v_k$ for $k \geq 0$ s.t.

$$\{p(n, v_1), p(v_1, v_2), \dots, p(v_{k-1}, v_k), p(v_k, m)\} \subseteq \Delta$$

$\Delta \models A_1, \dots, A_n$, if A_i is an atomic assertion, and $\Delta \models A_i$ for $i : 1, \dots, n$,
- if φ has no existential quantifiers and $FV(\varphi) = \{X_1, \dots, X_k\}$, then $\Delta \models \exists X_1, \dots, X_k.\varphi$ holds, if $\Delta \models \varphi\sigma$ for some injective mapping σ from $FV(\varphi)$ to the set of nodes.

The denotation of an assertion is defined as follows:

$$Den(\gamma) = \{\Delta \mid \Delta \models \gamma\}$$

In other words γ denotes all configurations obtained by extending the minimal requirements specified in γ in order to satisfy *path* formulas. The denotation of a finite set Γ (a disjunction) of assertions is defined as follows: $Den(\Gamma) = \bigcup_{\gamma \in \Gamma} Den(\gamma)$. For instance, given $\gamma = \exists X, Y.path(p, X, Y)$, $Den(\gamma)$ contains all configurations with at least a path with labels p from two distinct nodes. Given $\gamma_1 = \exists X.path(p, X, X)$, $Den(\gamma_1)$ contains all configurations with at least a loop with labels p in node n. Notice that in $\gamma_2 = \exists X.path(p, X, Y), link(p, X, Y)$, the existence of of a link connecting X and Y is stronger than the existence of a path. In other words, a graph with a link between instances of X and Y always satisfy the *path* constraint. A similar observation holds for more complex patterns involving a *path*-formula, e.g., in $\gamma_3 = \exists X.path(p, X, Y), link(p, X, Z), path(p, Z, Y)$ the assertion $path(p, X, Y)$ is entailed by the remaining ones (to satisfy them we need a path linking instances of X and Y). We formalize this idea as follows. An assertion γ is in redudant form if there are symbol p and existentially quantified variables $X, Y, V_1, \ldots, V_k$ for $k \geq 0$ s.t. γ contains the assertion $path(p, X, Y)$ and $\alpha_1(p, V_1, V_2), \alpha_2(p, V_2, V_3), \ldots, \alpha_{k-1}(p, V_{k-1}, V_k)$ s.t. $\alpha_i \in \{link, path\}$ for $i : 1, \ldots, k$ and either $V_1 = X$, $V_k = Y$, and $X \neq Y$, or $V_1 = X$ and $V_k = X$.

If the conditions in the previous definitions are satisfied for variables X (resp. X, Y) the atomic formula $path(p, X, X)$ (resp. $path(p, X, Y)$) is called redundant. An assertion is in reduced form, if it is not redundant. An assertion can be rewritten in reduced form by eliminating every occurrence of redundant atomic formulas. In the rest of the paper, when clear from the context, we will omit existential quantifiers.

Proposition 1. *If φ' is the reduced form of φ, then $Den(\varphi) = Den(\varphi')$.*

Decision Problem. Decision problems defined for ground configurations can be transferred to sets of assertions as follows.

Definition 3. *Given a protocol $\mathcal{P}$ a set I of initial configurations, and a set of assertions Γ, $\exists$-reachability is satisfied for $\mathcal{P}$, I and Γ, written $\exists Reach(\mathcal{P}, I, \Gamma)$, if there exists $\Delta \in Den(\Gamma)$ s.t. $\Delta \in Post^*(I)$.*

In other words $\exists Reach(\mathcal{P}, I, \Gamma)$ holds if there exists $\Delta_1 \in Den(\Gamma)$ s.t. $\Delta_0 \to^* \Delta_1$ for some $\Delta_0 \in I$. The undecidability proof in [5] can be reformulated when targets are expressed via assertions. The $\exists$-Reachability problem remains undecidable.

4   Symbolic Operations

In this section we define symbolic operations to manipulate our assertional language. We are interested in operations that can be used to implement symbolic exploration procedures, like union, intersection, containment, and computation of pre- and post-conditions w.r.t. update rules.

Containment Test. Let us first consider the containment test between two assertions in reduced form. Namely, given assertions γ_1 and γ_2, we would like to define a procedure *subset* s.t., at least, if $subset(\gamma_1, \gamma_2) = true$, then $Den(\gamma_1) \subseteq Den(\gamma_2)$. Assertions can be viewed as minimal constraints on configurations. In order for the denotation of γ_2 to include the denotation of γ_1, we must ensure that for every assertion in γ_2 there exists a stronger assertion in γ_1. This property ensures that every constraint enforced by atomic formulas in γ_1 will be satisfied in γ_2 possibly with stronger conditions. Since assertions are existentially quantified, we need to find an injection from variable in γ_2 to variables in γ_1 s.t. the above mentioned condition is satisfied.

Definition 4. *Let γ_1 be the reduced assertion $\exists X_1, \ldots, X_n.\eta_1$ and γ_2 be the reduced assertion $\exists Y_1, \ldots, Y_m.\eta_2$ with $m \leq n$. Withouth loss of generality, we assume that $Var(\eta_2) = \{Y_1, \ldots; Y_m\}$ and $Var(\eta_1) = \{X_1, \ldots, X_n\}$ are disjoint (we can apply variable renaming to ensure this property). We define the predicate $subset(\gamma_1, \gamma_2)$ evaluates to true if there exists an injective mapping σ from $Var(\eta_2)$ to $Var(\eta_1)$ that satisfies the following conditions:*

- *For every link-constraint φ in γ_2, $\varphi\sigma$ must occur in γ_1, i.e., every edge in γ_2 must be present in γ_1.*
- *For every path-constraint $\varphi - path(p, X, Y)$ in γ_2, there must exist variables $V_1, \ldots, V_k$ and the list of assertions (forming a chain)*

$$\alpha_1(p, V_1, V_2), \alpha_2(p, V_2, V_3), \ldots, \alpha_{k-1}(p, V_{k-1}, V_k)$$

in γ_1 s.t.
- *$\sigma(X) = V_1$, $\sigma(Y) = V_k$,*
- *$\alpha_i \in \{link, path\}$ for $i : 1, \ldots, k$.*

Notice that, by hypothesis, existentially quantified variables are always mapped to distinct nodes. In accord with our previous definition, the assertion $link(p, X, Y)$ does not subsume $link(p, X, X)$. Consider the assertion

$$link(p, X, Y), path(q, X, Y)$$

in γ_2 and the assertion

$$link(p, A, B), link(q, A, C), path(q, C, B)$$

in γ_1. We can map X, Y to A, B so as to satisfy $link(p, X, Y)$ with the atomic formula $link(p, A, B)$, and $path(q, X, Y)$ with the assertion $link(q, A, C), path(q, C, B)$. Notice that in order to satisfy $path(q, C, B)$ in γ_1, we need a path involving either *link* or *path* assertions in γ_2. Finally, consider the assertion $path(p, X, X)$ in γ_2 and the assertions

$$link(p, A, B), link(p, B, C), path(p, C, A)$$

in γ_1. By mapping X to A, we obtain an assertion

$$link(p, X, B), link(p, B, C), path(p, C, X)$$

which is less general than γ_2.

Proposition 2. *Let φ, φ' be two reduced assertions. Then, we have that $subset(\gamma_1, \gamma_2) = true$ if and only if $Den(\gamma_1) \subseteq Den(\gamma_2)$.*

The containment test can be extended to sets of assertions as follows. Let Γ_1, Γ_2 be two sets of reduced assertions, $subset(\Gamma_1, \Gamma_2)$ holds if and only if for each $\gamma_1 \in Gamma_1$ there exists $\gamma_2 \in \Gamma_2$ s.t. $subset(\gamma_1, \gamma_2)$. In other word, each assertion in Γ_1 is subsumed by at least one assertion in Γ_2.

Proposition 3. *Let Γ_1, Γ_2 be sets of reduced assertions. Then, we have that $subset(\Gamma_1, \Gamma_2) = true$ if and only if $Den(\Gamma_1) \subseteq Den(\Gamma_2)$.*

Pre-conditions. We now consider symbolic operations to compute assertions that represent preconditions of update rules. Starting from a set of assertions Γ and a set of update rules R, the goal is to compute a set of assertions Γ' s.t.

$$Den(\Gamma') = Pre(Den(\Gamma))$$

We consider here a restricted form of update rules, namely we only consider relabeling rules.

Definition 5. *A relabeling rule is an update rule of the form $\langle C, D, A \rangle$, where*

- $C = D = \{p_1(X_1, Y_1), \ldots, p_k(X_k, Y_k)\}$
- $A = \{q_1(X_1, Y_1), \ldots, q_k(X_k, Y_k)\}$

where $p_i, q_i \in P$ for $i : 1, \ldots, k$.

Observe that D is used both as enabling condition and deletion set so as to ensure the existence of all elements to be deleted. Free variables occurring in D and A are implicitly existentially quantified. For instance, the rule $\langle D, D, A \rangle$ with $D = \{p(X, Y)\}$ and $A = \{q(X, Y)\}$. This rule non-deterministically selects any pairs of links with label p and updates its label by changing it into q. Relabeling rules only change labels of existing links. We focus our attention on relabeling rules since our assertional language cannot represent arbitrary formulas as those allowed in conditions. Relabeling however induces very expressive transition systems.

Proposition 4. *$\exists$-reachability for relabeling rules is undecidable.*

Proof. In what follows we present a sketch of the proof containing the main intuitions. We first notice that edge addition and deletion can be simulated by introducing a special predicate name (i.e. edge label) ϵ. To simulate edge creation, we can use relabeling rules that update ϵ-edges. For instance, the rule $D = \{\epsilon(X, Y)\}, A = \{p(X, Y)\}$ non-deterministically introduces an occurrence of a p-edge. Similar constructions have been proposed for graph rewriting with addition/deletion of edges or with relabeling in [2]. Undecidability of $\exists$-reachability depends from the assumptions on the shape of initial states.

- Let us consider initial states consisting of (directed) paths (i.e. chains of atomic formulas) of arbitrary length with an initial label q_0 followed by ϵ labels only, then we can use such a configuration as initial structure on which to run a simulation of a Turing powerful model such a two counter machine.
- Every path corresponds to the maximum amount of memory needed during the execution of a machine.
- The initial state q_0 can then be transformed into a pointer to visit each element (an edge) of the memory and to modify its contents (e.g. flip it from one to zero or from zero to one). To represent the value k for counter c with use k occurrences of label c along the path.

More specifically, if the transition from q_1 to q_2 increments counter c we use the following set of rules:

$$
\begin{aligned}
D_1 &= \{q_1(X,Y), \epsilon(Y,Z)\}, & A_1 &= \{q_2(X,Y), c(Y,Z)\} \\
D_2 &= \{q_1(X,Y), c(Y,Z)\}, & A_2 &= \{q_1^1(X,Y), c^1(Y,Z)\} \\
D_3 &= \{q_1(X,Y), d(Y,Z)\}, & A_3 &= \{q_1^1(X,Y), d^1(Y,Z)\} \\
D_4 &= \{c^1(X,Y), c(Y,Z)\}, & A_4 &= \{c^1(X,Y), c^1(Y,Z)\} \\
D_5 &= \{c^1(X,Y), \epsilon(Y,Z)\}, & A_5 &= \{c^2(X,Y), c(Y,Z)\} \\
D_6 &= \{d^1(X,Y), \epsilon(Y,Z)\}, & A_6 &= \{d^2(X,Y), c(Y,Z)\} \\
D_7 &= \{d^1(X,Y), d(Y,Z)\}, & A_7 &= \{d^1(X,Y), d^1(Y,Z)\} \\
D_8 &= \{d^1(X,Y), c(Y,Z)\}, & A_8 &= \{d^1(X,Y), c^1(Y,Z)\} \\
D_9 &= \{c^1(X,Y), c^2(Y,Z)\}, & A_9 &= \{c^2(X,Y), c(Y,Z)\} \\
D_{10} &= \{c^1(X,Y), d^2(Y,Z)\}, & A_{10} &= \{c^2(X,Y), d(Y,Z)\} \\
D_{11} &= \{d^1(X,Y), d^2(Y,Z)\}, & A_{11} &= \{d^2(X,Y), d(Y,Z)\} \\
D_{12} &= \{c^1(X,Y), d^2(Y,Z)\}, & A_{12} &= \{c^2(X,Y), d(Y,Z)\} \\
D_{13} &= \{q_1^1(X,Y), c^2(Y,Z)\}, & A_{13} &= \{q_2(X,Y), c(Y,Z)\} \\
D_{13} &= \{q_1^1(X,Y), d^2(Y,Z)\}, & A_{13} &= \{q_2(X,Y), d(Y,Z)\}
\end{aligned}
$$

The rules just scan the chain passing through c and d labels until the first ϵ label is found. During the scan each label is marked to prepare the second phase of the simulation. When the ϵ label has been found, it is replaced with c and then the chain is traversed back in order to restore the original c and d labels and to move the control state to q_2. Decrement of counter d is handled in a simmetric way.

If the transition from q_1 to q_2 decrement counter c we use the following set of rules:

$$
\begin{aligned}
D_1' &= \{q_1(X,Y), c(Y,Z)\}, & A_1 &= \{q_2(X,Y), \epsilon(Y,Z)\} \\
D_2' &= \{q_1(X,Y), d(Y,Z)\}, & A_2 &= \{q_1^1(X,Y), d^3(Y,Z)\} \\
D_3' &= \{d^3(X,Y), d(Y,Z)\}, & A_3 &= \{d^3(X,Y), d^3(Y,Z)\} \\
D_4' &= \{d^3(X,Y), c(Y,Z)\}, & A_4 &= \{d^4(X,Y), \epsilon(Y,Z)\} \\
D_5' &= \{d^3(X,Y), d^4(Y,Z)\}, & A_5 &= \{d^4(X,Y), d(Y,Z)\} \\
D_6' &= \{q_1^1(X,Y), d^4(Y,Z)\}, & A_6 &= \{q_2(X,Y), d(Y,Z)\}
\end{aligned}
$$

The rules just scan the chain passing through d labels until the first c label is found. During the scan each label is marked to prepare the second phase of the simulation. When the c label has been found, it is replaced with ϵ and then the chain is traversed back in order to restore the original d labels and to move the control state to q_2. Decrement of counter d is simmetric.

Similarly, zero test on counter c is implemented by the rules

$$D_1'' = \{q_1(X,Y), \epsilon(Y,Z)\}, \quad A_1 = \{q_2(X,Y), \epsilon(Y,Z)\}$$
$$D_2'' = \{q_1(X,Y), d(Y,Z)\}, \quad A_2 = \{q_1^1(X,Y), d^5(Y,Z)\}$$
$$D_3'' = \{d^5(X,Y), d(Y,Z)\}, \quad A_3 = \{d^5(X,Y), d^5(Y,Z)\}$$
$$D_4'' = \{d^5(X,Y), \epsilon(Y,Z)\}, \quad A_4 = \{d^6(X,Y), \epsilon(Y,Z)\}$$
$$D_5'' = \{d^5(X,Y), d^6(Y,Z)\}, \quad A_5 = \{d^6(X,Y), d(Y,Z)\}$$
$$D_6'' = \{q_1^1(X,Y), d^6(Y,Z)\}, \quad A_6 = \{q_2(X,Y), d(Y,Z)\}$$

The rules scan the chain passing through all d labels in search of the first ϵ. The test fails if there are c labels (i.e. counter c is greater than one).

Rules of non-zero test are implemented in a similar way.

The simulation is successful only for paths with the necessary amount of memory (i.e. length). The halting problem for such a program can be formulated as an existential reachability problem via an assertion $\exists X, Y.link(halt, X, Y)$ used to single out the halting control state of the program.

The freedom in fixing the shape of the initial set of configurations is central here in order to give enough power to relabeling rules. Indeed, if the initial configurations are arbitrary graphs, e.g., with ϵ labels, then relabeling is not expressive enough to make existential reachability undecidable.

Proposition 5. $\exists$-reachability for relabeling rules is decidable if the set of initial configurations consists of arbitrary fully connected graphs with ϵ-transition.

Proof. Differently from the undecidability proof for special classes of initial configurations, The difficulty in building a perfect simulation of a (Turing or counter) machine when starting from arbitrary graphs with epsilon transitions is due to the fact that relabeling rules can non-deterministically be applied at any position.

- For every configuration in which a relabeling is applied to a given link, we can find another configuration with additional links attached to the same nodes, involved in the first application of the rule, in which the same relabeling can be applied several times.
- Since the additional links can be adjacent to the original ones, it is not possible to use chains of predicates to define lists of cells or other regular structures.

In other words, the effect of a relabeling rule is only that of enabling other possible rule applications. The same effect can be obtained by considering rewriting rules operating on a finite set of labels (predicate symbols). As a side effect there is no more difference between links and paths. $\exists$-reachability can then be reformulated as a reachability problem starting from the singleton containing ϵ and with the set of labels occurring in the target assertion as final configuration. Since we only consider finitely many predicate symbols, this kind of reachability problem becomes decidable. Similar reductions have been proposed for coverability in graph rewriting with relabeling rules, and in broadcast protocols with non deterministic reconfigurations of links [6].

The previous result shows that relabeling rules defined over finite alphabets are not very expressive. Indeed a more interesting classes of transition systems is obtained by adding relations over data associated to edges and nodes (e.g. sequence numbers as in AODV). We will discuss these extensions in the last section of the paper. We first consider the problem of computing pre-conditions of relabeling rules w.r.t. a set of assertions. The goal is to define a symbolic procedure to infer new assertions for this simple types of updates. More specifically, for a relabeling rule $r = \langle D, D, A \rangle$ and an assertion φ, we want to compute the effect of applying backwards r to configurations in $Den(\varphi)$. In order to infer new assertions, starting from φ we need to find minimal instantiations of the *path*-assertions that could be used to find a partial matching with the edges specified in A. The key point is to show that such minimal instantiations exist and that it is enough to consider finitely many of them. These two properties follow from the observation that *path*-assertions can be made more specific by using by chaining *link* assertions with other *path*-assertions. For instance, $path(p, X, Y)$ can be made more specific via the assertion $link(p, X, Z), path(p, Z, Y)$. This kind of concretization steps must be performed as long as needed to match a subset of edges occurring in the relabeling rules. In the worst case we have to consider all possible concretization involving as many edges as those occurring in A. This argument can be used to define an finite upper bound on the assertions that we have to considerto represent all predecessors.

Definition 6. *Let γ be a reduced assertion, and $r = \langle D, D, A \rangle$ be a relabeling rule s.t. D has cardinality k. Let W be a denumerable set of variables distinct from those in γ. The set of concretizations of $C(\gamma, A, W)$ is obtained by considering all assertions γ' in which every occurrence of a $path(p, X, Y)$-assertion is replaced a chain*

$$\alpha_1(p, X, Z_1), \alpha_2(p, Z_1, Z_2), \ldots, \alpha_q(p, Z_q, Y)$$

where $Z_i \in W$, $q \leq k$, and $\alpha_i \in \{link, path\}$ for $i : 1, \ldots, q$.

Notice that different *path*-formulas can generate chains sharing common variables. For instance,

$$path(p, X, Y), path(q, W, Z)$$

can generate the assertion

$$link(p, X, T), link(p, T, Y), path(p, W, T), link(p, T, Z)$$

in which the generated chain assertions share an intermediate node variable T.

As mentioned before, concretizations are the first step towards the generations of patterns used to match the right-hand side of a relabeling rule. To complete the definition, we introduce the following operators. We first interpret conjunctions of atomic formulas as sets of formulas and use $\ominus$ and $\oplus$ to compute set differences and union, respectively. Furthermore, we define

$$\overline{p_1(X_1, Y_1), \ldots, p_k(X_k, Y_k)} = link(p_1, X_1, Y_1), \ldots, link(p_k, X_k, Y_k)$$

to transform conjunctions of atomic formulas into an assertions.

We are ready now to define the set of preconditions $pre(\gamma, r)$ of an assertion γ and a relabeling rule r.

Definition 7. *Let γ be a reduced assertion and $r = \langle D, D, A \rangle$ be a relabeling rule. An assertion ξ belongs to $pre(\gamma, r)$ iff the following conditions are satisfied*

- *there exists a concretization $\gamma' \in C(\gamma, A, Vars)$ with $\gamma' = \exists X_1, \ldots, X_n.\eta$ s.t. $Var(D, A)$ and $Var(\eta)$ are disjoint,*
- *there exists a partial and injective mapping σ from $Var(\eta)$ to $Var(A)$ s.t. for every link-constraint φ in η, $\varphi\sigma$ occurs in A*
- *given $A' = \overline{A}$ and $D' = \overline{D}$, ξ is the assertion $\exists W_1, \ldots, W_n.\xi'$ where*

$$\xi' = ((\sigma(\eta) \oplus A') \ominus A') \oplus D'$$

and $FV(\xi') = \{W_1, \ldots, W_n\}$, i.e., ξ' is obtained by first merging A' and η, then sharing the common matching parts by applying σ to η, and, finally, by replacing $\overline{A}$ with the precondition $\overline{D}$. Notice that, by construction, $\overline{A}$ and $\overline{D}$ are defined on the same set of variables, and $\sigma(\eta)$ shares variables with $\overline{A}$.

The following proposition then holds.

Proposition 6. *Let γ be a reduced assertion and r be a relabeling rule. $\xi' \in pre(\gamma, r)$ if and only if $Den(\xi) = Pre_r(Den(\gamma))$, where Pre_r is the predecessor operator restricted to rule r.*

Proof. Assume that, given $A' = \overline{A}$ and $D' = \overline{D}$, ξ is defined by the assertion $\exists FV(\xi').\xi'$, where $\xi' = ((\sigma(\eta) \oplus A') \ominus A') \oplus D'$ and η is a concretization of the original assertion. Consider now a configuration $\Delta \in Den(\xi)$. By definition, there exists $\Delta' \subseteq \Delta$, an interpretation θ for $FV(\xi')$ and a further concretization ξ'' need to eliminate all path formulas in ξ' s.t. $\Delta' = \xi''\theta$. Concretization is used here to replace every *path*-predicate with a concrete path of atomic formulas of arbitrary length. The application of the two concretization steps is the key point in order to generate all possible chains of atomic formulas for which there could be a matching with instances of A. We observe that the two concretization steps give rise to a minimal set of ground formulas needed to generate $Den(\gamma)$. All denotations of γ can then be generated by taking the upward closure computed with respect to subset inclusion of the considered concretizations. By replacing, $A\theta$ with $D\theta$ we obtain predecessors of configurations in $Den(\gamma)$, i.e., $\Delta \in pre(Den(\gamma), r)$. The same argument can be applied to show that assertions $\xi \in Pre(\gamma, r)$ can generate all concretizations and instantiations needed to represent every predecessor configuration. $\qquad \square$

The operator is extended to sets of assertions as follows $pre(\Gamma, r) = \bigcup_{\gamma \in \Gamma} pre(\gamma, r)$.

Fixpoint Computation. Containment test and symbolic computation of preconditions are key operations to define infinite-state extensions to model checking algorithms. For instance, model checking algorithms perform backward search based on preconditions in order to verify invariants. More precisely, to verify that the property P is an invariant for a given transition system T with initial states I and predecessor operator Pre_T the following property must hold

$I \cap Pre_T^*(Bad_P) = \emptyset$, where Bad_P is the set of configurations that violate the invariant P. Violations of invariant properties are often upward closed with respect to orderings like set/multiset inclusion. Our assertional language can be applied to perform backward reasoning, i.e., to compute the set of assertions $pre^*(\Gamma)$ obtained by iterating the application of pre starting from an initial set of assertions representing bad configurations (e.g. all graphs that contain at least one occurrence of link $halt$ or that contain a loop with labels req on some node). Termination of the computation cannot be guaranteed in general. However we can apply the containment test as heuristics to stop the computation. The final step is checking intersection with the initial states. The effectiveness of this test depends on the class of graphs chosen to represent intial configurations.

5 Conclusions

We have presented an assertional language with reachability predicates for reasoning about infinite set of graphs. The assertional language is devised for a specification language that can be applied to specify properties of distributed protocols and algorithms for which it is important to state correctness properties like loop freedom. These properties require powerful assertions that can assert the existence of paths of arbitrary length in a configuration. In the paper we have defined a specification language to formally update graph-based transition systems and an assertional language consisting of existentially quantified formulas. Furthermore, we have studied symbolic operations operating over our assertions. This is a preliminary step towards the definition of symbolic procedure needed to explore the search space of our specification language.

Adding data and relations over data to rules and assertions is one possible extension of the framework presented in this paper. Our update rules can be viewed as rewriting rules with equality with conditions formulated again over a quantified logic with equality. Following the paradigm of constraint logic programming (CLP), it comes natural to extend update rules in order to consider variables ranging over (possibly infinite) data domains and conditions expressed by richer theories, e.g., equality, inequality, $<$, $>$, etc. A similar idea can be applied to the assertional language, i.e., assertions become existentially quantified formulas with constraints. Denotations are defined by extending the notion of instantiation in order to generate ground instances that satisfy constraints. An interesting direction here is the application of existing solvers as constraint solver to deal with assertions involving both reachability predicates and constraints in order to implement engines for symbolic search as MCMT based on SMT over the theory of arrays [16] and UNDIP [18] based on the PPL library.

References

1. Bardin, S., Finkel, A., Leroux, J., Petrucci, L.: FAST: acceleration from theory to practice. STTT **10**(5), 401–424 (2008)
2. Bertrand, N., Delzanno, G., König, B., Sangnier, A., Stückrath, J.: On the decidability status of reachability and coverability in graph transformation systems. In: 23rd International Conference on Rewriting Techniques and Applications (RTA 2012), Nagoya, Japan, 28 May – 2 June 2012, pp. 101–116 (2012)
3. Bouajjani, A., Dragoi, C., Enea, C., Jurski, Y., Sighireanu, M.: A generic framework for reasoning about dynamic networks of in nite-state processes. Logical Methods Comput. Sci. **5**(2), 1–29 (2009). http://arxiv.org/pdf/0903.3126.pdf
4. Das, S., Perkins, C., Belding-Royer, E.: Ad hoc on-demand distance vector (AODV) routing (2003)
5. Delzanno, G.: A logic-based approach to verify distributed protocols. To appear in the Proceedings of CILC (2016)
6. Delzanno, G., Sangnier, A., Traverso, R., Zavattaro, G.: On the complexity of parameterized reachability in recongurable broadcast networks. In: IARCS Annual Conference on Foundations of Software Technology and Theoretical Computer Science, FSTTCS 2012, Hyderabad, India, 15–17 December 2012, pp. 289–300 (2012)
7. Emerson, E.A., Namjoshi, K.S.: On model checking for non-deterministic in nite-state systems. In: Thirteenth Annual IEEE Symposium on Logic in Computer Science, Indianapolis, Indiana, USA, 21–24 June 1998, pp. 70–80 (1998)
8. Fioravanti, F., Pettorossi, A., Proietti, M., Senni, V.: Improving reachability analysis of in nite state systems by specialization. Fundam. Inform. **119**(3–4), 281–300 (2012)
9. German, S.M., Sistla, A.P.: Reasoning about systems with many processes. J. ACM **39**(3), 675–735 (1992)
10. Ghamarian, A.H., de Mol, M., Rensink, A., Zambon, E., Zimakova, M.: Modelling and analysis using groove. STTT **14**(1), 15–40 (2012)
11. König, B., Kozioura, V.: Augur 2 - a new version of a tool for the analysis of graph transformation systems. Electron. Notes Theor. Comput. Sci. **211**, 201–210 (2008)
12. Meyer, R., Strazny, T.: Petruchio: from dynamic networks to nets. In: Touili, T., Cook, B., Jackson, P. (eds.) CAV 2010. LNCS, vol. 6174, pp. 175–179. Springer, Heidelberg (2010)
13. Namjoshi, K.S., Trefler, R.J.: Uncovering symmetries in irregular process networks. In: Giacobazzi, R., Berdine, J., Mastroeni, I. (eds.) VMCAI 2013. LNCS, vol. 7737, pp. 496–514. Springer, Heidelberg (2013)
14. Stückrath, J.: Uncover: using coverability analysis for verifying graph transformation systems. In: Parisi-Presicce, F., Westfechtel, B. (eds.) ICGT 2015. LNCS, vol. 9151, pp. 266–274. Springer, Heidelberg (2015)
15. https://github.com/pierreganty/mist/
16. http://users.mat.unimi.it/users/ghilardi/mcmt/
17. http://www.it.uu.se/research/docs/fm/apv/tools/pfs/
18. http://www.it.uu.se/research/docs/fm/apv/tools/undip/
19. http://www.liafa.jussieu.fr/~sighirea/trex/
20. http://www.lsv.ens-cachan.fr/Software/fast/
21. http://www.montefiore.ulg.ac.be/~boigelot/research/lash/
22. http://www.ti.inf.uni-due.de/de/research/tools/uncover/

Occam's Razor Applied to the Petri Net Coverability Problem

Thomas Geffroy[1(✉)], Jérôme Leroux[2], and Grégoire Sutre[2]

[1] University of Bordeaux, LaBRI, UMR 5800, Talence, France
tgeffroy@labri.fr
[2] University of Bordeaux and CNRS, LaBRI, UMR 5800, Talence, France

Abstract. The verification of safety properties for concurrent systems often reduces to the *coverability* problem for Petri nets. This problem was shown to be ExpSpace-complete forty years ago. Driven by the concurrency revolution, it has regained a lot of interest over the last decade. In this paper, we propose a generic and simple approach to solve this problem. Our method is inspired from the recent approach of Blondin, Finkel, Haase and Haddad [3]. Basically, we combine forward invariant generation techniques for Petri nets with backward reachability for well-structured transition systems. An experimental evaluation demonstrates the efficiency of our approach.

1 Introduction

Context. The analysis of concurrent systems with unboundedly many processes classically uses the so-called *counter abstraction* [12]. The main idea is to forget about the identity of each process, so as to make processes indistinguishable. Assuming that each process is modeled by a finite-state automaton, it is then enough to count, for each state q, how many processes are in state q. The resulting model is a Petri net, with no a priori bound on the number of tokens. The verification of a safety property on the original concurrent system (e.g., mutual exclusion) translates into a *coverability* question on the Petri net: Is it possible to reach a marking that is component-wise larger than a given marking?

Related Work. Karp and Miller [14] proved in 1969 that coverability is decidable (but their algorithm is not primitive recursive), Lipton showed that it requires at least exponential space [15], and Rackoff showed that it only requires exponential space [17]. Despite these somewhat negative results, and driven by the concurrency revolution, the coverability problem has regained a lot of interest over the last decade. Recent efficient approaches include target set widening [13] and structural analysis mixed with SMT solving [3,7]. We believe that the time is ripe to experiment with new ideas and prototypes for coverability, and to apply them to real-world concurrent systems.

Our work builds notably on [3], which proposes a new approach to the coverability problem and its implementation. The approach of [3] is conceptually

© Springer International Publishing Switzerland 2016
K.G. Larsen et al. (Eds.): RP 2016, LNCS 9899, pp. 77–89, 2016.
DOI: 10.1007/978-3-319-45994-3_6

simple and exploits recent advances in the theory of Petri nets as well as the power of modern SMT-solvers. In a nutshell, they leverage recent results on coverability in continuous Petri nets [9] to over-approximate coverability under the standard semantics: any configuration that is not coverable in a continuous Petri net is also not coverable under the standard semantics. This observation is then exploited inside a backward-coverability framework [1].

Our Contribution. We present a generic backward coverability algorithm that relies on downward-closed (forward) invariants to prune the exploration of the state space. Our algorithm is in fact a family of algorithms parametrized by downward-closed invariants. It generalizes the algorithm presented in [3] and implemented in the promising tool QCover. We implemented our algorithm as a variant of QCover that we call ICover. Whereas QCover is based on invariants obtained from recent results on continuous Petri nets [9], our tool ICover is based on two classical methods: the *state equation* for Petri nets, and data-flow *sign analysis* [4]. On the 143 Petri net coverability questions that QCover solved, the tool QCover took 10318 s, while ICover used only 5517 s.

Outline. Section 2 recalls the Petri net coverability problem. Sections 3 and 4 present our backward coverability algorithm with pruning based on downward-closed invariants. In Sects. 5 and 6, we recall two classical methods for computing invariants, namely the state (in-)equation and sign analysis. Section 7 is dedicated to the experimental evaluation of the tool ICover. In Sect. 8, we provide mathematical foundations for explaining our empirical good results based on the notion of limit-reachability in continuous Petri nets [18].

2   The Coverability Problem for Petri Nets

A Petri net is a tuple $\mathcal{N} = (P, T, F, m_{init})$ comprising a finite set of *places* P, a finite set of *transitions* T disjoint of P, a *flow* function F from $(P \times T) \cup (T \times P)$ to $\mathbb{N}$, and an *initial* marking $m_{init} \in \mathbb{N}^P$. It is understood that $\mathbb{N}^P$ denotes the set of total maps from P to $\mathbb{N}$. Elements of $\mathbb{N}^P$ are called *markings*. Intuitively, a marking specifies how many *tokens* are in each place of the net. Tokens are consumed and produced through the firing of transitions. A transition $t \in T$ may fire only if it is enabled, meaning that each place p contains at least $F(p, t)$ tokens. Firing an enabled transition t modifies the contents of each place p by first removing $F(p, t)$ tokens and then adding $F(t, p)$ tokens. To clarify this intuitive description of the Petri net semantics, we introduce, for each transition $t \in T$, the t-step binary relation $\xrightarrow{t}$ over $\mathbb{N}^P$, defined by

$$m \xrightarrow{t} m' \Leftrightarrow \forall p \in P : m(p) \geq F(p, t) \wedge m'(p) = m(p) - F(p, t) + F(t, p)$$

The one-step binary relation $\rightarrow$ is the union of these t-step relations. Formally, $m \rightarrow m' \Leftrightarrow \exists t \in T : m \xrightarrow{t} m'$. The many-step binary relation $\xrightarrow{*}$ is the reflexive-transitive closure of $\rightarrow$.

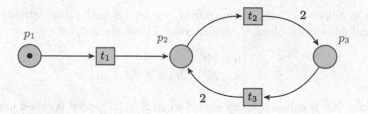

Fig. 1. Simple Petri net example

Example 2.1. Figure 1 depicts a simple Petri net $\mathcal{N} = (P, T, F, m_{init})$ with places $P = \{p_1, p_2, p_3\}$, transitions $T = \{t_1, t_2, t_3\}$ and flow function F such that $F(p_1, t_1) = 1$, $F(p_2, t_2) = 1$, $F(p_3, t_3) = 1$, $F(t_1, p_2) = 1$, $F(t_2, p_3) = 2$, $F(t_3, p_2) = 2$, and $F(p, t) = F(t, p) = 0$ for all other cases. The initial marking is $m_{init} = (1, 0, 0)$. The sequence of transitions $t_1 t_2 t_3$ may fire from the initial marking. Indeed, $(1, 0, 0) \xrightarrow{t_1} (0, 1, 0) \xrightarrow{t_2} (0, 0, 2) \xrightarrow{t_3} (0, 2, 1)$.

One of the most fundamental verification questions on Petri nets is coverability. In its simplest form, the coverability problem asks whether it is possible, by firing a sequence of transitions, to put a token in a given place. In essence, the coverability problem for Petri nets corresponds to the control-state reachability problem for other models of computation, such as counter machines, which are equipped with control states. The formal definition of coverability relies on a partial order over markings, defined hereafter.

Let $\leq$ denote the usual total order on $\mathbb{N}$. We extend $\leq$ over $\mathbb{N}^P$ componentwise, by $m \leq m' \Leftrightarrow \forall p \in P : m(p) \leq m'(p)$. This extension is a partial order over $\mathbb{N}^P$. Given two markings m and m' in $\mathbb{N}^P$, we say that m *covers* m' when $m \geq m'$. The *coverability problem* asks, given a Petri net $\mathcal{N} = (P, T, F, m_{init})$ and a *target* marking $m_{final} \in \mathbb{N}^P$, whether there exists a marking $m \in \mathbb{N}^P$ such that $m_{init} \xrightarrow{*} m$ and $m \geq m_{final}$. The main goal of this paper is to provide a simple, yet efficient procedure for solving this problem. Our method is inspired from the recent approach of [3]. Basically, we combine forward invariant generation techniques for Petri nets with backward reachability for well-structured transition systems [1,8]. Before delving into the details, we need some additional notations.

For a transition $t \in T$ and a set $S \subseteq \mathbb{N}^P$ of markings, we let $pre_{\mathcal{N}}^t(S)$ denote the predecessors of S via the transition t. Similarly, $pre_{\mathcal{N}}(S)$ and $pre_{\mathcal{N}}^*(S)$ denote the one-step and many-step predecessors of S, respectively. Formally, the functions $pre_{\mathcal{N}}^t$, $pre_{\mathcal{N}}$ and $pre_{\mathcal{N}}^*$ from $2^{\mathbb{N}^P}$ to $2^{\mathbb{N}^P}$ are defined by

$$pre_{\mathcal{N}}^t(S) = \{m \in \mathbb{N}^P \mid \exists m' \in S : m \xrightarrow{t} m'\}$$
$$pre_{\mathcal{N}}(S) = \{m \in \mathbb{N}^P \mid \exists m' \in S : m \to m'\}$$
$$pre_{\mathcal{N}}^*(S) = \{m \in \mathbb{N}^P \mid \exists m' \in S : m \xrightarrow{*} m'\}$$

Given a subset $S \subseteq \mathbb{N}^P$ of markings, we let $\uparrow S$ and $\downarrow S$ denote its *upward closure* and *downward closure*, respectively. These are defined by

$$\uparrow S = \{u \in \mathbb{N}^P \mid \exists m \in S : u \geq m\}$$
$$\downarrow S = \{d \in \mathbb{N}^P \mid \exists m \in S : d \leq m\}$$

A subset $S \subseteq \mathbb{N}^P$ is called *upward-closed* when $S = \uparrow S$, and it is called *downward-closed* when $S = \downarrow S$.

Notation 2.2. For the remainder of the paper, to avoid clutter, we will simply write m in place of $\{m\}$ for singletons, when this causes no confusion.

Recall that the coverability problem asks whether $m_{init} \xrightarrow{*} m \geq m_{final}$ for some marking $m \in \mathbb{N}^P$. This problem is equivalently phrased as the question whether m_{init} belongs to $pre_{\mathcal{N}}^*(\uparrow m_{final})$. This formulation can be seen as a backward analysis question. We may also phrase the coverability problem in terms of a forward analysis question, using the notion of coverability set.

Given a Petri net $\mathcal{N} = (P, T, F, m_{init})$, the *coverability set* of $\mathcal{N}$ is the set $Cov_{\mathcal{N}} = \downarrow\{m \in \mathbb{N}^P \mid m_{init} \xrightarrow{*} m\}$. It is readily seen that the coverability problem is equivalent to the question whether m_{final} belongs to $Cov_{\mathcal{N}}$. We are now equipped with the necessary notions to present our mixed forward/backward approach for the coverability problem.

3   Backward Coverability Analysis with Pruning

We now present our method to solve the coverability problem for Petri nets. This section gives the mathematical foundations of our approach, with no regard for implementability. We will focus on the implementation of this approach in Sect. 4.

The classical backward reachability approach for the coverability problem [1,8] consists in computing a growing sequence $U_0 \subseteq U_1 \subseteq \cdots$ of upward-closed subsets of $\mathbb{N}^P$ that converges to $pre_{\mathcal{N}}^*(\uparrow m_{final})$. Here, we modify this growing sequence in order to leverage an a priori known over-approximation of the coverability set. In practice, this means that we narrow the backward reachability search by pruning some markings that are known to be not coverable.

An *invariant* for a Petri net $\mathcal{N} = (P, T, F, m_{init})$ is any subset $I \subseteq \mathbb{N}^P$ that contains every reachable marking, i.e., every marking m with $m_{init} \xrightarrow{*} m$. Observe that a downward-closed subset of $\mathbb{N}^P$ is an invariant of $\mathcal{N}$ if, and only if, it contains $Cov_{\mathcal{N}}$. Sections 5 and 6 will discuss the automatic generation of downward-closed invariants.

For the remainder of this section, we consider a Petri net $\mathcal{N} = (P, T, F, m_{init})$ and we assume that we are given a downward-closed invariant I for $\mathcal{N}$. We introduce the sequence $U_0, U_1, \ldots$ of subsets of $\mathbb{N}^P$ defined as follows:

$$U_0 = \uparrow(m_{final} \cap I)$$
$$U_{k+1} = \uparrow(pre_{\mathcal{N}}(U_k) \cap I) \cup U_k$$

Observe that each U_k is upward-closed and that the sequence $(U_k)_k$ is growing for inclusion. On the contrary to the classical backward reachability approach [1,8], U_{k+1} does not consider all one-step predecessors of U_k, but discards those that are not in I. Note that by taking $I = \mathbb{N}^P$, which is trivially a downward-closed invariant, we obtain the same growing sequence as in the classical backward reachability approach [1,8]. The two following lemmas show that we can use the sequence $(U_k)_k$ to solve the coverability problem.

Lemma 3.1. *The sequence $(U_k)_k$ is ultimately stationary.*

Lemma 3.2. *It holds that $m_{final} \in Cov_\mathcal{N}$ if, and only if, $m_{init} \in \bigcup_k U_k$.*

We have presented in this section a growing sequence of upward-closed subsets of markings that is ultimately stationary and whose limit contains enough information to solve the coverability problem. Our next step is to transform this sequence into an algorithm.

4   The ICover Algorithm

In this section, we turn the growing sequence $(U_k)_k$ of upward-closed subsets of markings defined in Sect. 3 into an algorithm. Of course, we cannot directly compute the sets U_k since they may be infinite (in fact, they are either empty or infinite). Instead, we will compute finite sets $B_k \subseteq \mathbb{N}^P$ such that $U_k = \uparrow B_k$. The existence of such finite sets is guaranteed by the following lemma. A *basis* of an upward-closed subset $U \subseteq \mathbb{N}^P$ is any set $B \subseteq \mathbb{N}^P$ such that $U = \uparrow B$. Recall that a *minimal* element of a subset $S \subseteq \mathbb{N}^P$ is any $m \in S$ such that $u \le m \Rightarrow u = m$ for every $u \in S$.

Lemma 4.1. *For every subset $S \subseteq \mathbb{N}^P$, the set $\mathrm{Min}\, S$ of its minimal elements is finite and satisfies $\uparrow S = \uparrow \mathrm{Min}\, S$.*

Corollary 4.2. *Every upward-closed subset $U \subseteq \mathbb{N}^P$ admits a finite basis.*

We still need to show how to compute a finite basis of U_{k+1} from a finite basis of U_k. To this end we introduce, for each transition $t \in T$, the *covering predecessor* function $cpre_\mathcal{N}^t : \mathbb{N}^P \to \mathbb{N}^P$ defined by

$$cpre_\mathcal{N}^t(m)(p) = F(p,t) + \max(0, m(p) - F(t,p))$$

Informally, $cpre_\mathcal{N}^t(m)$ is the least marking that can cover m in one step by firing the transition t. This property will be formally stated in Lemma 4.3. The function $cpre_\mathcal{N}^t$ is extended to sets of markings by $cpre_\mathcal{N}^t(S) = \{cpre_\mathcal{N}^t(m) \mid m \in S\}$.

Lemma 4.3. *It holds that $pre_\mathcal{N}^t(\uparrow m) = \uparrow cpre_\mathcal{N}^t(m)$ for every marking $m \in \mathbb{N}^P$.*

The previous lemma can easily be extended to sets of markings. We extend it further, in Lemma 4.4, to bridge the gap with the definition of $(U_k)_k$. The lemma shows how to compute a finite basis of U_{k+1} from a finite basis of U_k.

$\text{ICover}(\mathcal{N}, m_{final}, I)$

Input: A Petri Net $\mathcal{N} = (P, T, F, m_{init})$, a target marking $m_{final} \in \mathbb{N}^P$ and a downward-closed invariant I for $\mathcal{N}$.

Output: Whether there exists a marking $m \in \mathbb{N}^P$ such that $m_{init} \xrightarrow{*} m$ and $m \geq m_{final}$.

```
1  begin
2  |  if m_final ∈ I then
3  |  |    B ← {m_final}
4  |  else
5  |  |    B ← ∅
6  |  while m_init ∉ ↑B do
7  |  |    N ← {cpre_N^t(m) | t ∈ T, m ∈ B} \ ↑B        /* new predecessors */
8  |  |    P ← N ∩ I                                     /* prune uncoverable markings */
9  |  |    if P = ∅ then
10 |  |    |    return False
11 |  |    B ← Min(B ∪ P)
12 |  return True
```

Lemma 4.4. *Let I be a downward-closed invariant for $\mathcal{N}$. For every subset $S \subseteq \mathbb{N}^P$, it holds that $\uparrow pre_{\mathcal{N}}^t((\uparrow S) \cap I) = \uparrow(cpre_{\mathcal{N}}^t(S) \cap I)$.*

Proof. The straightforward extension of Lemma 4.3 to sets of markings shows that $pre_{\mathcal{N}}^t(\uparrow S) = \uparrow cpre_{\mathcal{N}}^t(S)$ for every subset $S \subseteq \mathbb{N}^P$. Moreover, it is readily seen that, for every subset $S \subseteq \mathbb{N}^P$, $\uparrow((\uparrow S) \cap I) = \uparrow(S \cap I)$. This property follows from the assumption that I is downward-closed. We derive that

$$\begin{aligned} \uparrow(cpre_{\mathcal{N}}^t(S) \cap I) &= \uparrow((\uparrow cpre_{\mathcal{N}}^t(S)) \cap I) \\ &= \uparrow(pre_{\mathcal{N}}^t(\uparrow S) \cap I) \end{aligned}$$

This concludes the proof of the lemma.   □

The previous lemma leads to a backward coverability algorithm, called ICover and presented on page 6. Basically, this procedure symbolically computes the growing sequence $(U_k)_k$ of upward-closed sets. Let us make the relationship between the procedure and the sequence $(U_k)_k$ more precise. Consider an input instance $(\mathcal{N}, m_{final}, I)$ of ICover. Since the procedure is deterministic, $\text{ICover}(\mathcal{N}, m_{final}, I)$ has a unique maximal execution, that either terminates (at line 10 or 12) or iterates the **while** loop (lines 6–11) indefinitely. Let $\ell_B, \ell_P \in \mathbb{N} \cup \{\infty\}$ denote the numbers of executions of lines 6 and 9, respectively. It is understood that $l_P \leq l_B \leq l_P + 1$, with the convention that $\infty + 1 = \infty$. Let $(B_k)_{k < \ell_B}$ and $(P_k)_{k < \ell_P}$ denote the successive values at lines 6 and 9 of the variables B and P, respectively.

Lemma 4.5. *For every k with $0 \leq k < \ell_B$, the set B_k is a finite basis of U_k. For every k with $0 \leq k < \ell_P$, the set P_k is a finite basis of $\uparrow(U_{k+1} \setminus U_k)$.*

Theorem 4.6. *The procedure* ICover *terminates on every input and is correct.*

Remark 4.7. Petri nets obtained by translation from high-level concurrent programs often contain transitions that cannot be fired from any reachable marking. Downward-closed invariants can be used in a pre-processing algorithm to filter out some of them. Basically, if a transition t is not enabled in any marking of an invariant I, it can be safely removed without modifying the coverability set. Algorithmically, when I is downward-closed, detecting such a property just reduces to a membership problem in I. In fact a transition t is enabled in a downward-closed set of markings D if, and only if, D contains the marking m_t defined by $m_t(p) = F(p,t)$ for every place p.

The algorithm ICover is parametrized by an a priori known downward-closed invariant that is given as input. On the one hand, this invariant needs to be precise enough to discard markings (at line 8) and accelerate the main loop. On the other hand, we need to decide efficiently whether a marking is in the invariant, to avoid slowing down the main loop. The next two sections show how to generate downward-closed invariants with efficient membership testing.

5   State Inequation for Downward-Closed Invariants

The state equation provides a simple over-approximation of Petri net reachability relations that was successfully used in two recent algorithms for deciding the coverability problems [3,7]. This equation is obtained by introducing the total function $\Delta(t)$ in $\mathbb{Z}^P$ called the *displacement* of a transition t and defined for every place p by $\Delta(t)(p) = F(t,p) - F(p,t)$. Let us assume that a marking m_{final} is in the coverability set of a Petri net $\mathcal{N}$. It follows that there exists a word $t_1 \ldots t_k$ of transitions and a marking $m \geq m_{final}$ such that $m_{init} \xrightarrow{t_1} \cdots \xrightarrow{t_k} m$. We derive the following relation:

$$m_{init} + \Delta(t_1) + \cdots + \Delta(t_k) = m \geq m_{final}$$

By reordering the sum $\Delta(t_1) + \cdots + \Delta(t_k)$, we can group together the displacements $\Delta(t)$ corresponding to the same transition t. Denoting by $\lambda(t)$ the number of occurrences of t in the word $t_1 \ldots t_k$, we get:

$$m_{init} + \sum_{t \in T} \lambda(t)\Delta(t) \geq m_{final} \tag{1}$$

The relation (1) is called the *state inequation* for the coverability problem. Notice that a similar equation can be derived for the reachability problem by replacing the inequality by an equality. We do not consider this equality in the sequel since we restrict our attention to the coverability problem. We introduce the following set I_S where $\mathbb{Q}_{\geq 0}$ is the set of non-negative rational numbers.

$$I_S = \{m \in \mathbb{N}^P \mid \exists \lambda \in \mathbb{Q}_{\geq 0}^T : m_{init} + \sum_{t \in T} \lambda(t)\Delta(t) \geq m\} \tag{2}$$

Proposition 5.1. *The set I_S is a downward-closed invariant with a polynomial-time membership problem.*

A more precise downward-closed invariant can be obtained by requiring that $\lambda \in \mathbb{N}^T$. In particular, the pruned backward algorithm presented in Sect. 4 should produce smaller sets of configurations with this more precise invariant. In practice, we do not observe any significant improvement on a large set of benchmarks. Moreover, whereas the membership problem of a marking m is decidable in polynomial time when λ ranges over $\mathbb{Q}_{\geq 0}^T$, the problem becomes NP-complete when λ is restricted to $\mathbb{N}^T$.

6 Sign Analysis for Downward-Closed Invariants

In this section we introduce a downward-closed invariant based on data-flow sign analysis [4]. Rephrased in the context of Petri nets, an invariant I is said to be *inductive* if $m \overset{t}{\to} m'$ and $m \in I$ implies $m' \in I$. Sign analysis then reduces to the computation of the maximal (for the inclusion) set Z of places such that the following set I_Z is an inductive invariant:

$$I_Z = \{m \in \mathbb{N}^P \mid \bigwedge_{p \in Z} m(p) = 0\} \tag{3}$$

The unicity of that set is immediate since the class of sets Z such that I_Z is an invariant is clearly closed under union. In the sequel, Z denotes the maximal set satisfying this property, and this maximal set is shown to be computable in polynomial time thanks to a fixpoint propagation. We introduce the operator $\mathrm{prop}_t : 2^P \to 2^P$ associated to a transition t and defined for any set Q of places as follows:

$$\mathrm{prop}_t(Q) = \begin{cases} \{q \in P \mid F(t,q) > 0\} & \text{if } \bigwedge_{p \in P \setminus Q} F(p,t) = 0 \\ \emptyset & \text{otherwise} \end{cases}$$

Intuitively, if t is a transition such that $\bigwedge_{p \in P \setminus Q} F(p,t) = 0$ then from a marking with large number of tokens in each place of Q, it is possible to fire t. In particular places q satisfying $F(t,q) > 0$ cannot be in Z. This property is formally stated by the following lemma.

Lemma 6.1. *We have $\mathrm{prop}_t(Q) \subseteq P \setminus Z$ for every set $Q \subseteq P \setminus Z$.*

The set Z can be computed as a fixpoint by introducing the non-decreasing sequence $Q_0, Q_1, \ldots$ of places defined as follows:

$$Q_0 = \{q \in P \mid m_{init}(q) > 0\}$$

$$Q_{k+1} = Q_k \cup \bigcup_{t \in T} \mathrm{prop}_t(Q_k)$$

Let us notice that the set $Q = \bigcup_{k \geq 0} Q_k$ is computable in polynomial time. The following lemma shows that Q provides the set Z as a complement.

Lemma 6.2. *We have $Z = P \backslash Q$.*

Corollary 6.3. *The set Z is computable in polynomial time.*

7   Experimental Evaluation

We implemented our approach using the QCover [3] tool as a starting point. This tool, which implements a backward coverability algorithm for Petri nets, is written in Python and relies on the SMT-solver $z3$ [16]. QCover also uses some other heuristics that we kept unchanged. QCover was competitive with others tools especially for uncoverable Petri net. Only the BFC tool performs significantly better on coverable Petri net. We have made two modifications to QCover. First, we have added a pre-processing step (see Remark 4.7) based on sign analysis. Second, we have replaced their pruning technique, which is based on coverability in continuous Petri nets, by the one of our algorithm ICover presented in Sect. 4. ICover is available as a patch [11] for QCover [2].

To test our implementation, we used the same benchmark as Petrinizer [7] and QCover [3]. It comprises models from various sources: Mist [10], BFC [13], Erlang programs abstracted into Petri nets [6], as well as so-called medical and bug-tracking examples [7]. We let each tool work for 2000 s in a machine on Ubuntu Linux 14.04 with Intel(R) Core(TM) i7-4770 CPU at 3.40 GHz with 16 GB of memory for each benchmark. The computation times are the sum of the system and user times. Overall QCover solved 106 uncoverable instances on 115 Petri net and 37 coverable problems on 61 Petri nets. ICover was able to find one more coverable instance. In fact calling QCover on the Petri net computed by the pre-processing, that we will call QCover/Pp, can even solve one more uncoverable instance than ICover. On the 143 instances that QCover solved, the tool took 10318 s, QCover/Pp used 6479 s, and ICover used only 5162 s.

Figure 2(a) shows the comparison between ICover and QCover in time. The straight line represents when the two tools took the same time. Each dot represents a coverability question. When the dot is under the line, it means that ICover was faster than QCover and conversely. There are three instances where QCover performs very well, under a second, and where ICover took a few tens of seconds to answer. For the three cases, the formula used by QCover for coverability in $\mathbb{Q}$ was enough to discard the target as uncoverable and it didn't have to enter in the while loop. But ICover wasn't able to discard the target and had to enter the while loop in the three cases. We also see two dots above the line at the middle of the figure. The pre-processing took respectively 12 and 45 s while the initial Petri net was solved by QCover in respectively 16 and 33 s. The pre-processing has not been optimized yet, and it could probably run faster.

Figure 2(b) and (c) show the intermediate comparisons: ICover versus QCover/Pp and QCover/Pp versus QCover. We can observe that the pre-processing has a major impact on the good performance of ICover compared to QCover.

Figure 2(e) and (f) aims to show the effect of the pre-processing on the size of Petri nets. The former show the percentage of places left after pre-processing.

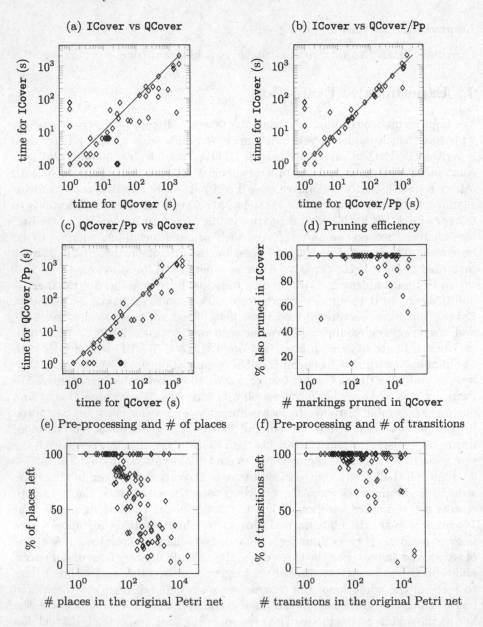

Fig. 2. Experimental results for ICover, QCover and QCover/Pp

Some Petri nets kept all their places but others were left with only 2.5 % of their initial places. And most of Petri nets lost a significant number of places. The latter shows the percentages of transitions left after the pre-processing. Overall less transitions were cut than places. Half of the Petri nets kept all their transitions, but some were left with only 4 % of their initial transitions.

Figure 2(d) compares the efficiency of pruning between ICover and QCover. Again, each dot represents a coverability question. As discussed in Sect. 8, QCover always prunes at least as many markings as ICover (but at the expense of more complex pruning tests). A value of 100 % means that ICover was able to prune the same markings as QCover. It turns out that on most instances, this perfect value of 100 % is obtained. This is rather surprising at first sight, and warrants an investigation, which is the focus of the next section.

8   Comparison with Continuous Petri Net

Continuous Petri nets are defined like Petri nets except that transitions can be fired a non-negative rational number of times. The firing of such a transition produces markings with non-negative rational numbers of tokens. Under such a semantics, called the *continuous semantics*, the reachability problem was recently proved to be decidable in polynomial time [9]. Based on this observation, the tool QCover implements the pruning backward coverability algorithm presented in Sect. 3 with a downward-closed invariant derived from the continuous semantics. Whereas this invariant is more precise than the downward-closed invariant obtained from the state inequation introduced in Sect. 5, we have seen in Sect. 7 that such an improvement is overall not useful in practice for the pruning backward algorithm. In this section, we provide a simple structural condition on Petri nets in such a way the two kinds of downward-closed invariants derived respectively from the continuous semantics and the state inequation are "almost" equal. This structural condition is shown to be natural since it is fulfilled by the Petri nets obtained after the pre-processing introduced in Remark 4.7.

A *continuous marking* is a mapping $m \in \mathbb{Q}_{\geq 0}^{P}$ where $\mathbb{Q}_{\geq 0}$ denotes the set of non-negative rational numbers, and P the set of places. Given $r \in \mathbb{Q}_{\geq 0}$ and a transition t, the continuous rt-step binary relation $\xrightarrow{\ rt\ }$ over the continuous markings is defined by

$$m \xrightarrow{\ rt\ } m' \iff \forall p \in P : m(p) \geq r.F(p,t) \wedge m'(p) = m(p) - r.F(p,t) + r.F(t,p)$$

The one-step continuous binary relation $\dashrightarrow$ is the union of these rt-step relations. Formally, $m \dashrightarrow m'$ if there exists $r \in \mathbb{Q}_{\geq 0}$ and $t \in T$ such that $m \xrightarrow{\ rt\ } m'$. The many-step continuous binary relation $\xdashrightarrow{*}$ is the reflexive-transitive closure of $\dashrightarrow$. We also introduce the binary relation $\xdashrightarrow{\infty}$ defined over the continuous markings by $m \xdashrightarrow{\infty} m'$ if there exists a sequence $(m_k)_{k \geq 0}$ of continuous markings that *converges* towards m' with the classical topology on $\mathbb{Q}_{\geq 0}^{P}$ and such that $m \xdashrightarrow{*} m_k$ for every k.

Example 8.1. Let us look back at the simple Petri net $\mathcal{N}$ depicted in Fig. 1. For every positive natural number k, we have:

$$(1,0,0) \xdashrightarrow{\frac{1}{k}t_1} (1 - \frac{1}{k}, \frac{1}{k}, 0) \xdashrightarrow{\frac{1}{k}t_2 \frac{1}{k}t_3} (1 - \frac{1}{k}, \frac{2}{k}, \frac{1}{k}) \dots \xdashrightarrow{\frac{1}{k}t_2 \frac{1}{k}t_3} (1 - \frac{1}{k}, 1 + \frac{1}{k}, 1)$$

It follows that $(1,0,0) \xrightarrow{\infty} (1,1,1)$. Notice that the relation $(1,0,0) \xrightarrow{*} (1,1,1)$ does not hold.

The downward-closed invariant used in the tool `QCover` for implementing the pruning backward algorithm is defined as follows:

$$I_C = \{m \in \mathbb{N}^P \mid \exists m' \in \mathbb{Q}_{\geq 0}^P : m_{init} \xrightarrow{*} m' \geq m\} \tag{4}$$

Recall that in Sect. 5 we introduced the set I_S for denoting the downward-closed invariant derived from the state inequation. The following result[1] provides a characterization of that invariant when the Petri net satisfies a structural condition.

Theorem 8.2 ([18, **Theorem 7**]). *If every transition is fireable from the downward-closed invariant I_Z introduced in Sect. 6, we have:*

$$I_S = \{m \in \mathbb{N}^P \mid \exists m' \in \mathbb{Q}_{\geq 0}^P : m_{init} \xrightarrow{\infty} m' \geq m\} \tag{5}$$

The two equalities Eqs. (4) and (5) show that I_S and I_C are very similar for Petri nets satisfying the structural condition stated in Theorem 8.2. This condition will be fulfilled by the Petri nets produced by the pre-processing algorithm introduced in Remark 4.7. Notice that even if the membership problem in I_S and I_C are both decidable in polynomial time, the extra computational cost for deciding the membership problem for the invariant I_C, even for efficient SMT solvers like Z3, is not neglectable. Naturally, if a marking is in I_C then it is also in I_S, and the converse property is false in general as shown by Example 8.1. However, in practice, we observed that configurations that are in I_S are very often also in I_C (see Fig. 2(d)), as already mentioned in Sect. 7.

9   Conclusion

Petri nets have recently been used as low-level models for model-checking concurrent systems written in high-level programming languages [5,6]. The original verification question on the concurrent program reduces to a coverability question on the resulting Petri net. We have proposed in this paper a family of simple coverability algorithms parametrized by downward-closed invariants. As future work, we intend to look for classes of downward-closed invariants with a good tradeoff between precision and efficient membership.

---

[1] The statement of Theorem 7 in [18] is wrong since it is based on a too strong definition of limit-reachability. However, the proof becomes correct with our definitions and notations.

References

1. Abdulla, P.A., Cerans, K., Jonsson, B., Tsay, Y.: Algorithmic analysis of programs with well quasi-ordered domains. Inf. Comput. **160**(1–2), 109–127 (2000)
2. Blondin, M., Finkel, A., Haase, C., Haddad, S.: QCover with benchmarks. http://www-etud.iro.umontreal.ca/~blondimi/doc/qcover_with_benchmarks.zip
3. Blondin, M., Finkel, A., Haase, C., Haddad, S.: Approaching the coverability problem continuously. In: Chechik, M., Raskin, J.-F. (eds.) TACAS 2016. LNCS, vol. 9636, pp. 480–496. Springer, Heidelberg (2016). doi:10.1007/978-3-662-49674-9_28
4. Cousot, P., Cousot, R.: Abstract interpretation: a unified lattice model for static analysis of programs by construction or approximation of fixpoints. In: POPL, pp. 238–252. ACM (1977)
5. Donaldson, A., Kaiser, A., Kroening, D., Wahl, T.: Symmetry-aware predicate abstraction for shared-variable concurrent programs. In: Gopalakrishnan, G., Qadeer, S. (eds.) CAV 2011. LNCS, vol. 6806, pp. 356–371. Springer, Heidelberg (2011)
6. D'Osualdo, E., Kochems, J., Ong, C.-H.L.: Automatic verification of Erlang-style concurrency. In: Logozzo, F., Fähndrich, M. (eds.) Static Analysis. LNCS, vol. 7935, pp. 454–476. Springer, Heidelberg (2013)
7. Esparza, J., Ledesma-Garza, R., Majumdar, R., Meyer, P., Niksic, F.: An SMT-based approach to coverability analysis. In: Biere, A., Bloem, R. (eds.) CAV 2014. LNCS, vol. 8559, pp. 603–619. Springer, Heidelberg (2014)
8. Finkel, A., Schnoebelen, P.: Well-structured transition systems everywhere!. Inf. Comput. **256**(1–2), 63–92 (2001)
9. Fraca, E., Haddad, S.: Complexity analysis of continuous Petri nets. Inf. Comput. **137**(1), 1–28 (2015)
10. Ganty, P.: Mist - a safety checker for petri nets and extensions. http://github.com/pierreganty/mist
11. Geffroy, T., Leroux, J., Sutre, G.: ICover patch. http://dept-info.labri.u-bordeaux.fr/~tgeffroy/icover/
12. German, S.M., Sistla, A.P.: Reasoning about systems with many processes. Inf. Comput. **39**(3), 675–735 (1992)
13. Kaiser, A., Kroening, D., Wahl, T.: A widening approach to multithreaded program verification. ACM Trans. Program. Lang. Syst. **36**(4), 14:1–14:29 (2014)
14. Karp, R.M., Miller, R.E.: Parallel program schemata. J. Comput. Syst. Sci. **3**(2), 147–195 (1969)
15. Lipton, R.J.: The reachability problem requires exponential space. Technical report 62, Yale University (1976)
16. de Moura, L., Bjørner, N.S.: Z3: an efficient SMT solver. In: Ramakrishnan, C.R., Rehof, J. (eds.) TACAS 2008. LNCS, vol. 4963, pp. 337–340. Springer, Heidelberg (2008)
17. Rackoff, C.: The covering and boundedness problems for vector addition systems. Theor. Comput. Sci. **6**(2), 223–231 (1978)
18. Recalde, L., Teruel, E., Silva, M.: Autonomous continuous P/T systems. In: Donatelli, S., Kleijn, J. (eds.) ICATPN 1999. LNCS, pp. 107–126. Springer, Heidelberg (1999)

Safety Property-Driven Stubborn Sets

Henri Hansen[✉] and Antti Valmari

Department of Mathematics, Tampere University of Technology,
PO-Box 553, 33101 Tampere, Finland
henri.hansen@tut.fi

Abstract. A new reduced state space construction method is presented
where in every constructed state, the set of transitions that are fired is
chosen based on the safety property that is being verified. Typical earlier
methods only take the property into account in one state of each cycle
or in one state of each terminal strong component of the reduced state
space. They may fire totally irrelevant transitions in the other states.
Where the property is taken into account, typically many or all enabled
transitions are fired. This has spoiled attempts to be property-driven in
every state. The present study exploits an idea that was published in
2016 with which this can be avoided. Furthermore, most earlier methods
classify the transitions to visible and invisible. The new method uses
a novel improved concept. An experiment is presented where the new
concept provides significant improvement to the reduction results.

1 Introduction

Stubborn sets and related methods reduce the size of a state space by eliminating unnecessary transitions (see [10] for a comparison of ample, persistent,
and stubborn sets). The state space of a system under verification is built by
including only a subset of its enabled transitions in each state. The set of necessary transitions depends on the property that is being verified. Previous work in
these methods has dealt with preservation of various property classes, from rep-
resentatives of terminating (deadlocking) executions to LTL_X and even CTL_X^*.

The preservation of a property class is achieved by establishing conditions
that make sure a sufficient set of different interleavings are explored. These
provisos are often of three types. The first ones are found in almost all stubborn
set methods independently of the property class. The second ones deal with
some concept of *visibility*, which means identifying transitions whose execution
order is potentially essential for the preservation of the property. This means,
for instance, transitions that may change the truth-value of some propositions
that appear in the property under verification. The third ones deal with the
so-called *ignoring problem*, and serve to prevent postponing relevant transitions
indefinitely.

Previous work [5] has shown that relaxing the visibility rule during state space
construction improves reduction results, and the approach can be seen as an
early property-driven method. Solutions to the ignoring problem [1] use different

© Springer International Publishing Switzerland 2016
K.G. Larsen et al. (Eds.): RP 2016, LNCS 9899, pp. 90–103, 2016.
DOI: 10.1007/978-3-319-45994-3_7

· conditions for the preservation of safety and liveness violations. A property-driven method was suggested already in [7], but it was not successful, because the closure approach used in it led to the investigation of too many transitions.

The stubborn set method has the unique feature that its formulation makes it possible to include disabled transitions in the set and we make use of it in this study. This and other differences between stubborn sets and other methods have been addressed in [10]. The main contribution of this study is the definition and proof of correctness of a set of property-driven conditions for safety violations. The combination of conditions is to the best of our knowledge the least restrictive that has been proposed. The conditions depend on the particular property and we also discuss how these conditions are implemented. We also provide motivating examples that demonstrate the potential of our method.

Section 2 gives the background definitions for transition systems and standard stubborn sets that preserve deadlocks. Proofs of the theorems are omitted in that section, as they are not novel results. Section 3 presents a property-driven solution to the ignoring problem. The solution improves upon one that has appeared in [11] by employing a powerful new idea presented in [10]. In this article we also explain with an example why the idea in [10] is powerful. Section 4 presents a property-driven relaxation of the visibility condition, and proves that together with the solution to the ignoring problem, it preserves all safety properties. Section 5 contains a brief discussion about implementation of the new ideas. Section 6 contains as an example a protocol and a property, and verification results that compare the performance of the traditional visibility condition and the novel conditions.

2   Technical Background

We make no strong assumptions about how systems under verification are expressed, only that the system executes deterministic *structural transitions*. The semantics are given over *transition systems* or TS. Given a set T of structural transitions, TS over T is the tuple $(S_M, \delta_M, \hat{s}_M)$ where S_M is the set of states, $\delta_M : S_M \times T \to S_M$ is a partial *transition function* and $\hat{s}_M \in S_M$ is the *initial state*. We use the subscript M to indicate that the transition system is a model under verification.

We write $\delta_M(s, a) = \bot$ if the transition is not defined at s. We write $\mathsf{en}(s) = \{t \mid \delta_M(s, t) \neq \bot\}$, for the set of *enabled transitions* at s. If $\mathsf{en}(s) = \emptyset$ we say that s is a *deadlock*. We write $s \xrightarrow{t} s'$ if $\delta(s, t) = s'$, and generalize this to $s_0 \xrightarrow{t_1 \cdots t_n} s_n$ in the natural way.

Properties of the system are expressed as languages over *events* Σ. Let Σ^* denote the set of finite words over Σ, and let ε denote the empty word. We assume $\varepsilon \notin \Sigma$. We assume each transition $t \in T$ is associated either with an event in Σ or ε. This is expressed by a mapping $e : T \to \Sigma \cup \{\varepsilon\}$. We extend the mapping e to $T^* \to \Sigma^*$. If $\rho = t_1 \cdots t_n$ for $n > 1$, $e(\rho)$ is defined $e(\rho) = e(t_1)e(t_2 \cdots t_n)$. A transition t such that $e(t) \neq \varepsilon$ is said to be *visible*, other transitions are *invisible*.

Model checking of safety properties of, say LTL_X, can be conducted with this approach [4]. We make use of automata in this article to express the properties under verification. An automaton is a tuple $(P, \delta_A, \hat{p}, F)$ where $\delta_A : P \times \Sigma \to P$ is a partial transition function, $\hat{p} \in P$ is the initial state, and $F \subseteq P$ is the set of *error states*. We use the same notation as with TS, and write $p_0 \xrightarrow{a_1 \cdots a_n} p_n$ for executions of automata. Given a property under verification, a *counterexample* is some $\sigma \in \Sigma^*$ that violates the property, and this corresponds to an execution $\hat{p} \xrightarrow{\sigma} p$ of the automaton such that $p \in F$.

An execution $\hat{s}_M \xrightarrow{t_1 \cdots t_n} s_n$ of a TS is a *violating execution* if and only if $e(t_1 \cdots t_n)$ is a counterexample. Model checking against an automaton can be done by constructing a *product automaton* (PA) $(S_M \times P, \delta, (\hat{s}_M, \hat{p}), S_M \times F)$ where $\delta((s, p), t) = (s', p')$ if $\delta_M(s, t) = s'$, and

1. $p = p'$ and $e(t) = \varepsilon$, or
2. $p \xrightarrow{a} p'$ and $e(t) = a$.

Given a TS and an automaton, if $a_1 a_2 \cdots a_n$ is a counterexample, $\hat{p} = p_0$ and $\hat{s}_M = s_0$ and $s_0 \xrightarrow{t_1 \cdots t_m} s_m$ is a violating execution such that $e(t_1 \cdots t_m) = a_1 \cdots a_n$, there exists a sequence $(s_0, p_0) \xrightarrow{t_1} \cdots \xrightarrow{t_m} (s_m, p_n)$ such that $p_0 \xrightarrow{a_1 a_2 \cdots a_n} p_n$ and $p_n \in F$. We use the terms *remaining counterexample* and *remaining violating execution* for suffixes of counterexamples such that if $e(t_1 \cdots t_j) = a_1 \cdots a_i$, we call $a_{i+1} a_{i+2} \cdots a_n$ a remaining counterexample at (s_j, p_i) and $s_j \xrightarrow{t_{j+1} t_{j+2} \cdots t_m} s_m$ a remaining violating execution. Through out the rest of this study, whenever the property is involved in the discussion, we apply the method to the product automaton. This is not a problem when there is no property, because the case without the automaton is equivalent to the case with a trivial one-state automaton, with $\Sigma = \emptyset$.

Given a PA $(S, \delta, \hat{s}, F)$, we define a *reduction function* as any function $R : S \to 2^T$, and a *reduced PA* as the smallest PA $(S_R, \delta_R, \hat{s}, F_R)$ that satisfies:

1. $\hat{s} \in S_R$,
2. if $s \in S_R$ and $t \in R(s)$ and $s \xrightarrow{t} s'$, then $s' \in S_R$, and
3. $\delta_R(s, t) = \delta(s, t)$ if $t \in R(s)$ and $\perp$ otherwise.
4. $F_R = F \cap S_R$

The traditional deadlock-preserving *stubborn sets* are defined as follows: A set $\mathsf{stubb}(s) \subseteq T$ is *stubborn* at the state s if it satisfies

D0 If $\mathsf{en}(s) \neq \emptyset$ then $\mathsf{stubb}(s) \cap \mathsf{en}(s) \neq \emptyset$.

D1 If $t \in \mathsf{stubb}(s)$, $t_i \notin \mathsf{stubb}(s)$ for $1 \leq i \leq n$, and $s \xrightarrow{t_1 \cdots t_n t} s'$, then $s \xrightarrow{t t_1 \cdots t_n} s'$.

D2 If $t \in \mathsf{stubb}(s) \cap \mathsf{en}(s)$ and $t_i \notin \mathsf{stubb}(s)$ for $1 \leq i \leq n$, then $s \xrightarrow{t_1 \cdots t_n t}$.

Condition **D2** states that enabled transitions in the stubborn set cannot be disabled by executing transitions that are outside the stubborn set. This version of stubborn sets is also known as *strong* stubborn sets. It is not the most general existing theory, but we use it as a reference as it is one that lends itself to a simple and effective implementation.

The following theorem is well-known, and the proof can be found in several publications, including [10]. We state it for reference.

Theorem 1. *Let $M = (S, \delta, \hat{s})$ be a PA and* stubb *be a reduction function that satisfies D0, D1, and D2 at every $s \in S_{stubb}$, and let $M_{stubb} = (S_{stubb}, \delta_{stubb}, \hat{s})$ be the reduced PA. Let $s_0 \in S_{stubb}$ and $s_0 \xrightarrow{t_1 \cdots t_n} s_n$ be an execution of M such that s_n is a deadlock. Then there is an execution $s_0 \xrightarrow{u_1 \cdots u_n} s_n$ of M_{stubb} where $u_1 \cdots u_n$ is a permutation of $t_1 \cdots t_n$.*

The definition of stubborn sets does not immediately yield an obvious method by which to compute stubborn sets. To this end, the literature often makes use of a concept of *independence*, a relation that is meant to capture the situation where pairs of transitions satisfy something akin to the definition of **D1** and **D2**. The following characterization makes it possible to compute stubborn sets, which will be discussed in Sect. 5. For every state s, let $\mathsf{reach}(s)$ denote the set of states reachable from s in $(S, \delta, \hat{s})$. We define a relation $\leadsto_s$ over T as any relation that satisfies the following:

1. For every $t \in \mathsf{en}(s)$, $t_1 \subset T$, and $s' \subset \mathsf{reach}(s)$, if $t, t_1 \in \mathsf{en}(s')$, then either $t \leadsto_s t_1$ or there is a state s'' such that $s' \xrightarrow{tt_1} s''$ and $s' \xrightarrow{t_1 t} s''$.
2. If $t \notin \mathsf{en}(s)$, then for every s' and $t_1, \ldots, t_n$, if $s \xrightarrow{t_1 \cdots t_n} s'$ and $t \in \mathsf{en}(s')$, there is some t_i such that $t \leadsto_s t_i$.

The purpose of the relation is made explicit in the following lemma:

Lemma 1. *Let U be a set such that at s, for every $t, u \in T$, if $t \in U$ and $t \leadsto_s u$ then $u \in U$. Then U satisfies D1 and D2 at s.*

This lemma makes it possible to devise algorithms for computing stubborn sets [10,11]. Different kinds of characterizations do exist, in which a relation similar to $\leadsto_s$ is used to compute different variants of stubborn sets [3], but they tend to be more complicated, so we do not address them in this article.

3   Property-Based Solution to the Ignoring Problem

Consider a concurrent system given in Fig. 1. The system consists of four concurrent processes over shared variables. We assume only the variable x is shared, and initially $x = 0$. Other features of the system are omitted. The transition v_1 is disabled unless $x > 0$. All other transitions are enabled whenever the process is in the appropriate control state. The resulting transition system has 14 states, given in the rightmost figure.

Assume that we are only interested in whether the transition v_1 can be executed. The conditions presented this far are not sufficient to establish this. The set $\{w_1\}$ satisfies **D0, D1,** and **D2** in every state, but it merely creates a loop. This phenomenon is known as the *ignoring problem*.

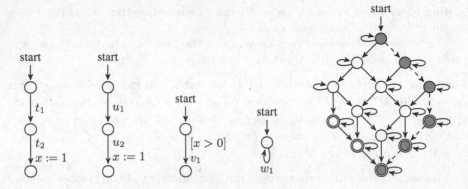

Fig. 1. Ignoring example

There are several conditions in the literature for solving the ignoring problem [1]. Solutions have been discussed in [10], but some discussion is warranted here. Alternatives in the case of safety properties include not completing a terminal strong component of the model before all the enabled transitions or all the visible transitions have been included in some stubborn set in the component. Such rules may include unnecessary transitions in the set for several reasons. As an example, we discuss the latter rule.

Let $\hat{s}$ be the initial state of the system in Fig. 1. Assume, for arguments sake, that an algorithm first explores the transition that closes the loop, and a cycle condition that includes all visible transitions – in this case v_1 – in the stubborn set at $\hat{s}$ is used. The transition v_1 is disabled at $\hat{s}$ and $\hat{s} \xrightarrow{t_1 t_2 v_1}$ holds. No matter what algorithm is used to construct the stubborn set, either t_1 or t_2 is in the result, because otherwise **D1** does not hold. If t_2 is chosen, and because $t_2 \notin \text{en}(\hat{s})$, also t_1 must be in the set. By similar reasoning, because $\hat{s} \xrightarrow{u_1 u_2 v_1}$ holds, also u_1 would be in the set. Repeating the reasoning in the resulting states, all the states (though not all the edges) in Fig. 1 are constructed.

We shall now proceed to introduce a better set of conditions, one that does not force us to include both t_1 and u_1 in the set at the same time. It was first introduced in [10], but we modify the theory by weakening the conditions further, using **N** instead of **D2**. The condition is based on the concept of a set of *interesting transitions*. In our example $\{v_1\}$ is the set of interesting transitions. The set of interesting transitions depends on the property that we are verifying. We shall elaborate the concept in the next section.

Given a set U of transitions, we define the following condition for state s:

Dd If $t \in U$, $t_i \notin U$ for $1 \leq i \leq n$, and $s \xrightarrow{t_1 \cdots t_n t} s'$, then $t \in \text{en}(s)$

A set that satisfies the condition **Dd** has the property that if a transition t of the set is disabled at s, then t cannot become enabled by firing only transitions outside the set.

We say that $t \in \mathsf{stubb}(s) \cap \mathsf{en}(s)$ is *neutral* if and only if for every $t_1, \ldots, t_n \notin \mathsf{stubb}(s)$, if $s \xrightarrow{t_1 \cdots t_n}$, then $s \xrightarrow{tt_1 \cdots t_n}$. The following condition will be used in place of **D2**.

N If $\mathsf{stubb}(s) \cap \mathsf{en}(s) \neq \emptyset$, then $\mathsf{stubb}(s)$ contains a neutral transition.

The condition **N** guarantees that the possibility of executing a given sequence of transitions that are outside the stubborn set is preserved. The rest of the theory then guarantees that if such a sequence is interesting in some way, it will be explored eventually.

For $s, s' \in S_{\mathsf{stubb}}$, we define $s \to_N s'$ if and only if there is an execution $s = s_0 \xrightarrow{t_1} s_1 \xrightarrow{t_2} \cdots \xrightarrow{t_n} s_n = s'$ in the reduced product, such that every t_i is a neutral transition at s_{i-1}.

We define the following condition for state s; it entails a set T_s, not itself necessarily stubborn.

S There exists some set $T_s \subseteq T$ that satisfies **Dd** and contains all interesting transitions, and for every $t \in T_s \cap \mathsf{en}(s)$ there is some s_t such that $s \to_N s_t$ and $t \in \mathsf{stubb}(s_t)$.

The intuition behind the condition **S** is best explained by the following lemma.

Lemma 2. *Assume $s_0 \in S_{\mathsf{stubb}}$, $\mathsf{stubb}(s_0)$ satisfies **S**, and $s_0 \xrightarrow{t_1 \cdots t_n} s_n$, where t_n is interesting. Then there are $s'_0, \ldots, s'_m$ and neutral transitions $u_1, \ldots, u_m$ such that $s'_0 = s_0$, $s'_0 \xrightarrow{u_1} s'_1 \xrightarrow{u_2} \cdots \xrightarrow{u_m} s'_m$, $\{t_1, \ldots, t_n\} \cap \mathsf{stubb}(s'_i) = \emptyset$ for every $0 \leq i < m$, and $\{t_1, \ldots, t_n\} \cap \mathsf{stubb}(s'_m) \neq \emptyset$.*

Proof. Because $t_n \in T_s$, there is $1 \leq i \leq n$ such that $t_i \in T_s$ but $t_j \notin T_s$ for $1 \leq j < i$. Due to **Dd** $t_i \in \mathsf{en}(s_0)$. The assumption says there is s_{t_i} such that $t_i \in \mathsf{stubb}(s_{t_i})$ and $s_0 \to_N s_{t_i}$. Let the states along this path be called $s'_0, \ldots, s'_h$. So $s'_0 = s_0$, $s'_h = s_{t_i}$ and $t_i \in \{t_1, \ldots, t_n\} \cap \mathsf{stubb}(s'_h)$. Thus there is the smallest m such that $\{t_1, \ldots, t_n\} \cap \mathsf{stubb}(s'_m) \neq \emptyset$, completing the proof. $\square$

In the initial state of our example, we would have $T_{\hat{s}} = \{v_1, t_2, t_1, u_2, u_1\}$ and $T_{\hat{s}} \cap \mathsf{en}(\hat{s}) = \{t_1, u_1\}$, so we may choose $\mathsf{stubb}(\hat{s}) = \{u_1\}$, constructing the grey state below the initial state. There we have $T_s = \{v_1, t_2, t_1, u_2\}$, and $T_s \cap \mathsf{en}(s) = \{t_1, u_2\}$, and we can have $\mathsf{stubb}(s) = \{u_2\}$. Continuing like this, only the 6 grey states are constructed, which is clearly better than the 14 states that we had before.

4   Property-Driven Visibility

Consider a very simple system given in Fig. 2. It is constructed from two concurrent processes, one can execute transition t and the other transitions u and v. Assume we have the events $\Sigma = \{a, b\}$, and that $e(t) = a$, $e(u) = \varepsilon$ and $e(v) = b$. The property under verification is "In any (partial) execution, the number of as

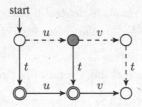

Fig. 2. Visibility example

never exceeds the number of bs", so that a counterexample to the property is any sequence where the number of as exceeds the number of bs.

The property can be violated by ab but not by ba, and the states where this is detected are drawn with double circles in the figure. If we consider stubborn sets with **D0**, **D1** and **D2** then a permissible stubborn set reduction might be to preserve only the dashed transitions of the system model, and this would omit the double circled states, which are exactly the states in which the property in question is violated. Use of **D1** and **S** will not help even if we declare both t and v interesting, because these conditions are similarly satisfied by the execution $\hat{s} \xrightarrow{uvt}$ which misses the counterexample.

The problem here is usually solved by requiring that visible transitions must preserve their order. Recall that a transition $t \in T$ was defined as being visible if $e(t) \in \Sigma$. The set of visible transitions is denoted T_v. In the example, the transitions t and v are visible, whereas u is not. Visibility is traditionally used in stubborn set theory by adding the following requirement:

V If $\mathsf{stubb}(s_0) \cap \mathsf{en}(s_0) \cap T_v \neq \emptyset$, then $T_v \subseteq \mathsf{stubb}(s_0)$. I.e., if a visible transition is enabled and stubborn, all visible transitions (including disabled ones) are stubborn.

D1, **D2**, **S** and **V** guarantee that for every deadlocking execution, the order between visible transitions is preserved, as stated by the following theorem.

Theorem 2. *Let* stubb *be a reduction function that satisfies* **D1**, **D2**, **S** *and* **V** *at every state,* $s_0 \in S_{\mathsf{stubb}}$, *and* $s_0 \xrightarrow{t_1 \cdots t_n}$. *Then* $s_0 \xrightarrow{u_1 \cdots u_n}$ *in* $(S_{\mathsf{stubb}}, \delta_{\mathsf{stubb}}, \hat{s})$, *and* $e(t_1 \cdots t_n) = e(u_1 \cdots u_n)$.

The proof can be found, for example in [10].

A closer inspection of the system in the example reveals a weakness in the use of **V**. From the initial state, the stubborn set may be constructed in such a way that it contains only u, but from the grey state, all enabled transitions are taken, so that the reduction will omit only one state. Even if construction is stopped when the counterexample $\hat{s} \xrightarrow{ut}$ is constructed, the algorithm may first explore the branch where v is taken first, so that five states are generated in total. If, on the other hand t is chosen in the initial state, then visibility forces the inclusion of v, which in turn forces the inclusion of u, and no reduction is gained. At worst five states end up being explored even if construction stops when an error is found.

If we analyse the property more closely, however, we notice that v, though visible, *can never appear before t in a violating execution*. This actually comes, not from the system behaviour, but from the property: if σ is any counterexample, $a\sigma$ is also a counterexample. Transitions that map to a and transitions that map to b, though all visible, need not preserve *all* orders in which they are explored, it suffices to explore the orders that lead to a counterexample.

Let $t \in \mathsf{stubb}(s) \cap \mathsf{en}(s), t_1, \ldots, t_n \notin \mathsf{stubb}(s)$ and $u_1, \ldots, u_m \in T$. We define the following conditions:

V1 if $e(t_1 \cdots t_n t u_1 \cdots u_m)$ is a remaining counterexample at s then some prefix of $e(t t_1 \cdots t_n u_1 \cdots u_m)$ is a remaining counterexample at s.

V2 if $e(t_1 \cdots t_n)$ is a remaining counterexample at s, then some prefix of $e(t t_1 \cdots t_n)$ is a remaining counterexample at s.

A set of interesting transitions needs to be defined for the remaining counterexample. Let $\Sigma_s^i \subseteq \Sigma$. It is *interesting* at s if every non-empty remaining counterexample at s contains at least one event from Σ_s^i. The set of *interesting transitions* is the set $\{t \in T \mid e(t) \in \Sigma_s^i\}$.

Theorem 3. *If* stubb *is a reduction function that satisfies* **D1, S, V1** *and* **V2** *at every state of* M_{stubb} *and* M *has a violating execution, then* M_{stubb} *has a violating execution.*

Proof. The proof is by induction. Let $s_0 \xrightarrow{t_1 t_2 \cdots t_n} s_n$ be a (remaining) violating execution at s_0, $s_0 \in S_{\mathsf{stubb}}$. If $n = 0$, the empty string is a counterexample and the claim holds trivially. Otherwise at least one of $t_1, \ldots, t_n$ is interesting, by definition.

Let t_i be the last interesting transition in the violating execution. Lemma 2 gives us $s_0 \xrightarrow{u_1 \cdots u_m} s'_m$ of neutral transitions. Neutrality guarantees that $s'_m \xrightarrow{t_1 t_2 \cdots t_i} s^i_m$ for some s^i_m. Applying **V2** m times guarantees that some prefix of $s_0 \xrightarrow{u_1 \cdots u_m t_1 t_2 \cdots t_i}$ is a remaining violating execution; note that the violating execution may even consist of some prefix of $s_0 \xrightarrow{u_1 \cdots u_m}$ which would complete the proof immediately.

Assume then that no prefix of $s_0 \xrightarrow{u_1 \cdots u_m} s'_m$ is a violating execution. By Lemma 2, there is a j, $1 \le j \le i$ such that $t_j \in \mathsf{stubb}(s'_m)$. Thus choosing the minimal such j, we have $s'_m \xrightarrow{t_j} s''_m$ for some $s''_m \in S_{\mathsf{stubb}}$, from which **D1** gives $s''_m \xrightarrow{t_1 t_2 \cdots t_{j-1} t_{j+1} \cdots t_i} s^i_m$. **V1** guarantees that some prefix of this execution is a remaining violating execution, completing the inductive step. $\square$

The conditions **V1** and **V2** are *property driven* conditions. They do not guarantee that *all orderings* of visible transitions are preserved, only that sufficiently many to detect violating executions if there are any. The $\leadsto_s$-characterization we gave in the previous section can be used here; if we can deduce, as in our example, that exploring only sequences where t occurs before v does not run the risk of missing remaining counterexamples, so we need *not* require that $t \leadsto_s v$. That is the case in our example. An example of analysing the properties of the automaton to determine a $\leadsto_s$ that guarantees **V1** and **V2** is discussed in Sect. 6.

5   On the Algorithmic Aspects of the Method

We suggest the following algorithm for implementing the method developed in Sects. 3 and 4. It has been adapted from [11]; please see it for further details. Its design aims at computing small stubborn sets that satisfy **D1**, **N**, **V1**, and **V2**, and making them gradually bigger as needed to satisfy **S**.

The algorithm uses two sub-algorithms, $\mathsf{clsr}(t)$ and $\mathsf{esc}(t)$, where t is a transition. They work on the $\leadsto_s$-relation from Sect. 2. $\mathsf{clsr}(t)$ simply computes the reflexive transitive closure of t. $\mathsf{esc}(t)$ ("enabled strong component") either computes a minimal closed subset of the closure that contains at least one enabled transition, or indicates that no enabled transition is reachable from t. It is based on Tarjan's algorithm [2,6].

It has been described in many publications (e.g., [10]) how an easily computable $\leadsto_s$ can be found such that each closure satisfies **D1**, **D2**, and **V**. The same idea immediately applies to **Dd**. The switch from **V** to **V1** and **V2** is trivial. How to exploit **N** is future work, but in the meantime **D2** can be used in its place, since **D1** and **D2** imply **N**.

The reduced product of the model and the automaton is constructed in depth-first order. Tarjan's algorithm is applied to recognize terminal strong components of the result. Let s be a state, T_s be as in the definition of **S**, and $t_1, \ldots, t_n$ be the enabled transitions in T_s. For each totally unprocessed state s and each time when the algorithm is about to backtrack from a terminal strong component by backtracking from s, the next sets in the following sequence are computed until either the list is exhausted or a new transition is fired in s: $\mathsf{esc}(t_1), \ldots, \mathsf{esc}(t_n)$, $\mathsf{clsr}(t_1), \ldots, \mathsf{clsr}(t_n)$. If all enabled transitions of the set have been fired inside the component, then the set is skipped, otherwise it is used as an extension of the stubborn set in s.

Unfortunately, our tool [8] does not yet have an implementation of this algorithm. Instead, it implements **D0**, **D1**, **D2**, **V1**, and **V2**. Fortunately, our example system has the property that from every reachable state, a deadlock is reachable. This trivially guarantees **S**. So the results from our experiments are correct, but the reduction that is obtained may be worse than would be obtained with a proper implementation.

6   An Example

We demonstrate the ideas using a modified alternating bit protocol and its specification. The example is closely related to the example in [11], with modifications to make certain specification issues relevant.

The alternating bit protocol provides reliable transmission of messages over unreliable channels. In Fig. 3 left, the channels are shown as Dchan, Achan, Dloss, and Aloss, where the former are reliable fifo queues of fixed finite capacity and the latter model the possibility of a data packet being lost in transmit. Sender and Receiver co-operate so that each message given to the protocol via sen is eventually delivered via rec, without being lost or duplicated and without the order of the messages being changed.

The only feature not drawn in the figure is that in all the states where Sender is ready to send a message, it may also decide to terminate. This feature makes sure the protocol can reach a terminating state from all its states, i.e., it is AG EF- terminating. This guarantees that stubborn sets that satisfy D1 and D2, trivially also satisfy S. Conversely, stubborn sets also guarantee [9] that the reduced system is AG EF- terminating if and only if the original is.

For each message that Receiver receives via Dchan, it sends an acknowledgement via Achan. If the acknowledgement does not arrive quickly enough, Sender sends the same message again. Each data packet in the channels contains an additional bit, *the alternating bit*, via which Sender and Receiver can distinguish relevant data packets from outdated ones. If either channel is totally broken (i.e., Dloss or Aloss consumes all data packets), the alternating bit protocol collapses into an unproductive infinite loop where Sender sends the same message again and again.

Our example studies a more complicated protocol that has an upper bound to the number of sending attempts. If Sender has tried that many times without getting the acknowledgement, it replies err. Otherwise, it replies ok. Now every received message must have a unique corresponding sent message in the right order, but not necessarily the other way round.

Unfortunately, this yields an infinite specification, because there is no bound to the number of messages that may still be in transmit. Therefore, we aim at incomplete verification results by using a finite specification that only keeps track of partial information on the messages that may still be in transmit. We use two different messages, N and Y.

Figure 3 shows part of the specification; the sequences starting with senY have been omitted, as they are symmetric to the ones drawn. The double circle indicates a state in which a counterexample has been found. The initial state is the situation where the protocol is empty. sen refers to sending and rec to receiving of a message by the respective clients. If any message is received from

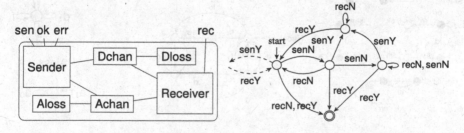

Fig. 3. Protocol architecture and part of the specification automaton

the empty protocol, this constitutes a violation of the property. In the middle state, the protocol contains exactly one message with content N. If more N-messages are sent, the automaton moves to the right-most state and remembers only that some number of N-messages have been sent. The automaton does not remember how many N messages have been sent so any number of them may be received. The topmost state indicates a situation where one message with Y was sent after either of these situations. The automaton does not consider situations where any more messages of any type are sent in this state. If a Y message is received, then all the messages with N content must have either been lost or received, meaning the protocol should be empty. In the three states in the middle, the protocol contains no messages with content Y, so receiving such a message constitutes a counterexample in these states.

It is immediately obvious that all counterexamples contain rec-events, so the set of interesting transitions is the set of transitions that receive from the protocol. An appropriate $\rightsquigarrow$-relation that guarantees **V1** and **V2** is easily computed for every state of the automaton.

The process models of the example system are shown in Fig. 4. From left to right and then top to bottom, the figures depict the processes Sender, Receiver, Dloss, and Aloss. Dchan and Achan are first-in first-out queues of finite capacity, their models are not shown separately. Each sen, rec, d_0, d_1, $\bar{d}_0$, and $\bar{d}_1$ carries a parameter that is either N or Y. Each grey state corresponds to two states, one for each parameter value. Each black state corresponds to $2r$ states, where r is the number of times that Sender tries to send before giving up. ta (try again) is only enabled when that number has not yet been reached, and err is only enabled in the opposite case. Each $\bar{x}$ synchronizes with x along a line in the architecture picture. The output of Dchan is consumed either by Receiver or Dloss, and similarly with Achan.

We implemented the model in ASSET [8] and model checked against the property given in the beginning of the section. Visibility conditions **V1** and **V2** and the classic visibility condition **V** were implemented for stubborn sets using **D0**, **D1** and **D2**. The model was parameterized by channel capacity ranging from 1 to 40, and $r = 2$ was used in all cases. The computation of stubborn

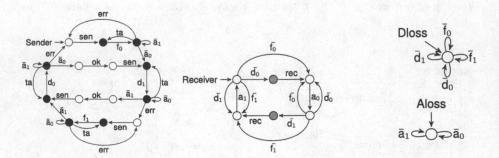

Fig. 4. The example system processes

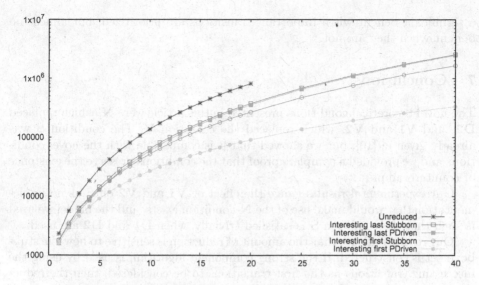

Fig. 5. Number of states as a function of channel capacity

sets is non-deterministic, in the sense that for a given state there may be several stubborn sets. The set that is generated depends on several factos, including the order in which transitions are considered in the computation. The way the model is written gives an order to the transitions. In our experiments, we also constructed stubborn sets by inverting this order. In the former, the interesting transitions (i.e. rec-transitions) are considered first.

The results are given in Fig. 5. The graph indicates how the number of states scales as a function of channel capacity for the original state space, the state space reduced using the old **V**-condition and the state space reduced by using the new conditions **V1** and **V2** instead. The reduction results are given for both transition orders. Table 1 reports some of the measurements in more detail.

Table 1. States and transitions

	Unreduced	V (I-last)	V (I-first)	V1 + V2 (I-last)	V1 + V2 (I-first)
States ($n = 20$)	680,383	310,661	233,839	295,425	80,129
Transitions ($n = 20$)	2,882,316	613,344	380,780	581,344	141,194
States ($n = 40$)	N/A	2,083,541	1,418,959	2,024,305	292,449
Transitions ($n = 40$)	N/A	4,140,264	2,238,660	4,015,624	514,994

We see from both the graph and the numbers that prioritizing the interesting transitions in the construction of stubborn sets has a high impact on the number of states. In particular, the property-driven visibility conditions provide a significant benefit when important transitions are prioritized, but almost no benefit when they are not.

7   Conclusions

The novel theoretical conditions presented in this article were **N**, which replaced **D2**, and **V1** and **V2**, which replaced the condition **V**. The condition **S** was already given in [10], but we showed that it is compatible with the novel conditions and we provided a complete proof that the conditions preserve the existence of counterexamples.

Our experimental results gauge the effect of **V1** and **V2** only, as no implementation that would make use of the **N**-condition exists, and the model we used is such that the condition **S** is satisfied trivially, when **D1** and **D2** are used.

Our results indicate that the amount of reduction is sensitive to how the stubborn set is constructed. If the strong component algorithm is used by using the interesting transitions as the first transitions to be considered, then the reduction is clearly better. Our novel conditions provide very little extra reduction if the interesting transitions are considered last, but a significant reduction if they are considered first.

The implementation of the **N**-condition is an important topic for future work. Virtually all existing methods preserve all deadlocks, whereas with the **N**-condition, only interesting executions are preserved. Further improvement in reduction is thus possible.

The theory in this article was restricted to safety properties, which always have finite counterexamples. An important question for future research is what changes are necessary for the preservation of infinite counterexamples.

References

1. Evangelista, S., Pajault, C.: Solving the ignoring problem for partial order reduction. Int. J. Softw. Tools Technol. Transf. **12**(2), 155–170 (2010)
2. Eve, J., Kurki-Suonio, R.: On computing the transitive closure of a relation. Acta Informatica **8**(4), 303–314 (1977)
3. Hansen, H., Wang, X.: Compositional analysis for weak stubborn sets. In: 11th International Conference on Application of Concurrency to System Design (ACSD), pp. 36–43. IEEE (2011)
4. Latvala, T.: Efficient model checking of safety properties. In: Ball, T., Rajamani, S.K. (eds.) SPIN 2003. LNCS, vol. 2648, pp. 74–88. Springer, Heidelberg (2003)
5. Peled, D., Valmari, A., Kokkarinen, I.: Relaxed visibility enhances partial order reduction. Formal Methods Syst. Des. **19**(3), 275–289 (2001)
6. Tarjan, R.: Depth-first search and linear graph algorithms. SIAM J. Comput. **1**(2), 146–160 (1972)
7. Valmari, A.: On-the-fly verification with stubborn sets. In: Courcoubetis, C. (ed.) Computer Aided Verification, vol. 697, pp. 397–408. Springer, Heidelberg (1993)
8. Valmari, A.: A state space tool for concurrent system models expressed in C++. In: SPLST 2015. CEUR Workshop Proceedings, vol. 1525, pp. 377–397 (2015)

9. Valmari, A.: Stop it, and be stubborn! In: 15th International Conference on Application of Concurrency to System Design (ACSD), pp. 10–19. IEEE (2015)
10. Valmari, A., Hansen, H.: Stubborn set intuition explained. In: Cabac, L., Kristensen, L.M., Rölke, H. (eds.) Proceedings of the International Workshop on Petri Nets and Software Engineering, PNSE 2016, CEUR Workshop Proceedings, vol. 1591, Toruń, Poland, 20–21 June 2016, pp. 213–232. CEUR-WS.org (2016). http://CEUR-WS.org/Vol-1591/
11. Valmari, A., Vogler, W.: Fair testing and stubborn sets. In: Bošnacki, D., Wijs, A. (eds.) SPIN 2016. LNCS, vol. 9641, pp. 225–243. Springer, Heidelberg (2016). doi:10.1007/978-3-319-32582-8_16

Characterizing Word Problems of Groups

Sam A.M. Jones[1] and Richard M. Thomas[2(✉)]

[1] School of Mathematics and Computer Science, University of Wolverhampton,
Wulfruna Street, Wolverhampton WV1 1LY, UK
[2] Department of Computer Science, University of Leicester, Leicester LE1 7RH, UK
rmt@mcs.le.ac.uk

Abstract. The word problem of a finitely generated group is a fundamental notion in group theory; it can be defined as the set of all the
words in the generators of the group that represent the identity element
of the group. This definition allows us to consider a word problem as
a formal language and a rich topic of research concerns the connection
between the complexity of this language and the algebraic structure of
the corresponding group.

Another interesting problem is that of characterizing which languages
are word problems of groups. There is a known necessary and sufficient
criterion for a language to be a word problem of a group; however a
natural question is what other characterizations there are. In this paper
we investigate this question, using sentences expressed in first-order logic
where the relations we consider are membership of the language in question and concatenation of words. We choose some natural conditions that
apply to word problems and then characterize which sets of these conditions are sufficient to guarantee that the language in question really is
the word problem of a group. We finish by investigating the decidability
of these conditions for the families of regular and one-counter languages.

1 Introduction

The word problem of a finitely generated group G is a fundamental notion in
group theory; it can be defined as the set of all the words in the generators of the
group that represent the identity element of G. This definition allows us to consider a word problem as a formal language and a rich topic of research concerns
the connection between the complexity of this language and the algebraic structure of the corresponding group. For example, the groups with a regular word
problem were classified in [1] and those with a context-free word problem in [11]
(modulo a subsequent result in [3]).

We will focus on the one-counter languages in this paper (see Sect. 2) which
are particularly interesting in the context of word problems of groups for the
following reason. Herbst showed in [4] that, if $\mathcal{F}$ is a subset of the context-free
languages which is a cone (in the sense of [2], i.e. $\mathcal{F}$ is a family of languages
closed under homomorphism, inverse homomorphism and intersection with regular languages), then the finitely generated groups whose word problem lies in
$\mathcal{F}$ are either those with a regular word problem, those with a one-counter word

© Springer International Publishing Switzerland 2016
K.G. Larsen et al. (Eds.): RP 2016, LNCS 9899, pp. 104–118, 2016.
DOI: 10.1007/978-3-319-45994-3_8

Characterizing Word Problems of Groups   105

problem or those with a context-free word problem. He also classified [4] the groups with a one-counter word problem (see also [5,6]). Note that, in all the cases mentioned here, whether or not the word problem of the group lies in the specified family of languages is independent of the choice of finite generating set for the group (see [5] for example).

Another interesting problem is that of characterizing which languages are word problems of groups. A simple necessary and sufficient criterion for a language to be a word problem was established in [13]. This involves the conjunction of two conditions, universal prefix closure and deletion closure (see Definition 2 below); a natural question is what other such characterizations there are. We investigate this problem, using sentences expressed in first-order logic where the only relations are membership of the language in question and concatenation of words. We choose some natural conditions that hold in all word problems (see Definition 2) and then characterize which sets of these conditions are sufficient to guarantee that the language really is the word problem of a group (see Theorem 25).

We then build on the work in [10] in Sect. 5 and investigate the decidability of these conditions for the families of regular and one-counter languages, noting that all the properties are decidable for the regular languages but undecidable for the one counter languages (and hence for the context-free languages as well).

2   Preliminaries

In this section we will survey some concepts, notation and results we need from formal language theory and group theory. For the background material on formal language theory the reader is referred to [2,7,8] and, for group theory, to [9,14].

As usual, we let Σ^* denote the set of all *words*, including the *empty word* ϵ, and Σ^+ denote the set of all non-empty words over the alphabet Σ. If $\alpha \in \Sigma^*$ and $x \in \Sigma$ we let $|\alpha|$ denote the length of α and $|\alpha|_x$ the number of occurrences of x in α. If $n \in \mathbb{N}$ then $\Sigma^{\leqslant n}$ is the set of words in Σ^* of length at most n and $\Sigma^{\geqslant n}$ is the set of words of length at least n.

If $\alpha = \beta\gamma$ for some $\beta, \gamma \in \Sigma^*$ then β is said to be a *prefix* of α and γ is a *suffix* of α; if $\alpha = \beta\gamma\delta$ for some $\beta, \gamma, \delta \in \Sigma^*$ then γ is said to be a *factor* of α. If α is the word $a_1 a_2 \dots a_{n-1} a_n$ with $n \geqslant 1$ and $a_i \in \Sigma$ for each i, then the *reversal* α^{rev} of α is the word $a_n a_{n-1} \dots a_2 a_1$ (and ϵ^{rev} is defined to be ϵ). For any language L we define L^{rev} to be the language $\{\alpha^{rev} : \alpha \in L\}$.

Given a language L over an alphabet Σ we define the *syntactic congruence* $\approx_L$ to be the congruence on Σ^* defined by:

$$\alpha \approx_L \beta \iff (\gamma\alpha\delta \in L \Leftrightarrow \gamma\beta\delta \in L \text{ for all } \gamma, \delta \in \Sigma^*),$$

and then the *syntactic monoid* M_L of L is the quotient $\Sigma^*/ \approx_L$. If φ is the natural map from Σ^* onto M_L then $L = S\varphi^{-1}$ for some subset S of M_L.

We will be discussing *one-counter languages*, which are the languages accepted by a *one-counter automaton*, i.e. a pushdown automaton where we have only a single stack symbol apart from a special symbol marking the bottom of the stack; these automata are nondeterministic and accept by final state.

A *group* is a set G together with a closed binary operation $*$ which is associative and where there is an identity element $1 = 1_G$ for $*$ and each g in G has an inverse g^{-1}. We often suppress the reference to $*$, simply referring to the group as G and writing gh for $g * h$. If G is a group, Σ is a finite set and $\varphi : \Sigma^* \to G$ is a surjective monoid homomorphism then we refer to Σ as a (monoid) *generating set* for G (via φ). For each $a \in \Sigma$ let $\bar{a}$ be an element of Σ^* such that $\bar{a}\varphi = (a\varphi)^{-1}$. We have that $a_1 a_2 \ldots a_n = b_1 b_2 \ldots b_m$ in G (where $a_i, b_j \in \Sigma$) if and only if $a_1 a_2 \ldots a_n \bar{b}_m \bar{b}_{m-1} \ldots \bar{b}_1$ represents 1_G; so we can focus on the set of the words in Σ^* representing the identity of G and we refer to this language as the *word problem* $W(G, \Sigma)$ of G with respect to the generating set Σ (via φ).

Remark 1. A group is the syntactic monoid of its word problem; see [5] for example. We will need a more general result here. Let Σ be a finite set, G be a group, $\varphi : \Sigma^* \to G$ be a surjective homomorphism, H be a subgroup of G (i.e. a subset of G that forms a group in its own right) such that there is no non-trivial normal subgroup of G contained in H (i.e. such that $\bigcap \{g^{-1}Hg : g \in G\} = \{1\}$) and $L = H\varphi^{-1}$; then G is the syntactic monoid of L (see [12]). □

3   Properties of Word Problems

As we said in the introduction, we are interested in determining which sets of properties of languages are sufficient to ensure that a language must be the word problem of a group. Obviously such properties must be ones that are satisfied by word problems; the ones we consider are listed in the following definition:

Definition 2. *The following are potential properties of a language L over an alphabet Σ:*

(UPP) *for all $\alpha \in \Sigma^*$ there exists $\beta \in \Sigma^*$ such that $\alpha\beta \in L$;*
  if L satisfies (UPP) we say that L has the universal prefix property*;*
(USP) *for all $\alpha \in \Sigma^*$ there exists $\beta \in \Sigma^*$ such that $\beta\alpha \in L$;*
  if L satisfies (USP) we say that L has the universal suffix property*;*
(UFP) *for all $\alpha \in \Sigma^*$ there exist $\beta, \gamma \in \Sigma^*$ such that $\beta\alpha\gamma \in L$;*
  if L satisfies (UFP) we say that L has the universal factor property*;*
(DC) *$\alpha\beta\gamma \in L, \beta \in L \Rightarrow \alpha\gamma \in L$;*
  if L satisfies (DC) we say that L is deletion closed*;*
(CRD) *$\alpha\beta \in L, \beta \in L \Rightarrow \alpha \in L$;*
  if L satisfies (CRD) we say that L is closed under right deletions*;*
(CLD) *$\alpha\beta \in L, \alpha \in L \Rightarrow \beta \in L$;*
  if L satisfies (CLD) we say that L is closed under left deletions*;*
(IC) *$\alpha\beta \in L, \gamma \in L \Rightarrow \alpha\gamma\beta \in L$;*
  if L satisfies (IC) we say that L is insertion closed*;*

(CCS) $\alpha\beta \in L \Rightarrow \beta\alpha \in L;$
   if L satisfies (CCS) we say that L is closed under cyclic shift*;*
(CC) $\alpha, \beta \in L \Rightarrow \alpha\beta \in L;$
   if L satisfies (CC) we say that L is closed under concatenation.   □

It is clear that all the properties in Definition 2 are satisfied by word problems of groups; we will use this fact from now on without further comment. We now introduce a concept that we will call (for the purposes of this paper) "duality".

Remark 3. Suppose we have (as in Definition 2) a sentence σ in first-order logic where the only relations in σ are membership of the language in question and concatenation of words. We can obtain a new sentence σ' by reversing the order of the words in any concatenation in σ (but leaving everything else fixed). For example, if we take the sentence representing the property (UPP), then the only concatenation in the sentence is $\alpha\beta \in L$; we reverse this to get $\beta\alpha \in L$ and we now have the sentence representing (USP). In this sense we say that (USP) is the *dual* of (UPP) (and that (UPP) is the dual of (USP)).

In a similar vein we see that (CRD) is the dual of (CLD) and that the other properties listed in Definition 2 are all self-dual. We sum these facts up in the following tables:

Dual properties	
(UPP)	(USP)
(CLD)	(CRD)

Self dual properties		
(UPP)	(DC)	(IC)
(CCS)	(CC)	

□

The motivation for introducing this concept is that, when characterizing word problems of groups, we will make extensive use of the following result:

Proposition 4. *If L is a language over some alphabet Σ, $S = \{\sigma_1, \sigma_2, \ldots, \sigma_n\}$ is a subset of the properties listed in Definition 2, σ_i' is the dual of σ_i for each i and $S' = \{\sigma_1', \sigma_2', \ldots, \sigma_n'\}$, then the following statements are equivalent:*

(i) L is the word problem of a group if and only if it satisfies S.
(ii) L is the word problem of a group if and only if it satisfies S'.

Proof. We will first show that L is a word problem of a group if and only if L^{rev} is a word problem of a group.

If $\Sigma = \{a_1, a_2, \ldots, a_n\}$ and $\varphi : \Sigma^* \to G$ is a surjective homomorphism from Σ^* onto a group G then we define a new homomorphism $\theta : \Sigma^* \to G$ by $a\theta = (a\varphi)^{-1}$ for all $a \in \Sigma$. If L is the word problem of G then, since $(g_1 \cdots g_n)^{-1} = g_n^{-1} \cdots g_1^{-1}$ in G and $\alpha\varphi = 1$ if and only if $(\alpha\varphi)^{-1} = 1$, we see that L^{rev} is also the word problem of G via the homomorphism θ. Applying the argument again shows that, if L^{rev} is the word problem of a group, then $L = (L^{rev})^{rev}$ is also the word problem of a group.

The result now follows from the observation that L satisfies the properties in S if and only if L^{rev} satisfies the properties in S'.   □

4   Characterizing Word Problems

The following result from [13] is the starting point for our investigations in this paper:

Proposition 5. *A language L over an alphabet Σ is the word problem of a group if and only if it satisfies properties (UPP) and (DC).*   □

Using Remark 3 and Proposition 4 we immediately have:

Corollary 6. *A language L over an alphabet Σ is the word problem of a group if and only if it satisfies properties (USP) and (DC).*   □

We note the following:

Proposition 7. *If a language L over an alphabet Σ satisfies properties (CCS) and (UFP) then it satisfies property (UPP).*

Proof. If $\alpha \in \Sigma^*$ then there exist $\beta, \gamma \in \Sigma^*$ such that $\beta\alpha\gamma \in L$ by (UFP). Then $\alpha\gamma\beta \in L$ by (CCS) and so there exists $\delta = \gamma\beta$ with $\alpha\delta \in L$ as required.   □

Using Remark 3 we immediately have:

Corollary 8. *If a language L over an alphabet Σ satisfies properties (CCS) and (UFP) then it satisfies property (USP).*   □

Given Propositions 5 and 7, we have the following immediate consequence:

Corollary 9. *A language L over an alphabet Σ is the word problem of a group if and only if it satisfies properties (DC), (CCS) and (UFP).*   □

We next note the following:

Proposition 10. *If a language L over an alphabet Σ satisfies properties (CCS) and (CRD) then it satisfies property (DC).*

Proof. If $\alpha\beta\gamma \in L$ and $\beta \in L$ then we apply (CCS), (CRD), (CCS) in turn to get that $\gamma\alpha\beta \in L$, $\gamma\alpha \in L$, and then $\alpha\gamma \in L$ as required.   □

Given Propositions 5 and 10, we have the following:

Corollary 11. *A language L over an alphabet Σ is the word problem of a group if and only if it satisfies properties (UPP), (CCS) and (CRD).*   □

By Remark 3 and Proposition 10, we have the following:

Corollary 12. *If a language L over an alphabet Σ satisfies properties (CCS) and (CLD) then it satisfies property (DC).*   □

Given Proposition 5 and Corollary 12 we have:

Corollary 13. *A language L over an alphabet Σ is the word problem of a group if and only if it satisfies properties (UPP), (CCS) and (CLD).* □

Given Propositions 5, 7 and 10 we have:

Corollary 14. *A language L over an alphabet Σ is the word problem of a group if and only if it satisfies properties (UFP), (CCS) and (CRD).* □

In a similar vein, Propositions 5, 7 and 12 give:

Corollary 15. *A language L over an alphabet Σ is the word problem of a group if and only if it satisfies properties (UFP), (CCS) and (CLD).* □

Given Corollaries 6 and 12 we have:

Corollary 16. *A language L over an alphabet Σ is the word problem of a group if and only if it satisfies properties (CCS), (USP) and (CLD).* □

In a similar way, Corollaries 6 and 10 give:

Corollary 17. *A language L over an alphabet Σ is the word problem of a group if and only if it satisfies properties (CCS), (USP) and (CRD).* □

Another such result is the following:

Proposition 18. *If a language L over an alphabet Σ satisfies properties (UPP), (IC) and (CRD) then it satisfies property (DC).*

Proof. Assume that L satisfies (UPP), (IC) and (CRD); we want to show that L satisfies (DC).

So assume that $\alpha\beta\gamma \in L$ and $\beta \in L$. By (UPP) there exists $\delta \in \Sigma^*$ such that $\alpha\gamma\delta \in L$. Since $\beta \in L$ we have by (IC) that $\alpha\beta\gamma\delta \in L$. Since $\alpha\gamma\delta \in L$ and $\alpha\beta\gamma \in L$, (IC) also gives us that $\alpha\gamma(\alpha\beta\gamma)\delta \in L$. Since $\alpha\gamma\alpha\beta\gamma\delta \in L$ and $\alpha\beta\gamma\delta \in L$, (CRD) gives that $\alpha\gamma \in L$ as required. □

Given Propositions 5 and 18 we have another characterization of word problems as follows:

Corollary 19. *A language L over an alphabet Σ is the word problem of a group if and only if it satisfies properties (UPP), (IC) and (CRD).*

Given Proposition 18 we can apply Remark 3 to deduce:

Proposition 20. *If a language L over an alphabet Σ satisfies properties (USP), (IC) and (CLD) then it satisfies property (DC).*

Given Propositions 6 and 20 we have another characterization as follows:

Corollary 21. *A language L over an alphabet Σ is the word problem of a group if and only if it satisfies properties (USP), (IC) and (CLD).*

Remark 22. For the convenience of the reader we show the implications between the conditions listed in Definition 2 which we have established in this section by means of the following diagrams:

$$(\text{UPP}) \Longleftarrow \boxed{\begin{array}{c} (\text{CCS}) \\ (\text{UFP}) \end{array}} \Longrightarrow (\text{USP}) \qquad \boxed{\begin{array}{c} (\text{CCS}) \\ (\text{CRD}) \end{array}} \Longrightarrow (\text{DC}) \Longleftarrow \boxed{\begin{array}{c} (\text{CCS}) \\ (\text{CLD}) \end{array}}$$

$$\boxed{\begin{array}{c} (\text{UPP}) \\ (\text{IC}) \\ (\text{CRD}) \end{array}} \Longrightarrow (\text{DC}) \Longleftarrow \boxed{\begin{array}{c} (\text{USP}) \\ (\text{IC}) \\ (\text{CLD}) \end{array}} \qquad\qquad\qquad \square$$

We now establish a result that will be crucial in establishing the minimality of certain sets of conditions from Definition 2 when characterizing word problems of groups:

Proposition 23. *There are languages L_1, L_2, L_3, L_4, L_5 and L_6 that satisfy respectively the following specified subsets of the set of the properties listed in Definition 2:*

	(UPP)	(DC)	(CCS)	(UFP)	(CRD)	(IC)	(CC)	(CLD)	(USP)
L_1	Yes	No	Yes	Yes	No	Yes	Yes	No	Yes
L_2	No	Yes	Yes	No	Yes	No	No	Yes	No
L_3	Yes	No	No	Yes	Yes	No	Yes	Yes	Yes
L_4	No	Yes	No	Yes	Yes	Yes	Yes	Yes	No
L_5	No	Yes	Yes	No	Yes	Yes	Yes	Yes	No
L_6	Yes	No	No	Yes	No	Yes	Yes	Yes	No

Proof. Let $\Sigma = \{a, b\}$, $n \geqslant 1$, $L_1 = \Sigma^{\geqslant n}$ and $L_2 = \Sigma^{\leqslant n}$. We see that L_1 satisfies (UPP), (USP), (UFP), (CCS), (CC) and (IC) but not (DC), (CLD) or (CRD). On the other hand, L_2 satisfies (DC), (CRD), (CLD) and (CCS) but not (UPP), (USP), (UFP), (CC) or (IC).

Let Ω be a finite set, G be a group, $\varphi : \Omega^* \to G$ be a surjective homomorphism, H be a non-trivial subgroup of G such that there is no non-trivial normal subgroup of G contained in H and $L_3 = H\varphi^{-1}$. By Remark 1, we see that G is the syntactic monoid of L_3. If L_3 were the word problem of a group then every element of L_3 would represent the identity in its syntactic monoid G, contradicting the fact that H is non-trivial.

Despite L_3 not being a word problem, it does satisfy some of the properties in Definition 2. For example, it satisfies (UPP) (and hence (UFP) as well): if $\alpha \in \Omega^*$ choose $g \in G$ such that $(\alpha\varphi)g \in H$ and then $\beta \in \Omega^*$ with $\beta\varphi = g$; since $(\alpha\beta)\varphi \in H$ we have that $\alpha\beta \in L_3$. A similar argument shows that L_3 also satisfies (USP).

L_3 also satisfies (CRD): if $\alpha\beta \in L$ and $\beta \in L$ then $(\alpha\varphi)(\beta\varphi) \in H$ and $\beta\varphi \in H$, so that $\alpha\varphi = (\alpha\varphi)(\beta\varphi)(\beta\varphi)^{-1} \in H$, and so $\alpha \in L$. Similarly L_3 satisfies (CLD). It is clear that L_3 satisfies (CC): if $\alpha, \beta \in L_3$ then $\alpha\varphi \in H$ and $\beta\varphi \in H$, so that $(\alpha\beta)\varphi = (\alpha\varphi)(\beta\varphi) \in H$ and hence $\alpha\beta \in L_3$. Given that L_3 is not the word problem of a group it cannot satisfy (DC) by Proposition 5, (CCS) by Corollary 14 or (IC) by Corollary 19.

For our next language we consider the bicyclic monoid B with the (monoid) presentation $\langle a, b : ab = 1 \rangle$. We let $\Sigma = \{a, b\}$ and let L_4 consist of all those words in Σ^* that represent the identity element of B; more formally, we have the natural homomorphism $\theta : \Sigma^* \to B$ and we let $L_4 = \{1\}\theta^{-1}$.

Each element of B is represented by a word of the form $b^i a^j$ (were $i, j \geqslant 0$) and we have that $(b^i a^j)\theta = (b^k a^\ell)\theta$ if and only if $i = k$ and $j = \ell$. If we consider the complete (i.e. the confluent and terminating) string rewriting system $\mathcal{R}$ over Σ where the only rule is $ab \to \epsilon$, we see that $\mathcal{R}$ reduces any word α in Σ^* to the word β of the form $b^i a^j$ that represents the same element of B as α (i.e. to the word β such that $\beta\theta = \alpha\theta$).

It is clear that L_4 satisfies (DC) (and hence (CRD) and (CLD) as well): if $\alpha\beta\gamma \in L_4$ and $\beta \in L_4$ then $(\alpha\beta\gamma)\theta = \beta\theta = 1$ and then

$$(\alpha\gamma)\theta = (\alpha\theta)(\gamma\theta) = (\alpha\theta)(\beta\theta)(\gamma\theta) = (\alpha\beta\gamma)\theta - 1,$$

so that $\alpha\gamma \in L_4$. Similarly L_4 satisfies (IC): if $\alpha\beta \in L_4$ and $\gamma \in L_4$ then $(\alpha\beta)\theta = \gamma\theta = 1$ and so

$$(\alpha\gamma\beta)\theta = (\alpha\theta)(\gamma\theta)(\beta\theta) = (\alpha\theta)(\beta\theta) = (\alpha\beta)\theta = 1,$$

and so $\alpha\gamma\beta \in L_4$. Given that L_4 satisfies (IC) it clearly satisfies (CC) as well.

We also have that L_4 satisfies (UFP): if $\alpha = a^{i_1} b^{j_1} \dots a^{i_n} b^{j_n}$ let

$$J = i_1 + \dots + i_n \text{ and } I = j_1 + \dots + j_n;$$

then $a^I a b^J$ reduces in $\mathcal{R}$ to ϵ and so $a^I a b^J \in L_4$. However, L_4 does not satisfy (UPP): if we let $\alpha = b$ then there is no word β such that $\alpha\beta \in L$ as any word in L can be reduced to ϵ through repeated uses of the rewriting rule $ab \to \epsilon$ and no word starting in b can be so reduced. A similar argument shows that no word ending in a can be so reduced and so L_4 does not satisfy (USP). The fact that no word starting in b can belong to L_4 also shows that L_4 does not satisfy (CCS) (since $ab \in L_4$ but $ba \notin L_4$).

We next consider $L_5 = \emptyset$. It is clear that L_5 satisfies (DC), (CCS), (CRD), (CLD), (IC) and (CC) but not (UPP), (USP) or (UFP).

Lastly we let $\Sigma = \{a, b\}$ and let $L_6 = \{\epsilon\} \cup \Sigma^*\{a\}$. It is clear that L_6 satisfies (UPP) and (UFP) but not (USP). L_6 also satisfies (IC) and (CC) but not (CCS). Lastly L_6 satisfies (CLD) but not (CRD) or (DC).   □

As we said above, the languages specified in Proposition 23 will be useful in establishing the minimality of certain sets of conditions from Definition 2. We can now show that the characterizations we have obtained so far are all minimal, in that no proper subset of any of the specified eleven sets of properties is sufficient to ensure that the language in question is a word problem:

Proposition 24. *For any non-empty proper subset S of any of the sets*

$$\{(UPP), (DC)\}, \qquad \{(DC), (CCS), (UFP)\},$$
$$\{(UPP), (CCS), (CRD)\}, \quad \{(CCS), (CRD), (UFP)\}$$
$$\{(UPP), (IC), (CRD)\}, \qquad \{(USP), (DC)\},$$
$$\{(IC), (CLD), (USP)\}, \quad \{(UPP), (CCS), (CLD)\},$$
$$\{(USP), (CCS), (CLD)\}, \quad \{(USP), (CCS), (CRD)\},$$
$$or \qquad \{(UFP), (CCS), (CLD)\}$$

there is a language satisfying all the conditions in S which is not a word problem of a group.

Proof. Throughout this proof we will refer to the six languages L_1, L_2, L_3, L_4, L_5 and L_6 introduced in Proposition 23.

To eliminate proper subsets of ...	...we consider ...
$\{(UPP), (DC)\}$	L_1 and L_2
$\{(DC), (CCS), (UFP)\}$	L_1, L_2 and L_4
$\{(UPP), (CCS), (CRD)\}$	L_1, L_2 and L_3
$\{(CCS), (CRD), (UFP)\}$	L_1, L_2 and L_3
$\{(UPP), (IC), (CRD)\}$	L_1, L_3 and L_4
$\{(USP), (DC)\}$	L_1 and L_2
$\{(IC), (CLD), (USP)\}$	L_1, L_3 and L_4
$\{(UPP), (CCS), (CLD)\}$	L_1, L_2 and L_3
$\{(USP), (CCS), (CLD)\}$	L_1, L_2 and L_3
$\{(USP), (CCS), (CRD)\}$	L_1, L_2 and L_3
$\{(UFP), (CCS), (CLD)\}$	L_1, L_2 and L_4

For each maximal proper subset S of one the eleven sets we have given a language satisfying all the properties in S which is not the word problem of a group. $\square$

Theorem 25. *The sets of properties listed in Proposition 24 are precisely those subsets S of the set of properties listed in Definition 2 such that satisfying the conditions in S is sufficient for a language L to be the word problem of a group but such that no proper subset of S has this property.*

Proof. To start with, notice that the empty set L_5 is not a characterisation and satisfies all of the properties except (UPP), (USP) and (UFP); so any characterisation must contain at least one of these three properties. Next we note that, if a language satisfies (CCS) and one of (UPP), (USP) and (UFP), then it satisfies all of them; so, in the first instance, we will consider languages which do not satisfy (CCS).

Note, also, that each of (USP) and (UPP) imply (UFP) so, when considering languages which satisfy two of (USP), (UPP) and (UFP), there is in fact only one pair to consider (taking minimality into account), namely (UPP) and (USP). The result of these considerations is that we have five cases to consider (with respect to minimal characterizations):

- Case 1. We specify (UPP) but not (CCS).
- Case 2. We specify (USP) but not (CCS).
- Case 3. We specify (UFP) but not (CCS).
- Case 4. We specify (UPP) and (USP) but not (CCS).
- Case 5. We specify (CCS) and one of (UPP), (USP) and (UFP).

Let us consider Case 1 where we specify (UPP) but not (CCS), (USP) or (UFP). Since (UPP) and (DC) is already a characterization by Proposition 5 there is no minimal characterization properly containing both of these properties; so we will exclude (DC). Since (IC) implies (CC) we do not include both of these; so we are looking at subsets of (UPP), (CLD), (CRD) and (CC) or of (UPP), (CLD), (CRD) and (IC). With regards to (UPP), (CLD), (CRD) and (CC), the language L_3 satisfies all these conditions, and so no subset of this is sufficient for a characterization.

Let us now consider (UPP), (CLD), (CRD) and (IC). Considering L_3 again we see that (IC) must be included. If we only have (UPP) and (IC) then this is not sufficient as is demonstrated by L_1. If we add (CLD) to (UPP) and (IC) we see that this is not a characterization as witnessed by L_6. If we add (CRD) to (UPP) and (IC) we have a characterization by Corollary 19, and this is minimal by Proposition 24.

Case 2 is the dual of Case 1 (in the sense of Remark 3). Using Proposition 4 we see that the only minimal sets of conditions here are $\{(USP),(DC)\}$ and $\{(USP),(IC),(CLD)\}$.

Case 3 cannot give rise to any characterizations as witnessed by L_4 which satisfies all the properties in Definition 2 except (UPP), (USP) and (CCS).

Let us now consider Case 4 where we specify (UPP) and (USP) but not (CCS) or (UFP). Again, using Proposition 5, we can exclude (DC) if we are considering minimal characterizations. Again, since (IC) implies (CC), we do not include both of these properties; so we are looking at subsets of (UPP), (USP), (CLD), (CRD) and (CC) or of (UPP), (USP), (CLD), (CRD) and (IC). With regards to (UPP), (USP), (CLD), (CRD) and (CC), the language L_3 satisfies all these conditions, and so no subset of this particular set is sufficient for a characterization.

Now consider (UPP), (USP), (CLD), (CRD) and (IC). Given L_3 we see that (IC) must be included. If we only have (UPP), (USP) and (IC) this is not sufficient as demonstrated by L_1. If we add (CRD) to (UPP), (USP) and (IC) then we have a proper superset of $\{(UPP),(IC),(CRD)\}$ which is a characterization as above, and, if we add (CLD) to (UPP), (USP) and (IC) then we have a proper superset of $\{(USP),(IC),(CLD)\}$ which is also a characterization; so no new minimal characterizations arise here.

Lastly consider Case 5. We first consider the case where we have (CCS) and (UPP). Again, by minimality, we can assume that (DC) is excluded.

Given Proposition 24, if we include (CRD), then we have a minimal characterization by Corollary 11 and, if we include (CLD), then we have a minimal characterization by Corollary 15. We must include one of these, however, as L_1 satisfies (UPP), (CCS), (IC) and (CC).

We next turn to the case where we specify (CCS) and (USP). This is the dual of the case where we specify (CCS) and (UPP) and so we get the minimal characterizations $\{(CCS), (USP), (CRD)\}$ and $\{(CCS), (USP), (CLD)\}$ here.

Lastly we look at the case where we specify (CCS) and (UFP). Given that (UPP), (USP) and (UFP) are all equivalent in the presence of (CCS), we get (using Proposition 24) the minimal characterizations $\{(CCS), (UFP), (CRD)\}$ and $\{(CCS), (UFP), (CLD)\}$. The only other possibility would be to include (DC) as, unlike (UPP) and (USP), (DC) is not sufficient to guarantee a word problem when taken in conjunction with (UFP) as witnessed by L_4. The set $\{(CCS), (UFP), (DC)\}$ is a characterization by Corollary 9 and is minimal by Proposition 24; so this is our last possibility (as we clearly cannot take any set properly containing it and preserve minimality).   □

5   Decidability Results

We now investigate the decidability of the properties listed in Definition 2. It is reasonably clear that these are all decidable for regular languages, i.e. given a finite automaton M we can decide whether or not $L(M)$ satisfies the property in question.

One possible approach for regular languages involves considering the syntactic monoid of $L(M)$. If $L = L(M) \subseteq \Sigma^*$ then we know that M_L is finite, that $L = S\varphi^{-1}$ for some $S \subseteq M$ (where φ is the natural map from Σ^* onto M_L) and that we can explicitly construct M_L and S from M. Given this (for example), (UPP) is equivalent to the sentence $\forall x \in M_L \exists y \in M_L : xy \in S$, which is decidable as M_L is finite. The decidability of the other properties listed in Definition 2 for regular languages can all be established in the same way.

When we consider the corresponding questions for one-counter languages then, as in [10], we will need the idea of a *counter machine*. There are several ways of describing these machines and we give one possibility here, following the approach taken in [10]. For the convenience of the reader we will reproduce the basic definitions and notation from [10] here.

A counter machine M (as distinct from a one-counter automaton) is a two-tape machine. The first tape is the input tape; it is read only and the head can only move to the right. The second tape is a stack: whenever we move left, M erases the symbol it moved away from. There is only one stack symbol, a say. Intuitively M can only store a natural number (so that we can think of M as having an input tape and a counter). As we will see, the stack is never empty.

More formally, a *counter machine* is a sextuple $M = (Q, \Sigma, a, \delta, q_0, q_f)$ where Q is a finite set of states containing two distinguished states, q_0, the start state, and q_f, the final state. The input alphabet Σ is a finite set of symbols such that $a \notin \Sigma$. A *configuration* of M is a word of the form qa^n where $q \in Q$ and $n > 0$ (where the current state is q and the current stack contents are a^n).

We take C to be $\{1, 2, 3, 5, 7, \frac{1}{2}, \frac{1}{3}, \frac{1}{5}, \frac{1}{7}\}$; there is no particular significance in our choice of 2, 3, 5 and 7, in that any four pair-wise coprime natural numbers would suffice. The transition relation δ is a function from $(Q - \{q_f\}) \times \Sigma \times C$ to $(Q - \{q_0\}) \times (Q - \{q_0\})$; the fact that δ is a function means that M is deterministic. M starts with just a on its stack (i.e. with the counter set to 1) and must set its counter to 1 again before entering q_f.

A move (p, b, x, q, r) in δ is interpreted as follows. If M is in state p reading an input b and if the result of multiplying the current value n of the counter (i.e. we have a^n on the stack) by the value x is an integer, then we set the counter to xn and move to state q; if xn is not an integer then the counter remains set at n and M moves to state r. We write $pa^n \vdash qa^{xn}$ or $pa^n \vdash ra^n$ as appropriate.

Given a Turing Machine, one can effectively construct a counter machine accepting the same language (see [7] for example). We now turn to the computations of a counter machine:

Definition 26. *Let M be a counter machine. A valid computation of M is a word $C_0 C_1 \dots C_n \in (Q \cup \{a\})^*$ where the C_i are configurations of M and*

$$C_0 = q_0 a \vdash C_1 \vdash \dots \vdash C_n = q_f a;$$

other elements of $(Q \cup \{a\})^*$ are said to be invalid computations. □

In any valid computation, any configuration qa^n will have $n = 2^b 3^c 5^d 7^e$ for some $b, c, d, e \geqslant 0$. Multiplying by 2, 3, 5 or 7 increases b, c, d or e respectively by 1 and multiplying by $\frac{1}{2}, \frac{1}{3}, \frac{1}{5}$ or $\frac{1}{7}$ (if possible) decreases b, c, d or e by 1; so we effectively have four counters each of which can be increased or decreased. The fact that we can only multiply by x if nx is an integer effectively says that we can test each counter individually for zero (e.g. if $n = 2^b 3^c 5^d 7^e$ and we want to multiply by $\frac{1}{2}$ then we must have that $b > 0$).

We will need the following result from [10]:

Proposition 27. *If $M = (Q, \Sigma, a, \delta, q_0, q_f)$ is a counter machine then the following language is a one-counter language:*

$K = \{qa^n pa^j :$ *the following conditions hold :*
   if (q, b, k, p, r) is a quintuple of δ and kn is an integer then $kn \neq j$;
   if (q, b, k, p, r) is a quintuple of δ and kn is not an integer then $j \neq n\}$

In [10] it was shown that the properties (UPP) and (DC) were undecidable for one-counter languages. Our aim here is to extend this result to the other properties listed in Definition 2. We will need the following technical result:

Proposition 28. *The following problem is undecidable:*
   Input: *a one-counter automaton M with input alphabet Σ of size at least two such that either $L(M) = \Sigma^*$ or $L(M) = \Sigma^* - \Sigma^* \{\alpha\} \Sigma^*$ for some word α such that α has length at least two and contains at least two different symbols.*
   Output: *"yes" if $L(M) = \Sigma^* - \Sigma^* \{\alpha\} \Sigma^*$;*
      "no" if $L(M) = \Sigma^*$.

Proof. Our aim is to describe a language L over an alphabet Σ which is closed under taking factors and which does not include a valid computation of a counter machine M (when reading a specified input β) as a factor. This way L will be equal to either Σ^* or $\Sigma^* - \Sigma^* \{\alpha\} \Sigma^*$, where α is the computation path of M accepting β, depending on whether or not M accepts β.

Since we want L to be closed under taking factors we need to ensure that no factor of a word in L is a valid computation of M. We do this by checking that, whenever an initial configuration occurs in α, a valid computation does not follow. Formally, we will consider the following three languages:

(i) $L_1 = \Sigma^* - \Sigma^* \{q_0 a\} \Sigma^*$. This is the set of all words in Σ^* which do not contain the unique initial configuration of M.

(ii) $L_2 = \Sigma^* - \Sigma^* \{q_f a\} \Sigma^*$. This is the set of all words which do not contain the unique halting configuration of M.

(iii) L_3. The set of all words which are invalid as computations of M after every instance of the unique initial configuration of M (i.e. words which do not contain a factor consisting of the unique initial configuration of M followed by a valid computation path ending in the unique halting configuration of M).

L_1 and L_2 are regular and so one-counter; we now show that L_3 is one-counter.

The machine accepting L_3 operates as follows: it scans its input doing nothing until it reads the unique initial configuration of M. At this point the machine changes state and attempts to detect an invalid computation step of M (as in Proposition 27). If the machine does not find a factor which is an invalid computation step of M before reading the unique halting configuration of M then the machine scans the rest of its input, doing nothing, and rejects. If it does find a factor which is an invalid computation step of M then the machine continues to scan its input until it finds another instance of the unique initial configuration and then repeats the process, accepting if and only if, after every instance of the initial configuration, we do not reach the halting configuration without finding an invalid computation step first. If, at any point, the machine finds another instance of the initial configuration before an instance of the halting configuration then the machine resets its state and attempts again to find an invalid computation step of M starting at the most recent initial configuration read.

So $L = L_1 \cup L_2 \cup L_3$ is a one-counter language as the family of one-counter languages is closed under union. Now $L = \Sigma^*$ if and only if M rejects β and $L = \Sigma^* - \Sigma^* \{\alpha\} \Sigma^*$ (for suitable α) if and only if M accepts β. So, if we could distinguish between Σ^* and $\Sigma^* - \Sigma^* \{\alpha\} \Sigma^*$ for one-counter languages, then we could solve the halting problem, a contradiction.   □

The condition in Proposition 28 that α can be assumed to have length greater than two and to consist of at least two symbols is included only to facilitate the undecidability results that follow. In a similar manner we can establish:

Proposition 29. *The following problem is undecidable:*

    Input: *a one-counter automaton M with input alphabet Σ of size at least two such that either $L(M) = \Sigma^*$ or $L(M) = \Sigma^* - \{\alpha\}$ for some α such that α has length at least two and contains at least two different symbols.*

    Output: "yes" *if $L(M) = \Sigma^* - \{\alpha\}$;*
                "no" *if $L(M) = \Sigma^*$.*

Having established Propositions 28 and 29 we can now prove our result:

Theorem 30. *All the properties listed in Definition 2 are undecidable for one-counter languages.*

Proof. Σ^* satisfies all the properties in Definition 2 but $K = \Sigma^* - \Sigma^*\{\alpha\}\Sigma^*$ (where α has length at least two and contains two different symbols) does not satisfy any of the conditions (UPP), (USP), (UFP), (IC), (CCS), (CC). These are reasonably clear. The word α is not a prefix, suffix or factor of any word in K, and so K does not satisfy (UPP), (USP) or (UFP). If $\alpha = \beta\gamma$ with $\beta \neq \epsilon \neq \gamma$ then $\beta, \gamma \in K$ but $\beta\gamma \notin K$; so K does not satisfy (IC) or (CC).

Given that α can be assumed to have two distinct symbols, we can write α in the form $a\delta b\zeta$ for some $a, b \in \Sigma$ with $a \neq b$ and $\delta, \zeta \in \Sigma^*$; if K satisfied (CCS) then, as $b\zeta a\delta \in K$, we would have that $\alpha = a\delta b\zeta \in K$, a contradiction. So all these conditions must be undecidable by Proposition 28.

The remaining properties are (DC), (RDC) and (LDC). If we could decide these then we would be able to distinguish between Σ^* (which satisfies all three properties) and $\Sigma^* - \{\alpha\}$ (which doesn't satisfy any of them; for example, for any character x in Σ, $\alpha x \in \Sigma^* - \{\alpha\}$ and $x \in \Sigma^* - \{\alpha\}$ but deleting x from αx yields α which is not a member of $\Sigma^* - \{\alpha\}$), contradicting Proposition 29.   □

Acknowledgments. The supportive comments from the referees and their suggestions about the presentation of the material were very welcome; we are grateful to them for their careful reading of the paper.

This paper was completed whilst the second author was on study leave from the University of Leicester and he would like to acknowledge the help and support of the university in this respect. The second author would also like to thank Hilary Craig for all her help and encouragement.

References

1. Anisimov, V.A.: The group languages. Kibernetika **4**, 18–24 (1971)
2. Berstel, J.: Transductions and Context-Free Languages. Teubner, Leipzig (1979)
3. Dunwoody, M.J.: The accessibility of finitely presented groups. Invent. Math. **81**, 449–457 (1985)
4. Herbst, T.: On a subclass of context-free groups. RAIRO Inform. Théor. Appl. **25**, 255–272 (1991)
5. Herbst, T., Thomas, R.M.: Group presentations, formal languages and characterizations of one-counter groups. Theoret. Comput. Sci. **112**, 187–213 (1993)

118   S.A.M. Jones and R.M. Thomas

6. Holt, D.F., Owens, M.D., Thomas, R.M.: Groups and semigroups with a one-counter word problem. J. Aust. Math. Soc. **85**, 197–209 (2008)
7. Hopcroft, J.E., Ullman, J.D.: Introduction to Automata Theory, Languages and Computation. Addison-Wesley, Reading (1979)
8. Ito, M.: Algebraic Theory of Automata and Languages. World Scientific Press, Singapore (2004)
9. Johnson, D.L.: Presentations of Groups. Cambridge University Press, Cambridge (1990)
10. Jones, S.A.M., Thomas, R.M.: Formal languages, word problems of groups and decidability. In: Abdulla, P.A., Potapov, I. (eds.) RP 2013. LNCS, vol. 8169, pp. 146–158. Springer, Heidelberg (2013)
11. Muller, D.E., Schupp, P.E.: Groups, the theory of ends, and context-free languages. J. Comput. Syst. Sci. **26**, 295–310 (1983)
12. Parkes, D.W., Thomas, R.M.: Syntactic monoids and word problems. Arab. J. Sci. Eng. **25**, 81–94 (2000)
13. Parkes, D.W., Thomas, R.M.: Groups with context-free reduced word problem. Comm. Algebra **30**, 3143–3156 (2002)
14. Rotman, J.L.: An Introduction to the Theory of Groups. Springer, Berlin (1995)

Distributed Synthesis of State-Dependent Switching Control

Adrien Le Coënt[1], Laurent Fribourg[2], Nicolas Markey[2(✉)], Florian De Vuyst[1], and Ludovic Chamoin[3]

[1] CMLA, ENS Cachan, CNRS, Université Paris-Saclay, 61 Av. du Président Wilson, 94235 Cachan Cedex, France
adrien.le-coent@ens-cachan.fr, devuyst@cmla.ens-cachan.fr
[2] LSV, ENS Cachan, CNRS, Université Paris-Saclay, 61 Av. du Président Wilson, 94235 Cachan Cedex, France
fribourg@lsv.ens-cachan.fr, markey@lsv.fr
[3] LMT, ENS Cachan, CNRS, Université Paris-Saclay, 61 Av. du Président Wilson, 94235 Cachan Cedex, France
chamoin@lmt.ens-cachan.fr

Abstract. We present a correct-by-design method of state-dependent control synthesis for linear discrete-time switching systems. Given an objective region R of the state space, the method builds a capture set S and a control which steers any element of S into R. The method works by iterated backward reachability from R. More precisely, S is given as a parametric extension of R, and the maximum value of the parameter is solved by linear programming. The method can also be used to synthesize a stability control which maintains indefinitely within R all the states starting at R. We explain how the synthesis method can be performed in a distributed manner. The method has been implemented and successfully applied to the synthesis of a distributed control of a concrete floor heating system with 11 rooms and $2^{11} = 2048$ switching modes.

1 Introduction

The importance of switched systems has grown up considerably these last years because of their ease of implementation for controlling cyber-physical systems. A switched system is a family of sub-systems, each with its own dynamics characterized by a parameter mode u whose values are in a finite set U (see [12]). However, due to the composition of many switched systems together, the global switched system has a number of modes and dynamics which increases exponentially. Take for example a heating system for a building of 11 rooms (see [9]): each room i has a heater with two modes values $\{off, on\}$. This makes a combination of $2^{11} = 2048$ mode values. If we want to analyze the evolution of a trajectory on a horizon of K units of discrete time, we have to consider the dynamics corresponding to 2^{11K} possible sequences of modes, which is intractable even for

Partly supported by EU project Cassting (FP7-601148).

K.G. Larsen et al. (Eds.): RP 2016, LNCS 9899, pp. 119–133, 2016.
DOI: 10.1007/978-3-319-45994-3_9

small values of K. It is therefore essential to design *compositional* methods in order to obtain control methods of switched systems that give formal guarantees on the correct behavior of the cyber physical systems.

In this paper, we give a symbolic compositional method which allows to synthesize a control of linear discrete-time switched systems that is guaranteed to satisfy *reachability* and *stability* properties. The method starts from an objective region R of the state space, which is rectangular (i.e., is a product of closed intervals of reals). It then generates in a backward manner, using linear programming techniques, an increasing sequence of nested rectangles $\{R^{(i)}\}_{i \geq 0}$ such that every trajectory issued from $R^{(i)}$ is guaranteed to reach $R^{(i-1)}$ in a bounded number of time units. Once $R^{(0)} = R$ is reached, the trajectory is also guaranteed to stay in R indefinitely (stability). The method relies on a simple operation of *tiling* of the rectangles $R^{(i)}$ in a finite number of sub-rectangles (tiles), using a standard operation of *bisection*. Although the method works in a backward fashion, it does not require to inverse the linear dynamics of the system (via matrix inversion), and does not compute *predecessors* of symbolic states (tiles), but only *successors* using the forward dynamics. This is useful in order to avoid numerical imprecisions, especially when the dynamics are *contractive*, which happens often in practical systems (see [14]).

Another contribution of this paper is a technique of state *over-approximation* which allows a distributed control synthesis: this over-approximation allows subsystem 1 to infer a correct value for its next local mode u_1 without knowing the exact value of the state of sub-system 2. This distributed synthesis method is computationally efficient, and works in presence of partial observability. This is at the cost of the performance of the control which usually makes the trajectories reach the objective area in more steps than with a centralized approach.

Related Work. In symbolic analysis and control synthesis methods for hybrid systems, the method of backward reachability and the use of polyhedral symbolic states, as used here, is classical (see, e.g., [2,5]). The use of tiling or partitioning the state-space using bisection is also classical (see, e.g., [6,7]). The main original contribution of this paper is to give a simple technique of over-approximation, which allows one component to estimate the symbolic state of the other component, in presence of partial information. This is similar in spirit to an assume-guarantee reasoning where the controller synthesis for each subsystems assumes that some safety properties are are satisfied by the others [1,13]. In contrast to [3], we do not need, for the mode selection of a sub-system, to explore blindly all the possible mode choices made by the other sub-system. This yields a drastic reduction of the complexity[1]. This approach allows us to treat a real case study which is intractable with a centralized approach. This case study comes from [9], and we use the same decomposition of the system in two parts (rooms 1–5 and rooms 6–11). In contrast to the work of [9] which uses an on-line

---

[1] This separability technique is made possible by the fact that the difference equation $x_1(t + 1) = f_1(x_1(t), x_2(t), u_1)$ (see Sect. 2.1) does not involve the control mode u_2.

and heuristic approach with no formal guarantees, we use here an off-line formal method which guarantees reachability and stability properties.

Implementation. The methods of control synthesis both in the centralized context and in the distributed context have been integrated to the tool MINIMATOR [4,8] written in Octave. All the computation times given in the paper have been performed on a 2.80 GHz Intel Core i7-4810MQ CPU with 8 GB of memory.

Plan. The structure of this paper is as follows. The class of systems considered and some preliminary definitions are given in Sect. 2. Our symbolic approach, which is based on the tiling of the state space and backward reachability, is explained in Sect. 3. In Sect. 4, we present a centralized method to synthesize a controller based on a "generate-and-test" tiling procedure. A distributed approach is then given in Sect. 5 where we introduce a state over-approximation technique in order to avoid the use of non-local information by the subsystem controllers. For both methods, we provide reachability and stability guarantees on the controlled trajectories of the system. We present a case study in Sect. 6: the aim of this case is to control the temperature of an eleven rooms house, heated by geothermal energy. We manage to apply our technique, and to synthesize a correct-by-construction control for this example.

2 State-Dependent Switching Control

2.1 Control Modes

Consider the discrete-time system with *finite control*:

$$x_1(t+1) = f_1(x_1(t), x_2(t), u_1) \qquad x_2(t+1) = f_2(x_1(t), x_2(t), u_2)$$

where x_1 (resp. x_2) is the first (resp. second) component of the state vector variable, which takes its values in $\mathbb{R}^{n_1}$ (resp. $\mathbb{R}^{n_2}$), and u_1 (resp. u_2) is the first (resp. second) component of the control *mode* variable, which takes its values in the *finite* set U_1 (resp. U_2). We will often use x for (x_1, x_2), u for (u_1, u_2), and n for $n_1 + n_2$. We will also abbreviate the set $U_1 \times U_2$ as U. Let N be the cardinal of U, and N_1 (resp. N_2) the cardinal of U_1 (resp. U_2). We have $N = N_1 \cdot N_2$.

More generally, we abbreviate the discrete-time system under the form:

$$x(t+1) = f(x(t), u)$$

where x is a vector state variable which takes its values in $\mathbb{R}^n = \mathbb{R}^{n_1} \times \mathbb{R}^{n_2}$, u is of the form (u_1, u_2) where u_1 takes its values in U_1 and u_2 in U_2. In this context, we are interested by the following *centralized* control synthesis problem: at each discrete-time t, select the appropriate mode $u \in U$ in order to satisfy a given property. In this paper we focus on *state-dependent* control, which means that, at each time t, the selection of the value of u is done by considering only the values of $x(t)$.

In the *distributed* context, the control synthesis problem consists in concurrently selecting the value of u_1 in U_1 according to the value of $x_1(t)$ *only*, and the value of u_2 in U_2 according to the value of $x_2(t)$ *only*.

The properties that we consider are *reachability* properties: given a set S and a set R, we look for a control which will steer any element of S to R in a bounded number of steps. We will also consider *stability* properties, which means, that once the state x of the system is in R at time t, the control will maintain it in R indefinitely at $t+1, t+2, \ldots$ Actually, given a state set R, we will present a method which does not start from a given set S, but *constructs* it, together with a control which steers all the elements of S to R within a bounded number of steps (S can be seen as a "capture set" of R).

In this paper, we consider that R and S are "rectangles" of the state space. More precisely, $R = R_1 \times R_2$ is a rectangle of reals, i.e., R is a product of n closed intervals of reals, and R_1 (resp. R_2) is a product of n_1 (resp. n_2) closed intervals of reals. Likewise, we assume that $S = S_1 \times S_2$ is a rectangular sub-area of the state space.

Example 1. The centralized and distributed approaches will be illustrated by the example of a two rooms apartment, heated by two heaters located in each room (adapted from [6]). In this example, the objective is to control the temperature of the two rooms. There is heat exchange between the two rooms and with the environment. The *continuous* dynamics of the system is given by the equation:

$$\begin{pmatrix} \dot{T_1} \\ \dot{T_2} \end{pmatrix} = \begin{pmatrix} -\alpha_{21} - \alpha_{e1} - \alpha_f u_1 & \alpha_{21} \\ \alpha_{12} & -\alpha_{12} - \alpha_{e2} - \alpha_f u_2 \end{pmatrix} \begin{pmatrix} T_1 \\ T_2 \end{pmatrix} + \begin{pmatrix} \alpha_{e1} T_e + \alpha_f T_f u_1 \\ \alpha_{e2} T_e + \alpha_f T_f u_2 \end{pmatrix}.$$

Here T_1 and T_2 are the temperatures of the two rooms, and the state of the system corresponds to $T = (T_1, T_2)$. The control mode variable u_1 (respectively u_2) can take the values 0 or 1 depending on whether the heater in room 1 (respectively room 2) is switched off or switched on (hence $U_1 = U_2 = \{0, 1\}$). Hence, here $n_1 = n_2 = 1$, $N_1 = N_2 = 2$ and $n = 2, N = 4$. T_e corresponds to the temperature of the environment, and T_f to the temperature of the heaters. The values of the different parameters are the following: $\alpha_{12} = 5 \times 10^{-2}$, $\alpha_{21} = 5 \times 10^{-2}$, $\alpha_{e1} = 5 \times 10^{-3}$, $\alpha_{e2} = 5 \times 10^{-3}$, $\alpha_f = 8.3 \times 10^{-3}$, $T_e = 10$ and $T_f = 35$.

We suppose that the heaters can be switched periodically at sampling instants $\tau, 2\tau, \ldots$ (here, $\tau = 5\,$s). By integration of the continuous dynamics between t and $t + \tau$, the system can be easily put under the desired *discrete-time* form:

$$T_1(t+1) = f_1(T_1(t), T_2(t), u_1) \qquad T_2(t+1) = f_2(T_1(t), T_2(t), u_2)$$

where f_1 and f_2 are affine functions.

Given an objective rectangle for $T = (T_1, T_2)$ of the form $R = [18.5, 22] \times [18.5, 22]$, the control synthesis problem is to find a rectangular capture set S as large as possible, from which one can steer the state T to R ("reachability"), then maintain T within R for ever ("stability").

2.2   Control Patterns

It is often easier to design a control of the system using several applications of f in a row rather than using just a single application of f at each time. We are thus led to the notion of "macro-step", and "control pattern". A *(control) pattern* $\pi = (\pi_1, \pi_2)$ *of length* k is a sequence of modes defined recursively by:

1. π is of the form $(u_1, u_2) \in U_1 \times U_2$ if $k = 1$,
2. π is of the form $(u_1 \cdot \pi_1', u_2 \cdot \pi_2')$, where u_1 (resp. u_2) is in U_1 (resp. U_2), and (π_1', π_2') is a (control) pattern of length $k - 1$ if $k \geq 2$.

The set of patterns of length k is denoted by Π^k (for length $k = 1$, $\Pi^1 = U$). Likewise, for $k \geq 1$, we denote by Π_1^k (resp. Π_2^k) the set of sequences of k elements of U_1 (resp. U_2). For a system defined by $x(t+1) = f(x(t), (u_1, u_2))$ and a pattern $\pi = (\pi_1, \pi_2)$ of length k, one can define recursively $x(t + k) = f(x(t), (\pi_1, \pi_2))$ with $(\pi_1, \pi_2) \in \Pi^k$, by:

1. $f(x(t), (\pi_1, \pi_2)) = f(x(t), (u_1, u_2))$, if (π_1, π_2) is a pattern of length $k = 1$ of the form $(u_1, u_2) \in U$,
2. $f(x(t), (\pi_1, \pi_2)) = f(f(x(t), (\pi_1', \pi_2')), (u_1, u_2))$, if (π_1, π_2) is a pattern of length $k \geq 2$ of the form $(u_1 \cdot \pi_1', u_2 \cdot \pi_2')$ with $(u_1, u_2) \in U$ and $(\pi_1', \pi_2') \in \Pi^{k-1}$.

One defines $(f(x, \pi))_1 \in \mathbb{R}^{n_1}$ and $(f(x, \pi))_2 \in \mathbb{R}^{n_2}$ to be the first and second components of $f(x, \pi) \in \mathbb{R}^{n_1} \times \mathbb{R}^{n_2} = \mathbb{R}^n$, i.e.: $f(x, \pi) = ((f(x, \pi))_1, f(x, \pi)_2)$.

In the following, we suppose that $K \in \mathbb{N}$ is an upper bound of the length of patterns. The value of K can be seen as a maximum number of time steps, for which we compute the future behavior of the system ("horizon"). We denote by $\Pi_1^{\leq K}$ (resp. $\Pi_2^{\leq K}$) the expression $\bigcup_{1 \leq k \leq K} \Pi_1^k$ (resp. $\bigcup_{1 \leq k \leq K} \Pi_2^k$). Likewise, we denote by $\Pi^{\leq K}$ the expression $\bigcup_{1 \leq k \leq K} \Pi^k$.

3   Control Synthesis Using Tiling

3.1   Tiling

Let $R = R_1 \times R_2$ be a rectangle. We say that $\mathcal{R}$ is a *(finite rectangular) tiling* of R if $\mathcal{R}$ is of the form $\{r_{i_1, i_2}\}_{i_1 \in I_1, i_2 \in I_2}$, where I_1 and I_2 are given finite sets of positive integers, each r_{i_1, i_2} is a sub-rectangle of R of the form $r_{i_1} \times r_{i_2}$, and r_{i_1}, r_{i_2} are closed sub-intervals of R_1 and R_2 respectively. Besides, we have $\bigcup_{i_1 \in I_1} r_{i_1} = R_1$ and $\bigcup_{i_2 \in I_2} r_{i_2} = R_2$ (hence $R = \bigcup_{i_1 \in I_1, i_2 \in I_2} r_{i_1, i_2}$). We will refer to r_{i_1}, r_{i_2} and r_{i_1, i_2} as "tiles" of R_1, R_2 and R respectively. The same notions hold for rectangle S.

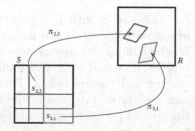

Fig. 1. Mapping of tile $s_{2,3}$ to R via pattern $\pi_{2,3}$, and mapping of tile $s_{3,1}$ via $\pi_{3,1}$.

In the centralized context, given a rectangle R, the *macro-step (backward reachability) control synthesis problem with horizon* K consists in finding a rectangle S and a tiling $\mathcal{S} = \{s_{i_1, i_2}\}_{i_1 \in I_1, i_2 \in I_2}$ of S such that, for each $(i_1, i_2) \in I_1 \times I_2$, there exists $\pi \in \Pi^{\leq K}$ such that: $f(s_{i_1, i_2}, \pi) \subseteq R$ (i.e., for all $x \in s_{i_1, i_2}$, it holds $f(x, \pi) \in R$). This is illustrated in Fig. 1.

3.2   Parametric Extension of Tiling

In the following, we assume that the set S we are looking for is a *parametric extension* of R, denoted by $R + (a, a)$, which is defined in the following.

Suppose that $R = R_1 \times R_2$ is given as well as a tiling $\mathcal{R} = \mathcal{R}_1 \times \mathcal{R}_2 = \{r_{i_1} \times r_{i_2}\}_{i_1 \in I_1, i_2 \in I_2} = \{r_{i_1, i_2}\}_{i_1 \in I_1, i_2 \in I_2}$. R_1 can be seen as a product of n_1 closed intervals of the form $[\ell, m]$. Consider a non negative real parameter a. Let $(R_1 + a)$ denote the corresponding product of n_1 intervals of the form $[\ell - a, m + a]$.[2] We define $(R_2 + a)$ similarly. Finally, we define $R + (a, a)$ as $(R_1 + a) \times (R_2 + a)$.

We now consider that S is a (parametric) superset of R of the form $R + (a, a)$. We define a tiling $\mathcal{S} = \mathcal{S}_1 \times \mathcal{S}_2$ of S of the form $\{s_{i_1} \times s_{i_2}\}_{i_1 \in I_1, i_2 \in I_2}$, which is obtained from $\mathcal{R} = \mathcal{R}_1 \times \mathcal{R}_2 = \{r_{i_1} \times r_{i_2}\}_{i_1 \in I_1, i_2 \in I_2}$ by a simple extension, as follows: a tile r_{i_1} (resp. r_{i_2}) of $\mathcal{R}_1$ (resp. $\mathcal{R}_2$) in "contact" with ∂R_1 (resp. ∂R_2) is prolonged as a tile s_{i_1} (resp. s_{i_2}) in order to be in contact with $\partial(R_1 + a)$ (resp. $\partial(R_2 + a)$); a tile "interior" to R_1 (i.e., with no contact with ∂R_1) is kept unchanged, and coincides with s_{i_1}, and similarly for R_2.

We denote the resulting tiling $\mathcal{S}$ by $\mathcal{R} + (a, a)$. We also denote s_{i_1} (resp. s_{i_2}) as $r_{i_1} + a$ (resp. $r_{i_2} + a$) even if r_{i_1} (resp. r_{i_2}) is "interior" to R_1 (resp. R_2). Likewise, we will denote $s_{i,j}$ as $r_{i,j} + (a, a)$. Note that a tiling of R of index set $I_1 \times I_2$ induces a tiling of $R + (a, a)$ with the same index set $I_1 \times I_2$, hence the same number of tiles as R, for any $a \geq 0$. This is illustrated in Fig. 2, where the tiling of R is represented with black continuous lines, and the extended tiling of $R + (a, a)$ with red dashed lines.

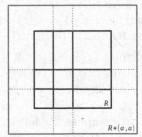

Fig. 2. Tiling of $R + (a, a)$ induced by tiling $\mathcal{R}$ of R. (Color figure online)

3.3   Generate and Test Tilings

By replacing S with $R + (a, a)$ in the notions defined in Sect. 3.1 the problem of macro-step control synthesis can now be reformulated as finding a tiling $\mathcal{R}$ of R which induces a macro-step control of $R + (a, a)$ towards R, for some $a \geq 0$; besides, if we find such $\mathcal{R}$, we want to compute the *maximum* value of a for which the induced control exists. This problem can be solved by a simple "generate and test" procedure: one *generates* a candidate tiling, then one *tests* if it satisfies the control property (the control test procedure is explained in Sect. 4.1); if the test fails, one generate another candidate, and so on iteratively.

In practice, the generation of a candidate $\mathcal{R}$ is done, starting from the trivial tiling (made of one tile equal to R), then using successive *bisections* of R until, either the control test succeeds ("success"), or the depth of bisection of the new candidate is greater than a given upper bound D ("failure"). See details of this procedure in [10].

---

[2] Actually, we will consider in the examples that $(R_1 + a)$ is a product of intervals of the form $[\ell - a, m]$ where the interval is extended only at its *lower* end, but the method is strictly identical.

Remark 1. Note that, if the generate-and-test process stops with "success" for a tiling $\mathcal{R}$, then the tiling $\mathcal{R}_{D,uniform}$ also solves the problem, where $\mathcal{R}_{D,uniform}$ is the "finest" tiling obtained by bisecting D times all the n components of R. Since $\mathcal{R}_{D,uniform}$ has exactly 2^{nD} tiles, it is in general impractical to perform directly the control test on it. From a theoretical point of view however, it is convenient to suppose that $\mathcal{R} = \mathcal{R}_{D,uniform}$ for reducing the *worst case time complexity* of the control synthesis procedure to the complexity of the control test part only (see Sect. 4.1).

4 Centralized Control

4.1 Tiling Test Procedure

As seen in Sect. 3.2, the *(macro-step) control synthesis problem with horizon* K consists in finding (the maximum value of) $a \geq 0$, and a tiling $\mathcal{R} = \{r_{i_1,i_2}\}_{i_1 \in I_1, i_2 \in I_2}$ of R such that, for each $(i_1, i_2) \in I_1 \times I_2$, there exists some $\pi \in \Pi^{\leq K}$ with $f(r_{i_1,i_2} + (a,a), \pi) \subseteq R$. In order to *test* if a tiling candidate $\mathcal{R} = \{r_{i_1,i_2}\}_{i_1 \in I_1, i_2 \in I_2}$ of R satisfies the desired property, we define, for each $(i_1, i_2) \in I_1 \times I_2$:

$$\Pi_{i_1,i_2}^{\leq K} = \{\pi \in \Pi^{\leq K} \mid f(r_{i_1,i_2}, \pi) \subset R\}.$$

When $\Pi_{i_1,i_2}^{\leq K} \neq \emptyset$, we define $A = \min_{(i_1,i_2) \in I_1 \times I_2} \{a_{i_1,i_2}\}$, where

$$1 a_{i_1,i_2} = \max_{\pi \in \Pi_{i_1,i_2}^{\leq K}} \max\{a \geq 0 \mid f(r_{i_1,i_2} + (a,a), \pi) \subseteq R\}$$

$$\pi_{i_1,i_2} = \operatorname*{argmax}_{\pi \in \Pi_{i_1,i_2}^{\leq K}} \max\{a \geq 0 \mid f(r_{i_1,i_2} + (a,a), \pi) \subseteq R\}$$

For each tile r_{i_1,i_2} of R and each $\pi \in \Pi^{\leq K}$, the inclusion test $f(r_{i_1,i_2}, \pi) \subseteq R$ can be done in time polynomial in n when f is affine. Hence the test $\Pi_{i_1,i_2}^{\leq K} \neq \emptyset$ can be done in $O(N^K \cdot n^\alpha)$ since $\Pi^{\leq K}$ contains $O(N^K)$ elements. The computation of $\max\{a \geq 0 \mid f(r_{i_1,i_2} + (a,a), \pi) \subseteq R\}$ can be done by *linear programming* in time polynomial in n, the dimension of the state space. The computation time of $\{a_{i_1,i_2}\}_{i_1 \in I, i_2 \in I_2}$, π_{i_1,i_2}, and A is thus in $O(N^K \cdot 2^{nD})$, where D is the maximal depth of bisection. Hence the complexity of testing a candidate tiling $\mathcal{R}$ is in $O(N^K \cdot 2^{nD})$. By Remark 1 above, the complexity of the control synthesis by generate-and-test is also in $O(N^K \cdot 2^{nD})$. We have:

Proposition 1. *Assume that there exists a tiling* $\mathcal{R} = \{r_{i_1,i_2}\}_{i_1 \in I_1, i_2 \in I_2}$ *of R such that* $\Pi_{i_1,i_2}^{\leq K} \neq \emptyset$ *for any* $(i_1, i_2) \in I_1 \times I_2$. *Then $\mathcal{R}$ induces a macro-step control of horizon K of $R + (A, A)$ towards R with:*

$$\forall (i_1, i_2) \in I_1 \times I_2. \ f(r_{i_1,i_2} + (A, A), \pi_{i_1,i_2}) \subseteq R.$$

Once a candidate tiling $\mathcal{R}$ satisfying the control test property is found, the generate-and-test procedure ends with *success* (see Sect. 3.3), and a set $S = R + (a^{(1)}, a^{(1)})$ with $a^{(1)} = A$ has been found. One can then *iterate* the "generate and test" procedure in order to construct an increasing sequence of nested rectangles of the form $R + (a^{(1)}, a^{(1)})$, $R + (a^{(1)} + a^{(2)}, a^{(1)} + a^{(2)})$, ..., which can all be driven to R, as explained in [10].

Example 2. Consider the specification of a two-rooms apartment given in Example 1. Set $R = [18.5, 22] \times [18.5, 22]$. Let $D = 1$ (the depth of bisection is at most 1), and $K = 4$ (the maximum length of patterns is 4). We look for a centralized controller which will steer the rectangle $S = [18.5 - a, 22] \times [18.5 - a, 22]$ to R with a as large as possible, and stay in R indefinitely. Using our implementation, the computation of the control synthesis takes 4.14 s of CPU time.

The method iterates successfully 15 times the macro-step control synthesis procedure. We find $S = R + (a, a)$ with $a = 53.5$, i.e. $S = [-35, 22] \times [-35, 22]$. This means that any element of S can be driven to R within 15 macro-steps of length (at most) 4, i.e., within $15 \times 4 = 60$ units of time. Since each unit of time is of duration $\tau = 5$ s, any trajectory starting from S reaches R within $60 \times 5 = 300$ s. Once the trajectory $x(t)$ is in R, it returns in R every macro-step of length (at most) 4, i.e., every $4 \times 5 = 20$ s.

These results are consistent with the simulation given in Fig. 3 for the time evolution of (T_1, T_2) starting from $(12, 12)$. Simulations of the control, starting from $(T_1, T_2) = (12, 12)$, $(T_1, T_2) = (12, 19)$ and $(T_1, T_2) = (22, 12)$ are also given in the state space plane in Fig. 3.

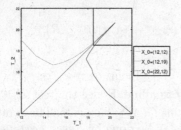 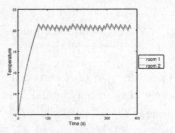

Fig. 3. Simulations of the centralized reachability controller for three different initial conditions plotted in the state space plane (left); simulation of the centralized reachability controller for the initial condition $(12, 12)$ plotted within time (right).

4.2 Stability as a Special Case of Reachability

Instead of looking for a set of the form $S = R + (a, a)$ from which R is reachable via a macro-step, let us consider the particular case where $S = R$ (i.e., $a = 0$).

The problem is now to construct a tiling $\mathcal{R} = \{r_{i_1, i_2}\}_{i_1 \in I_1, i_2 \in I_2}$ of R such that, for all $(i_1, i_2) \in I_1 \times I_2$, there exists a pattern $\pi_{i_1, i_2} \in \Pi^{\leq K}$ verifying $f(r_{i_1, i_2}, \pi_{i_1, i_2}) \subseteq R$. If such a tiling $\mathcal{R}$ exists, then $x(t) \in R$ implies $x(t + k) \in R$

for some $k \leq K$.[3] Actually, we can slightly modify the procedure in order to impose, additionally, that $\forall k \leq K \; x(t+k) \in R+\varepsilon$ for some $\varepsilon > 0$ (see Sect. 5.2). It follows that $R + (\varepsilon, \varepsilon)$ is *stable* under the control induced by $\mathcal{R}$. We can thus treat the stability control of R as a special case of reachability control.

5 Distributed Control

5.1 Background

In the distributed context, given a set $R = R_1 \times R_2$, the *(macro-step) distributed control synthesis problem with horizon K* consists in finding (the maximum value of) $a \geq 0$, and a tiling $\mathcal{R}_1 = \{r_{i_1}\}_{i_1 \in I_1}$ of R_1 which induces a (macro-step) control on $R_1 + a$, a tiling $\mathcal{R}_2 = \{r_{i_2}\}_{i_2 \in I_2}$ which induces a (macro-step) control on $R_2 + a$.

More precisely, we seek tilings $\mathcal{R}_1$ and $\mathcal{R}_2$ such that: there exists $\ell \in \mathbb{N}$ such that, for each $i_1 \in I_1$ there exists a sequence π_1 of ℓ modes in U_1, and for each $i_2 \in I_2$, a sequence π_2 of ℓ modes in U_2 such that:

$$f((r_{i_1} + a) \times (R_2 + a), (\pi_1, \pi_2))_{|1} \subseteq R_1 \; \wedge \; f((R_1 + a) \times (r_{i_2} + a), (\pi_1, \pi_2))_{|2} \subseteq R_2.$$

In order to synthesize a *distributed* strategy where the control pattern π_1 is determined only by i_1 (regardless of the value of i_2), and the control pattern π_2 only by i_2 (regardless of the value of i_1), we now define an *over-approximation* $X_{i_1}(a, \pi_1)$ for $f((r_{i_1} + a) \times (R_2 + a), (\pi_1, \pi_2))_{|1}$, and an *over-approximation* $X_{i_2}(a, \pi_2)$ for $f((R_1 + a) \times (r_{i_2} + a), (\pi_1, \pi_2))_{|2}$. The correctness of these over-approximations relies on the existence of a fixed positive value for parameter ε. Intuitively, ε represents the width of the additional margin (around $R + (a, a)$) within which all the intermediate states lie when a macro-step is applied to a point of $R + (a, a)$.

5.2 Tiling Test Procedure

Let π_1^k (resp. π_2^k) denote the prefix of length k of π_1 (resp. π_2), and $\pi_1(k)$ (resp. $\pi_2(k)$) the k-th element of sequence π_1 (resp. π_2).

Definition 1. *Consider an element r_{i_1} (resp. r_{i_2}) of a tiling $\mathcal{R}_1$ (resp. $\mathcal{R}_2$) of R_1 (resp. R_2), and a sequence $\pi_1 \in \Pi_1^{\leq K}$ (resp. $\pi_2 \in \Pi_2^{\leq K}$) of length ℓ_1 (resp. ℓ_2). The approximate first (resp. second) component sequence $\{X_{i_1}^k(a, \pi_1)\}_{0 \leq k \leq \ell_1}$ (resp. $\{X_{i_2}^k(a, \pi_2)\}_{0 \leq k \leq \ell_2}$) is defined as follows:*

- $X_{i_1}^0(a, \pi_1) = r_{i_1} + a$ *(resp. $X_{i_2}^0(a, \pi_2) = r_{i_2} + a$);*
- $X_{i_1}^k(a, \pi_1) = f_1(X_{i_1}^{k-1}(a, \pi_1), R_2 + a + \varepsilon, \pi_1(k))$ *for $1 \leq k \leq \ell_1$ (resp. $X_{i_2}^k(a, \pi_2) = f_2(R_1 + a + \varepsilon, X_{i_2}^{k-1}(a, \pi_2), \pi_2(k))$ for $1 \leq k \leq \ell_2$).*

---

[3] If $x(t) \in R$, then $x(t) \in r_{i,j}$ for some $(i,j) \in I_1 \times I_2$, hence $x(t+k) = f(x, \pi_{i,j}) \in R$ for some $k \leq K$.

We define the property $Prop(a, i_1, \pi_1)$ of $\{X_{i_1}^k(a, \pi_1)\}_{0 \leq k \leq \ell_1}$ as:

$$X_{i_1}^k(a, \pi_1) \subseteq R_1 + a + \varepsilon \text{ for } 1 \leq k \leq \ell_1 - 1, \text{ and } X_{i_1}^{\ell_1}(a, \pi_1) \subseteq R_1.$$

Likewise, we define the property $Prop(a, i_2, \pi_2)$ of $\{X_{i_2}^k(a, \pi_2)\}_{0 \leq k \leq \ell_2}$ as:

$$X_{i_2}^k(a, \pi_2) \subseteq R_2 + a + \varepsilon \text{ for } 1 \leq k \leq \ell_2 - 1, \text{ and } X_{i_2}^{\ell_2}(a, \pi_2) \subseteq R_2.$$

Given a tiling $\mathcal{R}_1 = \{r_{i_1}\}_{i_1 \in I_1}$ of R_1, for each $i_1 \in I_1$, and each $k \in \{1, \ldots, K\}$: we let $\Pi_{i_1}^k = \{\pi_1 \in \Pi_1^k \mid Prop(0, i_1, \pi_1)\}$.

When $\Pi_{i_1}^k \neq \emptyset$, we define:

$$a_{i_1}^k = \max_{\pi_1 \in \Pi_{i_1}^k} \max\{a \geq 0 \mid Prop(a, i_1, \pi_1)\}$$

$$\pi_{i_1}^k = \operatorname{argmax}_{\pi_1 \in \Pi_{i_1}^k} \max\{a \geq 0 \mid Prop(a, i_1, \pi_1)\}$$

Given $\mathcal{R}_2$, we define similarly: $\Pi_{i_2}^k$, $a_{i_2}^k$ and $\pi_{i_2}^k$. Suppose now, that:

(H1) there exists $k_1 \in \{1, \ldots, K\}$ such that $\forall i_1 \in I_1 : \Pi_{i_1}^{k_1} \neq \emptyset$.

(H2) there exists $k_2 \in \{1, \ldots, K\}$ such that $\forall i_2 \in I_2 : \Pi_{i_2}^{k_2} \neq \emptyset$.

Then we define: $a_1^{k_1} = \min_{i_1 \in I_1}\{a_{i_1}^{k_1}\}$, $a_2^{k_2} = \min_{i_2 \in I_2}\{a_{i_2}^{k_2}\}$, $A = \min\{a_1^{k_1}, a_2^{k_2}\}$.

Remark 2. Given a tiling $\mathcal{R} = \mathcal{R}_1 \times \mathcal{R}_2$, (H1) means that the points of $R_1 + A$ can be (macro-step) controlled to R_1 using patterns which all have the *same length* k_1; in other terms, all the macro-steps controlling $R_1 + A$ contain the same number k_1 of elementary steps. Symmetrically for (H2).

Remark 3. The determination of an appropriate value for ε is for the moment done by hand, and is the result of a compromise: if ε is too small, then $f_1(r_{i_1} + a, R_2 + a, u_1) \not\subseteq R_1 + a + \varepsilon$; if ε is too large, $f_1(X_{i_1}^{k-1}, R_2 + a + \varepsilon, \pi_1(k)) \not\subseteq R_1 + a$.

Given a tiling $\mathcal{R} = \mathcal{R}_1 \times \mathcal{R}_2$ of R and a real $\varepsilon > 0$, the problem of existence and computation of k_1, k_2, $\{\pi_{i_1}^{k_1}\}_{i_1 \in I_1}$, $\{\pi_{i_2}^{k_2}\}_{i_2 \in I_2}$, and A can be solved by *linear programming* since f_1 and f_2 are affine. Using the same kinds of calculation as in the centralized case (see Sect. 4.1), one can see that the complexity of testing $\Pi_{i_1}^k \neq \emptyset$ and $\Pi_{i_2}^k \neq \emptyset$ for $1 \leq k \leq K$, checking (H1)–(H2), generating k_1, k_2, A and $\{\pi_{i_1}\}_{i_1 \in I_1}$, and $\{\pi_{i_2}\}_{i_2 \in I_2}$ is in $O((\max(N_1, N_2))^K \cdot 2^{\max(n_1, n_2)D})$. Hence the complexity of the control test procedure is also in $O((\max(N_1, N_2))^K \cdot 2^{\max(n_1, n_2)D})$.

Lemma 1. *Consider a tiling $\mathcal{R} = \mathcal{R}_1 \times \mathcal{R}_2$ of the form $\{r_{i_1} \times r_{i_2}\}_{(i_1, i_2) \in I_1 \times I_2}$. Let $a \geq 0$. We suppose that (H1) and (H2) hold, and that, for all $i_1 \in I_1$, $Prop(a, i_1, \pi_1)$ holds for some $\pi_1 \in \Pi_1^{k_1}$, and for all $i_2 \in I_2$, $Prop(a, i_2, \pi_2)$ holds for some $\pi_2 \in \Pi_2^{k_2}$, then we have:*

– *in case $k_1 \leq k_2$:*

$f((r_{i_1} + a) \times (R_2 + a), (\pi_1^k, \pi_2^k))_{|1} \subseteq X_{i_1}^k(a, \pi_1) \subseteq R_1 + a + \varepsilon$ *and*

$f((R_1 + a) \times (r_{i_2} + a), (\pi_1^k, \pi_2^k))_{|2} \subseteq X_{i_2}^k(a, \pi_2) \subseteq R_2 + a + \varepsilon,$

for all $1 \leq k \leq k_1$, *and*

$f((r_{i_1} + a) \times (R_2 + a), (\pi_1^{k_1}, \pi_2^{k_1}))_{|1} \subseteq X_{i_1}^{k_1}(a, \pi_1) \subseteq R_1,$

– *in case $k_2 \leq k_1$:*

$f((r_{i_1} + a) \times (R_2 + a), (\pi_1^k, \pi_2^k))_{|1} \subseteq X_{i_1}^k(a, \pi_1) \subseteq R_1 + a + \varepsilon$ *and*

$f((R_1 + a) \times (r_{i_2} + a), (\pi_1^k, \pi_2^k))_{|2} \subseteq X_{i_2}^k(a, \pi_2) \subseteq R_2 + a + \varepsilon,$

for all $1 \leq k \leq k_2$, *and*

$f((R_1 + a) \times (r_{i_2} + a), (\pi_1^{k_2}, \pi_2^{k_2}))_{|2} \subseteq X_{i_2}^{k_2}(a, \pi_2) \subseteq R_2.$

At $t = 0$, consider a point $x(0) = (x_1(0), x_2(0))$ of $R + (A, A)$, and let us apply concurrently the strategy induced by $\mathcal{R}_1$ on x_1, and $\mathcal{R}_2$ on x_2. After k_1 steps, by Lemma 1, we obtain a point $x(k_1) = (x_1(k_1), x_2(k_1)) \in R_1 \times (R_2 + A + \varepsilon)$. Then, after k_1 steps, we obtain again a point $x(2k_1) \in R_1 \times (R_2 + A + \varepsilon)$, and so on iteratively. Likewise, we obtain points $x(k_2), x(2k_2), \ldots$ which all belong to $(R_1 + A + \varepsilon) \times R_2$. It follows that, after $\ell = lcm(k_1, k_2)$ steps, we obtain a point $x(\ell)$ which belongs to $R_1 \times R_2 = R$.

Theorem 1. *Assume there are tilings* $\mathcal{R}_1 = \{r_{i_1}\}_{i_1 \in I_1}$ *of* R_1 *and* $\mathcal{R}_2 = \{r_{i_2}\}_{i_2 \in I_2}$ *of* R_2, *and a positive real* ε *such that (H1) and (H2) hold, and let* k_1, k_2, A *be defined as above. Let* $\ell = lcm(k_1, k_2)$ *with* $\ell = \alpha_1 k_1 = \alpha_2 k_2$ *for some* $\alpha_1, \alpha_2 \in \mathbb{N}$.

Then $\mathcal{R}_1$ *induces a sequence of* α_1 *macro-steps on* $R_1 + A$, *and* $\mathcal{R}_2$ *a sequence of* α_2 *macro-steps on* $R_2 + A$, *such that, applied concurrently, we have, for all* $i_1 \in I_1$ *and* $i_2 \in I_2$:

$$f((r_{i_1} + A) \times (R_2 + A), \pi)_{|1} \subseteq R_1 \;\wedge\; f((R_1 + A) \times (r_{i_2} + A), \pi)_{|2} \subseteq R_2,$$

for some $\pi = (\pi_1, \pi_2) \in \Pi^\ell$ *where* π_1 *(resp.* π_2*) is of the form* $\pi_1^1 \cdots \pi_1^{\alpha_1}$ *(resp.* $\pi_2^1 \cdots \pi_2^{\alpha_2}$*) with* $\pi_1^i \in \Pi_1^{k_1}$ *for all* $1 \leq i \leq \alpha_1$ *(resp.* $\pi_2^i \in \Pi_2^{k_2}$ *for all* $1 \leq i \leq \alpha_2$*). Besides, for all prefix* π' *of* π, *we have*

$$f((r_{i_1} + A) \times (R_2 + A), \pi')_{|1} \subseteq R_1 + A + \varepsilon \;\wedge\; f((R_1 + A) \times (r_{i_2} + A), \pi')_{|2} \subseteq R_2 + A + \varepsilon.$$

If (H1)–(H2) hold, there exists a control that steers $R + (A, A)$ to R in ℓ steps. Letting $R' = R + (A, A)$, it is then possible to iterate the process on R' and, in case of success, generate a rectangle $R'' = R' + (A', A')$ from which R' would be reachable in ℓ' steps, for some $A' \geq 0$ and $\ell' \in \mathbb{N}$. And so on, iteratively, one generates an increasing sequence of nested control rectangles, as in Sect. 4.1.

Example 3. Consider again the specification of a two-rooms appartment given in Example 1. We consider the distributed control synthesis problem where the first (resp. second) state component corresponds to the temperature of the first (resp. second) room T_1 (resp. T_2), and the first (resp. second) control mode component corresponds to the heater u_1 (resp. u_2) of the the first (resp. second) room.

Set $R = R_1 \times R_2 = [18.5, 22] \times [18.5, 22]$. Let $D = 3$ (the depth of bisection is at most 3), and $K = 10$ (the maximum length of patterns is 10). The parameter

ε is set to value $1.5\,^\circ C$. We look for a distributed controller which steers any temperature state in $S = S_1 \times S_2 = [18.5 - a, 22] \times [18.5 - a, 22]$ to R with a as large as possible, then maintain it in R indefinitely.

Using our implementation, the computation of the control synthesis takes 220 s of CPU time. The method iterates 8 times the macro-step control synthesis procedure. We find $S = [18.5 - a, 22] \times [18.5 - a, 22]$ with $a = 6.5$, i.e. $S = [12, 22] \times [12, 22]$. This means that any element of S can be driven to R within 8 macro-steps of length (at most) 10, i.e., within $8 \times 10 = 80$ units of time. Since each unit of time is of duration $\tau = 5\,s$, any trajectory starting from S reaches R within $80 \times 5 = 400\,s$. The trajectory is then guaranteed to always stay (at each discrete time t) in $R + (\varepsilon, \varepsilon) = [17, 23.5] \times [17, 23.5]$.

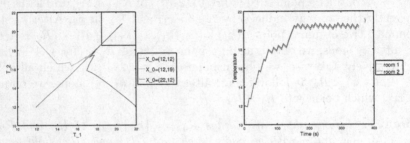

Fig. 4. Simulations of the distributed reachability controller for three different initial conditions plotted in the state space plane (left); simulation of the distributed reachability controller for the initial condition $(12, 12)$ plotted within time (right).

These results are consistent with the simulation given in Fig. 4 showing the time evolution of (T_1, T_2) starting from $(12, 12)$. Simulations of the control are also given in the state space plane, in Fig. 4, for initial states $(T_1, T_2) = (12, 12)$, $(T_1, T_2) = (12, 19)$ and $(T_1, T_2) = (22, 12)$. Not surprisingly, the performance guaranteed by the distributed approach ($a = 6.5$, reachability of R in 400 s) are worse than those guaranteed by the centralized approach of Example 2 ($a = 53.5$, reachability of R in 300 s). However, unexpectedly, the CPU computation time in the distributed approach (220 s) is here worse than the CPU time of the centralized approach (4.14 s). This relative inefficiency is due to the small size of the example.

6   Case Study

This case study, proposed by the Danish company Seluxit, aims at controlling the temperature of an eleven rooms house, heated by geothermal energy.

The *continuous* dynamics of the system is the following:

$$\frac{d}{dt} T_i(t) = \sum_{j=1}^{n} A_{i,j}^d (T_j(t) - T_i(t)) + B_i(T_{env}(t) - T_i(t)) + H_{i,j}^v \cdot v_j \qquad (1)$$

The temperatures of the rooms are the T_i. The matrix A^d contains the heat transfer coefficients between the rooms, matrix B contains the heat transfer coefficients betweens the rooms and the external temperature, set to $T_{env} = 10°C$ for the computations. The control matrix H^v contains the effects of the control on the room temperatures, and the control variable is here denoted by v_j. We have $v_j = 1$ (resp. $v_j = 0$) if the heater in room j is turned on (resp. turned off). We thus have $n = 11$ and $N = 2^{11} = 2048$ switching modes.

Note that the matrix A^d is parametrized by the open of closed state of the doors in the house. In our case, the average between closed and open matrices was taken for the computations. The exact values of the coefficients are given in [9]. The controller has to select which heater to turn on in the eleven rooms. Due to a limitation of the capacity supplied by the geothermal device, the 11 heaters cannot be turned on at the same time. In our case, we set to 4 the maximum number of heaters turned on at the same time.

We consider the distributed control synthesis problem where the first (resp. second) state component corresponds to the temperatures of rooms 1 to 5 (resp. 6 to 11), and the first (resp. second) control mode component corresponds to the heaters of rooms 1 to 5 (resp. 6 to 11). Hence $n_1 = 5, n_2 = 6, N_1 = 2^5, N_2 = 2^6$. We impose that at most 2 heaters are switched on at the same time in the first sub-system, and at most 2 in the second sub-system.

Let $D = 1$ (the depth of bisection is at most 1), and $K = 4$ (the maximum length of patterns is 4). The parameter ε is set to value $0.5°C$. The sampling time is $\tau = 15$ min. We look for a distributed controller which steers any temperature state in the rectangle $S = [18 - a, 22]^{11}$ to $R = [18, 22]^{11}$ with a as large as possible, then maintain the temperatures in R indefinitely.

Using our implementation, the computation of the control synthesis takes around 20 h of CPU time. The method successfully iterates the macro-step control synthesis procedure 15 times. We find $S = [18 - a, 22]^{11}$ with $a = 4.2$, i.e. $S = [13.8, 22]^{11}$. This means that any element of S can be driven into R within 15 macro-steps of length (at most) 4, i.e., within $15 \times 4 = 60$ units of time. Since each timeunit has duration $\tau = 15$ min, any trajectory starting from S reaches R within $60 \times 15 = 900$ min. The trajectory is then guaranteed to stay in $R + (\varepsilon, \varepsilon) = [17.5, 22.5]^{11}$. These results are consistent with the simulation of Fig. 5, showing the time evolution of the temperature of the rooms, starting from 14^{11}.

We also performed the same simulations as in Fig. 5, except that the environment temperature is not fixed at 10 °C but follows scenarios of soft winter and spring (Fig. 6). The environment temperature is plotted in green in the figures. The spring scenario is taken from [9], and the soft winter scenario is the winter scenario of [9] with 5 additional degrees. We see that our controller, which has been designed for $T_{env} = 10$ °C, still satisfies the properties of reachability and stability. These simulations are very close those obtained in [9].

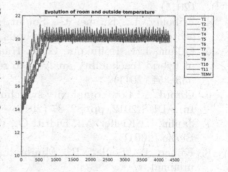

Fig. 5. Simulation of the Seluxit case study plotted with time (in min) for $T_{env} = 10°C$.

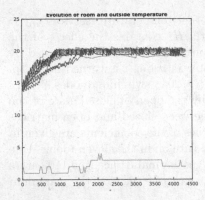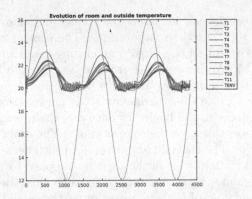

Fig. 6. Simulation of the Seluxit case study in the soft winter scenario (left), and in the spring scenario (right).

7   Final Remarks

In this paper, we have proposed a distributed approach for control synthesis and applied it to a real floor heating system. To our knowledge, this is the first time that reachability and stability properties are guaranteed for a case study of this size. The method can be extended to take into account obstacles and safety constraints. We are currently investigating an extension of the method to systems with non linear dynamics and varying parameters, see [11].

References

1. Alur, R., Henzinger, T.A.: Reactive modules. Formal Methods Syst. Des. **15**(1), 7–48 (1999)
2. Asarin, E., Bournez, O., Dang, T., Maler, O., Pnueli, A.: Effective synthesis of switching controllers for linear systems. Proc. IEEE **88**(7), 1011–1025 (2000)
3. Fribourg, L., Kühne, U., Markey, N.: Game-based synthesis of distributed controllers for sampled switched systems. In: SynCoP 2015, OASIcs 44, pp. 48–62 (2015)
4. Fribourg, L., Kühne, U., Soulat, R.: Finite controlled invariants for sampled switched systems. Formal Methods Syst. Des. **45**(3), 303–329 (2014)
5. Gillula, J.H., Hoffmann, G.M., Huang, H., Vitus, M.P., Tomlin, C.: Applications of hybrid reachability analysis to robotic aerial vehicles. Int. J. Rob. Res. **30**(3), 335–354 (2011)
6. Girard, A.: Low-complexity switching controllers for safety using symbolic models. In: ADHS 2012, pp. 82–87 (2012)
7. Jaulin, L., Kieffer, M., Didrit, O., Walter, E.: Applied Interval Analysis. Springer, Berlin (2001)
8. Kühne, U., Soulat, R.: Minimator 1.0 (2015). https://bitbucket.org/ukuehne/minimator/

9. Larsen, K.G., Mikučionis, M., Muñiz, M., Srba, J., Taankvist, J.H.: Online and compositional learning of controllers with application to floor heating. In: Chechik, M., Raskin, J.-F. (eds.) TACAS 2016. LNCS, vol. 9636, pp. 244–259. Springer, Heidelberg (2016). doi:10.1007/978-3-662-49674-9_14
10. Le Coënt, A., Fribourg, L., Markey, N., De Vuyst, F., Chamoin, L.: Distributed synthesis of state-dependent switching control. Technical report, March 2016. https://hal.archives-ouvertes.fr/hal-01295738
11. Le Coent, A., Alexandre Dit Sandretto, J., Chapoutot, A., Fribourg, L.: Control of nonlinear switched systems based on validated simulation. In: SNR 2016. IEEE (2016)
12. Liberzon, D.: Switching in Systems and Control. Springer, Berlin (2012)
13. Meyer, P.-J., Girard, A., Witrant, E.: Safety control with performance guarantees of cooperative systems using compositional abstractions. In: ADHS 2015, pp. 317–322 (2015)
14. Mitchell, I.M.: Comparing forward and backward reachability as tools for safety analysis. In: Bemporad, A., Bicchi, A., Buttazzo, G. (eds.) HSCC 2007. LNCS, vol. 4416, pp. 428–443. Springer, Heidelberg (2007)

Compositional Analysis of Boolean Networks Using Local Fixed-Point Iterations

Adrien Le Coënt[1(✉)], Laurent Fribourg[2], and Romain Soulat[3]

[1] CMLA, ENS Cachan, CNRS, Université Paris-Saclay, 61 Av. du Président Wilson, 94235 Cachan Cedex, France
adrien.le-coent@ens-cachan.fr
[2] LSV, ENS Cachan, CNRS, Université Paris-Saclay, 61 Av. du Président Wilson, 94235 Cachan Cedex, France
fribourg@lsv.ens-cachan.fr
[3] Thales Research & Technology, 1 Av. Augustin Fresnel, 91767 Palaiseau, France
romain.soulat@thalesgroup.com

Abstract. We present a compositional method which allows to over-approximate the set of attractors and under-approximate the set of basins of attraction of a Boolean network (BN). This merely consists in replacing a global fixed-point computation by a composition of local fixed-point computations. Once these approximations have been computed, it becomes much more tractable to generate the exact sets of attractors and basins of attraction. We illustrate the interest of our approach on several examples, among which is a BN modeling a railway interlocking system with 50 nodes and millions of attractors.

1 Introduction

Boolean Networks (BNs) have been widely used to model biological systems [15]. The BN is a discrete model that comprises a number of nodes and corresponding update rules. Classically, each node represents a gene and takes a value of 1 or 0, meaning that the gene is expressed or not. Each update rule represents interactions between genes. BNs have also been used in industrial networks such as railway yards [10]. The states of objects in a railway yard (railway interlocking system) can be captured by means of Boolean variables. The control and management of such systems can then be expressed under the form of rules of BNs.

We consider here *synchronous* BNs, which means that the updates are performed synchronously. Synchronous BNs can be considered as a class of deterministic finite state machines. Any sequence of consecutive states eventually converges to a cycle of states, called an *attractor*. In biological systems, attractors capture long-term behaviors of biological systems (e.g., growth, differentiation, and apoptosis) [15]. In railway interlocking systems, attractors also convey important information.

Practically, all algorithms for computing attractors in Boolean networks face a potential state-space explosion that must be addressed to handle large-scale models. (The problem of finding attractors in BNs is NP-hard [1]). A common

© Springer International Publishing Switzerland 2016
K.G. Larsen et al. (Eds.): RP 2016, LNCS 9899, pp. 134–147, 2016.
DOI: 10.1007/978-3-319-45994-3_10

approach is to use *symbolic* algorithms (Binary Decision Diagrams (BDDs) [3] or SAT-based methods) which avoid representing explicit states and transitions.

Algorithms based on BDDs are usable to process BNs with up to a hundred of state variables [17]. However for larger networks, BDDs become too memory-consuming. Propositional decision procedures (SAT) do not suffer from the potential space explosion of BDDs and can handle propositional satisfiability with thousands of variables [8]. The approach in [9] relies on SAT-based bounded model checking [2] to compute attractors. Those algorithms enable to scale up hundreds of nodes with K (maximum indegree or maximum node connectivity) ≤ 3 (i.e., low maximum connectivity). However, in case of BNs with higher Ks, a state explosion still occurs. The same phenomenon occurs when the number of attractors N_a increases, which makes the problem of finding attractors impracticable for the case studies that we consider here (for which N_a increases exponentially with the number n of state variables).

To expand the range of feasible BNs, partitioning-based attractor detection algorithms have been published recently [12,19]. Both works use a partitioning strategy based on strongly connected component (SCC). Attractors are independently detected in each block, and then combined to construct the attractors of the original BN. Therefore better scalability can be achieved, but still for low K (≤ 3). For BNs with large K, the size of the largest SCC is too large to be analyzed within a reasonable time.

In order to overcome this problem, in [14], the authors propose a partitioning not based on SCC. They are thus able to find attractors for networks with a number n of nodes up to 1000 and $K = 5$. Unfortunately the method generates only "steady states", i.e., cyclic attractors of length 1, and ignores cyclic attractors of greater length.

Here, we propose a method which uses the same kind of partitioning as in [14] but we use a different algorithm for detecting the local attractors inside each component: while [14] uses SAT-based bounded model checking methods for finding local attractors, we use an "iterative reduction" method (similar to [6], Sect. 11.2 and [7], Sect. VIII.B). For constructing the global attractors, we first combine the results obtained by the local iterative reductions similarly to [7]. This allows us to compute an *over-approximation* of the union of all the attractors (not only the steady states). In a second step, starting from this over-approximation, we then compute the *exact set* of all the attractors using global fixed-point iterations.

We have implemented the method in Octave. Using this prototype, we are able to find all the attractors of a BN with $n = 50$ and $K = 6$, which models a portion of the New York City subway [11].

We also explain how our compositional method can be adapted to construct (under-approximations of) basins of attraction.

Plan. We explain how to find (a superset of) all the attractors in a compositional way in Sect. 2 and (subsets of) basins of attraction in Sect. 3. We present some experiments performed with a prototype implementation in Sect. 4. We conclude in Sect. 5.

2   Attractors

2.1   Concrete Functions

A *synchronous Boolean Control Network (BCN)* is a discrete-time dynamical system subject to the rules

$$x(t+1) = f(x(t), u(t)) \tag{1}$$

where x is a vector of n Boolean variables (called *state*), u is a vector of m Boolean variables (called *control input*), and f is a vector of n Boolean functions on these variables and inputs. We denote by S the set of all possible instantiations of variables x $(S = \{0,1\}^n)$. We denote by U the set of all possible instantiations of inputs u $(U = \{0,1\}^m)$.

In the following, we will consider that a BCN can be decomposed into two systems of the form

$$x_1(t+1) = f_1(x_1(t), x_2(t), u_1(t)) \tag{2}$$
$$x_2(t+1) = f_2(x_1(t), x_2(t), u_2(t)) \tag{3}$$

where x_1 and x_2 are vectors of respectively n_1 and n_2 Boolean variables with $n = n_1 + n_2$, u_1 and u_2 are vectors of respectively m_1 and m_2 Boolean inputs with $m = m_1 + m_2$, and f_1 and f_2 are vectors of respectively n_1 and n_2 Boolean functions on these variables and inputs. We denote by S_1 the set of all possible instantiations of variables x_1 $(S_1 = \{0,1\}^{n_1})$, and by S_2 the set of all possible instantiations of variables x_2 $(S_2 = \{0,1\}^{n_2})$. Likewise, we denote by U_1 the set of all possible instantiations of inputs u_1 $(U_1 = \{0,1\}^{m_1})$, and by U_2 the set of all possible instantiations of inputs u_2 $(U_2 = \{0,1\}^{m_2})$.

Remark. The way of finding interesting splittings of the system into two subsystems is beyond the scope of this paper. It can be done using the method of [14].

A *BN* is a BCN without control inputs:

$$x(t+1) = f(x(t)). \tag{4}$$

For the sake of simplicity, we will focus in the sequel of this section on BN.

The definitions of f, f_1 and f_2 can naturally be "lifted" to the powerset level. We will use the same notation f for the functions and their lifted versions. For $X \in 2^S$, we have: $f(X) = \{f(x) \mid x \in X\}$. Likewise, given a set $X_1 \in 2^{S_1}$ and a set $X_2 \in 2^{S_2}$, we have for $i = 1, 2$: $f_i(X_1, X_2) = \{f_i(x_1, x_2) \mid x_1 \in X_1, x_2 \in X_2\}$.

In the rest of the paper, all the fixed-point results will concern functions lifted at the powerset level.

We have:

Proposition 2.1. *Suppose:* $F^\times \subseteq X \subseteq S$. *Then* $F^\times = \bigcap_{k \geq 0} f^k(X)$.

Proof. Suppose $F^\times \subseteq X \subseteq S$. Then $\bigcap_{k \geq 0} f^k(F^\times) \subseteq \bigcap_{k \geq 0} f^k(X) \subseteq \bigcap_{k \geq 0} f^k S$. Hence: $F^\times \subseteq \bigcap_{k \geq 0} f^k(X) \subseteq F^\times$. It follows: $F^\times = \bigcap_{k \geq 0} f^k(X)$. $\qquad \square$

As already mentioned, since a BN is subject to deterministic rules (applied here synchronously) and since the number of elements is finite (equal to 2^n), every derivation from an arbitrary element ends to a cycle. The set of elements composing this cycle is called an *attractor*. We have:

Proposition 2.2. *The union of the attractors of the BN is equal to $F^\times$.*

2.2 Abstract Functions

We are going to give a method for computing an *over-approximation* (i.e., a superset) of $F^\times$. This will be done by constructing the greatest fixed-point of an "abstraction" $\tilde{f}$ of f. Let $\tilde{S} = (S_1, S_2)$.

Definition 2.3. *The function $\tilde{f} \colon 2^{S_1} \times 2^{S_2} \to 2^{S_1} \times 2^{S_2}$ is defined for all $X_1 \in 2^{S_1}$ and $X_2 \in 2^{S_2}$, by:*

$$\tilde{f}(X_1, X_2) = (f_1(X_1, X_2), f_2(X_1, X_2))$$
$$= \{(f_1(x_1, x_2), f_2(w_1, w_2)) \mid x_1 \in X_1, x_2 \in X_2, w_1 \in X_1, w_2 \in X_2\}.$$

At the concrete (resp. abstract) level, we consider the finite lattice of functions from 2^S to 2^S (resp. from $2^{S_1} \times 2^{S_2}$ to $2^{S_1} \times 2^{S_2}$). We say that two abstract functions φ and ψ are *ordered*, and write $\varphi \leq_a \psi$ if for any $(X_1, X_2) \in 2^{S_1} \times 2^{S_2}$: $\varphi(X_1, X_2) = (Y_1, Y_2), \psi(X_1, X_2) = (Z_1, Z_2)$ with $Y_i \subseteq_i Z_i$ for $i = 1, 2$, where '$\subseteq_i$' denotes the inclusion ordering between elements of 2^{S_i}. Likewise, we say that two concrete functions f and g are *ordered*, and write $f \leq_c g$ if $f(X) \subseteq_c g(X)$ where '$\subseteq_c$' denotes the inclusion ordering between elements of 2^S. Without loss of understanding, we will omit the indices of symbols '$\leq$' and '$\subseteq$'. Context will make it clear. The identity function at the abstract (resp. concrete) level will be denoted by Id_a (resp. Id_c). Note that, abstract functions and concrete functions are *monotonic* since they are lifted at the powerset level. We have (see [7]):

Definition 2.4. *The abstraction function $\alpha \colon 2^S \to 2^{S_1} \times 2^{S_2}$ and the concretization function $\gamma \colon 2^{S_1} \times 2^{S_2} \to 2^S$ are defined as follows:*

– for all $X \in 2^S = 2^{S_1 \times S_2}$,

$$\alpha(X) = (\pi_1(X), \pi_2(X)),$$

where π_i is (the lift of) the i-th projection of S to S_i $(i = 1, 2)$.
– for all $X_1 \in 2^{S_1}$ and $X_2 \in 2^{S_2}$,

$$\gamma(X_1, X_2) = X_1 \times X_2 = \{(x_1, x_2) \mid x_1 \in X_1, x_2 \in X_2\}.$$

The abstraction function α "separates" an element of 2^S, i.e., a set X of n-vectors of bits into two elements X_1 and X_2 of 2^{S_1} and 2^{S_2} respectively, i.e., into a set of n_1-vectors and a set of n_2-vectors with $n = n_1 + n_2$. Conversely, the concretization function γ "gathers" two elements X_1 and X_2 of 2^{S_1} and 2^{S_2} into an element of $2^S = 2^{S_1 \times S_2}$.

It is easy to show that the function $\alpha f \gamma \colon 2^{S_1} \times 2^{S_2} \to 2^{S_1} \times 2^{S_2}$ coincides with the definition of $\tilde{f}$ given in Definition 2.3, i.e.: $\tilde{f} = \alpha f \gamma$. We have:

Proposition 2.5. $\gamma \alpha \geq Id_c$, *i.e., for all* $X \in 2^S \colon \gamma(\alpha(X)) \supseteq X$.

Proof. Let $X \in 2^S$. Write $\alpha(X) = (X_1, X_2)$. If $x = x_1 x_2 \in X$ then $x_1 \in X_1$ and $x_2 \in X_2$, thus $x \in \gamma(X_1, X_2) = \gamma \alpha(X)$.

Intuitively, this inclusion expresses the fact that by separating the arguments at the abstract level, we lose the information of interdependence between these arguments. The functions f, $\tilde{f}$, α and γ satisfy basic properties of Abstract Interpretation (see [7]):

Lemma 2.6. *We have:*

1. $\alpha \gamma \leq Id_a$, *i.e., for all* $(X_1, X_2) \in 2^{S_1} \times 2^{S_2} \colon \alpha(\gamma(X_1, X_2)) \subseteq (X_1, X_2)$.
2. $f \gamma \leq \gamma \tilde{f}$, *i.e., for all* $(X_1, X_2) \in 2^{S_1} \times 2^{S_2} \colon f \gamma(X_1, X_2) \subseteq \gamma \tilde{f}(X_1, X_2)$.

Proof. 1. Write $(Y_1, Y_2) = \alpha \gamma(X_1, X_2)$. Assume $y_i \in Y_i$ for $i = 1, 2$. Then $\exists y \in \gamma(X_1, X_2) \colon y_i = \pi_i(y)$ for $i = 1, 2$. Since $y \in X_1 \times X_2$, $y_i \in X_i$ for $i = 1, 2$. We have shown $Y_i \subseteq X_i$ for $i = 1, 2$, i.e.: $(Y_1, Y_2) \subseteq (X_1, X_2)$.
2. Since $Id_c \leq \gamma \alpha$ by Proposition 2.5 and $\tilde{f} = \alpha f \gamma$, we have: $\gamma \tilde{f} = \gamma \alpha f \gamma \geq f \gamma$. $\square$

Remark. In general we do not have $\alpha \gamma(X_1, X_2) = (X_1, X_2)$ because, in the case $X_1 = \emptyset$, we have $\alpha \gamma(\emptyset, X_2) = \alpha(\emptyset \times X_2) = (\emptyset, \emptyset)$ which is distinct from (X_1, X_2) when $X_2 \neq \emptyset$.

Let us write the greatest fixed-point gfp($\tilde{f}$) of $\tilde{f}$ as $(F_1^\times, F_2^\times)$.

Proposition 2.7. *We have:*

1. *gfp*$(f) \leq \gamma$ *gfp*$(\tilde{f})$, *i.e.:* $F^\times \subseteq F_1^\times \times F_2^\times$.
2. $F^\times = \bigcap_{k \geq 0} f^k(F_1^\times \times F_2^\times)$.

This proposition is a consequence of Theorem 2.8 that is given below. The pair $(F_1^\times, F_2^\times)$ can be thus used as a 'seed' for the computation of the greatest fixed-point $F^\times$ of f: one starts the iteration of f from $F_1^\times \times F_2^\times$ instead of starting from S. It may be easier to compute $F^\times$ starting from $F_1^\times \times F_2^\times$ rather than S because $|F_1^\times \times F_2^\times|$ is sometimes much smaller than $|S| = 2^n$.

For a given integer $\ell \geq 1$, let us define g and $\tilde{g}$ by: $g = f^\ell$ and $\tilde{g} = \alpha g \gamma$.

Let us write the greatest fixed-point of $\tilde{g}$ as $(G_1^\times, G_2^\times)$. We have:

Theorem 2.8. *For all integer* $\ell \geq 1$:

1. $F^\times = G^\times$.
2. $G^\times \subseteq G_1^\times \times G_2^\times$.
3. $F^\times = \bigcap_{k \geq 0} f^k(G_1^\times \times G_2^\times) = \bigcap_{k \geq 0} g^k(G_1^\times \times G_2^\times)$.
4. $G_1^\times \times G_2^\times \subseteq F_1^\times \times F_2^\times$.

Proof. 1. We have: $F^\times = \bigcap_{k \geq 0} f^k(S) = \bigcap_{k \geq 0} f^{k\ell}(S) = G^\times$.

2. By Lemma 2.6.3 with g in place of f, we have: $g\gamma \subseteq \gamma\tilde{g}$. One can then prove by induction on k: for all $k \geq 0$, $g^k\gamma(\tilde{S}) \subseteq \gamma\tilde{g}^k(\tilde{S})$. Passing to the limit and using $\gamma\tilde{S} = S_1 \times S_2 = S$, it follows: $G^\times \subseteq G_1^\times \times G_2^\times$.

3. By items 1 and 2, we have: $F^\times \subseteq G_1^\times \times G_2^\times \subseteq S$. It follows by Proposition 2.1: $F^\times = \bigcap_{k \geq 0} f^k(G_1^\times \times G_2^\times)$.

4. Using $\tilde{f} = \alpha f\gamma$ and $\gamma\alpha \supseteq Id_c$ (Proposition 2.5), we can prove by induction on ℓ: $\tilde{f}^\ell \supseteq \alpha f^\ell\gamma$, for $\ell \geq 0$. Passing to the limit, we have: $(F_1^\times, F_2^\times) \supseteq (G_1^\times, G_2^\times)$. Hence: $G_1^\times \times G_2^\times \subseteq F_1^\times \times F_2^\times$.

$\square$

It can be interesting to perform the computation of $F^\times$, starting from $G_1^\times \times G_2^\times$ rather than $F_1^\times \times F_2^\times$, because $|G_1^\times \times G_2^\times|$ may be much smaller than $|F_1^\times \times F_2^\times|$. Note that, for $\ell = 1$, g coincides with f, $G^\times$ with $F^\times$, and $G_i^\times$ with $F_i^\times$ ($i = 1, 2$). Hence Proposition 2.7 is an immediate consequence of Theorem 2.8.

2.3   Example

We will illustrate our approach with the Example 6.2 of [4], which is a BN given by the rules:

$$A(t + 1) = 1 \wedge H(t),$$
$$B(t + 1) = A(t) \wedge (A(t) \vee C(t)),$$
$$C(t + 1) = I(t),$$
$$E(t + 1) = 1 \wedge C(t) \wedge (C(t) \vee F(t)),$$
$$F(t + 1) = E(t) \wedge (E(t) \vee G(t)),$$
$$G(t + 1) = 1 \wedge (B(t) \vee E(t)),$$
$$H(t + 1) = F(t) \wedge (F(t) \vee G(t)),$$
$$I(t + 1) = H(t) \wedge (H(t) \vee I(t)).$$

This corresponds to state variable $x = (A, B, C, E, F, G, H, I)$ and $S = \{0,1\}^8$. The system is split in two as follows: $x_1 = (A, F, G, H, I)$, $x_2 = (B, C, E)$, $S_1 = \{0,1\}^5$, $S_2 = \{0,1\}^3$.

Computation of $F_1^\times \times F_2^\times$. In order to compute gfp($\tilde{f}$)$= (F_1^\times, F_2^\times)$, we use a strategy related to the application of Bekić-Leszczyłowski theorem (see [16]). Roughly speaking, we compute at step i an intermediate fixed-point $F_{1,i+1}$ starting from the current value $F_{1,i}$ of the 1st component using the current value $F_{2,i}$ of the 2nd component as a parameter. Then, we compute a new intermediate fixed-point $F_{2,i+1}$ starting from $F_{2,i}$ using $F_{1,i+1}$ as a parameter, and so on alternatively until stabilization. We have:

$$F_{1,0} = S_1,$$
$$F_{2,0} = S_2.$$

$F_{1,1} = \{00000, 00001, 00010, 00011, 00100, 00101, 00110, 00111, 01000, 01001,$
$01010, 01011, 01100, 01101, 01110, 01111, 10000, 10001, 10010, 10011, 10100,$
$10101, 10110, 10111, 11000, 11001, 11010, 11011, 11100, 11101, 11110, 11111\},$

$F_{2,1} = \{000, 001, 010, 011, 101, 111\}.$

$F_{1,2} = \{00000, 00010, 00100, 00110, 01000, 01010, 01011, 01100, 01101,$
$01110, 01111, 10000, 10010, 10100, 10110, 11000, 11010, 11011, 11100, 11101,$
$11110, 11111\},$
$F_{2,2} = F_{2,1}.$

$F_{1,3} = F_{1,2}.$

Hence $F_1^\times \times F_2^\times = F_{1,2} \times F_{2,1}$ has $22 \times 6 = 132$ elements. The computation of $(F_1^\times, F_2^\times)$ is obtained in 2 iterations and 0.87 s of CPU time using our prototype implementation (see Sect. 4). The computation of $F^\times$ by iteration of f starting from $F_1^\times \times F_2^\times$ is then obtained in 11 iterations and takes 0.11 s of CPU time.

Computation of $G_1^\times \times G_2^\times$, with $g = f^2$
We have:

$G_{1,0} = S_1,$
$G_{2,0} = S_2.$

$G_{1,1} = \{00000, 00001, 00100, 00101, 00110, 00111, 01010, 01011, 01110,$
$01111, 10000, 10100, 10110, 11000, 11010, 11100, 11110\},$
$G_{2,1} = \{000, 001, 011, 101\}.$

$G_{1,2} = \{10000, 11000, 11010, 01011, 01010, 01111, 00100, 10100, 10100\},$
$G_{2,2} = G_{2,1}.$

$G_{1,3} = G_{1,2}.$

Hence $G_1^\times \times G_2^\times = G_{1,2} \times G_{2,1}$ has only $9 \times 4 = 36$ elements. This shows that the over-approximation $G_1^\times \times G_2^\times$ of $F^\times$ is much finer than $F_1^\times \times F_2^\times$. The computation of $(G_1^\times, G_2^\times)$ is obtained in 2 iterations and 0.84 s of CPU time with our prototype implementation. The fixed point $F^\times$ of f is then obtained from $G_1^\times \times G_2^\times$ via 11 applications of f, which takes 0.10 s of CPU time. This yields:

$F^\times = \{01111 \cdot 001, 00100 \cdot 011, 01010 \cdot 011, 01011 \cdot 101, 10100 \cdot 000, 10000 \cdot$
$101, 10100 \cdot 101, 11000 \cdot 101, 11010 \cdot 101\}$

where each element of $F^\times$ is an instance of $x = x_1 \cdot x_2 = AFGHI \cdot BCE$. It is easy to see that all the elements of $F^\times$ here belong to a *unique* attractor of length 9 (i.e., $F^\times$ is of the form $\{\sigma_1, \ldots, \sigma_9\}$ with $f(\sigma_i) = \sigma_{i+1}$ for $1 \leq i \leq 8$, and $f(\sigma_9) = \sigma_1$).

By comparison, the global computation of $F^\times$ by iterated application of f to S takes 12 iterations and 0.92 s of CPU time. On such a small example, the compositional approach does not bring a significant difference with the global approach, neither in terms of number of iterations nor in terms of computation time.

Remark. We have described here a method which computes attractors for a system split into two sub-systems. The extension to more than two sub-systems is straightforward.

3   Basins of Attraction

We now reintroduce the set U of control variables.

3.1   Concrete Functions

Given a *stationary point* σ of f (i.e., an element σ of $S = S_1 \times S_2$ such that $f(\sigma, u) = \sigma$ for some $u \in U$), it is interesting to compute the *basin of attraction* of σ, i.e.: the set of elements x such that $f(\cdots f(f(x, u_1), u_2), \ldots, u_k) \cdots) = \sigma$ for some $k > 0$ and $(u_1, u_2, \ldots, u_k) \in U^k$.

Classically, *backward reachability* procedures are used (see, e.g., [18]) to compute basins of attraction. Let us define the *predecessor* operator. For all $X \subseteq S$:

$$p(X) = \{y \in S \mid \exists u \in U : f(y, u) \in X\}.$$

As usual, we define $p^k(X)$ by: $p^0(X) = X$ and $p^{k+1}(X) = p(p^k(X))$ for $k \geq 0$. Since σ is a stationary point, the sequence $\{p^i(\{\sigma\})\}_{k \geq 0}$ is increasing. When the fixed-point $p^*(\{\sigma\})$ is reached, at step j (i.e. $p^{j+1}(\{\sigma\}) = p^j(\{\sigma\})$), we have: $p^*(\{\sigma\}) = \bigcup_{k \geq 0} p^k(\{\sigma\}) = p^j(\{\sigma\})$. Since $\{\sigma\} \subseteq p(\{\sigma\})$, the set $p^*(\{\sigma\})$ is, by Kleene fixed-point theorem, the *least fixed-point* of p containing σ; it coincides with the smallest *prefixed-point* of p containing σ, i.e., the smallest set $X \in 2^S$ containing σ such that $\forall x \in X \exists u \in U \; f(x, u) \in X$. We have:

Proposition 3.1. *The basin of attraction of σ is equal to*

$$p^*(\{\sigma\}) = \bigcup_{k \geq 0} p^k(\{\sigma\}).$$

The counterpart of Proposition 2.1 is:

Proposition 3.2. *Suppose:* $\{\sigma\} \subseteq X \subseteq p^*(\{\sigma\})$. *Then:* $p^*(\{\sigma\}) = \bigcup_{k \geq 0} p^k(X)$.

The proof is analogous to that of Proposition 2.1.

3.2   Abstract Functions

We now focus on systems of the form (2)–(3), i.e. that can be decomposed in two parts, this along S and along U. A stationary point σ is of the form (σ_1, σ_2) with $\sigma_1 \in S_1 = \{0, 1\}^{n_1}$, $\sigma_2 \in S_2 = \{0, 1\}^{n_2}$. Let $\tilde{\sigma} = (\{\sigma_1\}, \{\sigma_2\})$.

We are going to introduce two abstractions $\tilde{p}_{X_2}(X_1)$ and $\tilde{p}_{X_1}(X_2)$ of p. We will then compute least fixed-points, denoted by $\tilde{p}_{S_2}^*(\{\sigma_1\})$ and $\tilde{p}_{S_1}^*(\{\sigma_2\})$, of $\tilde{p}_{S_2}(\cdot)$ and $\tilde{p}_{S_1}(\cdot)$ containing $\{\sigma_1\}$ and $\{\sigma_2\}$ respectively. We will show that $\tilde{p}^*(\tilde{\sigma}) = (\tilde{p}_{S_2}^*(\{\sigma_1\}), \tilde{p}_{S_1}^*(\{\sigma_2\}))$ satisfies $\{\sigma\} \subseteq \gamma \tilde{p}^*(\tilde{\sigma}) \subseteq p^*(\{\sigma\})$. Hence, by Proposition 3.2, the basin of σ can be obtained by iteratively applying p to $\gamma \tilde{p}^*(\tilde{\sigma})$ instead of $\{\sigma\}$. This may reduce the computation time of the basin of σ.

We introduce the following (controlled) abstract predecessor operators:

$$\tilde{p}_{X_2}(X_1) = \{y_1 \in S_1 \mid \exists u_1 \in U_1, \forall x_2 \in X_2, f_1(y_1, x_2, u_1) \in X_1\}, \tag{5}$$

$$\tilde{p}_{X_1}(X_2) = \{y_2 \in S_2 | \ \exists u_2 \in U_2, \ \forall x_1 \in X_1, f_2(x_1, y_2, u_2) \in X_2\}. \qquad (6)$$

We denote by $\tilde{p}^*_{S_2}(\{\sigma_1\})$ and $\tilde{p}^*_{S_1}(\{\sigma_2\})$ the least fixed-points obtained by iterative application of $\tilde{p}_{S_2}(\cdot)$ and $\tilde{p}_{S_1}(\cdot)$ starting from $\{\sigma_1\}$ and $\{\sigma_2\}$ respectively. Finally, we write $\tilde{p}^*(\tilde{\sigma}) = (\tilde{p}^*_{S_2}(\{\sigma_1\}), \tilde{p}^*_{S_1}(\{\sigma_2\}))$.

Lemma 3.3. *For all* $(X_1, X_2) \in 2^{S_1} \times 2^{S_2}$, *we have* $\gamma(\tilde{p}_{S_2}(X_1), \tilde{p}_{S_1}(X_2)) \subseteq p\gamma(X_1, X_2)$.

Proof. Let $w = (w_1, w_2) \in \gamma(\tilde{p}_{S_2}(X_1), \tilde{p}_{S_1}(X_2))$. We know that:

$$\exists u_1 \in U_1, \ \forall x_2 \in S_2, f_1(w_1, x_2, u_1) \in X_1$$

and

$$\exists u_2 \in U_2, \ \forall x_1 \in S_1, f_2(x_1, w_2, u_2) \in X_2.$$

In particular:

$$\exists u_1 \in U_1, \ f_1(w_1, w_2, u_1) \in X_1$$

and

$$\exists u_2 \in U_2, \ f_2(w_1, w_2, u_2) \in X_2.$$

Hence:

$$\exists u = (u_1, u_2) \in U, \ f((w_1, w_2), u) = (f_1(w_1, w_2, u_1), f_2(w_1, w_2, u_2)) \in X_1 \times X_2,$$

i.e. $w \in p\gamma(X_1, X_2)$. □

Theorem 3.4. *We have:*

1. $\{\sigma\} \subseteq \gamma\tilde{p}^*(\tilde{\sigma}) \subseteq p^*(\{\sigma\})$.
2. $p^*(\{\sigma\}) = \bigcup_{k \geq 0} p^k(\gamma\tilde{p}^*(\tilde{\sigma}))$.

Proof. 1. Ones proves that, for all $k \geq 0$, $\{\sigma\} \subseteq \bigcup_{j \leq k} \gamma(\tilde{p}^j_{S_2}(X_1), \tilde{p}^j_{S_1}(X_2)) \subseteq \bigcup_{j \leq k} p^j \gamma(\tilde{\sigma})$ by induction on k, using Lemma 3.3. Passing to the limit, it follows: $\{\sigma\} \subseteq \gamma\tilde{p}^*(\tilde{\sigma}) \subseteq p^*(\{\sigma\})$, using $\gamma(\tilde{\sigma}) = \{\sigma\}$.
2. Since $\{\sigma\} \subseteq \gamma\tilde{p}^*(\tilde{\sigma}) \subseteq p^*(\{\sigma\})$ by item 1, it follows by Proposition 3.2: $p^*(\{\sigma\}) = \bigcup_{k \geq 0} p^k(\gamma\tilde{p}^*(\tilde{\sigma}))$. □

Remark. Note that it is possible to extend the definitions (5) and (6) to the use of sequences of control inputs using the following definitions:

$$\tilde{p}^{\ell_1}_{X_2}(X_1) = \{y_1 \in S_1 \mid \exists u^1_1 \ldots u^{\ell_1}_1 \in U^{\ell_1}_1, \forall u^1_2 \ldots u^{\ell_1}_2 \in U^{\ell_1}_2$$
$$\pi_1 f(\ldots f(f((y_1, S_2), (u^1_1, u^1_2)), (u^2_1, u^2_2)) \ldots, (u^{\ell_1}_1, u^{\ell_1}_2)) \in X_1\},$$

$$\tilde{p}^{\ell_2}_{X_1}(X_2) = \{y_2 \in S_2 \mid \exists u^1_2 \ldots u^{\ell_2}_2 \in U^{\ell_2}_2, \forall u^1_1 \ldots u^{\ell_2}_1 \in U^{\ell_2}_1$$
$$\pi_2 f(\ldots f(f((S_1, y_2), (u^1_1, u^1_2)), (u^2_1, u^2_2)) \ldots, (u^{\ell_2}_1, u^{\ell_2}_2)) \in X_2\}.$$

4   Experiments

The experiments presented here have been performed with our prototype written in Octave. The computation times given below have been performed on an Intel Core i7-4810MQ CPU running at 2.80 GHz with 8 GB of RAM memory.

4.1   Attractors

In industrial case studies, such as railway interlocking, it is important to show that all the attractors are cycles of length 1 (*stationary states*). We have tested our method on an example of a railway interlocking system taken from "NXSYS, Signalling and Interlocking Simulator" [11]. The dynamics of the BN model of the system is given in Appendix. This example has 28 variables and 22 para-meters. The objective of the analysis is to show that for any valuation ν of the parameters in $\{0,1\}^{22}$, all the attractors are stationary states. We divide the system into 4 sub-systems as explained in Appendix. The computation of the over-approximated set of attractors $\{F_{1,\nu}^{\times} \times F_{2,\nu}^{\times} \times F_{3,\nu}^{\times} \times F_{4,\nu}^{\times}\}_{\nu \in \{0,1\}^{22}}$ took 2 h. The computation of the exact set of attractors $\mathcal{A} = \{F_{\nu}^{\times}\}_{\nu \in \{0,1\}^{22}}$ then took 12 more hours. The total number of attractors is $|\mathcal{A}| \simeq 24.10^6$, and we check that all the elements of $\mathcal{A}$ are stationary states. By comparison, for a single instantiation ν, the state-of-art program BNS (available at https://people.kth.se/~dubrova/bns.html) takes 0.02 s, which seems to indicate that BNS would take at least twice more time for computing the whole set of attractors of the 2^{22} instantiations of the problem.

4.2   Basins of Attraction

We have experimented the compositional computation of basins of attraction on small examples of the literature, e.g.:

- regulation of the mammalian cell cycle [13] (9 variables, 1 input),
- Example 29 of [5] (5 variables and 2 control inputs).

We present here the example of the regulation of the mammalian cell cycle [13], which dynamics is the following:

$$Y_1(t+1) = (\bar{U}(t) \wedge \bar{Y}_3(t) \wedge \bar{Y}_4(t) \wedge \bar{Y}_9(t)) \vee (Y_5(t) \wedge \bar{U}(t) \wedge \bar{Y}_9(t)),$$
$$Y_2(t+1) = (\bar{Y}_1(t) \wedge \bar{Y}_4(t) \wedge \bar{Y}_9(t)) \vee (Y_5(t) \wedge \bar{Y}_1(t) \wedge \bar{Y}_9(t)),$$
$$Y_3(t+1) = Y_2(t) \wedge \bar{Y}_1(t),$$
$$Y_4(t+1) = (Y_2(t) \wedge \bar{Y}_1(t) \wedge \bar{Y}_6(t) \wedge (\overline{Y_7(t) \wedge Y_8(t)}))$$
$$\vee (Y_4(t) \wedge \bar{Y}_1(t) \wedge \bar{Y}_6(t) \wedge (\overline{Y_7(t) \wedge Y_8(t)})),$$
$$Y_5(t+1) = (\bar{U}(t) \wedge \bar{Y}_3(t) \wedge \bar{Y}_4(t) \wedge (\bar{Y}_9(t))$$
$$\vee (Y_5(t) \wedge (\overline{Y_3(t) \wedge Y_4(t)}) \wedge \bar{U}(t) \wedge \bar{Y}_9(t)),$$
$$Y_6(t+1) = Y_9(t+1),$$

$$Y_7(t + 1) = (\bar{Y}_4(t) \wedge \bar{Y}_9(t)) \vee Y_6(t) \vee (Y_5(t) \wedge \bar{Y}_9(t)),$$
$$Y_8(t + 1) = \bar{Y}_7(t) \vee (Y_7(t) \wedge Y_8(t) \wedge (Y_6(t) \vee Y_4(t) \vee Y_9(t))),$$
$$Y_9(t + 1) = \bar{Y}_6(t) \wedge \bar{Y}_7(t).$$

For this example, it is known that there exists a stationary point σ (associated to a sequence of inputs equal to 1), with $\sigma = \{100010100\}$.

Let us explain how we compute the basin of attraction of σ with the compositional method. We split the system in two: $x_1 = (Y_1, Y_2, Y_3, Y_5)$ and $x_2 = (Y_4, Y_6, Y_7, Y_8, Y_9)$, $S_1 = \{0,1\}^4$ and $S_2 = \{0,1\}^5$. The fixed-points $\tilde{p}^*_{S_2}(\{\sigma_1\})$ and $\tilde{p}^*_{S_1}(\{\sigma_2\})$ are obtained in 2 iterations and 1.71 s of CPU time, with sequences of control inputs of length lower than 5. The size of $\tilde{p}^*(\sigma_1, \sigma_2)$ is $16 \times 21 = 336$. By computing the iterated predecessors of $\gamma\tilde{p}^*(\sigma_1, \sigma_2)$ via p, we find in 3.03 s and 3 iterations, that the basin of attraction is equal to S. By comparison, the global computation of $p^*(\sigma)$ takes 4.15 s and 4 iterations. On such a small example, the results of the two approaches in terms of computation times and number of iterations are similar.

5   Final Remarks

We proposed a compositional method based on local fixed-point iterations. The method has been successfully applied to an example with 50 variables modeling a part of New York City subway, which allows us to identify more than 24 millions of attractors. We believe that such a finding of all the attractors would be difficult using a global approach with state-of-the-art tools. Our current implementation of the method is a simple prototype with explicit representation of Boolean states. We are currently integrating symbolic structures (BDDs) to the code in order to treat larger examples. One of our objectives is to find the attractors of a real railway interlocking system provided by Thales.

Acknowledgement. We are most grateful to Philippe Schnoebelen for insightful explanations on Abstract Interpretation and numerous comments on an earlier draft of this paper.

This work is supported by Institut Farman (ENS Cachan) and by the French National Research Agency through the "iCODE Institute project" funded by the IDEX Paris-Saclay, ANR-11-IDEX-0003-02.

Appendix: Railway Interlocking System

Railway Interlocking is one part of a complete railway system that ensures the safety of all trains and passengers. Given the routes that trains wish to travel along and current train positions (among other information), the Interlocking computes a safe environment for trains (mainly signals indications, and switches positions).

A part of the railway interlocking functioning can be translated to boolean equations. In this example, we have taken the boolean variables and equations associated with protection, movement command and locking of two railway switches while abstracting away all the timed components of those systems. Computing the attractors allows to find what states those switches will reach upon reception of a new command.

The dynamics of the system tested in Sect. 4.1 is given by the rules:

23NLP = !23RLP (OR (AND 23ANN 23ANS) (AND 23BNN 23BNS) 18PBS 23NL)
23RLP = !23NLP (OR (AND 23RN 23RS) 23RL)
23ANS = (OR 16PBS 16XR) !23RS !23RWK
23BNS = (OR 25ANS 25RS) !23RN !23RWK
23ANN = (OR 25BNN 25RN) !23RS !23RWK
23BNN = (OR 32XS 32PBS) !23RN !23RWK
23RS = 25ANS !23ANS !23BNN !23NWK
23RN = 25BNN !23ANS !23BNN !23NWK
23NWZ = (OR (AND 23NWZ !23RWZ) (AND 23NLP 23LS))
23RWZ = (OR (AND 23RWZ !23NWZ) (AND 23RLP 23LS))
23NWC = (AND 23NWZ 23NWP)
23RWC = (AND 23RWZ 23RWP)
23NWK = 23NWC (OR 23NLP !23LS)
23RWK = 23RWC (OR 23RLP !23LS)
25ANS = (OR 22PBS 28ZS 22XS 22XR) !25RS !25RWK
25BNS = (OR 23ANS 23RS) !25RN !25RWK
25ANN = (OR 23BNN 23RN) !25RS !25RWK
25BNN = (OR 34XS 34PBS) !25RN !25RWK
25RN = 23BNN !25ANS !25BNN !25NWK
25RS = 23ANS !25ANS !25BNN !25NWK
25NLP = !25RLP (OR (AND 25ANN 25ANS) (AND 25BNN 25BNS) 28XS 25NL)
25RLP = !25NLP (OR (AND 25RN 25RS) 25RL)
25NWZ = (OR (AND 25NWZ !25RWZ) (AND 25NLP 25LS))
25RWZ = (OR (AND 25RWZ !25NWZ) (AND 25RLP 25LS))
25NWC = (AND 25NWZ 25NWP)
25RWC = (AND 25RWZ 25RWP)
25NWK = 25NWC (OR 25NLP !25LS)
25RWK = 25RWC (OR 25RLP !25LS)

The left-hand sides of these equations correspond to the 28 state variables. The other expressions appearing in the right-hand sides correspond to the 22 parameters.

The system is split into 4 sub-systems as follows:

– For sub-system 1, the state variables are: 23NLP, 23RLP, 23ANS, 23BNS, 23ANN, 23BNN, 23RS and 23RN.
  The parameters are: 18PBS, 23RL, 16PBS, 16XR, 32XS, 32PBS and 23NL.
– For sub-system 2, the state variables are: 23NWZ, 23RWZ, 23NWC, 23RWC, 23NWK and 23RWK.
  The parameters are: 23LS, 23NWP and 23RWP.

– For sub-system 3, the state variables are: 25ANS, 25BNS, 25ANN, 25BNN, 25RN, 25RS and 25NLP.
The parameters are: 22PBS, 28ZS, 22XS, 22XR, 34XS, 34PBS, 28XS and 25NL.
– For sub-system 4, the state variables are: 25RLP, 25NWZ, 25RWZ, 25NWC, 25RWC, 25NWK and 25RWK.
The parameters are: 25RL, 25LS, 25NWP and 25RWP.

References

1. Akutsu, T., Kosub, S., Melkman, A.A., Tamura, T.: Finding a periodic attractor of a Boolean network. IEEE/ACM Trans. Comput. Biol. Bioinform. 9(5), 1410–1421 (2012)
2. Biere, A., Cimatti, A., Clarke, E.M., Fujita, M., Zhu, Y.: Symbolic model checking using SAT procedures instead of BDDs. In: DAC, pp. 317–320 (1999). http://doi.acm.org/10.1145/309847.309942
3. Bryant, R.E.: Graph-based algorithms for Boolean function manipulation. IEEE Trans. Comput. 100(8), 677–691 (1986)
4. Cheng, D., Qi, H.: A linear representation of dynamics of Boolean networks. IEEE Trans. Autom. Control 55(10), 2251–2258 (2010)
5. Cheng, D., Qi, H., Zhao, Y.: On Boolean control networks - an algebraic approach. In: Proceedings of the 18th IFAC World Congress, Milano, pp. 8366–8377 (2011)
6. Cousot, P.: The calculational design of a generic abstract interpreter. In: Broy, M., Steinbrüggen, R. (eds.) Calculational System Design. NATO ASI Series F. IOS Press, Amsterdam (1999)
7. Cousot, P.: Compositional separate modular static analysis of programs by abstract interpretation. In: Proceedings of SSGRR - Advances in Infrastructure for Electronic Business, Science, and Education on the Internet, pp. 6–10 (2001)
8. Davis, M., Putnam, H.: A computing procedure for quantification theory. J. ACM 7(3), 201–215 (1960). http://doi.acm.org/10.1145/321033.321034
9. Dubrova, E., Teslenko, M.: A SAT-based algorithm for finding attractors in synchronous Boolean networks. IEEE/ACM Trans. Comput. Biol. Bioinform. (TCBB) 8(5), 1393–1399 (2011)
10. Fokkink, W., Hollingshead, P., Groote, J., Luttik, S., van Wamel, J.: Verification of interlockings: from control tables to ladder logic diagrams. In: Proceedings of FMICS, vol. 98, pp. 171–185 (1998)
11. Greenberg, B.S.: NXSYS, Signaling and Interlocking Simulator. http://www.nycsubway.org/wiki/NXSYS,_Signalling_and_Interlocking_Simulator
12. Guo, W., Yang, G., Wu, W., He, L., Sun, M.: A parallel attractor finding algorithm based on Boolean satisfiability for genetic regulatory networks. PLoS ONE 9(4), e94258 (2014)
13. Hochma, G., Margaliot, M., Fornasini, E., Valcher, M.E.: Symbolic dynamics of Boolean control networks. Automatica 49(8), 2525–2530 (2013)
14. Hong, C., Hwang, J., Cho, K.-H., Shin, I.: An efficient steady-state analysis method for large boolean networks with high maximum node connectivity. PLoS ONE 10(12) (2015). doi:10.1371/journal.pone.0145734
15. Kauffman, S.A.: The Origins of Order: Self Organization and Selection in Evolution. Oxford University Press, New York (1993). http://opac.inria.fr/record=b1077782

16. Kuncak, V., Rustan, K. Leino, M.: On computing the fixpoint of a set of Boolean equations (2004). http://arXiv.org/abs/cs.PL/0408045
17. Naldi, A., Thieffry, D., Chaouiya, C.: Decision diagrams for the representation and analysis of logical models of genetic networks. In: Calder, M., Gilmore, S. (eds.) CMSB 2007. LNCS (LNBI), vol. 4695, pp. 233–247. Springer, Heidelberg (2007)
18. Wuensche, A., et al.: Discrete dynamical networks and their attractor basins. Complex. Int. **6**, 3–21 (1998)
19. Zhao, Y., Kim, J., Filippone, M.: Aggregation algorithm towards large-scale Boolean network analysis. IEEE Trans. Autom. Control **58**(8), 1976–1985 (2013)

Decidable Models of Integer-Manipulating Programs with Recursive Parallelism

Matthew Hague[1]([⊠]) and Anthony Widjaja Lin[2]([⊠])

[1] Royal Holloway, University of London, London, UK
matthew.hague@rhul.ac.uk
[2] Yale-NUS College, Singapore, Singapore
anthony.w.lin@yale-nus.edu.sg

Abstract. We study safety verification for multithreaded programs with recursive parallelism (i.e. unbounded thread creation and recursion) as well as unbounded integer variables. Since the threads in each program configuration are structured in a hierarchical fashion, our model is state-extended ground-tree rewrite systems equipped with shared unbounded integer counters that can be incremented, decremented, and compared against an integer constant. Since the model is Turing-complete, we propose a decidable underapproximation. First, using a restriction similar to context-bounding, we underapproximate the global control by a weak global control (i.e. DAGs possibly with self-loops), thereby limiting the number of synchronisations between different threads. Second, we bound the number of reversals between non-decrementing and non-incrementing modes of the counters. Under this restriction, we show that reachability becomes NP-complete. In fact, it is poly-time reducible to satisfaction over existential Presburger formulas, which allows one to tap into highly optimised SMT solvers. Our decidable approximation strictly generalises known decidable models including (i) weakly-synchronised ground-tree rewrite systems, and (ii) synchronisation/reversal-bounded concurrent pushdown systems with counters. Finally, we show that, when equipped with reversal-bounded counters, relaxing the weak control restriction by the notion of senescence results in undecidability.

1. Introduction

Verification of multithreaded programs is well-known to be a challenging problem. One approach that has proven effective in addressing the problem is to bound the number of context switches [36,38]. [Recall that a *context switch* occurs when the CPU switches from executing one thread to executing a different thread.] When the number of context switches is fixed, one may adopt pushdown systems as a model of a single thread and show that reachability for the concurrent extension of the abstraction (i.e. multi-pushdown systems) is NP-complete [38]. This result has paved the way for an efficient use of highly optimised SMT solvers in verifying concurrent programs (e.g. see [1,18,24]). Note that without bounding the number of context switches the model is undecidable [37].

In the past decade the work of Qadeer and Rehof [38] has spawned a lot of research in underapproximation techniques for verifying multithreaded

© Springer International Publishing Switzerland 2016
K.G. Larsen et al. (Eds.): RP 2016, LNCS 9899, pp. 148–162, 2016.
DOI: 10.1007/978-3-319-45994-3_11

programs, e.g., see [1,2,4,5,7,14,18,20,22,24,27,28,31,33,35,40,42,42] among many others. Other than unbounded recursions, some of these results simultaneously address other sources of infinity, e.g., unbounded thread creation [5,22,31], unbounded integer variables [24], and unbounded FIFO queues [1,2].

Contributions. In this paper we generalise existing underapproximation techniques [23,31] so as to handle both shared unbounded integer variables and recursive parallelism (unbounded thread creation and unbounded recursions). The paper also provides a cleaner proof of the result in [24]: an NP upper bound for synchronisation/reversal-bounded reachability analysis of concurrent pushdown systems with counters. We describe the details below.

We adopt state-extended ground-tree rewrite systems (sGTRS) [31] as a model for multithreaded programs with recursive parallelism (e.g. programming constructs including fork/join, parbegin/parend, and Parallel.For). Ground-tree rewrite systems (GTRS) are known (see [21]) to strictly subsume other well-known sequential and concurrent models like pushdown systems [11], PA-processes [19], and PAD-processes [34], which are known to be suitable for analysing concurrent programs. [One may think of GTRS as an extension of PA and PAD processes with return values to parent threads [21].] We then equip sGTRS with unbounded integer counters that can be incremented, decremented, and compared against an integer constant.

Since our model is Turing-powerful, we provide an underapproximation of the model for which safety verification becomes decidable. First, we underapproximate the global control by a weak global control [26,31] (i.e. DAGs possibly with self-loops), thereby limiting the number of synchronisations between different threads. To this end, we may simply unfold the *underlying control-state graph* of the sGTRS (see Sect. 3) in the standard way, while preserving self-loops. This type of underapproximation is similar to *loop acceleration* in the symbolic acceleration framework of [8]. Second, we bound the number of reversals between non-decrementing and non-incrementing modes of the counters [25]. Under these two restrictions, reachability is shown to be NP-complete; in fact, it is poly-time reducible to satisfaction over existential Presburger formulas, which allows one to tap into highly optimised SMT solvers. Our result strictly generalises the decidability (in fact, NP-completeness) of reachability for (i) weakly-synchronised ground-tree rewrite systems [31,41], and (ii) synchronisation/reversal-bounded concurrent pushdown systems with counters [24].

Finally, we show one negative result that delineates the boundary of decidability. If we relax the weak control underapproximation by the notion of senescence (with age restrictions associated with nodes in the trees) [22], then the resulting model becomes undecidable.

Related Work. Recursively-parallel program analysis was analysed in detail by Bouajjani and Emmi [10]. However, in contrast to our systems, their model does not allow processes to communicate during execution. Instead, processes hold handles to other processes which allow them to wait on the completion of others, and obtain the return value. They show that when handles can be passed to child processes (during creation) then the state reachability problem is undecidable. When handles may only be returned from a child to its parent, state reachability is decidable, with the complexity depending on which of a number of restrictions are imposed.

The work of Bouajjani and Emmi is closely related to branching vector addition systems [43] which can model a stack of counter values which can be incremented and decremented (if they remain non-negative), but not tested. While it is currently unknown whether reachability of a configuration is decidable, control-state reachability and boundedness are both 2ExpTime-complete [17].

Another variant of vector addition systems with recursion are pushdown vector addition systems, where a single (sequential) stack and several global counters are permitted. As before, these counters can be incremented and decremented, but not compared with a value. Reachability of a configuration, and control-state reachability in these models remain open problems, but termination (all paths are finite) and boundedness are known to be decidable [30]. For reachability of a configuration, an under-approximation algorithm is proposed by Atig and Ganty where the stack behaviour is approximated by a *finite index* context-free language [6].

Lang and Löding study boundedness problems over sequential pushdown systems [29]. In this model, the pushdown system is equipped with a counter that can be incremented, reset, or recorded. Their model differs from ours first in the restriction to sequential systems, and second because the counter cannot effect execution or be decremented: it is a recording of resource usage. These kind of cost functions have also been considered over static trees [9,13], however, to our knowledge, they have not been studied over tree rewrite systems.

2 Preliminaries

We write $\mathbb{N}$ to denote the set of natural numbers and $\mathbb{Z}$ the set of integers.

Trees. A *ranked alphabet* is a finite set of characters Σ together with a rank function $\rho : \Sigma \mapsto \mathbb{N}$. A *tree domain* $D \subset \mathbb{N}^*$ is a non-empty finite subset of $\mathbb{N}^*$ that is both *prefix-closed* and *younger-sibling-closed*. That is, if $\eta i \in D$, then we also have $\eta \in D$ and, for all $1 \leq j \leq i$, $\eta j \in D$ (respectively). A *tree* over a ranked alphabet Σ is a pair $t = (D, \lambda)$ where D is a tree domain and $\lambda : D \mapsto \Sigma$ such that for all $\eta \in D$, if $\lambda(\eta) = a$ and $\rho(a) = n$ then η has exactly n children (i.e. $\eta n \in D$ and $\eta(n+1) \notin D$). Let $\mathcal{T}_\Sigma$ denote the set of trees over Σ.

Context Trees. A *context tree* over the alphabet Σ with a set of context variables $x_1, \ldots, x_n$ is a tree $C = (D, \lambda)$ over $\Sigma \uplus \{x_1, \ldots, x_n\}$ such that for each $1 \leq i \leq n$ we have $\rho(x_i) = 0$ and there exists a unique *context node* η_i such that $\lambda(\eta_i) = x_i$. By unique, we mean $\eta_i \neq \eta_j$ for all $i \neq j$. We will denote such a tree $C[x_1, \ldots, x_n]$. Given trees $t_i = (D_i, \lambda_i)$ for each $1 \leq i \leq n$, we denote by $C[t_1, \ldots, t_n]$ the tree t' obtained by filling each variable x_i with t_i. That is, $t' = (D', \lambda')$ where

$$D' = D \cup \eta_1 \cdot D_1 \cup \cdots \cup \eta_n \cdot D_n \quad \text{and} \quad \lambda'(\eta) = \begin{cases} \lambda(\eta) & \text{if } \eta \in D \wedge \forall i.\eta \neq \eta_i \\ \lambda_i(\eta') & \text{if } \eta = \eta_i\eta'. \end{cases}$$

Tree Automata. A *bottom-up non-deterministic tree automaton* (NTA) over a ranked alphabet Σ is a tuple $\mathcal{T} = (\mathcal{Q}, \Delta, \mathcal{F})$ where $\mathcal{Q}$ is a finite set of states, $\mathcal{F} \subseteq \mathcal{Q}$ is a set of final (accepting) states, and Δ is a finite set of rules of the form $(q_1, \ldots, q_n) \xrightarrow{a} q$ where $q_1, \ldots, q_n, q \in \mathcal{Q}$, $a \in \Sigma$ and $\rho(a) = n$. A *run* of $\mathcal{T}$ on a tree $t = (D, \lambda)$ is a mapping $\pi : D \mapsto \mathcal{Q}$ such that for all $\eta \in D$ labelled $\lambda(\eta) = a$ with $\rho(a) = n$ we have $(\pi(\eta 1), \ldots, \pi(\eta n)) \xrightarrow{a} \pi(\eta)$. It is accepting if $\pi(\varepsilon) \in \mathcal{F}$. The *language* defined by a tree automaton $\mathcal{T}$ over alphabet Σ is a set $\mathcal{L}(\mathcal{T}) \subseteq \mathcal{T}_\Sigma$ of trees over which there exists an accepting run of $\mathcal{T}$.

Parikh Images. Given an alphabet $\Sigma = \{\gamma_1, \ldots, \gamma_n\}$ and a word $w \in \Sigma^*$, we write $\mathcal{P}(w)$ to denote a mapping $\rho : \Sigma \to \mathbb{N}$, where $\rho(a)$ is defined to be the number of occurrences of a in w. Given a language $L \subseteq \Sigma^*$, we write $\mathcal{P}(L)$ to denote the set $\{\mathcal{P}(w) \mid w \in L\}$. We say that $\mathcal{P}(L)$ is the *Parikh image* of L.

Presburger Arithmetic. Presburger formulas are first-order formulas over integers with addition. Here, we use existential Presburger formulas $\varphi(\mathbf{x}, \mathbf{y}) := \exists \mathbf{x}\varphi$, where (i) $\mathbf{x}$ and $\mathbf{y}$ are sets of variables, and (ii) φ is a boolean combination of expressions $\sum_{i=1}^{m} a_i z_i \sim b$ for variables $z_1, \ldots, z_m \in \mathbf{x} \cup \mathbf{y}$, constants $a_1, \ldots, a_m, b \in \mathbb{Z}$, and $\sim \in \{\leq, \geq, <, >, =\}$ with constants represented in binary. A *solution* to φ is a valuation $\mathbf{b} : \mathbf{y} \mapsto \mathbb{Z}$ to $\mathbf{y}$ such that $\varphi(\mathbf{x}, \mathbf{b})$ is true. The formula φ is *satisfiable* if it has a solution. Satisfiability of existential Presburger formulas is known to be NP-complete [39].

3 Formal Models

In this section, we will define our formal models, which are based on ground-tree rewrite systems. Ground-tree rewrite systems (GTRSs) [15] permit subtree rewriting where rules are given as a pair of ground-trees. In the sequel, we use the extension proposed by Löding [32] where NTA (instead of ground trees) appear in the rewrite rules. Hence, a single rule may correspond to an infinite number of *concrete rules* (i.e. containing concrete trees).

Ground Tree Rewrite Systems with State and Reversal-Bounded Counters. To capture synchronisations between different subthreads, we follow [26,31,41] and extend GTRS with state (a.k.a. global control). The resulting model is denoted by sGTRS (state-extended GTRS). To capture integer variables, we further extend the model with unbounded integer counters, which can be incremented, decremented, and compared against an integer constant. Since Minsky's machines can easily be encoded in such a model, we apply a standard underapproximation technique: *reversal-bounded analysis of the counters*

[23, 25]. This means that one only analyses executions of the machines whose number of reversals between nondecrementing and nonincrementing modes of the counters is bounded by a given constant $r \in \mathbb{N}$ (represented in unary). The resulting model will be denoted by rbGTRS. We will now define this model in more detail.

An *atomic counter constraint* on counter variables $C = \{c_1, \ldots, c_k\}$ is an expression of the form $c_i \sim v$, where $v \in \mathbb{Z}$ and $\sim \in \{<, \leq, =, \geq, >\}$. A *counter constraint* θ on C is a boolean combination of atomic counter constraints on C. Given a valuation $\nu : C \mapsto \mathbb{Z}$ to the counter variables, we can determine whether $\theta[\nu]$ is true or false by replacing a variable c by $\nu(c)$ and evaluating the resulting boolean expressions in the obvious way. Let Cons_C denote the set of all counter constraints on C. Intuitively, these formulas will act as guards to determine whether certain transitions can be fired. Given two counter valuations ν and μ we define $\nu + \mu$ as the pointwise addition of the valuations. That is, $(\nu + \mu)(c) = \nu(c) + \mu(c)$.

Given a sequence of counter values, a reversal occurs when a counter switches from being incremented to being decremented or vice-versa. For example, if the values of a counter c along a run are $1, 1, 1, 2, 3, 4, 4, \overline{4}, \overline{3}, 2, \overline{2}, \overline{3}$, then the number of reversals of c is 2 (reversals occur in between the overlined positions). A sequence of valuations is reversal-bounded whenever the number of reversals is the sequence is bounded.

Definition 1 (*r*-Reversal-Bounded). *For a counter c from a set of counters C, a sequence $\nu_1, \ldots, \nu_n$ of counter valuations over C is r-reversal-bounded for c whenever we can partition $\nu_1, \ldots, \nu_n$ into $(r + 1)$ sequences $A_1, \ldots, A_{r+1}$ (with $\nu_0, \ldots, \nu_n = A_1, \ldots, A_{r+1}$) such that for all $1 \leq i \leq r$ there is some $\sim \in \{\leq, \geq\}$ such that for all ν_j, ν_{j+1} appearing together in A_i, we have $\nu_j(c) \sim_c \nu_{j+1}(c)$.*

We define sGTRS with reversal-bounded counters (rbGTRS).

Definition 2 (sGTRSs with *r*-Reversal-Bounded Counters). *We define state-extended ground tree rewrite system with r-reversal-bounded counters (rbGTRS) as a tuple $G = (\mathcal{P}, \Sigma, \Gamma, \mathcal{R}, C, r)$ where $\mathcal{P}$ is a finite set of control-states, Σ is a finite ranked alphabet, Γ is a finite alphabet of output symbols (i.e. transition labels), C is a finite set of counters, $\mathcal{R}$ is a finite set of rules of the form $(p_1, \mathcal{T}_1, \theta) \xrightarrow{\gamma} (p_2, \mathcal{T}_2, \mu)$ where $p_1, p_2 \in \mathcal{P}$, $\gamma \in \Gamma$, $\theta \in \mathrm{Cons}_C$, $\mu \in C \mapsto \mathbb{Z}$, and $\mathcal{T}_1, \mathcal{T}_2$ are NTAs over Σ.*

In the sequel, we will omit mention of the number r in the tuple G if it is clear from the context.

A *configuration* of an sGTRS with counters is a tuple $\alpha = (p, t, \nu)$ where p is a control-state, t a tree, and ν a valuation of the counters. We have a *transition* $(p_1, t_1, \nu_1) \xrightarrow{\gamma} (p_2, t_2, \nu_2)$ whenever there is a rule $(p_1, \mathcal{T}_1, \theta) \xrightarrow{\gamma} (p_2, \mathcal{T}_2, \mu) \in \mathcal{R}$ such that: (i) *(dynamics of counters)* $\theta[\nu_1]$ is true and $\nu_2 = \nu_1 + \mu$, and (ii) *(dynamics of trees)* $t_1 = C[t_1']$ for some context C and tree $t_1' \in \mathcal{L}(\mathcal{T}_1)$ and $t_2 = C[t_2']$ for some tree $t_2' \in \mathcal{L}(\mathcal{T}_2)$. A *run* π over $\gamma_1 \ldots \gamma_{n-1}$ is a sequence

$$(p_1, t_1, \nu_1) \xrightarrow{\gamma_1} \cdots \xrightarrow{\gamma_{n-1}} (p_n, t_n, \nu_n)$$

such that for all $1 \leq i < n$ we have $(p_i, t_i, \nu_i) \xrightarrow{\gamma_i} (p_{i+1}, t_{i+1}, \nu_{i+1})$ is a transition of G and for each $c \in C$ the sequence $\nu_1, \dots, \nu_n$ is r-reversal-bounded for c. We say that $\gamma_1 \dots \gamma_{n-1}$ is the output string of π. We write $(p, t, \nu) \xrightarrow{\gamma_1 \dots \gamma_n} (p', t', \nu')$ (or simply $(p, t, \nu) \rightarrow^* (p', t', \nu')$) whenever there is a run from (p, t, ν) to (p', t', ν') over $\gamma_1 \dots \gamma_n$. Let ε denote the empty output symbol.

Whenever we wish to discuss sGTRSs without counters, we simply omit the counter components. That is, we have configurations of the form (p, t) and transitions of the form $(p_1, \mathcal{T}_1) \xrightarrow{\gamma} (p_2, \mathcal{T}_2)$. The standard notion of GTRS (i.e. not state-extended) [32] is simply sGTRS without counters with only one state.

We next define the problems of *(global) reachability*. To this end, we use a tree automaton $\mathcal{T}$ (resp. an existential Presburger formula φ) to represent the tree (resp. counter) component of a configuration. More precisely, a *symbolic config-set* of an rbGTRS $G = (\mathcal{P}, \Sigma, \Gamma, \mathcal{R}, C, r)$ is a tuple $(p, \mathcal{T}, \varphi)$, where $p \in \mathcal{P}$, $\mathcal{T}$ is an NTA over Σ, and $\varphi(\bar{x})$ is an existential Presburger formula with free variables $\bar{x} = \{x_c\}_{c \in C}$ (i.e. one free variable for each counter). Each symbolic config-set $(c, \mathcal{T}, \varphi)$ represents a set of configurations of G defined as follows: $[\![(p, \mathcal{T}, \varphi)]\!] := \{(p, t, \nu) : t \in \mathcal{L}(\mathcal{T}), \varphi(\nu) \text{ is true}\}$.

GLOBAL REACHABILITY

Instance: an rbGTRS G and two symbolic config-sets $(p_1, \mathcal{T}_1, \varphi_1)$ $(p_2, \mathcal{T}_2, \varphi_2)$
Question: Decide whether $(\mu_1, \iota_1, \nu_1) \rightarrow^* (p_2, t_2, \nu_2)$, for some $(p_1, t_1, \nu_1) \in [\![(p_1, \mathcal{T}_1, \varphi_1)]\!]$ and $(p_2, t_2, \nu_2) \in [\![(p_2, \mathcal{T}_2, \varphi_2)]\!]$

The problem of *control-state reachability* can be defined by restricting (i) the tree automata $\mathcal{T}_1$ and $\mathcal{T}_2$ to accept, respectively, a singleton tree and the set of all trees, and (ii) the solutions to the formulas φ_1 and φ_2 are, respectively, $\{\nu_0\}$ (where ν_0 is the valuation assigning 0 to all counters) and the set of all counter valuations.

Remark 3. When we measure the complexity of reachability for rbGTRS, the number r of reversals is represented in unary, while the numbers in counter constraints and valuations are represented in binary. This is consistent with the standard representation of numbers in previous work on reversal-bounded counter machines (e.g. see [23,24]). The unary representation for r can be justified by the fact that bugs can often be discovered within a small number of reversals.

Weakly-Synchronised Ground Tree Rewrite Systems. The control-state and global reachability problems for sGTRS are known to be undecidable [12, 21]. The problems become NP-complete for *weakly-synchronised* sGTRS [31,41], where the underlying control-state graph (where there is an edge between p_1 and p_2 whenever there is a transition $(p_1, \mathcal{T}_1) \xrightarrow{\gamma} (p_2, \mathcal{T}_2)$) may only have cycles of length 1 (i.e. self-loops), i.e., a DAG (directed acyclic graph) possibly with self-loops. Underapproximation by a weak control is akin to loop acceleration in the symbolic acceleration framework of [8]. We extend the definition to rbGTRSs. The original definition can be easily obtained by omitting the counter components.

We define the *underlying control graph* of an rbGTRS $G = (\mathcal{P}, \Sigma, \Gamma, \mathcal{R}, C)$ as a tuple $(\mathcal{P}, \Delta)$ where $\Delta = \left\{ (p_1, p_2) \mid (p_1, \mathcal{T}_1, \theta) \xrightarrow{\gamma} (p_1, \mathcal{T}_2, \mu) \in \mathcal{R} \right\}$.

Definition 4 (Weakly-Synchronised rbGTRS). *An rbGTRS is said to be weakly-synchronised if its underlying control graph* $(\mathcal{P}, \Delta)$ *is a DAG possibly with self-loops.*

4   Decidability

In this section we will prove the main result of the paper:

Theorem 5. *Global reachability for weakly synchronised rbGTRS is NP-complete. In fact, it is poly-time reducible to satisfiability over existential Presburger formulas.*

To prove this theorem, we fix notation for the input to the problem: an rbGTRS $G = (\mathcal{P}, \Sigma, \Gamma, \mathcal{R}, C, r)$ and two symbolic config-sets $(p_1, \mathcal{T}_1, \varphi_1)$, $(p_2, \mathcal{T}_2, \varphi_2)$ of G. Let $C = \{c_i\}_{i=1}^{k}$. The gist of the proof is as follows. From G, we construct a new sGTRS G' (without counters) by encoding the dynamics of the counters in the output symbols of G'. Of course, G' has no way of comparing the values of counters with constants. [In this sense, G' only overapproximates the behavior of G.] To deal with this problem, we use the result of [31] to compute an existential Presburger formula ψ capturing the Parikh images of the set of all output strings of G' from $(p_1, \mathcal{T}_1, \varphi_1)$ to $(p_2, \mathcal{T}_2, \varphi_2)$. The final formula is $\psi \wedge \psi'$, where ψ is a constraint asserting that the desired counter comparisons are performed throughout runs of G'. We sketch the details of the construction below.

Modes of the Counters. The first notion that is crucial in our proof is that of *mode* of a counter [23,25], which is an abstraction of the values of a counter in a run of an rbGTRS containing three pieces of information: (i) the *region* of the counter value (i.e. how it compares to constants occurring in counter constraints), (ii) the number of reversals that has been performed by each counter (between 0 and r), and (iii) whether a counter is currently non-decrementing ($\uparrow$) or non-incrementing ($\downarrow$). A *mode vector* is simply a k-tuple of modes, one mode for each of the k counters. We now formalise these notions.

Let $d_1 < \ldots < d_m$ be the integer constants appearing in the counter constraints in G. This sequence of constants gives rise to the set REG of *regions* defined as REG $:= \{A_0, \ldots, A_m, B_1, \ldots, B_m\}$, where $B_i := \{d_i\}$ (where $1 \leq i \leq m$), $A_i := \{n \in \mathbb{Z} : d_i < n < d_{i+1}\}$ (where $1 \leq i < m$), $A_0 := \{n \in \mathbb{Z} : n < d_1\}$, and $A_m := \{n \in \mathbb{Z} : n > d_m\}$. A *mode* is simply a tuple in REG $\times [0, r] \times \{\uparrow, \downarrow\}$. A *mode vector* is simply a tuple in **Modes** $:= \text{REG}^k \times [0, r]^k \times \{\uparrow, \downarrow\}^k$.

Building the sGTRS G'. We might be tempted to build G' by first removing the counters from G and then embedding **Modes** into the control-states G'. This, however, causes two problems. First, the number of control-states becomes exponential in k. Second, the resulting system is no longer weakly synchronised even though G originally was weakly synchronised. To circumvent this problem, we adapt a technique from [23]. Every run π of G from $(p_1, \mathcal{T}_1, \varphi_1)$ to $(p_2, \mathcal{T}_2, \varphi_2)$ can be associated with a sequence σ of mode vectors recording the information (i)–(iii) for each counter. The crucial observation is that there are at most $N_{\max} := 2mk(r + 1)$ different mode vectors in σ. This is because a counter can only go through at most $2m$ regions without incurring a reversal. For this reason, we may use the control-states of G' to store the number of mode vectors that G has gone through, while the actual mode vector guessed by G' will be made "visible" in the output strings of G'. That way, we can use an additional existential Presburger formula ψ' (see below) to enforce that the run of G' faithfully simulates runs of G. In addition, the shape of the control-states (DAG with self-loops) of G' is preserved. [The product graph of two DAGs with self-loops is also a DAG with self-loops.] We detail the construction below.

Define the weakly-synchronised sGTRS $G' = (\mathcal{P}', \Sigma, \Gamma', \mathcal{R}')$ as follows. Let $\mathcal{P}' := \mathcal{P} \times [0, N_{\max}]$. The output alphabet Γ' is defined as $\Gamma \times \mathcal{R} \times [0, N_{\max}] \times \{0, 1\}$, where the boolean flag is used to denote whether the transition taken changes the mode. We define $\mathcal{R}'$ as follows. For each rule $\tau = (p, \mathcal{T}, \theta) \xrightarrow{\gamma} (p', \mathcal{T}', \mu)$ in $\mathcal{R}$, we add the rule $((p, i), \mathcal{T}) \xrightarrow{(\gamma, \tau, i, 0)} ((p', i), \mathcal{T}')$ for each $i \in [0, N_{\max}]$, and $((p, i), \mathcal{T}) \xrightarrow{(\gamma, \tau, i, 1)} ((p', i + 1), \mathcal{T}')$ for each $i \in [0, N_{\max})$. Since G is weakly-synchronised and the mode counter never decreases, it follows that G' is weakly-synchronised too. Note also that this construction can be performed in polynomial-time.

Constructing the Formula $\psi \wedge \psi'$. As we mentioned, ψ is an existential Presburger formula encoding the Parikh image $\mathcal{P}(L)$ of the set L of all output strings of G' from $((p_1, 0), \mathcal{T}_1)$ to $(S, \mathcal{T}_2)$, where $S = \{p_2\} \times [0, N_{\max}]$. More precisely, the set $\mathbf{z}$ of free variables of ψ include z_a for each $a \in \Gamma'$. Furthermore, for each valuation $\mu \in \mathbf{z} \mapsto \mathbb{Z}$, it is the case that $\psi(\mu)$ is true iff $\mu \in \mathcal{P}(L)$. Such a formula is known to be polynomial-time computable since G' is a weakly-synchronised sGTRS [31].

Recall that ψ' should assert that the desired counter comparisons are performed throughout runs of G'. To this end, the formula ψ' will have extra variables for guessing the existence of a sequence of $N_{\max}$ distinct mode vectors through runs of G'. More precisely, the formula ψ' is the conjunction

$$\varphi_1(\mathbf{x}) \wedge \varphi_2(\mathbf{y}) \wedge \mathtt{Dom}(\mathbf{m}_0, \dots, \mathbf{m}_{N_{\max}}) \wedge \mathtt{Init}(\mathbf{m}_0) \wedge$$
$$\mathtt{GoodSeq}(\mathbf{m}_0, \dots, \mathbf{m}_{N_{\max}}) \wedge \mathtt{Respect}(\mathbf{z}, \mathbf{m}_0, \dots, \mathbf{m}_{N_{\max}}) \wedge \mathtt{EndVal}(\mathbf{x}, \mathbf{y}, \mathbf{z}).$$

The set $\mathbf{x}$ consists of variables x_i $(1 \leq i \leq k)$ which contain the initial value of the ith counter. Similarly, the set $\mathbf{y}$ consists of variables y_i $(1 \leq i \leq k)$ which contain the final value of the ith counter. Each $\mathbf{m}_i$ denotes a set of variables for the ith mode vector defined as follows:

- reg_j^i (for each $j \in [1, k]$) — to encode which of the $2m + 1$ possible regions the jth counter is in.
- rev_j^i (for each $j \in [1, k]$) — to encode how many reversals have been used up by the jth counter.

– arr_j^i (for each $j \in [1,k]$) — to encode whether the jth counter is non-incrementing or non-decrementing.

We detail each subformula below.

The subformula Dom asserts that each variable in $\mathbf{m}_i$ (for each i) has the right domain (i.e. range of integer values). More precisely, for each $j \in [1,k]$, we add the conjuncts: (i) $0 \le reg_j^i \le 2m$, (ii) $0 \le rev_j^i \le r$, and (iii) $0 \le arr_j^i \le 1$. For the first constraint, we use an even number of the form $2i$ to represent the region A_i, and an odd number $2i - 1$ to represent the region B_i. The last constraint simply encodes non-decrementing ($\uparrow$) as 1, and non-incrementing ($\downarrow$) as 0.

The subformula Init asserts that $\mathbf{m}_0$ is an initial mode vector. More precisely, for each $j \in [1,k]$, we add the conjuncts $rev_j^0 = 0$.

The subformula GoodSeq asserts that $\mathbf{m}_0, \ldots, \mathbf{m}_{N_{\max}}$ forms a valid sequence of mode vectors. More precisely, for each $i \in [0, N_{\max})$ and each $j \in [1,k]$, we add the conjuncts: (i) $arr_j^i \ne arr_j^{i+1} \Rightarrow rev_j^{i+1} = rev_j^i + 1$, (ii) $arr_j^i = arr_j^{i+1} \Rightarrow rev_j^{i+1} = rev_j^i$, (iii) $reg_j^i < reg_j^{i+1} \Rightarrow arr_j^{i+1} = 1$, and (iv) $reg_j^i > reg_j^{i+1} \Rightarrow arr_j^{i+1} = 0$. For example, the first constraint asserts that a change in the direction (non-incrementing or non-decrementing) of the counter incurs one reversal. The other constraints are similar.

The subformula Respect asserts that the Parikh image $\mathbf{z}$ of the run of G' respects the sequence $\mathbf{m}_0, \ldots, \mathbf{m}_{N_{\max}}$ of mode vectors. In effect, this subformula ensures that G' faithfully simulates G. Firstly, we need to assert that the jth counter values at the *start* and at the *end* of the ith mode of G' (which are encoded in $\mathbf{z}$) are in the right regions reg_j^i. To state this more precisely, for each rule $\tau = (p, \mathcal{T}, \theta) \xrightarrow{\gamma} (p', \mathcal{T}', \mu)$ in $\mathcal{R}$, we let $\mu_j(\tau)$ denote the value $\mu(c_j)$. For each $i \in [0, N_{\max}]$ and $j \in [1,k]$, we denote by the notation StartCounter$_j^i$ the term $x_j + \sum_{s=0}^{i-1} \sum_{(\gamma,\tau,s,l)} \mu_j(\tau) \times z_{(\gamma,\tau,s,l)}$, where γ, τ, and l, range over, respectively, Γ, $\mathcal{R}$, and $\{0,1\}$. Similarly, we denote by EndCounter$_j^i$ the term StartCounter$_j^i +$ $\sum_{(\gamma,\tau,i,0)} \mu_j(\tau) \times z_{(\gamma,\tau,i,0)}$. We add the conjuncts: (i) $reg_j^i = 2h \Rightarrow$ EndCounter$_j^i \in A_h$, for each $h \in [0,m]$, and (ii) $reg_j^i = 2h + 1 \Rightarrow$ EndCounter$_j^i \in B_h$, for each $h \in [0,m)$. [Note that formulas of the form $g \in A$, for a Presburger term g and a set $S \in \{A_0, \ldots, A_m, B_1, \ldots, B_m\}$, can be easily replaced by quantifier-free Presburger formulas, e.g., $g \in A_0$ stands for $g < d_1$.] To ensure that the initial condition is correct, for each $j \in [1,k]$, we add the following conjuncts: (1) StartCounter$_j^0 \in A_h \Rightarrow reg_j^0 = 2h$, and (2) StartCounter$_j^0 \in B_h \Rightarrow reg_j^0 = 2h + 1$. Secondly, we need to state that the transitions executed in each mode are valid (i.e. satisfy the counter constraints). More precisely, for each $\gamma \in \Gamma$, $\tau \in \mathcal{R}$, $i \in [0, N_{\max}]$, and $l \in \{0,1\}$, if θ is the counter constraint in τ, we add the conjunct $z_{(\gamma,\tau,i,l)} > 0 \Rightarrow \theta(\text{StartCounter}_1^i, \ldots, \text{StartCounter}_k^i)$. Next we assert that, when the jth counter is non-incrementing (resp. non-decrementing), only non-negative (resp. non-positive) counter increments are permitted. More precisely, for each $i \in [0, N_{\max}]$, $j \in [1,k]$, $l \in \{0,1\}$, and $\tau \in \mathcal{R}$, if $\mu_j(\tau) > 0$, then add the conjunct $arr_j^i = 0 \Rightarrow z_{(\gamma,\tau,i,l)} = 0$; if $\mu_j(\tau) < 0$, then add the conjunct $arr_j^i = 1 \Rightarrow z_{(\gamma,\tau,i,l)} = 0$.

Finally, the subformula `EndVal` simply asserts that, starting from the initial counter value $\mathbf{x}$ and following the transitions $\mathbf{z}$, the end counter values are $\mathbf{y}$. To this end, we can simply add the conjunct $y_j = \mathtt{EndCounter}_j^{N_{\max}}$ for each $j \in [1, k]$.

This concludes the formula construction. It is immediate that G' faithfully simulates G iff $\psi \wedge \psi'$ is true. In addition, the formula construction runs in polynomial-time. Since satisfiability over existential Presburger formulas is NP-complete [39], the NP upper bound for Theorem 5 follows. NP-hardness already holds for the restricted model where the tree component is a stack [23].

5   Senescent Ground-Tree Rewrite Systems

A natural question arising from the result on weakly synchronised rbGTRS is whether the "weakly synchronised" restriction can be relaxed while maintaining decidability. It is known that allowing arbitrary underlying control-state graphs leads to undecidability of reachability even without reversal bounded counters. In this section we explore the notion of *senescence* [22], which is more general than the weakly synchronised restriction, but still permits a decidable reachability problem (without counters). After giving the formal definition of senescent GTRS, we show the following result.

Theorem 6 (Control-State Reachability of Senescent rbGTRS). *The control-state reachability problem for senescent rbGTRS is undecidable.*

5.1   Model Definition

Senescence allows the underlying control-state graph to have arbitrary cycles (instead of only self-loops). For sGTRS, control-state reachability is decidable under an "age restriction" that is imposed on the nodes that can be rewritten. That is, when the control-state changes, the nodes in the tree age by one timestep. Once a node reaches an *a priori* fixed age r, it becomes fixed (i.e. cannot be rewritten by further transitions in the run).

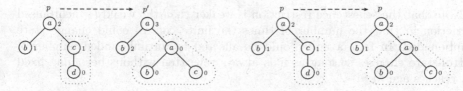

(a) A transition changing the control-state.   (b) A transition that does not change the control-state.

Fig. 1. Transitions of a senescent GTRS.

Before the formal definition, two example transitions of a senescent rbGTRS are shown in Fig. 1. A configuration is written as its control-state and counter values $((p, \nu)$ or $(p', \nu'))$ with the tree appearing below. In the tree, the label of each node appears in the centre of the node. The ages of each node is depicted as a subscript on the right. Dotted lines are used to indicate the part of the tree rewritten by a rule. In Fig. 1a the transition changes the control-state, causing the age of the nodes that are not rewritten to increase by 1. The rewritten nodes are given the age 0 as they are new, *fresh*, nodes. The situation when the control-state does not change is shown in Fig. 1b. In this case, the nodes that are not rewritten maintain the same age. The senescence restriction disallows runs where nodes older than a fixed age are rewritten.

More formally, given a run

$$(p_1, t_1, \nu_1) \xrightarrow{\gamma_1} \cdots \xrightarrow{\gamma_{n-1}} (p_n, t_n, \nu_n)$$

of an rbGTRS, let $C_1, \ldots, C_{n-1}$ be the sequence of tree contexts used in the transitions from which the run was constructed. That is, for all $1 \leq i < n$, we have $t_i = C_i[t_i^{\text{out}}]$ and $t_{i+1} = C_i[t_{i+1}^{\text{in}}]$ where $(p_i, \mathcal{T}_i, \theta_i) \xrightarrow{\gamma_i} (p_{i+1}, \mathcal{T}_i', \mu_i)$ was the rewrite rule used in the transition and $t_i^{\text{out}} \in \mathcal{L}(\mathcal{T}_i)$, $t_{i+1}^{\text{in}} \in \mathcal{L}(\mathcal{T}_i')$ were the trees that were used in the tree update.

For a given position (p_i, t_i, ν_i) in the run and a given node η in the domain of t_i, the *birthdate* of the node is the largest $1 \leq j \leq i$ such that η is in the domain of $C_j[t_j^{\text{in}}]$ and η is in the domain of $C_j[x]$ only if its label is x. The *age* of a node is the cardinality of the set $\{i' \mid j \leq i' < i \wedge p_{i'} \neq p_{i'+1}\}$. That is, the age is the number of times the control-state changed between the jth and the ith configurations in the run.

A lifespan-restricted run with a lifespan of r is a run such that each transition $(p_i, C_i[t_i^{\text{out}}], \nu_i) \xrightarrow{\gamma_i} (p_{i+1}, C_i[t_{i+1}^{\text{in}}], \nu_{i+1})$ has the property that all nodes η in t_i^{out} have an age of at most r. That is, more precisely, that all nodes η in the domain of $C_i[t_i^{\text{out}}]$ but only in the domain of $C_i[x]$ if the label is x have an age of at most r.

Definition 7 (Senescent rbGTRS). *A* senescent rbGTRS *with* lifespan r *is an rbGTRS $G = (\mathcal{P}, \Sigma, \mathcal{R}, C)$ where runs are lifespan-restricted with a lifespan of r.*

Note that the senescence restriction is weaker than the weakly-synchronised restriction in that the number of times the finite control could change state is unbounded. In fact, a node could be affected by an unbounded number of control-state changes so long as it is always rewritten without becoming fixed (i.e. reaches age r).

5.2   Undecidability

We show control-state reachability for senescent rbGTRSs is undecidable in the full version, and give the intuition here. In the following, we refer to nodes whose age is within the age bound as *live*. We refer to nodes that are not live as *fixed*. Note, each time a node is rewritten, its age is reset to zero. Thus, we can keep leaves of the tree live by allowing them to rewrite to themselves. That is, for all symbols a we wish to keep live and all control-states p, we have a transition $(p, a, \theta) \xrightarrow{\gamma} (p, a, \mu)$ where θ is a formula that is always satisfied, and μ assigns 0 to all counters (i.e. the rule does not depend on, nor change the counter values). In addition, by omitting the above rules for certain control-states, we can prevent a node from keeping itself fresh in certain situations.

We follow the proof that reachability for reset Petri nets is undecidable [3]. We simulate a two-counter machine. Testing whether such a machine can reach a given control-state while having counters with value zero is undecidable.

Let the two counters be c_1 and c_2. In the tree, we track the value of a counter $c \in \{c_1, c_2\}$ by the number of live leaves labelled with the counter name c. E.g. the tree $\bullet(c_1, \bullet(c_2, *))$ represents the situation where both counters have value 1, assuming these leaves are live. We will always use internal nodes labelled $\bullet$. The node $*$ is for adding new leaves when required. To increment a counter we add a new leaf labelled c. To decrement a counter, we rewrite a leaf labelled c to a null label. Thus, we can easily increment and decrement counters. Zero tests, however, are more subtle. To help with this, we track, using reversal-bounded counters, the number of increments made to each counter, and in separate reversal-bounded counters, the number of decrements. That is, we have reversal bounded counters $\{c_1^+, c_1^-, c_2^+, c_2^-\}$. When we simulate an increment of c_1 we add a leaf and increment c_1^+. When we simulate a decrement of c_2 we rewrite a leaf to a null character and increment c_1^-. Similarly for c_2. We simulate zero tests as follows.

To simulate a zero test on a counter c we perform the following checks. First, we "reset" the counter to zero by forcing enough control-state changes to fix the nodes corresponding to the counter. That is, we move to a control-state p where all leaf labels may rewrite to themselves, except those labelled c. After the move to p all leaves will have age 1. Leaves not labelled c can refresh their age to 0 by rewriting themselves. Leaves labelled c will stay aged 1. Then, we move to the target control-state of the transition we are simulating. Thus, after these moves, all leaves labelled c will reach age 2, while all other nodes will only reach age 1. Thus, if our lifespan is 2, nodes labelled c will no longer be live. That is, the simulated value of c in the tree has been forced to 0.

After this reset operation, the counter value is definitely zero. However, we did not enforce that the counter value was zero before the transition. Recall, we track the number of increments and decrements to c in the reversal bounded counters. If the counter was not zero before the test, there will be a discrepancy with the reversal bounded counters: more increments will be recorded than decrements. E.g. for counter c_1 we will have $c_1^+ > c_1^-$. This cannot be corrected by the simulation. Thus, at the end of the run, we check whether the number of increments is equal to the number of decrements. If not, we know the run made a spurious transition. That is, it performed a zero test transition when the counter was not zero. If no spurious transitions were made, we know the two-counter machine has a corresponding run. This completes the gist of the simulation of a two-counter machine.

6   Extensions and Future Work

We proposed sGTRS with counters as a model of recursively parallel programs with unbounded recursion, thread creation, and integer variables. To obtain decidability, we gave an underapproximation in the form of weak sGTRS with reversal-bounded counters. We showed that the reachability problem for this model is NP-complete; in fact, polynomial-time reducible to satisfiability of linear integer arithmetic, for which highly optimised SMT solvers are available (e.g. Z3 [16]). Additionally, we explored the possibility of relaxing the weakly-synchronised constraint to that of senescence, and showed that the resulting model has an undecidable control-state reachability problem.

One possible avenue of future work is to investigate what happens when *local* integer values are permitted. That is, reversal-bounded counters can be stored on the nodes of the tree. We may also study techniques that allow nodes to contain multiple labels, permitting the modelling of multiple local variables without an immediate exponential blow up.

Acknowledgments. We thank anonymous reviewers for their helpful feedback. This work was supported by the Engineering and Physical Sciences Research Council [EP/K009907/1] and Yale-NUS College Startup Grant.

References

1. Abdulla, P.A., Atig, M.F., Cederberg, J.: Analysis of message passing programs using SMT-solvers. In: Van Hung, D., Ogawa, M. (eds.) ATVA 2013. LNCS, vol. 8172, pp. 272–286. Springer, Heidelberg (2013)
2. Aiswarya, C., Gastin, P., Narayan Kumar, K.: Verifying communicating multi-pushdown systems via split-width. In: Cassez, F., Raskin, J.-F. (eds.) ATVA 2014. LNCS, vol. 8837, pp. 1–17. Springer, Heidelberg (2014)
3. Araki, T., Kasami, T.: Some decision problems related to the reachability problem for petri nets. Theor. Comput. Sci. **3**(1), 85–104 (1977)
4. Atig, M.F., Bollig, B., Habermehl, P.: Emptiness of multi-pushdown automata is 2ETIME-complete. In: Ito, M., Toyama, M. (eds.) DLT 2008. LNCS, vol. 5257, pp. 121–133. Springer, Heidelberg (2008)
5. Atig, M.F., Bouajjani, A., Qadeer, S.: Context-bounded analysis for concurrent programs with dynamic creation of threads. Log. Methods Comput. Sci. **7**(4), 4:1–4:48 (2011)
6. Atig, M.F., Ganty, P.: Approximating petri net reachability along context-free traces. In: FSTTCS, pp. 152–163 (2011)
7. Atig, M.F., Kumar, K.N., Saivasan, P.: Adjacent ordered multi-pushdown systems. Int. J. Found. Comput. Sci. **25**(8), 1083–1096 (2014)
8. Bardin, S., Finkel, A., Leroux, J., Schnoebelen, P.: Flat acceleration in symbolic model checking. In: Peled, D.A., Tsay, Y.-K. (eds.) ATVA 2005. LNCS, vol. 3707, pp. 474–488. Springer, Heidelberg (2005)
9. Blumensath, A., Colcombet, T., Kuperberg, D., Parys, P., Vanden Boom, M.: Two-way cost automata, cost logics over infinite trees. In: CSL-LICS, pp. 16:1–16:9 (2014)

10. Bouajjani, A., Emmi, M.: Analysis of recursively parallel programs. ACM Trans. Program. Lang. Syst. **35**(3), 10 (2013)
11. Bouajjani, A., Esparza, J., Maler, O.: Reachability analysis of pushdown automata: application to model-checking. In: Mazurkiewicz, A., Winkowski, J. (eds.) CONCUR 1997. LNCS, vol. 1243, pp. 135–150. Springer, Heidelberg (1997)
12. Bozzelli, L., Kretínský, M., Rehák, V., Strejcek, J.: On decidability of LTL model checking for process rewrite systems. Acta Inform. **46**(1), 1–28 (2009)
13. Colcombet, T., Löding, C.: Regular cost functions over finite trees. In: LICS, pp. 70–79 (2010)
14. Czerwinski, W., Hofman, P., Lasota, S.: Reachability problem for weak multipushdown automata. Log. Methods Comput. Sci. **9**(3), 1–29 (2013)
15. Dauchet, M., Tison, S.: The theory of ground rewrite systems is decidable. In: LICS, pp. 242–248 (1990)
16. de Moura, L., Bjørner, N.S.: Z3: an efficient SMT solver. In: Ramakrishnan, C.R., Rehof, J. (eds.) TACAS 2008. LNCS, vol. 4963, pp. 337–340. Springer, Heidelberg (2008)
17. Demri, S., Jurdzinski, M., Lachish, O., Lazic, R.: The covering and boundedness problems for branching vector addition systems. J. Comput. Syst. Sci. **79**(1), 23–38 (2013)
18. Esparza, J., Ganty, P., Poch, T.: Pattern-based verification for multithreaded programs. ACM Trans. Program. Lang. Syst. **36**(3), 9:1–9:29 (2014)
19. Esparza, J., Podelski, A.: Efficient algorithms for pre* and post* on interprocedural parallel flow graphs. In: POPL, pp. 1–11 (2000)
20. Ganty, P., Majumdar, R., Monmege, M.: Bounded underapproximations. FMSD **40**(2), 206–231 (2012)
21. Göller, S., Lin, A.W.: Refining the process rewrite systems hierarchy via ground tree rewrite systems. In: Katoen, J.-P., König, B. (eds.) CONCUR 2011. LNCS, vol. 6901, pp. 543–558. Springer, Heidelberg (2011)
22. Hague, M.: Senescent ground tree rewrite systems. In: CSL-LICS, pp. 48:1–48:10 (2014)
23. Hague, M., Lin, A.W.: Model checking recursive programs with numeric data types. In: Gopalakrishnan, G., Qadeer, S. (eds.) CAV 2011. LNCS, vol. 6806, pp. 743–759. Springer, Heidelberg (2011)
24. Hague, M., Lin, A.W.: Synchronisation- and reversal-bounded analysis of multithreaded programs with counters. In: Madhusudan, P., Seshia, S.A. (eds.) CAV 2012. LNCS, vol. 7358, pp. 260–276. Springer, Heidelberg (2012)
25. Ibarra, O.H.: Reversal-bounded multicounter machines and their decision problems. J. ACM **25**(1), 116–133 (1978)
26. Kretínský, M., Rehák, V., Strejcek, J.: Extended process rewrite systems: expressiveness and reachability. In: Gardner, P., Yoshida, N. (eds.) CONCUR 2004. LNCS, vol. 3170, pp. 355–370. Springer, Heidelberg (2004)
27. La Torre, S., Napoli, M., Parlato, G.: Scope-bounded pushdown languages. In: Shur, A.M., Volkov, M.V. (eds.) DLT 2014. LNCS, vol. 8633, pp. 116–128. Springer, Heidelberg (2014)
28. Lal, A., Touili, T., Kidd, N., Reps, T.: Interprocedural analysis of concurrent programs under a context bound. In: Ramakrishnan, C.R., Rehof, J. (eds.) TACAS 2008. LNCS, vol. 4963, pp. 282–298. Springer, Heidelberg (2008)
29. Lang, M., Löding, C.: Modeling and verification of infinite systems with resources. Log. Methods Comput. Sci. **9**(4), 1–39 (2013)
30. Leroux, J., Praveen, M., Sutre, G.: Hyper-ackermannian bounds for pushdown vector addition systems. In: CSL-LICS, pp. 63:1–63:10 (2014)

31. Lin, A.W.: Weakly-synchronized ground tree rewriting. In: Rovan, B., Sassone, V., Widmayer, P. (eds.) MFCS 2012. LNCS, vol. 7464, pp. 630–642. Springer, Heidelberg (2012)

32. Löding, C.: Reachability problems on regular ground tree rewriting graphs. Theory Comput. Syst. **39**(2), 347–383 (2006)

33. Madhusudan, P., Parlato, G.: The tree width of auxiliary storage. In: POPL, pp. 283–294 (2011)

34. Mayr, R.: Decidability and complexity of model checking problems for infinite-state systems. Ph.D. thesis, TU-Munich (1998)

35. Musuvathi, M., Qadeer, S.: Iterative context bounding for systematic testing of multithreaded programs. In: PLDI, pp. 446–455 (2007)

36. Qadeer, S.: The case for context-bounded verification of concurrent programs. In: Havelund, K., Majumdar, R., Palsberg, J. (eds.) SPIN 2008. LNCS, vol. 5156, pp. 3–6. Springer, Heidelberg (2008)

37. Ramalingam, G.: Context-sensitive synchronization-sensitive analysis is undecidable. Trans. Program. Lang. Syst. (TOPLAS) **22**, 416–430 (2000)

38. Qadeer, S., Rehof, J.: Context-bounded model checking of concurrent software. In: Halbwachs, N., Zuck, L.D. (eds.) TACAS 2005. LNCS, vol. 3440, pp. 93–107. Springer, Heidelberg (2005)

39. Scarpellini, B.: Complexity of subcases of Presburger arithmetic. Trans. AMS **284**(1), 203–218 (1984)

40. Suwimonteerabuth, D., Esparza, J., Schwoon, S.: Symbolic context-bounded analysis of multithreaded Java programs. In: Havelund, K., Majumdar, R., Palsberg, J. (eds.) SPIN 2008. LNCS, vol. 5156, pp. 270–287. Springer, Heidelberg (2008)

41. To, A.W., Libkin, L.: Algorithmic metatheorems for decidable LTL model checking over infinite systems. In: Ong, L. (ed.) FOSSACS 2010. LNCS, vol. 6014, pp. 221–236. Springer, Heidelberg (2010)

42. Torre, S.L., Madhusudan, P., Parlato, G.: A robust class of context-sensitive languages. In: LICS, pp. 161–170. IEEE Computer Society (2007)

43. Verma, K.N., Goubault-Larrecq, J.: Karp-Miller trees for a branching extension of VASS. Discret. Math. Theor. Comput. Sci. **7**(1), 217–230 (2005)

Robot Games with States in Dimension One

Reino Niskanen[✉]

Department of Computer Science, University of Liverpool, Liverpool, UK
r.niskanen@liverpool.ac.uk

Abstract. A robot game with states is a two-player vector addition game played on integer lattice $\mathbb{Z}^n$. Both players have their own control states and in each turn the vector chosen by a player, according to his/her internal control structure, is added to the current configuration vector of the game. One of the players, called Eve, tries to play the game from the initial configuration to the origin while the other player, Adam, tries to avoid the origin. The problem is to decide whether or not Eve has a winning strategy. In this paper we prove that deciding the winner in a robot game with states in dimension one is **EXPSPACE**-complete. Additionally we study a subclass of robot games with states where deciding the winner is in **EXPTIME**.

Keywords: Reachability games · Vector addition game · Decidability · Winning strategy

1 Introduction

There is a growing interest in the area of infinite-state games. Two-player games provide a powerful framework for problems related to verification and refinement of reactive systems [3], and have deep connections with automata theory and logic [17,23]. Infinite-state games can be classified according to the winning conditions, such as parity [2], energy [12], counter reachability, or a combination of two or more winning conditions [7].

Counter reachability games are two-player games played on a labelled directed graph. The vertices of the graph are partitioned into two sets, one for Eve, another for Adam. Starting from the initial vertex, the owner of a current vertex chooses an outgoing edge and adds its label to the counters. The goal of Eve is to reach a particular vertex with a particular counter value, while Adam tries to avoid it. The associated decision problem is to decide whether Eve has a winning strategy from a given initial configuration to the target configuration. Counter reachability games, and closely related variants, have been extensively studied [1,5,6,14–16,22].

In [22], it was proved that counter reachability games are undecidable starting from dimension two (as are most of the variants). For one-dimensional games it was proven that they are in **EXPSPACE**, and in [16] that the games are **EXPSPACE**-hard and thus **EXPSPACE**-complete. *Robot games* are a minimalistic subclass of counter reachability games, proposed by Doyen and Rabinovich [11], where the graph consists of two vertices, one for Eve and one

© Springer International Publishing Switzerland 2016
K.G. Larsen et al. (Eds.): RP 2016, LNCS 9899, pp. 163–176, 2016.
DOI: 10.1007/978-3-319-45994-3_12

for Adam, and no self-loops. In other words, the players have no internal structure and each move is available in every turn. As the state structure is very simple, it was hoped that robot games would be significantly easier to solve than general counter reachability games. Unfortunately, that did not hold for higher dimensions. First, it was proved in [21] that robot games are undecidable starting from dimension three and later it was improved to two in [20]. In dimension one, robot games are indeed easier than counter reachability games as was shown in [4] where an **EXPTIME** algorithm was presented along with a matching lower bound.

In this paper, we consider an extension of robot games, where both players have internal control states, called *robot games with states* (RGS). It was proved in [21], and restated in [20], that robot games with states are undecidable starting from dimension two. Unlike counter reachability games and robot games, one-dimensional robot games with states have not been studied before. Our main result is to prove that robot games with states in dimension one are **EXPSPACE**-complete by presenting a mutual reduction between robot games with states and counter reachability games. Note that this is not obvious as the games have essential differences. In a counter reachability game, since the game is played on a graph, a choice of a player, say Eve, affects from which state Adam moves next. In fact, it is not guaranteed that Adam will move at all, as it is possible for Eve to move only between her states. On the other hand, in robot games with states, the next state of a player is determined only by his or her previous move.

We construct a one-dimensional robot game with states that can simulate any one-dimensional counter reachability game such that Eve has a winning strategy in the RGS if and only if she has a winning strategy in the counter reachability game. In the constructed robot game with states Eve has $n+1$ states, where the counter reachability game has n vertices, and Adam has only one state.

Seeing how adding states for Eve increases complexity from robot games' **EXPTIME** to robot games with states' **EXPSPACE**, we consider a state structure of Adam that does not increase the complexity of the game. We show that deciding the winner in one-dimensional robot game with states, where Eve is stateless and Adam's states are *flat*, is in **EXPTIME**. Flat automata have been studied in various contexts [8–10,18,19] and have been shown to be a fruitful tool in verification of counter automata. Flat automata is a subclass of automata where the automaton does not have nested loops. This particular structure allows us to break a robot game with states into several stateless games, that can be solved in **EXPTIME**. The main challenge is in connecting these separate games. As Adam's underlying state structure is flat, there are only finitely many transitions from one game to another. This fact together with the particular structure of winning sets constructed by the algorithm for a stateless game of [4] provide us with necessary tools to decide the winner in **EXPTIME**.

The paper is organized as follows. In the next section we introduce the notation and definitions used throughout the paper. In the third section, we prove that deciding the winner in one-dimensional robot games with states is

EXPSPACE-complete. In the fourth section, we consider flat robot games with states and prove that, in dimension one, deciding the winner is **EXPTIME**-complete.

2 Notation and Definitions

We denote the sets of all integers, non-negative and non-positive integers by $\mathbb{Z}, \mathbb{Z}^-$ and $\mathbb{Z}^+$ respectively. By 0_n we denote the n-dimensional zero vector. An open interval (a, b) is a subset of $\mathbb{Z}$ containing all the integers larger than a and smaller than b. A closed interval $[a, b]$ is $(a, b) \cup \{a, b\}$ and half-open intervals are defined similarly. Let $X \subseteq \mathbb{Z}$. By $X + d$ and dX, where $d \in \mathbb{Z}$, we denote the sets $\{x + d \mid x \in X\}$ and $\{dx \mid x \in X\}$.

A n-dimensional *counter reachability game* (nCRG) consists of a directed graph $G = (V, F)$, where the set of vertices is partitioned into two parts, V_E and V_A, each edge $e \in F \subseteq V \times \mathbb{Z}^n \times V$ is labelled with vectors in $\mathbb{Z}^n$. A *configuration* of the game is $[v, \mathbf{x}]$, a successive configuration is $[v', \mathbf{x} + \mathbf{x}']$, where an edge $(v, \mathbf{x}', v') \in F$ is chosen by player 1 if $v \in V_E$ or by player 2 if $v \in V_A$. A *play* is a sequence of successive configurations. The goal of the first player, called *Eve*, is to reach the *final configuration* $[v_f, 0_n]$ for some $v_f \in V$ from a given *initial configuration* $[v_0, \mathbf{x}_0]$, while the goal of the second player, called *Adam*, is to keep Eve from reaching $[v_f, 0_n]$. A *strategy* for a player is a function that maps a configuration to an edge that can be applied. We say that Eve has a *winning strategy* if she can reach the final configuration regardless of the strategies of Adam. On the other hand, we say that Adam has a winning strategy if Eve does not have a winning strategy. In the figures we use ◯ for Eve's states and □ for Adam's states (diamonds represent arbitrary vertices).

A n-dimensional *robot game* (nRG) [11] is a special case of the counter reachability games, where graph consists of only two vertices, v_0 of Adam and v of Eve. The goal of the game is the configuration $[v_0, 0_n]$. That is, a robot game consists of two players, *Eve* and *Adam*, having a set of vectors E, A over $\mathbb{Z}^n$, respectively, and an *initial vector* $\mathbf{x}_0$. Starting from $\mathbf{x}_0$ players add a vector from their respective sets to the current configuration of the game in turns. As in counter reachability game, Eve tries to reach the origin while Adam tries to keep Eve from reaching the origin. The decision problem concerning robot games is, for a given robot game (A, E) and $\mathbf{x}_0$, to decide whether Eve has a winning strategy to reach 0_n from $\mathbf{x}_0$.

An extension of robot games where players have control states is called *robot games with states* (RGS). A nRGS consists of (A, E) where A is a finite subset of $Q_A \times \mathbb{Z}^n \times Q_A$ that Adam can apply during his turn and E is a finite subset of $Q_E \times \mathbb{Z}^n \times Q_E$ of Eve, and an initial configuration $[s_0, t_0, \mathbf{x}_0] \in Q_E \times Q_A \times \mathbb{Z}^n$. The configuration is now a triple $[s, t, \mathbf{v}]$ consisting of Eve's control state s, Adam's control state t and a counter vector $\mathbf{v} \in \mathbb{Z}^n$. Eve updates her control state when she makes a move: in the configuration $[s, t, \mathbf{v}]$, for any vector $\mathbf{v}$, only moves of the form $(s, \mathbf{x}, s')$ are enabled, and with one such move the new configuration is $[s', t, \mathbf{v} + \mathbf{x}]$. Similarly Adam updates his control state when he makes a move.

Eve wins if, and only if, after her turn, the configuration is $[s, t, 0_n]$ for some $s \in F \subseteq Q_E$. The decision problem associated with robot games with states asks whether Eve has a winning strategy from a given configuration.

In order to indicate whose turn it is in the configuration $[s, t, \mathbf{v}]$, we put a dot above s if it is Eve's turn, or above t if it is Adam's turn. That is, the respective configurations are $[\dot{s}, t, \mathbf{v}]$ and $[s, \dot{t}, \mathbf{v}]$. In the figures, the dot is placed inside the state (e.g., $\boxdot$ if it is Adam's turn).

Flat robot games with states (FRGS) is a subclass of the RGS where Eve is stateless, that is, all the moves of Eve are of form (s, z, s), and Adam's states are flat, i.e., without nested loops. In other words, we have an ordering of states of Adam $\{t_0, \ldots, t_k\}$ such that $(t_i, z, t_j) \in A$ only if $i \leq j$. Note that, unlike the usual definition of flat systems, we allow several self-loops for a state.

3   Robot Games with States in Dimension One

In this section we consider games in dimension one. First, we recall some known results.

Theorem 1 [16]. *Deciding which player wins in a one-dimensional counter reachability game is* **EXPSPACE**-*complete.*

Theorem 2 [4]. *Deciding which player wins in a one-dimensional robot game is* **EXPTIME**-*complete.*

As robot games are a special case of robot games with states, we can inherit the lower bound. That is, the 1RGS are **EXPTIME**-hard. On the other hand it is easy to construct a counter reachability game out of a robot game with states by storing information on the state of Eve in the 1RGS in the states of Adam and vice versa. That is, robot games with states are in **EXPSPACE**.

Lemma 3. *Deciding which player wins in a one-dimensional robot game with states is* **EXPSPACE**.

Proof. Let (A, E) be a 1RGS and $z_0 \in \mathbb{Z}$ the initial integer. We construct a counter reachability game (V, F) where Eve has a winning strategy if and only if Eve has a winning strategy in (A, E). Eve's states are $V_E = \{s_t \mid s \in Q_E, t \in Q_A\}$ and Adam's states are $V_A = \{t_s \mid t \in Q_A, s \in Q_E\}$. The edges of the graph are $F = \{(s_t, z, t_{s'}) \mid (s, z, s') \in E\} \cup \{(t_s, z, s_{t'}) \mid (t, z, t') \in A\}$. It is clear that Eve has a winning strategy in (A, E) from z_0 if and only if Eve has a winning strategy in (V, F) from z_0. As deciding the winner in the 1CRG is **EXPSPACE**-complete, also deciding the winner in the 1RGS is **EXPSPACE**.   □

We provide the matching tight lower bound, showing that one-dimensional robot games with states are **EXPSPACE**-complete. That is, we show that the 1RGS are **EXPSPACE**-hard. To prove this, we show how, for any one-dimensional counter reachability game, to construct a one-dimensional robot game with states such that the same player wins in both games. The idea is for Eve to

have the whole graph, including Adam's states, as her states and Adam have no
states. Adam has three moves, two to tell Eve which edge to pick if the state
was initially Adam's, and one to do nothing if that's not the case.

Theorem 4. *One-dimensional robot games with states are **EXPSPACE**-complete.*

First we consider a simple modification to a 1CRG. We can assume that in
every Adam's state there are at most two outgoing edges. Indeed, let t be Adam's
vertex with k outgoing edges, we replace it by a chain $t_1, \ldots, t_{k-1}$ such that ith
edge (t, z, t') is (t_i, z, t'). Finally, we connect the vertices with edges $(t_i, 0, t_{i+1})$
for $i \in \{1, \ldots, k-1\}$ and $(t, 0, t_1)$.

Next, we show the gadgets for different moves in the 1CRG. At this state, for
simplicity, we assume that both players will play in good faith and will simulate
the 1CRG correctly. Later on, we'll construct an additional gadget for Eve and
show that if one of the player cheats, then the other can catch the cheating and
has a winning strategy.

Now, there are three types of transitions: from Eve's state or from Adam's
state which has either one or two outgoing transitions. We construct gadgets for
each case. Let's first consider the cases where Adam does not make a decision.
That is moves (s, z, r) and (t, z, r), where $z \in \mathbb{Z}$, $s \in V_E$, $r \in V$, $t \in V_A$ and
$\deg(t) = 1$. In robot game with states, Eve has moves $(s, 4z, r)$ and $(t, 4z, r)$,
where $s, r, t \in Q_E$, respectively, and Adam has a move $(\top, 0, \top)$. The moves are
depicted in Fig. 1.

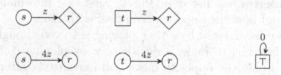

Fig. 1. Moves in a 1CRG (top) and the corresponding moves in the 1RGS (bottom)

The final case where Adam has to make a choice is slightly more complicated.
As Eve is simulating the whole graph of the 1CRG, Adam needs to indicate to her
which edge he would have picked. In the 1CRG the moves are $(t, y, p), (t, x, q)$,
where $p, q \in V$ and $t \in V_A$ and $\deg(t) = 2$. In robot game with states, Eve has a
gadget with moves $(t, 4y - 1, p)$, $(t, 4x + 1, q)$, and Adam has moves $(\top, 1, \top)$ and
$(\top, -1, \top)$. The moves are depicted in Fig. 2. By multiplying all the old labels
by 4, we have created extra space to store the information about which edge Eve
is supposed to pick.

Finally, we need to make sure that Adam does not abuse his moves, i.e.,
does not indicate his choice when he should not. For this, we create a gadget
similar to Adam's state transition, which Eve can enter and add ± 4 emptying
the counter while at the same time cancelling whatever Adam plays. To do so,
we design an emptying gadget of Eve consisting of one state $\bot$. The moves are
$(\bot, \pm 4 + 1, \bot)$, $(\bot, \pm 4 - 1, \bot)$ and $(\bot, \pm 4, \bot)$. The emptying gadget is connected

Fig. 2. Moves in a 1CRG (left) and the corresponding moves in the 1RGS (right)

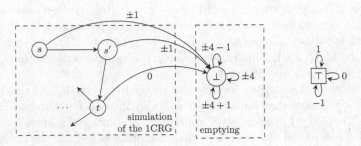

Fig. 3. An illustration of state transitions of Eve and Adam

to states of Eve with moves $(s, \pm 1, \perp)$ for every state $s \in V_E$ or $s \in V_A$ and $\deg(s) = 1$, and with $(t, 0, \perp)$, where $t \in V_A$ and $\deg(t) = 2$. The control states of the players are depicted in Fig. 3.

Next we consider all possible plays of Adam and Eve, and show that if the player plays incorrectly, the opponent has a winning strategy. The possible ways the game can progress are listed in Fig. 4. First, we informally describe the incorrect moves and how the opponent can deal with them.

Adam can play incorrectly by either playing ± 1 even though Eve is not in a state where Adam has to make a decision, or by playing 0 if Eve is. In the first case, Eve can play the opposite move and move to $\perp$, after which she can counter any move Adam plays whilst emptying the counter. In the latter case, Eve moves to $\perp$ without modifying the counter and again she can empty the counter while nullifying the moves of Adam.

Eve can play incorrectly by either moving to the emptying gadgets before Adam made an incorrect move or by not making the correct decision according to what Adam has played, that is, playing $4y - 1$ after Adam played -1 or $4x + 1$ after Adam played 1. In the both cases, Adam can ensure that the counter will never be 0 (mod 4).

First we prove two lemmas regarding incorrect moves by Adam and prove that Eve has winning strategies.

Lemma 5. *Let the configuration be $[s, \top, 4z]$, where $z \in \mathbb{Z}$ and $s \in V_E$ or $s \in V_A$ and $\deg(s) = 1$. If Adam plays $(\top, 1, \top)$, then Eve has a winning strategy starting with $(s, -1, \perp)$. Similarly, if Adam plays $(\top, -1, \top)$, then Eve has a winning strategy starting with $(s, 1, \perp)$.*

Proof. After Adam's move, the configuration is $[\dot{s}, \top, 4z+1]$ and after Eve's move, the configuration is $[\perp, \dot{\top}, 4z]$. After this, Eve can cancel Adam's move while

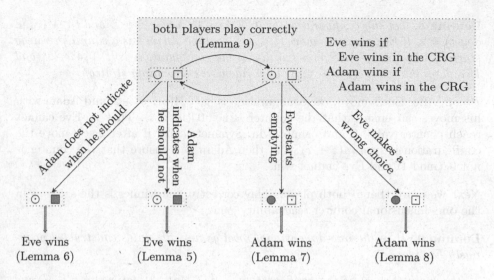

Fig. 4. Progress of a one-dimensional robot game with states

emptying the counter at the same time. In the case Adam played $(\top, -1, \top)$, then Eve's winning strategy is the same after she played $(s, 1, \bot)$. □

Lemma 6. *Let the configuration be* $[t, \dot{\top}, 4z]$, *where* $z \in \mathbb{Z}$ *and* $t \in V_A$ *and* $\deg(t) = 2$. *If Adam plays* $(\top, 0, \top)$ *then Eve has a winning strategy starting with* $(t, 0, \bot)$.

Proof. After Adam's move, the configuration is $[\dot{t}, \top, 4z]$ and after Eve's move, the configuration is $(\bot, \dot{\top}, 4z)$. As in previous lemma, Eve can empty the counter while cancelling Adam's move. □

Next we prove a lemma, where Eve moves to her emptying gadget and prove that Adam has a winning strategy.

Lemma 7. *Let the configuration be* $[\dot{s}, \top, 4z]$ *where* $z \in \mathbb{Z}$ *and* $s \in V_E$ *or* $s \in V_A$ *and* $\deg(s) = 1$. *If Eve moves to* $\bot$ *with a move* $(s, 1, \bot)$ *or a move* $(s, -1, \bot)$, *then Adam has a winning strategy starting with* $(\top, 1, \top)$ *or* $(\top, -1, \top)$ *respectively.*

Proof. After Eve's move, the configuration is $[\bot, \dot{\top}, 4z \pm 1]$ and after Adam's move, the configuration is $[\dot{\bot}, \top, 4z \pm 2]$. From this moment onward, Adam can ensure that the counter is not 0 (mod 4). Thus, Eve cannot reach counter value 0 and cannot win. □

Finally, we consider the case where Adam tells Eve his non-deterministic choice with 1 or -1, and Eve responds incorrectly by playing a move with 1 or -1, respectively.

Lemma 8. *Let the configuration be $[\dot{t}, \top, 4z+1]$, where $z \in \mathbb{Z}$ and $t \in V_A$ and $\deg(t) = 2$. If Eve plays the move $(t, 4y+1, p)$, then Adam has a winning strategy starting with $(\top, 0, \top)$. Symmetrically, if the configuration is $[\dot{t}, \top, 4z-1]$ and Eve plays the move $(t, 4x-1, q)$, then Adam has a winning strategy.*

Proof. After Eve's move, the configuration is $[p, \dot{\top}, 4(z+y)+2]$ and Adam with his moves can ensure that the counter is not 0 (mod 4). That is, Eve cannot reach counter value 0 and cannot win. Symmetrically, if after Eve's move the configuration is $[p, \dot{\top}, 4(z+x)-2]$, then Adam can ensure that the counter is not 0 (mod 4) and Eve cannot win.   □

Next we prove that if both players play correctly, the winner is the same as in the one-dimensional counter reachability game.

Lemma 9. *If in the one-dimensional robot game with states constructed previously Eve plays*

- *the move $(t, 1, p)$ if the configuration is $[\dot{t}, \top, 4z-1]$ for some $z \in \mathbb{Z}$ and $t \in V_E$ and $\deg(t) = 2$,*
- *the move $(t, -1, p)$ if the configuration is $[\dot{t}, \top, 4z+1]$ for some $z \in \mathbb{Z}$ and $t \in V_E$ and $\deg(t) = 2$*

and never moves to $\bot$, and Adam plays

- *the move $(\top, 0, \top)$ if the configuration is $[s, \dot{\top}, 4z]$, for some $z \in \mathbb{Z}$ and $s \in V_E$ or $s \in V_A$ and $\deg(s) = 1$,*
- *a move $(\top, -1, \top)$ or $(\top, 1, \top)$ if the configuration is $[t, \dot{\top}, 4z]$, for some $z \in \mathbb{Z}$ and $t \in V_A$ and $\deg(t) = 2$,*

then Eve has a winning strategy if and only if she has a winning strategy in the one-dimensional counter reachability game.

Proof. It is easy to see that these moves simulate the counter reachability game and that Eve has a winning strategy to reach the configuration $[f, 0]$ of the 1CRG if and only if she has a winning strategy to reach the configuration $[\dot{f}, \top, 0]$ in the 1RGS.   □

We are ready to prove the main theorem.

Theorem 3. *The one-dimensional robot games with states are **EXPSPACE**-complete.*

Proof. By Lemma 3, deciding the winner is in **EXPSPACE**. It remains to be proven that it is also **EXPSPACE**-hard. Let (V, F) be a 1CRG with an initial counter z_0. Let (A, E) be the robot game with states constructed from (V, F). Assume first that Eve has a winning strategy in (V, F). Now, Eve's winning strategy in the one-dimensional robot game (A, E) is to play according to the winning strategy of (V, F) if the configuration $[\dot{s}, \top, 4z]$ where $s \in V_E$ or $s \in V_A$ and $\deg(s) = 1$. If the configuration is $[\dot{t}, \top, 4z-1]$ or $[\dot{t}, \top, 4z+1]$ where

$t \in V_A, \deg(t) = 2$, then moves $(t, 4x+1, q)$ or $(t, 4y-1, p)$, respectively. This is a winning strategy by Lemma 9. If the configuration is $[\dot{s}, \top, 4z \pm 1]$ where $s \in V_E$ or $s \in V_E$ and $\deg(s) = 1$, then Eve has a winning strategy by Lemma 5. If the configuration is $[\dot{t}, \top, 4z]$ where $t \in V_A$ and $\deg(t) = 2$, then Eve has a winning strategy by Lemma 6.

Assume then that Adam has a winning strategy in (V, F) and Eve has a winning strategy in (A, E). By Lemma 9, Adam has a winning strategy if the players simulate the 1CRG correctly. That is, Eve has to, at some point, either move to an emptying gadget, or play $(t, 4x \pm 1, s)$ when the configuration is $[\dot{t}, \top, 4z \mp 1]$. By Lemmas 7 and 8, Adam has winning strategies for both cases. As we have analysed all the possible moves of Eve, we have shown that Eve does not have a winning strategy. $\qquad\square$

4   Flat Robot Games with States

There is an interesting complexity difference between games of Theorems 2 and 3. When the (stateless) robot game is extended by allowing Eve to have an internal state structure and keeping Adam stateless, the complexity of deciding the winner increases from **EXPTIME** to **EXPSPACE**. In this section we study a natural dual question — does keeping Eve stateless and allowing Adam to have an internal structure result in a similar increase? We study this question by considering robot games where Eve is stateless and Adam's states are flat (i.e., the underlying graph is directed acyclic graph with self-loops), called flat robot games with states (FRGS). The state structure of a FRGS is depicted in Fig. 5. The main result of the section is that deciding the winner in the FRGS is in **EXPTIME**. Note, that as the stateless robot games are also flat robot games with states, we have inherited **EXPTIME**-hard lower-bound.

Remark 4. Let (A, E) be a robot game. If the winning set is non-trivial then it is either $d\mathbb{Z}$, for some integer d, or $R \cup U \subseteq \mathbb{Z}^+$, where $U = \{x \in d\mathbb{Z} \mid x > b\}$ and R consists of the winning values on the finite arena $[0, b]$, or $R' \cup U' \subseteq \mathbb{Z}^-$, where $U' = \{x \in d\mathbb{Z} \mid x < b\}$ and R' consists of the winning values on the finite arena $[b, 0]$.

Before considering arbitrary flat graphs of Adam, we consider a simpler case where there are three types Adam's moves: self-loops in state t_0, self-loops in state t_1 and transitions from t_0 to t_1.

The idea is that there are two stateless robot games when moves are restricted to self-loops and additional moves connecting the games. The algorithm of [4]

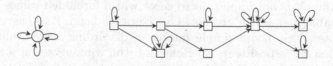

Fig. 5. An example of a flat robot game with states (FRGS)

not only computes whether the given initial value z_0 is winning for Eve, but it computes the set of all winning values. We can use the algorithm to compute winning sets for both games and then connect the two games using the transitions between t_0 and t_1.

Example 5. Consider a one-dimensional flat robot game with states where Eve's moves are $\{(s, -3, s), (s, -6, s), (s, -7, s), (s, -8, s)\}$ and Adam's moves are

$$\{(t_0, -3, t_0), (t_0, -6, t_0), (t_0, 0, t_1), (t_1, -7, t_1), (t_1, -8, t_1)\}.$$

It is easy to compute the winning sets for games restricting to t_0 and t_1: $W_0 = 9\mathbb{N}$ and $W_1 = \{0, 14, 15, 25, 28, 29, 30, 39, 40, 41, 42, 43, 44, 45, \} \cup \{x \mid x \geq 50\}$, respectively.

We notice that, for example, 9 is not a winning value in the flat robot game with states. Indeed, while by staying in t_0, Adam loses, if he instead moves to t_1, then after Eve's turn the counter will be $1, 2, 3$ or 6. None of which is a winning value when restricting to t_1. On the other hand, all the other winning values, that is $9k$ where $k > 1$, can reach 0 only by reaching 9 first. That is, Eve does not have any winning values. This is illustrated in Fig. 6.

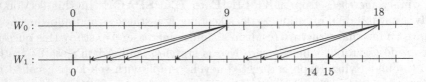

Fig. 6. An illustration of connecting winning sets in a flat robot game with states

For this special case, there are three steps needed to compute the winning set of the game.

– Compute the winning sets of restricted games, W_0 and W_1.
– Compute the forbidden values F in W_0, that is, all the values in W_0 from which there exists a move (t_0, z, t_1) of Adam such that for any move (s, x, s) of Eve, the resulting value is not in W_1.
– Finally, check whether values of F are avoidable in W_1. That is, whether there exists a winning strategy from the initial value z_0 to 0 that does not visit any values of F.

The first step can be done in **EXPTIME** using the algorithm for robot games. The second and third steps require some additional considerations as the sets are potentially infinite. In the game of the previous example, if the initial value is z_0, then it is not important to check which forbidden values larger than z_0 are avoidable and which are not. On the other hand, it is easy to see that in general case, it is not a simple matter of discarding larger values than z_0 (assuming that z_0 is positive). By Remark 4, the winning set of a robot game has a particular structure. In a similar manner, the set of forbidden values constructed from two winning sets have some structure which allows us to compute whether the values are avoidable. Now, there are two sets of forbidden values, one resulting from the finite set of R, $F_{fin} = \{f_1, \ldots, f_k\}$, and a regular but infinite set of values resulting from U, F_{inf}. Even though, F_{inf} is infinite, it is semi-linear (and in fact linear when Adam has two states). We can extract a finite set of forbidden values, F', such that $F_{inf} = \bigcup_{i=0}^{\infty} F' + i\ell$ for some $\ell \in \mathbb{Z}$. Now, we have two finite sets of forbidden values for which it is easy to check whether the values are avoidable. We can use the attractor construction of [13, Chap. 2] which solves the game in polynomial time. In our example, $F = \{9, 27\}$ and 9 is reachable only from one winning value, namely 18. On the other hand, 9 is the only winning value reachable from 18, so 9 is not avoidable.

Lemma 6. *Let (A_0, E) and (A_1, E) be two robot games and T a set of Adam's moves connecting the two games. Let W_0 and W_1 be their respective winning sets. The set $F = \{x \in W_0 \mid \exists z \in T \, \forall (s, y, s) \in E : x + z + y \notin W_1\}$ can be computed in polynomial time.*

Proof. There are several cases to consider. First we have two trivial cases when one of the winning sets is trivial, i.e., $\{0\}$. If the winning set W_0 is trivial, then $F = \{0\}$. If the winning set W_1 is trivial, then $F = W_0$. Another obvious case is when the winning set $W_0 \subseteq \mathbb{Z}^+$ and $W_1 \subseteq \mathbb{Z}^-$ (or the symmetric situation), then there are only finitely many points in W_0 from which it is possible to reach W_1. Thus $F = W_0 \setminus X$ where X is a finite subset of $(0, a]$ for some a bounded by $\min(E) + \min(T)$. There remains four cases.

1. $W_0 = d\mathbb{Z}$ and $W_1 = d'\mathbb{Z}$, or
2. $W_0 = R \cup U$ and $W_1 = d'\mathbb{Z}$, or
3. $W_0 = R \cup U$ and $W_1 = R' \cup U'$, or
4. $W_0 = d\mathbb{Z}$ and $W_1 = R' \cup U'$.

Recall that R and R' are finite and $U = \{x \in d\mathbb{Z} \mid x > b\}$. Consider the first case. Let $\ell = \text{lcm}(d, d')$. We can partition the integer line into intervals of length ℓ and effectively compute all the forbidden values F' in the interval. Clearly, the forbidden values in one interval, will be also forbidden in the other intervals. The set of all forbidden values is $F = \{f + \ell i \mid f \in F', i \in \mathbb{Z}\}$.

The next case can be divided into two parts, first finding forbidden values in R and then in U. Finding the forbidden values in R is easy as there are only finitely many possible values. Finding the forbidden values in U can be done as for the first case. The third and fourth cases are done similarly but now we also have to take the finite set R' into account. In all three cases, the set of forbidden values is $F = \{f_1 \ldots, f_k\} \cup \left[\bigcup_{i=0}^{\infty} F' + i\ell \right]$, where $|F'| < \infty$ and $f > f_j$ for all indexes j and $f \in F'$. $\square$

Lemma 7. *Let (A_0, E) be a robot game and $W_0 \subseteq \mathbb{Z}^+$ its winning set. Let $F_{fin} \subseteq (0, a] \subseteq W_0$ be a subset of forbidden values in W_0 and $F_{inf} \subseteq (a, b] \subseteq W_0$ such that the set of all forbidden values is $F_{fin} \cup \left[\bigcup_{i=0}^{\infty} F_{inf} + i(b - a) \right]$. There exists a finite set X such that $F_{fin} \cup F_{inf} \subseteq X \subseteq W_0$ and we can compute the values of X avoiding the values of F in polynomial time. Symmetrical claim holds if the winning set consists of only negative values.*

Proof. Let $m = \min(A_0)$ and $M = \max(A_0)$ be the smallest and the largest moves of Adam. Let $X = (m, b + (b - a) + M]$. Clearly $F_{\text{fin}} \cup F_{\text{inf}} \subseteq X$. We can construct a reachability game on a finite arena X by having two copies of the interval X, one for Eve and one for Adam. We connect integers in Eve's (Adam's) interval to integers in Adam's (Eve's) interval corresponding to her (his) moves.

The interval X can be partitioned into three parts, $(-m, a]$, $(a, b]$ and $(b, b + (b - a) + M]$. Intuitively, the first interval $(-m, a]$ corresponds to F_{fin}, the second interval $(a, b]$ to F_{inf} and the final interval to the set $\bigcup_{i=1}^{\infty} F_{\text{inf}} + i(b - a)$. As the finite interval corresponds to several sets, Eve can also move from $x \in (b + m, 2b - a + M]$ to y if there exists a move from $x + (b - a)$ to y. Additionally, if $f \in F_{\text{fin}} \cup F_{\text{inf}}$, then Adam can move to the sink state $\top$ which is losing for Eve. Finally, there exists an edge from a state x if the owner of the state has a move y in the robot game such that $x + y < 0$.

More formally, Adam has states $Q_A = \{\square \times [0, 2b - a]\} \cup \{\top\}$ and Eve has states $Q_E = \{\bigcirc \times [m, 2b - a + M]\}$. The transitions of the game are

$$T = \{((\square, x), (\bigcirc, y)) \in Q_A \times Q_E \mid y - x \in A\}$$
$$\cup \{((\bigcirc, x), (\square, y)) \in Q_E \times Q_A \mid y - x \in E\}$$
$$\cup \{((\bigcirc, x), (\square, y)) \in Q_E \times Q_A \mid y - (x + b - a) \in E, x \in (b + m, 2b - a + M]\}$$
$$\cup \{((\square, x), \top) \mid x \in F_{\text{fin}} \cup F_{\text{inf}} \cup F_{\text{inf}} + b - a\}$$
$$\cup \{((\bigcirc, x), \top) \in Q_E \times Q_A \mid \exists e \in E, x + e < 0\} \cup \{(\top, \top)\}.$$

Eve wins the game if she can reach $(\square, 0)$. The winning values of this game can be computed using the attractor construction in polynomial time [13].   □

Example 8. Let $(\{(t, -1, t)\}), (\{(s, -1, s), (s, -2, s)\})$ be a robot game. Let $F = \{3\} \cup \{x \in \mathbb{N} \mid x \equiv 2 \pmod{3}, x > 2\}$ be the set of forbidden values. By Lemma 7 we can construct a reachability game G depicted in Fig. 7.

Now we are ready to extend Adam's state structure to flat graphs. The algorithm is essentially the same as the one described previously. We utilize the topological sorting to remove forbidden points from the winning sets starting from the end of the graph using Lemma 6. Then we construct the set of avoidable values using Lemma 7.

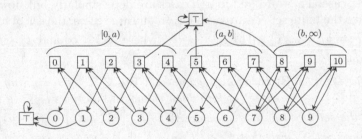

Fig. 7. A reachability game on finite arena constructed from a robot game and a set of forbidden values

Theorem 9. *One-dimensional flat robot games with states are* **EXPTIME-***complete.*

Proof. Let (A, E) be a FRGS where Adam has k states, $t_1, \ldots, t_k$, such that $(t_i, z, t_j) \in A$ only if $i \leq j$. Denote by $A_i = \{(t_i, z, t_i) \in A\}$. Using the algorithm of [4], we compute the winning set for each pair (A_i, E). Then, starting from k, we compute sets of forbidden values using Lemma 6. After computing the forbidden values, we compute the avoidable values using Lemma 7. Finally, we update the sets of winning values using the forbidden and avoidable values.   □

5   Conclusion

In this paper we proved that one-dimensional robot games with states are **EXPSPACE**-complete. In our construction Eve had states, while Adam was stateless. Motivated by this, we considered games where Adam had states and Eve was stateless. When limiting Adam's state structure to flat automata, we showed that the games are **EXPTIME**-complete.

In the future, it would be interesting to see whether non-flatness is the property that increases the complexity of deciding the winner from **EXPTIME** of robot games to **EXPSPACE** of robot games with states. It would be also interesting to see whether the complexity increases if Adam is stateless or has flat state structure and Eve has flat state structure as well.

Acknowledgements. The author would like to thank Igor Potapov for proposing the topic and helpful discussions.

References

1. Abdulla, P.A., Bouajjani, A., d'Orso, J.: Monotonic and downward closed games. J. Log. Comput. **18**(1), 153–169 (2008)
2. Abdulla, P.A., Mayr, R., Sangnier, A., Sproston, J.: Solving parity games on integer vectors. In: D'Argenio, P.R., Melgratti, H. (eds.) CONCUR 2013 – Concurrency Theory. LNCS, vol. 8052, pp. 106–120. Springer, Heidelberg (2013)
3. Alur, R., Henzinger, T.A., Kupferman, O.: Alternating-time temporal logic. J. ACM **49**(5), 672–713 (2002)
4. Arul, A., Reichert, J.: The complexity of robot games on the integer line. In: Proceedings of QApPL 2013, EPTCS, vol. 117, pp. 132–148 (2013)
5. Brázdil, T., Brozek, V., Etessami, K.: One-counter stochastic games. In: Proceedings of FSTTCS 2010, LIPIcs, vol. 8, pp. 108–119 (2010)
6. Brázdil, T., Jančar, P., Kučera, A.: Reachability games on extended vector addition systems with states. In: Abramsky, S., Gavoille, C., Kirchner, C., Meyer auf der Heide, F., Spirakis, P.G. (eds.) ICALP 2010. LNCS, vol. 6199, pp. 478–489. Springer, Heidelberg (2010)
7. Chatterjee, K., Doyen, L.: Energy parity games. Theor. Comput. Sci. **458**, 49–60 (2012)
8. Comon, H., Cortier, V.: Flatness is not a weakness. In: Clote, P.G., Schwichtenberg, H. (eds.) CSL 2000. LNCS, vol. 1862, p. 262. Springer, Heidelberg (2000)

9. Comon, H., Jurski, Y.: Multiple counters automata, safety analysis and presburger arithmetic. CAV'98. LNCS, vol. 1427, pp. 268–279. Springer, Heidelberg (1998)

10. Comon, H., Jurski, Y.: Timed automata and the theory of real numbers. In: Baeten, J.C.M., Mauw, S. (eds.) CONCUR 1999. LNCS, vol. 1664, p. 242. Springer, Heidelberg (1999)

11. Doyen, L., Rabinovich, A.: Robot games. Personal website, 2011. Technical report LSV-13-02, LSV, ENS Cachan (2013). http://www.lsv.ens-cachan.fr/Publis/RAPPORTS_LSV/PDF/rr-lsv-2013-02.pdf

12. Fahrenberg, U., Juhl, L., Larsen, K.G., Srba, J.: Energy games in multiweighted automata. In: Cerone, A., Pihlajasaari, P. (eds.) ICTAC 2011. LNCS, vol. 6916, pp. 95–115. Springer, Heidelberg (2011)

13. Grädel, E., Thomas, W., Wilke, T. (eds.): Automata, Logics, and Infinite Games: A Guide to Current Research. LNCS, vol. 2500. Springer, Heidelberg (2002)

14. Halava, V., Harju, T., Niskanen, R., Potapov, I.: Weighted automata on infinite words in the context of attacker-defender games. In: Beckmann, A., Mitrana, V., Soskova, M. (eds.) CiE 2015. LNCS, vol. 9136, pp. 206–215. Springer, Heidelberg (2015)

15. Halava, V., Niskanen, R., Potapov, I.: On robot games of degree two. In: Dediu, A.-H., Formenti, E., Martín-Vide, C., Truthe, B. (eds.) LATA 2015. LNCS, vol. 8977, pp. 224–236. Springer, Heidelberg (2015)

16. Hunter, P.: Reachability in succinct one-counter games. In: Bojanczyk, M., Lasota, S., Potapov, I. (eds.) RP 2015. LNCS, vol. 9328, pp. 37–49. Springer, Heidelberg (2015). doi:10.1007/978-3-319-24537-9_5

17. Kupferman, O., Vardi, M.Y., Wolper, P.: An automata-theoretic approach to branching-time model checking. J. ACM **47**(2), 312–360 (2000)

18. Leroux, J., Penelle, V., Sutre, G.: The context-freeness problem is coNP-complete for flat counter systems. In: Cassez, F., Raskin, J.-F. (eds.) ATVA 2014. LNCS, vol. 8837, pp. 248–263. Springer, Heidelberg (2014)

19. Leroux, J., Sutre, G.: Flat counter automata almost everywhere!. In: Peled, D.A., Tsay, Y.-K. (eds.) ATVA 2005. LNCS, vol. 3707, pp. 489–503. Springer, Heidelberg (2005)

20. Niskanen, R., Potapov, I., Reichert, J.: Undecidability of two-dimensional robot games. In: Proceedings of MFCS 2016, LIPIcs, vol. 58, pp. 74:1–74:13 (2016)

21. Reichert, J.: Reachability games with counters: decidability and algorithms. Doctoral thesis, Laboratoire Spécification et Vérification, ENS Cachan, France (2015)

22. Reichert, J.: On the complexity of counter reachability games. Fundam. Inform. **143**(3–4), 415–436 (2016)

23. Walukiewicz, I.: Pushdown processes: games and model-checking. Inf. Comput. **164**(2), 234–263 (2001)

Insertion-Deletion Systems over Relational Words

Igor Potapov[1], Olena Prianychnykova[2(✉)], and Sergey Verlan[3]

[1] Department of Computer Science, University of Liverpool, Liverpool, UK
potapov@liverpool.ac.uk
[2] Technische Universität Ilmenau, Ilmenau, Germany
olena.prian@tu-ilmenau.de
[3] LACL, Departement Informatique, Université Paris Est Créteil, Créteil, France
verlan@u-pec.fr

Abstract. We introduce a new notion of a relational word as a finite totally ordered set of positions endowed with two binary relations that describe which positions are labeled by equal data, by unequal data and those having an undefined relation between their labels. We define the operations of insertion and deletion on relational words generalizing corresponding operations on strings. We prove that the transitive and reflexive closure of these operations has a decidable reachability problem for the case of short insertion-deletion rules (of size two/three and three/two). At the same time, we show that in the general case such systems can produce a coding of any recursively enumerable language leading to undecidability of reachability questions.

1 Introduction

Nowadays there is a sufficiently broad research activity in the area of logic and automata for words and trees over infinite alphabets [1,3,4,9,11–13,19,29]. It is mainly motivated by the need to analyse and verify infinite-state systems, which for example can use infinite alphabet of natural numbers 1, 2, 3, . . . instead of finite number of symbols like a, b, c. In the seminal paper of Kaminski and Francez [9] a very restricted memory structure of the automaton (Register Automaton) working with words over infinite alphabets was introduced. The use of explicit references to the names of symbols in the process of accepting words over an infinite alphabet leads to a construction of an infinite automaton. In order to avoid it the register automaton is operating by keeping a finite number of symbols (from the working tape) in its memory and making their comparison to other observed symbols (i.e. checking whether they are equal or not). The model allows to recognize a large class of languages over an infinite alphabet and at the same time it is not taking an advantage of its memory capabilities beyond

I. Potapov — The author was partially supported by EPSRC grant (EP/M00077X/1)

O. Prianychnykova — Supported by the DFG-Project "Speichermechanismen als Monoide", KU 1107/9-1.

K.G. Larsen et al. (Eds.): RP 2016, LNCS 9899, pp. 177–191, 2016.
DOI: 10.1007/978-3-319-45994-3_13

what is needed for that purposes. A particular path in a register automaton accepting a word over an infinite alphabet can be seen as a template endowed with equivalence relation on the subset of positions that specifies which symbols should be considered as equal and non-transitive inequality relation specifying positions with unequal symbols. Note that such templates allow specifying an infinite number of concrete words, so in some sense it defines the structural properties of words from corresponding infinite language.

Extending the model by updating data can be in the form of adding new symbols when some prior information is known (i.e. generating fresh symbols which are different from anything has been used before) or adding data when there is no available prior and explicit information (i.e. when data is defined externally like in open systems). In both cases the analysis of computational processes which add and remove data can be quite non-trivial.

The first case can be illustrated by an example of using words over infinite alphabet in combinatorial topology [14,15]. Knot transformations can be implemented with a set of Reidemeister moves [28] represented by a fixed set of insertion/deletion and swapping operations on Gauss words [23,24], where the creation of new fresh symbols corresponds to appearance of new crossings. The complexity is coming from the fact that unknotting (reduction to the empty word) sometimes requires to increase significantly the number of crossing before the reduction to the empty word is possible [6,22].

The second case of adding/removing data with only local relations can be even more complex as the insertion of new data creates undefined relations, the deletion of undefined data may remove some uncertainties in other part of data and the outcome depends on assumptions about deleted data relations, yielding non-commutative sequences of deletions. Let us consider a simple "pick and place" robot arm control in the factory line [2,5,31]. For example, the control mechanism is allowing a robot arm to place three identical items (of unknown type) at some place on the conveyor (linear or circular) or pick two consecutive different items from the conveyor, see Fig. 1. As the domain of items is not fixed we have a process operating with unbounded sequence of items (on the conveyor) and item types from unbounded domain. In order to guarantee the correctness of some technological process we might be interested in checking reachability properties for a template, corresponding to the infinite number of possibilities, rather than reachability for concrete words.

In this paper we introduce the new concept of *relational words* and analyze their evolution under two types of updates defined for these structures: the insertion operation and the deletion operation. In a relational word any pair of

Fig. 1. Pick and place robot arm and its control system.

positions corresponds to symbols which can be either equal, or not equal or have an undefined relation (i.e. an absence of any of two relations) and if the domain of elements is unbounded (i.e. in case of an infinite alphabet) the relational word describes an infinite language over infinite alphabet or an infinite union of languages over finite alphabets. We consider the operations of insertion and deletion on relational words as the transformation of word templates and hence of corresponding languages. Another motivation comes from the fact that they are simpler than the corresponding rewriting counterpart and they allow to point out the main problems needed to properly define it. Similar idea of representing data over a finite alphabet as a set of relations was named as a "relational code" in [7], which generalize "partial words" in the area of nonstandard stringology [18] and DNA sequence processing [10].

The insertion of relational words creates new undefined relations as there is no prior information about inserted data, however the deletion operation can reduce the number of undefined relations introducing some non-local changes when we apply it to partially defined relational words (i.e. words containing undefined relations). For example, we allow the deletion of two adjacent symbols with undefined relation as equal adjacent symbols in a word. In this case we can conclude that all symbols (un)equal to the left symbol should be (un)equal to all symbols equal to the right symbol. Hence, such a deletion (beside deleting corresponding symbols from the word template) eventually induces new relations between remaining parts of the word. The complexity of deletion mainly follows from the original flexibility of insertions and unknown nature of data types. In fact a particular assumption on deleted data not only limiting original possibility of input data but also influence the future possibilities of further derivations. In contrast, when inserting new symbols no deduction about their relation to the others can be done, but it includes all the possibilities at once.

We are particularly interested in the following reachability problem: for a given set of insertion/deletion operations defined on relational words decide whether a relational word w can be derived from a relational word v. We show that for any system having rules inserting (resp. deleting) 3 symbols and rules deleting (resp. inserting) 2 symbols the reachability problem is decidable, contrary to the case of the finite alphabet. Moreover, the same result holds if only one insertion and one deletion rule is considered. We note that there exist 20 such combinations, however they correspond to an infinite number of underlying languages. Obviously, unrestricted and very general rules allowing rewriting over arbitrary infinite alphabet are too powerful making most of the computational problems to be undecidable [4]. However we show that if only insertion and deletion rules of relatively large size are considered, then the reachability problem on these templates (relational words) is undecidable. This result is obtained by encoding a finite alphabet by the structure of relational words. The obtained encoding is not trivial, because a structure does not specify individual symbols and can eventually match any corresponding sequence in the word; moreover there is no possibility to relate symbols (by equality or inequality) from several insertion or deletion rules.

2   Relational Words

A finite sequence of elements of a finite alphabet Σ is called a finite word over Σ, or just a word. We denote by Σ^* the set of words over Σ and by Σ^+ the set of nonempty words. The empty word is denoted by ε.

Let Δ be an infinite set. A word over an infinite alphabet Δ is a finite sequence of elements of Δ [9,16,19,29]. Elements of a finite alphabet Σ are defined explicitly and could be accessed directly, while elements of an infinite alphabet Δ could be only tested for equality. Then a word over an infinite alphabet may be viewed as a finite totally ordered set of positions endowed with an equivalence relation. Now the idea of this paper is to extend the notion of a word over an infinite alphabet by allowing the equivalence relation to be defined on a subset of the set of positions of the word. We define a relational word as a finite set of positions equipped with partial binary relations that describe which positions are labeled by equal and by inequal data.

Definition 1. *A relational word is the quadruple* $W = (X^W, \prec, E^W, N^W)$ *where*

- $(X^W, \prec)$ *is a finite totally ordered set;*
- E^W *and* N^W *(for equal and not equal) are binary relations on* X^W *such that*
  - *they are mutually exclusive:* $E^W \cap N^W = \emptyset$;
  - E^W *is an equivalence relation;*
  - N^W *is a symmetric relation;*
  - *for any* $x, y, z \in X^W$, *if* $(x, y) \in E^W$ *and* $(y, z) \in N^W$, *then* $(x, z) \in N^W$.

For technical reasons we shall consider the relation $U^W = X^W \times X^W \setminus (E^W \cup N^W)$ corresponding to an undefined relation between pairs of positions.

We denote by $|W| = |X^W|$ the *length* of the relational word W and by $W[i]$ the i-th element from the ordering of X^W. The empty relational word is denoted by ε, $|\varepsilon| = 0$.

A relational word W is *fully defined* if $U^W = \emptyset$. We denote *the set of all relational words* by $\mathbb{RW}$ and *the set of all fully defined relational words* is denoted by $\mathbb{FDRW}$.

A relational word can be viewed as a kind of a template. For an alphabet A (finite or infinite) a relational word W defines a language $L_A(W) \subseteq A^*$ which is the set of all words $w = a_1 a_2 .... a_n$, where $a_i \in A$, $1 \leq i \leq n$, with n being the length of W, such that for every pair of positions i and j in W we have

- if (i, j) belongs to the equality relation, then $a_i = a_j$,
- if (i, j) belongs to the inequality relation, then $a_i \neq a_j$

With every relational word W we can associate a graph $G^W = (Q, T)$ and an edge labeling function $Lab_{G^W} : T \rightarrow \{0, 1\}$ such that

- $Q = \{q_1, q_2, ..., q_n\}$ is an ordered set of nodes, n is the length of W,
- $T \subseteq Q \times Q$ is the set of edges such that $(q_i, q_j) \in T$ iff there is a relation (equality or inequality) between positions i and j.

– Lab_{G^W} is defined as follows
  - $Lab_{G^W}(q_i, q_j) = 1$ if the labels of the positions i and j are equal,
  - $Lab_{G^W}(q_i, q_j) = 0$ iff the labels of the positions i and j are not equal.

We will use the following convention for the graphical representation of G^W. The nodes of the graph will be aligned horizontally and the order of nodes taken from left to right will correspond to their ordering within the word. We will depict edges labeled by 1 below the axis induced by the node alignment and the edges labeled by 0 on the top of it. We also note that for any q_i, there exist an edge (q_i, q_i) labeled by 1. In order to simplify the pictures we will not draw corresponding self-loops.

With every relational word W we associate the matrix $M^W \in \{0, 1, 2\}^{n \times n}$ where n is the length of W, as follows:

$$M^W[i,j] = \begin{cases} 1 & \text{iff the labels of the positions } i \text{ and } j \text{ are equal} \\ 0 & \text{iff the labels of the positions } i \text{ and } j \text{ are not equal} \\ 2 & \text{iff the relation between the labels of the positions } i \text{ and } j \text{ is not defined} \end{cases}$$

Example 1. Let us consider the relational word W of length 4 such that the labels of the first and the third position are equal, the label of the second position is not equal to them, and the relations of the label of the fourth position to all others are undefined. We have that $X^W = \{x_1, x_2, x_3, x_4\}$; $x_1 \prec x_2 \prec x_3 \prec x_4$; and

– $E^W = \{(x_1, x_1), (x_2, x_2), (x_3, x_3), (x_4, x_4), (x_1, x_3), (x_3, x_1)\}$;
– $N^W = \{(x_1, x_2), (x_2, x_1), (x_2, x_3), (x_3, x_2)\}$;

If $A = \{a\}$, then $L_A(W) = \emptyset$. If $A = \{a, b\}$, then $L_A(W) = \{abaa, abab, baba, baba\}$. If $A = \{a, b, c\}$, then $L_A(W) = \{abaa, abab, abac, baba, babb, babc, acaa, acab, acac, caca, cacb, cacc, bcba, bcbb, bcbc, cbca, cbcb, cbcc\}$. The graph representing W and the corresponding matrix are shown on Fig. 2.

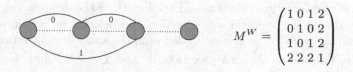

$$M^W = \begin{pmatrix} 1 & 0 & 1 & 2 \\ 0 & 1 & 0 & 2 \\ 1 & 0 & 1 & 2 \\ 2 & 2 & 2 & 1 \end{pmatrix}$$

Fig. 2. An example of a relational word.

We introduce the notions of equality and contradiction for relational words as follows. We say that two relational words V and W are *equal* if $|V| = |W| = n$, and for every $1 \leq i, j \leq n$ we have $(V[i], V[j]) \in R^V$ iff $(W[i], W[j]) \in R^W$, $R \in \{E, N\}$, i.e. V and W are isomorphic relational structures. For every alphabet A if $V = W$, then $L_A(V) = L_A(W)$.

A relational word V *contradicts* a relational word W if $|V| = |W| = n$ and there are $1 \le i, j \le n$ such that either $(V[i], V[j]) \in E^V$ and $(W[i], W[j]) \in N^W$, or $(V[i], V[j]) \in N^V$ and $(W[i], W[j]) \in E^W$. For every alphabet A if V contradicts W, then $L_A(V) \cap L_A(W) = \emptyset$.

We say that a relational word V is a *scattered subword* of W if V is a substructure of W, i.e., $X^V \subseteq X^W$ and for every $x, y \in X^V$ we have $(x, y) \in R^V$ iff $(x, y) \in R^W$, $R \in \{E, N\}$. If V is a scattered subword of W, then G^V is an induced subgraph of G^W.

A relational word V is a *subword* of W if it is a scattered subword of W and for every $x, y, z \in X^W$ if $x \prec y \prec z$ and $x, z \in X^V$, then $y \in X^V$.

Example 2. Figure 3 depicts the above notions. Consider the relational word from Fig. 3(a). The word from Fig. 3(b) is its scattered subword and from Fig. 3(c) is its subword.

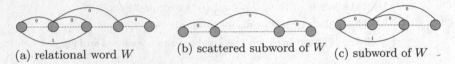

(a) relational word W (b) scattered subword of W (c) subword of W

Fig. 3. An example of a relational word with its scattered subword and subword

With every relational word W we associate its *numerical characteristics*:

1. $FD_{max}(W)$ is the length of the longest fully defined scattered subword of W;
2. $E_{max}(W)$ is the size of the largest equivalence class of the relation E^W, i.e., the length of the longest scattered subword of W such that every two elements of that subword are equal.

Definition 2. *An insertion-deletion scheme S is a pair $S = (INS, DEL)$ where $INS \subseteq \mathbb{FDRW}$ is the set of insertion rules and $DEL \subseteq \mathbb{FDRW}$ is the set of deletion rules.*

Scheme $S = (INS, DEL)$ is called *simple* if it contains only one insertion rule and only one deletion rule, i.e., $INS = \{I\}$, $DEL = \{D\}$ where $I, D \in \mathbb{FDRW}$.

We denote by $I_n D_m$ the set of all simple insertion-deletion schemes such that the length of the insertion rule is n and the length of the deletion rule is m.

Now we define the operations of insertion and deletion on relational words.

Informally, given $V, W \in \mathbb{RW}$ we understand the single-step insertion relation $W \overset{\text{ins}}{\underset{S}{\Longrightarrow}} V$ as follows: to obtain V, we take W and $Y \in INS$ and "insert" Y as a subword between any two symbols of W (Fig. 4). We assume that after such insertion for every pair (x, y), where x is a symbol of W and y is a symbol of Y, the relation between x and y is undefined.

Formally, we define this relation as follows. For every $k, m \in \mathbb{N}$ let the function $s_{k,m} : \mathbb{N} \to \mathbb{N}$ be defined as

$$s_{k,m}(i) = \begin{cases} i & \text{if } 1 \le i \le k, \\ i + m & \text{otherwise.} \end{cases}$$

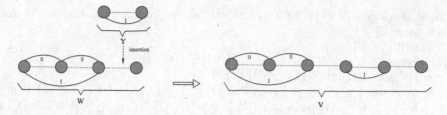

Fig. 4. The single-step insertion relation $W \underset{S}{\overset{\text{ins}}{\Rightarrow}} V$

Definition 3. *The single-step insertion relation on* $\mathbb{RW}$ *that is induced by* $S = (INS, DEL)$ *is defined as follows. For any* $V, W \in \mathbb{RW}$, $Y \in INS$, *and an integer* $0 \le k \le |W|$ *we have* $W \underset{Y}{\overset{ins_k}{\Rightarrow}} V$ *iff* $|V| = |W| + |Y|$ *and for every* $1 \le i, j \le |V|$

- *if* $i, j \in [k+1, k+m]$, *then* $(V[i], V[j]) \in R^V$ *iff* $(Y[i-k], Y[j-k]) \in R^Y$, *where* $m = |Y|$ *and* $R \in \{E, N\}$,
- *if* $i, j \notin [k+1, k+m]$, *then* $(V[i], V[j]) \in R^V$ *iff* $(W[s_{k,m}^{-1}(i)], W[s_{k,m}^{-1}(j)]) \in R^W$, *where* $m = |Y|$ *and* $R \in \{E, N\}$,
- *otherwise* $(V[i], V[j]) \in U^V$.

If we are not interested by the site of the insertion or by the concrete insertion rule, then we will write $W \underset{S}{\overset{\text{ins}}{\Rightarrow}} V$, meaning that there exists $Y \in INS$ and $k \ge 0$ such that $W \underset{Y}{\overset{ins_k}{\Rightarrow}} V$.

Definition 4. *The insertion relation on* $\mathbb{RW}$ *that is induced by* $S = (INS, DEL)$ *is the reflexive, transitive closure of* $\underset{S}{\overset{\text{ins}}{\Rightarrow}}$ *and is denoted by* $\underset{S}{\overset{\text{ins}}{\Rightarrow}}{}^{*}$.

Now we explain the deletion relation. Informally, the application of the deletion rule $W \underset{S}{\overset{\text{del}}{\Rightarrow}} V$ consists of two steps: expansion and deletion (Fig. 5). First, we have to find a subword Y' in the relational word W that does not contradict a relational word $Y \in DEL$ and to "expand" it to Y: for every symbol x and y in Y' such that the relation between them is undefined, we set this relation to be the same as the relation between the corresponding symbols of Y (a thick line on Fig. 5). In order to preserve transitivity, if we define that x is equal to y, then we have to connect to x all nodes incoming to y and using the same label (dotted lines on Fig. 5). Next, we take the "expanded" subword out of the word W and obtain the word V.

Definition 5. *The single-step deletion relation on* $\mathbb{RW}$ *that is induced by* $S = (INS, DEL)$ *is defined as follows. Let* $V, W \in \mathbb{RW}$, $Y \in DEL$, *and* $1 \le k \le |W|$. *We denote* $|Y| = m$. *Then* $W \underset{Y}{\overset{del_k}{\Rightarrow}} V$ *iff*

- *there is a subword of W of length m that starts from the position k and does not contradict Y;*
- $|V| = |W| - |Y|$;
- *for every $1 \leq i, j \leq |V|$ we have $(V[i], V[j]) \in E^V$ iff*
  - $(W[s_{k-1,m}(i)], W[s_{k-1,m}(j)]) \in E^W$ *or*
  - *there are $1 \leq p, q \leq |Y|$ such that $(Y[p], Y[q]) \in E^Y$, $(W[p+k-1], W[q+k-1]) \in U^W$, $(W[s_{k-1,m}(i)], W[p+k-1]), (W[s_{k-1,m}(j)], W[q+k-1]) \in E^W$;*
- *for every $1 \leq i, j \leq |V|$ we have $(V[i], V[j]) \in N^V$ iff*
  - $(W[s_{k-1,m}(i)], W[s_{k-1,m}(j)]) \in N^W$ *or*
  - *there are $1 \leq p, q \leq |Y|$ such that $(Y[p], Y[q]) \in E^Y$, $(W[p+k-1], W[q+k-1]) \in U^W$, $(W[s_{k-1,m}(i)], W[p+k-1]) \in E^W$, $(W[s_{k-1,m}(j)], W[q+k-1]) \in N^W$ or*
  - *there are $1 \leq p, q \leq |Y|$ such that $(Y[p], Y[q]) \in N^Y$, $(W[p+k-1], W[q+k-1]) \in U^W$, $(W[s_{k-1,m}(i)], W[p+k-1]), (W[s_{k-1,m}(j)], W[q+k-1]) \in E^W$.*

We will write $W \overset{del}{\underset{S}{\Rightarrow}} V$ meaning that there exists $Y \in DEL$ and $k \geq 1$ such that $W \overset{del_k}{\underset{Y}{\Rightarrow}} V$.

Definition 6. *The deletion relation on $\mathbb{RW}$ that is induced by $S = (INS, DEL)$ is the reflexive, transitive closure of $\overset{del}{\underset{S}{\Rightarrow}}$ and is denoted by $\overset{del}{\underset{S}{\Rightarrow}}{}^*$.*

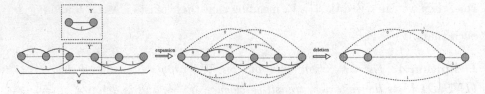

Fig. 5. The single-step deletion relation $W \overset{del}{\underset{S}{\Rightarrow}} V$

Union of the relations $\overset{ins}{\underset{S}{\Rightarrow}}$ and $\overset{del}{\underset{S}{\Rightarrow}}$ is denoted by $\underset{S}{\Rightarrow}$ and the reflexive, transitive closure of $\underset{S}{\Rightarrow}$ is denoted by $\underset{S}{\Rightarrow}{}^*$.

Definition 7. *An insertion-deletion system is the tuple $S = (V, INS, DEL, A)$, where V is an alphabet, (INS, DEL) is an insertion-deletion scheme, and $A \subseteq \mathbb{FDRW}$ is the initial language (the axioms) of the system.*

If $A = \emptyset$ then we will use a shorthand notation denoting the corresponding system as $S = (INS, DEL)$, i.e. we will identify it by the corresponding insertion-deletion scheme.

Definition 8. *For an insertion-deletion system $S = (V, INS, DEL, A)$ we define the language set $L(S) = \{W \in \mathbb{RW} \mid Z \underset{S}{\Rightarrow}{}^* W, Z \in A\}$ and the set $FDL(S) = \{W \in \mathbb{FDRW} \mid Z \underset{S}{\Rightarrow}{}^* W, Z \in A\}$.*

3   Decidability of Reachability Problem

Definition 9. *The reachability problem for insertion-deletion systems is, for a given insertion-deletion system S and two fully defined relational words V and W, to determine whether $W \Longrightarrow_S^* V$.*

Let $S = (\{I\}, \{D\})$ be a simple insertion-deletion system from $I_2 D_3 \cup I_3 D_2$, i.e., both sets INS and DEL contain only one rule and either the length of the insertion rule is 2 and the length of deletion rule is 3, or the length of the insertion rule is 3 and the length of deletion rule is 2.

We prove that for given simple insertion-deletion system $S \in I_2 D_3 \cup I_3 D_2$ and two fully defined relational words V and W the reachability problem is decidable.

Lemma 1. *For every insertion-deletion system S and every $W, V \in \mathbb{RW}$ if $W \Longrightarrow_S^* V$, then there is $Y \in \mathbb{RW}$ such that $W \xRightarrow[S]{ins}^* Y \xRightarrow[S]{del}^* V$.*

From now on, we consider only simple systems from $I_2 D_3 \cup I_3 D_2$. Because of the transitivity of the relation E, there are only 2 different fully defined relational words of length 2 and 5 different fully defined relational words of length 3, yielding 10 insertion-deletion systems in each $I_3 D_2$ and $I_2 D_3$. Below are the associated matrices.

$$M_1^2 = \begin{pmatrix} 1 & 0 \\ 0 & 1 \end{pmatrix}, M_2^2 = \begin{pmatrix} 1 & 1 \\ 1 & 1 \end{pmatrix}, M_1^3 = \begin{pmatrix} 1 & 1 & 1 \\ 1 & 1 & 1 \\ 1 & 1 & 1 \end{pmatrix}, M_2^3 = \begin{pmatrix} 1 & 1 & 0 \\ 1 & 1 & 0 \\ 0 & 0 & 1 \end{pmatrix},$$

$$M_3^3 = \begin{pmatrix} 1 & 0 & 0 \\ 0 & 1 & 1 \\ 0 & 1 & 1 \end{pmatrix}, M_4^3 = \begin{pmatrix} 1 & 0 & 1 \\ 0 & 1 & 0 \\ 1 & 0 & 1 \end{pmatrix}, M_5^3 = \begin{pmatrix} 1 & 0 & 0 \\ 0 & 1 & 0 \\ 0 & 0 & 1 \end{pmatrix}.$$

Lemma 2. *For every simple insertion-deletion system $S \in I_2 D_3 \cup I_3 D_2$ and every relational word W we have $W \Longrightarrow_S^* \varepsilon$.*

Proof. Let $S = (\{I\}, \{D\})$. First we show that it is possible to delete a relational word that consists of only one symbol, i.e., if $V \in \mathbb{RW}$ such that $|V| = 1$, then $V \Longrightarrow_S^* \varepsilon$. We have to consider three cases:

(1) $|I| = 2$, $|D| = 3$, and the matrix that associated with I is a submatrix of the matrix associated with D;
(2) $|I| = 3$, $|D| = 2$, and the matrix that associated with D is a submatrix of the matrix associated with I;
(3) The matrix associated with I is not a submatrix of the matrix associated with D and vice versa.

Let us consider the first case. If I can be obtained from D by removing the first row and the first column, then we insert I after V and get a matrix that does not contradict with D and hence we can apply the deletion rule to it. Similarly, if I can be obtained from D by removing the third row and the third column, then we insert I before V and again get a matrix that can be deleted.

Next, consider the case (2). In this case we first insert I after V, then apply the deletion rule to the part of I which coincide with D. As a result we obtain a word that consists of two symbols with undefined relation between them and hence can be deleted.

Finally, consider the case (3). Assume that $S \in I_3D_2$. Then $I = M_1^3$ and $D = M_1^2$ or $I = M_4^3$ and $D = M_2^2$ or $I = M_5^3$ and $D = M_2^2$. For each of these tree combinations the following derivation is possible:
$$V \overset{\text{ins}_1}{\underset{I}{\Rightarrow}} V_1 \overset{\text{ins}_1}{\underset{I}{\Rightarrow}} V_2 \overset{\text{ins}_1}{\underset{I}{\Rightarrow}} V_3 \overset{\text{del}_2}{\underset{D}{\Rightarrow}} V_4 \overset{\text{del}_4}{\underset{D}{\Rightarrow}} V_5 \overset{\text{del}_4}{\underset{D}{\Rightarrow}} V_6 \overset{\text{del}_3}{\underset{D}{\Rightarrow}} V_7 \overset{\text{del}_1}{\Rightarrow} \varepsilon.$$
Now assume that $S \in I_2D_3$. Then again there is a derivation that is possible for all the combinations of I and D: $V \overset{\text{ins}_1}{\underset{I}{\Rightarrow}} V_1 \overset{\text{ins}_3}{\underset{I}{\Rightarrow}} V_2 \overset{\text{ins}_4}{\underset{I}{\Rightarrow}} V_3 \overset{\text{ins}_5}{\underset{I}{\Rightarrow}} V_4 \overset{\text{del}_4}{\underset{D}{\Rightarrow}} V_5 \overset{\text{del}_3}{\underset{D}{\Rightarrow}} V_6 \overset{\text{del}_1}{\underset{D}{\Rightarrow}} \varepsilon.$

Now, since we can delete any isolated symbol, we can apply these sequences to each symbol of the relational word W and thus we can delete the whole word, i.e., for each simple $S \in I_2D_3 \cup I_3D_2$ and every relational word W we have $W \underset{S}{\Longrightarrow}^* \varepsilon$.

Corollary 1. *Let S be a simple insertion-deletion system such that $S \in I_2D_3 \cup I_3D_2$. For any fully defined relational words V and W we have $V \underset{S}{\Longrightarrow}^* W$ iff there is $W' \in \mathbb{RW}$ such that W is a fully defined scattered subword of W' and $V \underset{S}{\Longrightarrow}^* W'$.*

In the next lemma we analyze the behavior of insertion-deletion systems such that either I or D contains unequal symbols.

Lemma 3. *Let $S = (\{I\}, \{D\})$ be a simple insertion-deletion system such that $S \in I_2D_3 \cup I_3D_2$ and either I or D contains unequal symbols. Then for every $W \in \mathbb{FDRW}$ there is a constant $k \in \mathbb{N}$ such that for every $V \in \mathbb{FDRW}$ if $W \underset{S}{\Longrightarrow}^* V$, then $|V| \le k$.*

Now we consider the case when all symbols in both insertion and deletion rules are equal. For this, we define a mapping $Str: \mathbb{FDRW} \to \mathbb{FDRW}$ such that for every fully defined relational word W a fully defined relational word $Str(W)$ is obtained from W in the following way: from each maximal subword u of W that consists of only equal elements we remove $|u| - 1$ elements and corresponding relations. Then we can say that $Str(W)$ describe the structure of W.

Lemma 4. *Let $S = (\{I\}, \{D\})$ be a simple insertion-deletion system from $I_2D_3 \cup I_3D_2$ such that all symbols in both insertion and deletion rules are equal. Then for every $V, W \in \mathbb{FDRW}$ we have $W \underset{S}{\Longrightarrow}^* V$ if and only if $Str(V) = Str(W')$ where W' is a subword of W.*

Proof. First we prove that $V \in \mathbb{FDRW}$ could be derived from the empty word if and only if all its symbols are equal.

Next we show that if there is a subword W' of W such that $Str(V) = Str(W')$, then $W \underset{S}{\Longrightarrow}^* V$. Lemma 2 implies that $W \underset{S}{\Longrightarrow}^* W' \underset{S}{\Longrightarrow}^* Str(W')$ and hence $W \underset{S}{\Longrightarrow}^* Str(V)$. Then by the definition of the deletion rule we can obtain V from $Str(V)$ in the following way: for every symbol x of $Str(V)$ that corresponds to a group of equal symbols of size k in V we insert into $Str(V)$ a subword of $k + |D|$ equal symbols after x and then apply the deletion rule to $|D| - 1$ of them and the symbol x. Therefore $Str(V) \underset{S}{\Longrightarrow}^* V$ and hence $W \underset{S}{\Longrightarrow}^* V$.

Finally we show that if $W \underset{S}{\Longrightarrow}^* V$ and $Str(W) \neq Str(V)$, then there is $W' \in \mathrm{FDRW}$ such that W' is a subword of W and $Str(V) = Str(W')$.

Theorem 1. *Given a simple insertion-deletion system $S \in I_2D_3 \cup I_3D_2$ and fully defined relational words V and W, it is decidable, whether $W \underset{S}{\Longrightarrow}^* V$.*

Proof. Let $S = (\{I\}, \{D\})$ be a simple insertion-deletion system such that $S \in I_2D_3 \cup I_3D_2$. Then there are 2 cases:

(1) all symbols in both insertion and deletion rules are equal;
(2) either I or D contains unequal symbols.

In the first case by Lemma 4 we have that $W \underset{S}{\Longrightarrow}^* V$ if and only if there is a subword W' in W such that W' and V have the same structure, i.e., $S(V) = S(W')$. Then it is obvious that it is decidable, if $W \underset{S}{\Longrightarrow}^* V$.

In the second case it follows from Lemma 3 that the set $FDL_S(W) = \{V \in \mathrm{FDRW} \mid W \underset{S}{\Longrightarrow}^* V\}$ is finite since the length of words in this set is bounded by a constant k that depends only on parameters of S and W. Then we can get all the words in $FDL_S(W)$ in finite time by building the derivation tree.

4   Universality

In this section we show that if the length of the inserted and deleted words can be large, then corresponding insertion-deletion systems can produce a coding of any recursively enumerable language. We will abuse the terminology and we will call a function $f : \mathcal{A}^* \to \mathrm{RW}$ (where $\mathcal{A}$ is an alphabet) a morphism, if it satisfies $f(uv) = f(u)f(v)$. We will further restrict this notion and consider only those morphisms having $f(a) \in \mathrm{FDRW}$, for any $a \in \mathcal{A}$. Since any $w \in \mathrm{FDRW}$ can be uniquely identified by a string, we will use such a representation to define corresponding morphisms. Notice, that $f(u) \notin \mathrm{FDRW}$ for $|u| > 1$.

Theorem 2. *For any recursively enumerable language $\mathcal{L}$ over a finite alphabet $\mathcal{A}$ and for any (possibly infinite) alphabet $\mathcal{V}$ with $|\mathcal{V}| > 2$, there exists an insertion-deletion system over relational words $S = (\mathcal{V}, INS, DEL, \mathcal{A})$ and a morphism h such that $\mathcal{L} = h^{-1}(L(S))$.*

Proof. It is known that any recursively enumerable language can be generated by a context-free insertion-deletion system using strings over a finite alphabet with the size of the inserted, resp. deleted, words being equal to 3, resp. 2 [17]. Hence, there exists an insertion-deletion system $S' = (V', T', INS', DEL', A')$ with parameters above such that $L(S') = \mathcal{L}$. We recall that $L(S')$ contains words over T' reachable from the axioms of A'.

Let $c : \mathcal{A} \rightarrow$ FDRW be the morphism defined as follows: $c(\mathfrak{a}_i) = (ab)^K a^i (ba)^K$, $1 \leq i \leq n$, where $n = |\mathcal{A}|$ and $K > n + 2$, see Fig. 6. We will call $c(\mathfrak{a}_i)$ the *code* of the letter $\mathfrak{a}_i$. We say that $w \in \mathbb{RW}$ is in *canonical* form if $c^{-1}(w) \neq \emptyset$. Consider the extension of c to languages and let $INS = c(INS')$, $DEL = c(DEL')$ and $A = c(A')$. We also define $h(a) = c(a)$, if $a \in T'$.

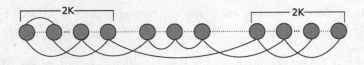

Fig. 6. The word $(ab)^K a^3 (ba)^K$ coding $\mathfrak{a}_3$. For simplicity, only the inequality relation between first a and b is depicted.

We claim that $\mathcal{L} = h^{-1}(L(S))$. Clearly, due to the construction of S we immediately obtain that $L(S)$ contains the image by c of all sentential forms used to obtain a word from $L(S')$. Next, we remark that the inverse morphism h^{-1} permits to select only relational words in canonical form corresponding to the concatenation of codes of terminal letters from T', therefore its application yields a word from $L(S')$. Thus we obtain that $\mathcal{L} \subseteq h^{-1}(L(S))$.

In order to show the converse inclusion $\mathcal{L} \supseteq h^{-1}(L(S))$ it is sufficient to prove that no other words except those corresponding to derivations of S' can be obtained. This can be formalized as follows.

Claim. For any derivation $\delta : u \Rightarrow x_1 \Rightarrow \ldots \Rightarrow x_m \Rightarrow v$ in S, where u and v are in canonical form and $m > 0$ it is possible to construct a derivation $\gamma : u \Rightarrow w_1 \Rightarrow \ldots \Rightarrow w_n \Rightarrow v$ in S, with all w_i being in canonical form, $1 \leq i \leq n$.

We will sketch the proof of this claim. We assume that all x_j, $1 \leq j \leq m$ are not in canonical form, that all insertions precede deletions and that δ does not have idempotent subderivations (*i.e.* for any partition of $u = u'xu''$ we have $\delta : u'xu'' \Rightarrow^+ v'x'v''$ implies $x \neq x'$, where $u' \Rightarrow^* v', u'' \Rightarrow^* v'', x \Rightarrow^+ x'$).

Now we will show that δ cannot be a valid derivation. We shall prove this statement by contradiction. We observe that x_1 can only be obtained by an insertion from u at a position not corresponding to the codeword boundary. Hence, in order to obtain a canonical word a sequence of codewords should be "broken" into pieces by insertion and new different codewords should be reconstructed from these pieces. Since the deletion operation is performed for words in canonical form only, a new subword in canonical form should be obtained using the insertion operation.

We recall that each codeword $c(\mathfrak{a}_i)$ is composed from 3 different parts: the left part – $(ab)^K$, the middle part – a^i and the right part – $(ba)^K$. By considering a and b as two kind of parentheses we can see that $\dot{c}(\mathfrak{a}_i)$ produces K pairs of alternating nested parentheses and the insertion as above produces several new unbalanced pairs. Clearly, in order to balance any of them again new unbalanced pairs are introduced, hence the number of incorrect patterns does not decrease. The value of K guarantees that no codeword can be accidentally constructed from several middle parts of the word.

Now to conclude the proof of the theorem we remark that if every derivation in S is using words in canonical form, then this directly corresponds to a derivation in S' (by applying c^{-1} to each word). Hence, no new words can be obtained yielding $\mathcal{L} \supseteq h^{-1}(L(S))$, which concludes the proof.

Since the membership problem for recursively enumerable languages is undecidable we obtain the following corollary.

Corollary 2. *Given an insertion-deletion system $S - (\mathcal{V}, INS, DEL, A)$ and a relational word X, it is undecidable, whether $X \in L(S)$, i.e., whether $Z \underset{S}{\Longrightarrow}^* X$, $Z \in A \cup \{\varepsilon\}$.*

5 Further Remarks

The concept of a relational word is very rich as it is allowing to reason about computational processes where both the size of strings as well as the domain of elements are not bounded, like in "pick and place" robot example presented in the introduction. Obviously the proposed operations on relational words could be interpreted in terms of graph rewriting [25–27] however the decidability and undecidability results presented in the paper do not follow from any known to us translation to graph rewriting.

Also we propose below two extensions of the model of insertion-deletion on relational words introduced in this paper. First we remark that a rewriting rule $u \to v$ can be seen as the deletion of u and an insertion of v at the corresponding place. So, with small technical changes, the Definitions 3 and 5 can be combined into a single definition for the rewriting operation. We remark that in the case of rewriting, the counterpart of Theorem 2 becomes trivial as the synchronization of the insertion and the deletion operation allows only rewriting of adjacent codewords.

Another extension is to consider the counterpart of the contextual or controlled variants of the insertion and deletion operation on strings [8,20,21,30]. In this case, the insertion or the deletion is performed is a specific context. The Definition 3 can be adapted by first combining the left and right contexts into a single word, using a pattern-matching step like in Definition 5 and then inserting the new word at the position given by contexts and keeping the relations between the context and the inserted word. For example, a rule (a, ab, b) would find an occurrence of two unequal symbols in the word and then would insert exactly between them two symbols equal to the symbol at left (resp. right) of the current position. The deletion operation can be defined similarly. In the case of contextual insertion and deletion the counterpart of Theorem 2 is also trivial, because it is possible to use the codes of entire symbols as left and right context. This means, that the operations can only be performed if the codewords are adjacent, i.e. in canonical form.

References

1. Abdulla, P.A., Atig, M.F., Kara, A., Rezine, O.: Verification of dynamic register automata. In: FSTTCS 2014, pp. 653–665
2. Ayob, M., Kendall, G.: A triple objective function with a Chebychev dynamic pick-and-place point specification approach to optimise the surface mount placement machine. Eur. J. Oper. Res. **164**, 609–626 (2005)
3. Bouajjani, A., Dragoi, C., Jurski, Y., Sighireanu, M.: Rewriting systems over nested data words. In: MEMICS 2009
4. Bouajjani, A., Habermehl, P., Jurski, Y., Sighireanu, M.: Rewriting systems with data. In: Csuhaj-Varjú, E., Ésik, Z. (eds.) FCT 2007. LNCS, vol. 4639, pp. 1–22. Springer, Heidelberg (2007)
5. Hackenberg, G., Campetelli, A., Legat, C., Mund, J., Teufl, S., Vogel-Heuser, B.: Formal technical process specification and verification for automated production systems. In: Amyot, D., Fonseca i Casas, P., Mussbacher, G. (eds.) SAM 2014. LNCS, vol. 8769, pp. 287–303. Springer, Heidelberg (2014)
6. Hayashi, C.: A lower bound for the number of Reidemeister moves for unknotting. J. Knot Theor. Ramif. **15**(3), 313–325 (2006)
7. Halava, V., Harju, T., Karki, T.: Relational codes of words. Theoret. Comput. Sci. **389**(1–2), 237–249 (2007)
8. Ivanov, S., Verlan, S.: Random context and semi-conditional insertion-deletion systems. Fundamenta Informaticae. **138**(1–2), 127–144 (2015)
9. Kaminski, M., Francez, N.: Finite-memory automata. Theor. Comput. Sci. **134**(2), 329–363 (1994)
10. Leupold, P.: Partial Words for DNA coding. In: Ferretti, C., Mauri, G., Zandron, C. (eds.) DNA 2004. LNCS, vol. 3384, pp. 224–234. Springer, Heidelberg (2005)
11. Lisitsa, A., Potapov, I.: Temporal logic with predicate lambda-abstraction. In: TIME 2005, pp. 147–155 (2005)
12. Lisitsa, A., Potapov, I.: In time alone: on the computational power of querying the history. In: TIME 2006, pp. 42–49 (2006)
13. Lisitsa, A., Potapov, I.: On the computational power of querying the history. Fundamenta Informaticae **91**(2), 395–409 (2009)
14. Lisitsa, A., Potapov, I., Saleh, R.: Planarity of knots, register automata and LogSpace computability. In: Dediu, A.-H., Inenaga, S., Martín-Vide, C. (eds.) LATA 2011. LNCS, vol. 6638, pp. 366–377. Springer, Heidelberg (2011)
15. Lisitsa, A., Potapov, I., Saleh, R.: Automata on Gauss words. In: Dediu, A.H., Ionescu, A.M., Martín-Vide, C. (eds.) LATA 2009. LNCS, vol. 5457, pp. 505–517. Springer, Heidelberg (2009)
16. Manuel, A., Ramanujam, R.: Automata over infinite alphabets. In: D'Souza, D., Shankar, P. (eds.) Modern Applications of Automata Theory, pp. 529–554. World Scientific, Singapore (2012)

17. Margenstern, M., Paun, G., Rogozhin, Y., Verlan, S.: Context-free insertion-deletion systems. Theor. Comput. Sci. **330**(2), 339–348 (2005)
18. Muthukrishnan, S., Palem, K.: Non-standard stringology: algorithms and complexity. In: Proceedings of the Twenty-Sixth Annual ACM Symposium on Theory of Computing, pp. 770–779. ACM, New York (1994)
19. Neven, F., Schwentick, T., Vianu, V.: Finite state machines for strings over infinite alphabets. ACM Trans. Comput. Log. **5**(3), 403–435 (2004)
20. Rozenberg, G., Salomaa, A.: Dna computing: new ideas and paradigms. In: Wiedermann, J., Emde Boas, P., Nielsen, M. (eds.) ICALP 1999. LNCS, vol. 1644, pp. 106–118. Springer, Heidelberg (1999)
21. Petre, I., Verlan, S.: Matrix insertion-deletion systems. Theor. Comput. Sci. **456**, 80–88 (2012)
22. Potapov, I.: Composition problems for braids. In: Leibniz International Proceedings in Informatics, LIPIcs, FSTTCS 2013, vol. 24, pp. 175–187. Leibniz-Zent. Inform (2013)
23. Saleh, R.: On the length of knot transformations via Reidemeister moves I, II. In: RP 2012, pp. 121–136
24. Saleh, R.: Computational aspects of knots and knot transformations. Ph.D. thesis, University of Liverpool (2011)
25. Rozenberg, G.: Handbook of Graph Grammars and Computing by Graph Transformation: Volume 1 i-xv. World Scientific, Singapore (1997)
26. Ehrig, H., Engels, G., Kreowski, H.-J., Rozenberg, G.: Handbook of Graph Grammars and Computing by Graph Transformation: Volume 2 i-xix. World Scientific, Singapore (1997)
27. Ehrig, H., Kreowski, H.-J., Montanari, U., Rozenberg, G.: Handbook of Graph Grammars and Computing by Graph Transformation: volume 3 i-xiii. World Scientific, Singapore (1997)
28. Reidemeister, K.: Elementare Berndang der Knotentheorie. Abh. Math. Sem. Univ. Hamburg **5**, 24–32 (1926)
29. Segoufin, L.: Automata and logics for words and trees over an infinite alphabet. In: Ésik, Z. (ed.) CSL 2006. LNCS, vol. 4207, pp. 41–57. Springer, Heidelberg (2006)
30. Verlan, S.: Recent developments on insertion-deletion systems. Comput. Sci. J. Moldova **18**(2), 210–245 (2010)
31. Vogel-Heuser, B., Legat, C., Folmer, J., Feldmann, S.: Researching evolution in industrial plant automation: Scenarios and documentation of the pick and place unit. Technical report TUM-AIS-TR-01-14-02, Institute of Automation and Information Systems, Technische Universitat Munchen (2014)

Author Index

Printed in the United States
By Bookmasters